T0220389

Humanizing the Digital Economy

Victor Glass

Humanizing the Digital Economy

Connecting Religious Humanism with Platforms for a Collaborative Society

 Springer

Victor Glass
Rutgers Business School
Newark, NJ, USA

ISBN 978-3-031-37506-4   ISBN 978-3-031-37507-1 (eBook)
https://doi.org/10.1007/978-3-031-37507-1

This Springer imprint is published by the registered company Springer Nature Switzerland AG
The registered company address is: Gewerbestrasse 11, 6330 Cham, Switzerland

Paper in this product is recyclable.

To my wife, Professor Ellen Susanna Cahn: thank you so much for helping me develop my ideas.
To my sons: thank you for prodding me to finish my book.
To the authors I have read: thank you for the virtual reality you opened to me by your written words.

Contents

1

The Roots of Political Gridlock and Foreshadowing a Way Out

Abstract This chapter is a prelude to the book. The aim is to outline basic themes about political splintering associated with hardening ideologies that emerged since World War II and a way forward to help Americans cooperate again. The chapter begins with an overview of the three sections of the book. Part 1 examines America's ideologies, Part 2 examines societal disruptions caused by what I call the Coding Revolution, and the third section describes pathways to reconciliation. The remaining part of the chapter gives a brief overview of America's three major ideologies and the general disaffection with them. It ends by outlining a strategy for ideological reconciliation.

1.1 Introduction

It is hard to recall a decade in the United States that did not experience social turmoil. During the twentieth century, the mass immigration from Eastern and Southern Europe, the rise of unions, wars, the Great Depression, the Civil Rights movement, and the counterculture and in the twenty-first century, the Great Recession, are easy examples. The 1960s–1970s seem especially similar to the social discord we are experiencing now. Like the extremists in Antifa, the violent members of Students for a Democratic Society (SDS), Weathermen, and Black Panthers wanted to overthrow American society. On the extreme right were the Minutemen, John Birch Society, and the Ku Klux Klan replaced now by the Proud Boys and Alt-Right. Black Lives Matter resembles the breadth of the Civil Rights movement that ranged from non-violent and civil disobedience to militant confrontations with police and street riots. Will America right itself after it absorbs recent social shocks? History suggests it will. Many of the people of the counterculture who tuned in and dropped out during the 1960s and 1970s, for example, have become solid, tax-paying citizens. In important ways, social turmoil has made the American culture more open and diverse, more accommodating to different lifestyles.

Nonetheless, this book takes a more wary view of America's ability to absorb these new protest movements because mainstream America is losing faith in its own core values, traditions, and institutions. Many Americans are not confident that scientific progress and economic growth are still working as unifying forces. Economic inequality has widened in the last few decades. While software engineers have seen their salaries balloon, production workers have lost their jobs to robots and clerical workers to copying machines and word processing packages. Scientists fear that humanity is destroying the environment and artificially inducing climate changes that are triggering more frequent and severe droughts, hurricanes, and wildfires. Plenty of white and non-white Americans are not sure that America can free itself from a racist and colonialist past. They accept to some extent beliefs that freedom means rejecting the tyranny of Western values associated with money and progress; and equality means allowing non-white minorities to get even with white male oppressors who kept them down. They stand by when protest groups pull down statues of Jefferson because he was a slaveowner.

Many grand plans for reform do not feel right or practical. In Western culture, overcoming a form of original sin looms large, but the sin differs depending on outlook. Western religions believe hubris destroys civilizations. The antidote is to treat everyone with respect and try to love thy neighbor. Economists believe the original sin is poverty. Faith in the market system or scientific management will usher in an age of personal growth and fulfillment. Environmentalists believe that despoiling nature is the original sin and that restoring nature to its pristine condition will reproduce the Garden of Eden. Freedom lovers believe the lust for power is the original sin and that democracy would dissipate hatred and lead toward peaceful and thoughtful compromise. Nationalists find salvation in the Volk instead of bickering individuals. Multiculturalists imagine a rainbow society of peace and pride in differences that will overcome the pride of cultural superiority. Add to the list nihilists who want to tear down society and reconstruct it from its foundations because it is hopelessly corrupt.

To paraphrase the author Robert Harris, the British novelist, they seem to their detractors like factories of superstition and invective. Love thy neighbor led to burning at the stake to save souls. Economic progress has not stopped wars or ended conflicts. Environmentalists forget that nature is a struggle of tooth and claw for survival that humans have won; no pristine Garden ever existed. Democracy did not settle the slavery question, nor has discussion and compromise prevented major wars. The Volk is a fiction, a sorry excuse for eliminating undesirables. Multicultural societies simmer with ethnic and racial hatreds. The "tear down" groups are too frightening to take seriously.

This spiritual dislocation has sped up enormously because of the Genetic Revolution and Digital Revolution. Bits of information are unlocking nature's genetic secrets and creating a new virtual reality dimension. Old rules and customs no longer anchor people to secure places. Online communication shortens attention spans and with it the patience to seek common ground. People can find information and like minds to support the most distorted views of society.

Below the crude sniping that goes on daily in the federal government and media lies a familiar deep-seated religious hatred among ideologies like that which existed for centuries in Europe among the Abrahamic religions and still is flaring in the Middle East and Asia. Ironically, religions in America are at peace – at least outwardly. Jewish, Christian, and Muslim clerics and students of religion point to their common spiritual messages that a righteous society depends on love, compassion, judgment, and mercy. Their unifying theme is that religions follow different paths to the same God who reveals different images of Self to separate faiths. The problem is that religions have little voice in calming American souls these days. Nonetheless, religious hatreds among the Abrahamic religions should remind everyone that different interpretations of text used to justify different religious imagery can produce holy wars.

Political fanaticism is not a new phenomenon, but it has gripped large segments of the population in recent decades. Looking back to the 1950s, political animosities were apparent. Cold Warriors like Joseph McCarthy were branding Americans as communist traitors, and overt racists like Strom Thurmond in Congress had political power. Politicians were overwhelmingly white males with WASPs at the top of the hierarchy. Diversity was an unknown political term. Despite these terrible failings, there was a sense of community among most congressmen and the president, possibly because WASP culture was firmly embedded in the political process, possibly because most Senators and House members were of WASP background or tried to emulate their WASP colleagues. Politicians had official labels – Republican and Democrat – but they were willing to listen and talk civilly to each other. They were on a common mission to tell the world that America was the City on the Hill, the nation glittering with thousands of points of lights, the nation that would lead the world to a better future than anyone could imagine. They boasted that America saved the world from fascism and would protect it from communism. Many politicians felt confident that together they would overcome America's character flaws rooted in distrust of minorities and racism.

Arguably, a sad decline in courtesy and respect began to occur beginning in the 1960s when young people rebelled against the draft and African Americans demanded justice that politicians had not delivered. This lack of faith in government authority led to political rifts that continue to widen as Americans question whether America is truly a noble society or one that talks nobly but is at heart corrupt.

The question is why the growing rifts? An easy answer is that a barrage of sociological and economic problems resulting from fragmenting communities, identity politics, the Great Recession, and loss of faith in America's purity during the ensuing decades after the 1960s explains why political community was being replaced by gated political communities, each with its watchtowers and code words. Politicians took on ideological beliefs of a growing radicalized constituency that hardened their political positions into nonnegotiable dogma by the turn of the twenty-first century. As a result, ideologies became fundamentalist religions that labeled nonbelievers as heretics who were destroying America instead of offering an alternative vision.

A more complete answer recognizes underlying disruptors created by technology. In past decades, social upheaval was associated with the Bomb, the Pill, television, and more recently the digital age of computers and online networks have sped up spiritual dislocations. Bits of information are unlocking nature's genetic secrets and creating a new virtual reality dimension. Online communications are shortening attention spans and with it the patience to seek common ground. Media influencers are producing lurid stories to attract eyeballs. And in this virtual landscape are haters spreading false information. Not surprisingly, old rules and customs are no longer anchoring people to secure places.

Despite these lurid descriptions of America falling apart, my belief is that reconciliation is not only possible but also likely if we change the way we look at social problems and at each other. If people recognize that fierce differences of opinion can exist despite having common objectives, then there is hope. Families sometimes fight over how to spend their money in pursuit of the good life, which they want for each other. The hope burns away when family members or politicians cannot agree on basic common values. In a family, it would lead to a divorce. In a state, it could lead to revolution.

1.2   Book Sections Overview

My aim is to counter the forces separating Americans. I want to reunite Americans who have almost stopped speaking to each other by restoring the power of American culture. My basic premise is that people will not change their basic life narrative by persuasion or factual evidence. People do change when their eyes open to a new set of challenges they can't explain or new possibilities they want to pursue. My objective is to offer new ways of seeing the world without threatening a person's core values. In this expanded field of vision lie the possibilities for ideologues to cooperate.

To build the case for a new unity, I divided the book into three sections. The first part shows America's traditional ideologies share a common core of ideas but different perspectives on solving social problems. Many of the grandees who shaped these ideologies were much more flexible than one would think. They had plenty of intellectual space for compromise with people with differing opinions. But like religions, America's ideologies have their fundamentalists who cannot compromise because their beliefs are divine, and any others strike them as profane. Unfortunately, the extremes can become the influencers of public policy in this new axial age – an age of massive dislocation of peoples caused by massive migration, rapid technological change, and, in America's case, loss of world prestige and power. During periods of turmoil, people tend to rush to find solutions that will restore stability and peace, which may be destructive in the long-term. Part 2 describes a major technological cause of societal disruption, and Part 3 attempts to open pathways to reconciliation.

1.2.1 Part 1: The Ideologies

To document America's current ideological divide, my starting point is some-what arbitrary. I connect the current ideological turmoil to the decades of disil-lusion following World War I that led to the rise of Naziism and communism, two ideologies that wanted to sweep away traditional culture to usher in a sup-posed golden age. I contrast these disastrous ideologies with America's major ones to show that they aim at ennobling the individual instead of a race or particular economic class. I show that Americans have a great deal in common for respectful collaboration, but in times of stress, their differences in perspec-tive can lead to political paralysis and name-calling. I reinforce this commonal-ity by contrasting the Nazi and communist violent internal revolutions to the King-led Civil Rights movement that made its case for equal rights for African Americans by rooting itself in traditional American ideals.

1.2.2 Part 2: Coding Revolution Disruptions

The second part describes the massive disruptions to American society caused by what I call the Coding Revolution, a revolution that has been building up for a while. It spans the effects of a range of massive changes in American society caused by new approaches to programming in the digital age, by the rise of the Internet and artificial intelligence, and by the breaking of the genetic code. I make the case that no ideology has easy answers to its challenges in part because the Coding Revolution upends traditional notions of privacy, security, and even the integrity of the human body and soul. It sometimes creates societal bubbles that form quickly and then burst causing economic and social damage.

I cover topics to show that the Coding Revolution has made American society more fragile and potentially more fearful. I show that America's financial system is at risk because a stampede to withdraw deposits from failing financial institutions can occur as fast as a few thousand investors tapping out their withdrawal requests. Like giant corporations of the twentieth century, online platforms such as Google or Amazon are enormous in size. Unlike their predecessors, these new giants gather information that allows them to see our every move and perhaps manipulate our behavior. The media has always vied for readers and viewers by sometimes producing sensational stories. In the digital world, with so many more channels, and with a growing stockpile of data that tracks every person in the online economy, everyone, especially media favorites, is under constant surveillance. The explosion of communication channels also allows many groups to form with similar interests. The downside is that many channels of communication can also splinter society into groups that do not speak to each other. Intelligence agencies now have huge databases they use to prevent terrorist attacks. J. Edgar Hoover had his dossiers to influence politicians. Now the intelligence agencies can potentially target anyone they deem a threat to America. They can also advise the government to outlaw the import and export of sensitive equipment and software to unfriendly foreign regimes. Finally, selective breeding of plants and animals, and in an informal way among humans, is now giving way to genetic engineering that would allow humans to reshape the substance and essence of life itself.

1.2.3 Part 3: Pathways to Reconciliation

The final part offers a new but oddly familiar approach for reanchoring and refocusing American society's visions of a good society that should appeal in an open, multicultural society trying to navigate in both virtual and physical reality. The centerpiece of this section is a philosophical view of American culture, which I define as Religious Humanism. It is an extension of the philosophical view of the Founders who viewed the colonists as having a common culture but diverse expressions of it. For example, the great majority of colonists were Christian, but they practiced Christianity differently. As a result, the Founders sought social harmony through religious freedom that protected religious beliefs.

In the spirit of inclusiveness, Religious Humanism is a philosophical framework contains moral behavior, ethics, and visions drawn from sources of wisdom that underlay America's ideologies. The "Humanist" part stresses the importance of an I and Thou relationship among Americans from all backgrounds that respects diversity that rests on a deeper unity. The "Religious" part has its roots in covenants and visions of society embedded in the Bible and the Constitution but are also consistent with other worldly covenants that suggest we have obligations that extend beyond self. Within this broad philosophical framework, Religious Humanism also recognizes the dark side of the human condition. The will to control, to form factions, to get even were well-known to the Founders of America. They wanted to disperse power to lessen these threats. Within the confines of justice and mercy, for example, I suggest there are many paths consistent with the advance of American civilization toward composing unifying narratives and pictures of America as a model for humanity.

Next, I identify four basic sources of wisdom that feed America's ideologies: rationalism/pragmatism, romanticism, deism, and mysticism. Because these sources are evolving to understand new challenges, America's ideologies could benefit from being sensitive to their new insights.

A few of my discoveries from this wisdom search are from unusual sources. While modern religion is mainly associated now with ceremonies and proper moral behavior of individuals and humanism with treating others with respect and dignity, I focused on the mystical template that underpins many great religions and ideologies. It is in the mystical regions of spiritual thought where one finds a sense of self that extends beyond physical self to a Self that connects a person to a grand purpose that spans peoples and generations and nurtures all humanity. At its core this mystical Self is often not subject to negotiation. When threatened, a person will sometimes die for a cause rather than submit to another religion or culture. As Patrick Henry said, "Give me liberty or give me death." The willingness to die I call the Samson Complex. A person is sometimes willing to bring down a threatening society by sacrificing his life rather than to survive as a converso or slave. This striving to connect with a Self is common in all ideologies. For example, Adam Smith saw an "Invisible Hand" nudging a group of self-seekers who like to truck and barter into uplifting society through voluntary trading. The American mystical tradition stresses a process of improving humanity rather than a fixed description of a utopia, which the Nazis and communists tried to imprint upon the masses.

This wider view of Self is the basis the "soulful" model used by Jewish mystics. I use it to explain in a unified way an amazing variety of values and beliefs, from art appreciation to government policy design. This model has a broader view of human needs that goes beyond usefulness and profit associated with rationalism. I suggest that America's current ideologies focus too much on the self and personal satisfaction. They undervalue the importance of creative meaning to us as individuals and as members of historical ethnic and racial groups. The soulful model expects groups to differ in approach to building a meaningful life, but they all aim at enhancing life. The soulful model tries to show that "I" and "We" are necessary to create a better life and spread newfound riches across humanity. Instead of evil being rooted in a corrupt soul, the model stresses that evil is often the product of the demand for strict justice for past wrongs, or the desire to excuse every breach of human civility. In the extreme, too much mercy breaks down society.

This expansive view helps identify limits of political negotiations that go beyond mutual gain from trading. For example, I use mystical levels of reality to explain why the West's conflict with Islamic countries is not solely to control oil reserves. The conflict is also over moral behavior and the path to redemption. The West favors material progress and democracy. Islamic countries ruled by fundamentalists favor theocracy and obedience to Allah. Knowing the limits to negotiation could prevent the clash of civilizations that we see today around the world and at home. The mystical tradition also offers a way out of the nonnegotiable dilemma by pointing out that there are many pathways to honoring Self that allow the Self to adapt its outer features to fit the times. The key to social reconciliation and cooperation is to allow each culture or religion to change on its own terms, as if the change is an organic outcome of its own traditions.

With the insights of Religious Humanism explained, the next challenge is to explain how the online world is developing and connect it with Religious Humanism. I outline a new social contract fit for the digital age. While large online platforms such as Amazon and Google are targets for government policies to reign in their power, I also suggest they represent the future of society in a way that the great industrial firms did in the twentieth century. I show that in many respects, they face similar challenges to America's ideologies.

Unlike traditional firms, but similar to political movements, platforms are open systems because outsiders contribute to maintaining and updating them. They serve many more customer groups than a traditional firm, so their market segmenting strategy resembles to some extent accommodating many cultures. In some respects, they resemble nation states more than ideologies because they set their own rules, monitor behavior on their platforms, and develop treaties with key suppliers and users.

As a platform develops, its culture emerges to fit its corporate mission, an ideological statement of the purpose of the platform. Culture, with a vision, focuses a platform's energies but also limits its ability to enter new markets that are dissimilar from its core base. For example, Amazon is unlikely to enter the social media business. America's ideologies have similar limitations in attracting new constituencies with different perspectives on life. Nonetheless, platforms continue to try to reinvent themselves incrementally and sometimes with bold initiatives like Meta trying to develop a virtual reality platform that supersedes its social media platform.

Meta's bet of billions on a new virtual reality platform is a test case on whether incrementalism or grand plans work best in the fast-changing digital world. In the past, Meta was successful in expanding its social media business by buying startups such as Instagram and WhatsApp that were extensions of Meta's business. Its metaverse system aims at being an immersive virtual reality filled with Avatars. The difference in strategy is reminiscent of America's open, incremental private enterprise system that moves forward in incremental steps versus the Soviet Union's 5-year plans. While it is only one test case, it may be a lesson for comparing sweeping legislative proposals like the Green New Deal versus government research support programs such as ARPA-E that funds promising new energy technologies that hold promise of commercialization but lack private funding sources.

In the online world, sometimes new markets open quickly and do not fit neatly into a service category that fits the business culture of a platform. When the payoffs are big and government does not block them, platforms will collaborate for mutual gain. Verizon and Amazon are developing products for the next generation wireless companies. This type of collaboration is missing among America's ideologies.

Separately, the insights from Religious Humanism and platform operations are insufficient to encourage ideological collaboration in this axial age. I also rely heavily on Daniel Bell's way of analyzing societal disruptions. He was a famous sociologist in the 1950s and 1960s who identified three realms of society: techno-economic, cultural, and polity.[1] I use his categories combined with the mystical soulful model as a grid for developing analytical and narrative tools that ideologues can use productively.

I use Bell's techno-economic realm to show how the economy is transitioning to a "smart" systems approach that can explain cultural changes that can carry over into policymaking. For example, platforms symbolize the transition of business society from the regimented corporate manager in a gray flannel suit to the creative software designer in jeans and a t-shirt. As an emerging

---

[1] Daniel Bell, D. (1978), *The Cultural Contradictions of Capitalism: Twentieth Anniversary Edition*. Basic Books, NY, pp. 11–12.

subculture, it is not clear how they connect with America's evolving social contract aimed at honoring an expanding number of ethnic, religious, and racial groups in America. Religious Humanism offers visions of harmony but, by itself, is too abstract. It needs grounding in real-world and real-time issues to come alive. But together Religious Humanism and platform practices and strategies can help define elements of a new American social contract that will enable Americans of all ideological backgrounds to collaborate on formulating and solving Coding Revolution problems.

The new social contract I outline recognizes that geographic borders are becoming less important for binding a people together. Software, data, and digital services are all highly mobile, and people are becoming increasingly mobile. Virtual reality becomes the norm. ChatGPT puts the analytical power of artificial intelligence at everyone's fingertips.

The online record so far suggests that incremental and decentralized experimentation paradoxically can produce powerhouse platforms. Government policies to protect the vibrancy of the online economy are important but require a deep understanding of the surprising evolution of the online economy and current trends in its evolution.

Religious Humanism can help humanize the Coding Revolution so that it becomes a new source for revitalizing American society by allowing all groups to imagine a new, more inclusive society that has a global reach with a personalized feel. The Humanism side suggests that two paradoxes are the key to political harmony. Political collaboration requires that ideological voters seek candidates that are centrists within their ideology. They are the type that can work together with ideologues of a different type. Again, paradoxically, voters need to elect candidates that are performers instead of reflexively voting for someone of the same race or ethnic background. The mystical side of Religious Humanism envisions the harmony of a cultural rainbow, the harmony of peoples gliding on nature's currents but choosing their own course, and the harmony of a Garden where all forms of life flourish. It warns against unleashing the dark side of the human soul. Together, Religious Humanism and platforms should give American society the vision and pathways to reimagine "Soul, Statutes, Sales, and Systems" that underpin our culture and, by doing so, add large increases in bandwidth for collaborative dialogue.

1.3   Background Information on America's Ideologies and Disaffections

This remaining part of the chapter is a prelude to the rest of the book. The aim is to outline basic themes about political splintering and fanaticism that have emerged since World War II and pathways to reconciliation. In this section, I offer a basic overview of America's three basic political ideologies – liberalism, conservatism, and libertarianism – that were debated during the Cold War and decades beyond. The intent is to describe their common core values, but different interpretations of them that have led to political conflict. The descriptions lack the historical rise of the ideologies and nuances that I discuss later in Part 1 of the book, but it is a start. After describing the debate on the meaning of core values, I explore historical events that caused America's major ideologies to harden and become increasingly less credible to many Americans. I offer three types of explanations: the first includes a series of rational explanations associated with historical events that may explain why Americans are losing faith in America's ideologies. The second delves into deeper psychological dislocations often not discussed and the resulting search for moorings for justifying a personal narrative. In fearful times, people may cling to personal narratives that are almost impossible to overturn with reasoned analysis. The third describes the effects of the Digital Revolution and related genetic revolution that I define together as the Coding Revolution. This revolution is overturning the "order of the soul" as Leonard Cohen, the poet, might describe it by opening a new dimension, virtual reality, and God-like possibilities to alter creation itself. Finally, in the last section, I briefly describe pathways to reconciliation and collaboration among many of America's factions. These pathways are based on two premises: the first is that you cannot convince a person with strongly held beliefs that they are wrong. People are willing to change if they voluntarily change their own personal narrative. This is more likely to happen when an innovative expansion of the narrative is possible. This is where Religious Humanism comes in. It serves as a framework for including a wide range of moral sentiments, rules, and visions that are compatible with America's core culture and for developing new rules and visions of America that are compatible with the emerging Coding Revolution that includes both digital and genetic coding.

1.3.1 America's Three Ideologies

To start, I offer a brief overview of America's ideologies to understand their perspectives on the right way to organize society. I claim America has three major ones – liberalism, conservatism, and libertarianism. Like offshoots of a common religious source, I want to show that their differences in interpretation of core beliefs can flare into major political conflicts when America is under stress. In practice, Liberals believe government action is a major tool for improving society. Conservatives believe that family and traditions are the backbone of society and government policy should aim at strengthening them. Libertarians believe that society works best when government gets out of the way and allows people to build their own lives. Despite their different approaches, all three ideologies want to build a unified and vital American society that shows the world how diverse peoples can live in harmony.

Their political fights center on four basic core values they hold in common: liberty, equality, property, and security. Others could be added such as dignity and honor, but I believe the four are the distinguishing values of Western Civilization. The basic tool that society has for upholding these values is the law. Each ideology interprets core values differently, which affects their views of the proper role for the law and by extension for government actions. As you will see, each of America's ideologies interprets these core values in a consistent way to weave an American story of why America is a Great Society. The narratives are a tapestry of logic, imagination, beliefs, and passions woven into a recognizable storyline.

1.3.1.1   Freedom

The first among equals is the core value freedom. In the American tradition, the struggle for freedom spans millennia and invokes different imagery. The ancient Israelites believed God's strong arm overthrew their Egyptian oppressors and allowed them to live free and follow God's path. Protestants fought to liberate themselves from the Catholic Church. Liberty was the battle cry in the French and American revolutions. Emancipating slaves was at the heart of both the American Civil War and British policy beginning with the Slavery Abolition Act of 1833. Wars of liberation against colonialism expanded globally during the twentieth century and the Civil Rights movement at home, post-World War II. Historically, the fight for freedom was bloody, and for centuries the sword was the weapon of choice, being upgraded as technology permitted.

I want to examine freedom and the other core values from an intellectual perspective to gain precision about the causes of the ideological clashes without losing sight that rational explanations often justify different imagery of a good society. In my case, I will use Lady Liberty in different poses as America's icon. Although her statute at the mouth of New York City's harbor looks the same to all, her true Self is quite different to different Americans.

A major American economist, Frank Knight, a founding member of the Chicago School of Economics, said that freedom is the opposite of coercion, the wrongful use of power to manipulate the choices open to others. But he also said freedom presupposes both the means and power to exercise choice.[2] He recognized that many associations are not free. A person has no choice of family and no choice of national origin, and the exercise of freedom is a product of social processes.[3] Nonetheless, Knight said that a person must have the ability to exercise freedom even if he does not want it. Slavery is not an option in modern society.

Lady Liberty, America's goddess of freedom, is the incarnation of Knight's definition of protecting and nurturing her children. Standing in New York's harbor, she looks serene, steadfast, and unchanging, above ideological conflict. Superficially America's ideologues agree broadly on her outward features, the features that define a free people. She symbolizes America's mission to let people live their lives as they see fit, to allow them to be what they want to be as the Army slogan goes, and, as a nation, to redeem humanity, not by imposing a dogma or way of living but by offering a compelling lifestyle that others would want to adopt. Freedom requires open access to opportunities, to objects of desire, and to destinations. The best use of freedom requires fair rules, fairly applied, and transparency – ease of access to information that allows someone to make informed decisions. Freedom requires self-discipline and a developed sense of what is important in life as opposed to satisfying wants as they arise. Order and security rest on free cooperation instead of on a "big brother" with police powers. Yet, some people need a helping hand to enjoy the promise of freedom. Circumstances often beyond comprehension and control can leave someone helpless and alone.

Archibald MacLeish in his poem *Liberty* imagined that Lady Liberty's soul was maturing from a woman of action to a nurturing mother:

---

[2] Frank H. Knight, F.H. (1960) *Intelligence and Democratic Action*. Harvard University Press, MA, pp. 123–124.
[3] Id., pp. 116–117.

When liberty is a headlong girl
  And runs her roads and wends her ways
Liberty will shriek and whirl
  Her showery torch to see it blaze.
When liberty is a wedded wife
  And keeps the barn and counts the byre
Liberty amends her life.
  She drowns her torch for fear of fire.[4]

Isaiah Berlin, an English philosopher, translated MacLeish's two images of Lady Liberty into two definitions of freedom: "freedom from" and "freedom to."[5] These definitions set the terms for America's ideological confrontations.

Freedom from (negative freedom) – is freedom from others imposing their will using external restraints. It is an open space that allows people freedom to act as they please without fear of retribution. This is the Lady Liberty of action.

Freedom to (positive freedom) – is freedom aided by resources that open possibilities to all people regardless of origins and situation and guiding them to intelligent use of their freedoms. Positive freedom is based on nurturing and often associated with government using its authority to improve the lot of private citizens, especially those in distress because of personal disabilities or because of systematic prejudice. This is Lady Liberty as a caring mother.

Although MacLeish clearly favors the mature, motherly image of Lady Liberty, almost all scholars who have examined these definitions agree that "freedom from" is the more basic freedom. People need the power to shape their own lives. The real debate centers on promoting positive freedom.

America's ideological skirmishes begin when liberals put forward government as the instrument for giving people enough resources to enable them to act on their own behalf to better themselves. Both libertarians and conservatives believe free markets will solve most problems but for different reasons. Libertarians believe voluntary individual choices allow people to build their own lives as they please. Conservatives fear that government safety nets will rob the family, community, and religious institutions of their reasons for existing. Like libertarians, they do not want government to put its hands in their pockets and spend their money as it sees fit instead of the way private citizens

---

[4] MacLeish, A (1985), *Liberty*. In Collected Poems 1917–1982. Reprinted with the permission of Houghton Mifflin Company. Poetry Foundation *https://www.poetryfoundation.org/poems/43008/liberty-56d221ad3a741*.Accessed 30 April 2023.
[5] Berlin, I. (1969), *Two Concepts of Liberty*, in I. Berlin, *Four Essays on Liberty*. Oxford University Press, UK, pp. 118–172.

see fit. They do not want government handouts to destroy families by paying people to have children out of wedlock because single-parent families lead to increased school drop-out rates, poverty, and crime.

1.3.1.2 Law

The debate over government's role in promoting freedom fans out into a wider struggle over other core values and national imagery. Libertarians and conservatives believe in the rule of law: fair rules, fairly applied, are the great protector of freedom. They imagine Lady Liberty putting on a blindfold and swapping her torch for scales of justice. The goal of Lady Liberty is to protect personal freedom. "Freedom from" oppression is associated with laws that set ground rules. These laws are of the "do not" variety that set limits on acceptable behavior. Within a protected sphere carved out by these types of laws, people can act as they choose. Laws defined in the negative are the products of court rulings to settle conflicts. Judges apply legal precedents to new cases, which embody the morals of a nation. In some instances, they may have to add a bit of interpretation to previous court rulings to apply to the case at hand. Over time, the common law adapts to changing conditions.

Liberals wouldn't disagree with this image. However, when Lady Liberty has a corrupt stand in, law becomes one of the most potent instruments for destroying freedom. The Nazis and communists used laws to hunt down and eliminate their innocent victims. Many of these dazed targets never made it to a courtroom; they were rushed to prison camps instead. The few who faced inquisitors probably knew full well that no matter what they said, they were guilty of crimes against the state. African Americans in the South must have felt that way during the Jim Crow years, when the law kept them separated from whites and confined them to servile roles long after slavery ended. Since life is a series of struggles and reconciliation, when conflict occurs, liberals agree that the law should appeal to the sense of fair play of a disinterested party. In this sense, liberals championed federal action to end systematic racism by local and state governments and by private industry that served the public.

The liberal belief in empowering oppressed people led them to support policies in the category of "Freedom to." Here Lady Liberty takes a long look at society after she takes off her blindfold and does not like what she sees. She wants to scold those who make others vulnerable and ashamed. In this role she supports laws of the "Do" variety, ones that require socially acceptable behavior. These types of laws have their source typically in legislation with government agencies adding regulations in harmony with legislative intent. Examples of positive laws are fair housing laws and equal opportunity laws. They aim to promote the health, welfare, and dignity of society when private citizens lack power to defend their interests.

1.3.1.3 Equality

Adding to her attributes, Lady Liberty is also an incarnation of another core value: equality. Liberals think of her as a mother who cherishes all her children but realizes that some need more nurturing than others. To the oppressed, this role of symbolizing equality is arguably a more potent rallying cry than liberty. Revolutions were fought over inequality of condition as much as for freedom. Both the French and American revolutions championed liberty and equality, but the accents were quite different. The French middle class and peasants fought to level society. They wanted to rid themselves of a king and aristocracy that had dominated politics and economic affairs for centuries. The pitched battle began with storming the Bastille and ended with the reign of terror. These events have fascinated and repelled revolutionaries throughout the world ever since. In the French Revolution, one can find the seeds of all future revolutions aimed at getting rid of the elite and replacing them with rule by the masses.

America's ideologies point to the American Revolution as their ideal. On the surface, the American Revolution was far more prosaic than its French counterpart because it was basically a struggle to gain local control of laws and administration – for equal protection under the law – as opposed to a class struggle for food and fraternity. No entrenched aristocracy existed in America. The colonists never wanted to level society but simply to pursue their own happiness following democratic principles already accepted in England. To do this, the colonists wanted to govern themselves. Nothing is very romantic about this goal. It is almost too rational. Yet, the American Revolution is the shining example of the well-conceived revolution that brought not only liberty but also equality to its citizens.

Liberals agree that America's Revolution was a proper fight for freedom, but they are mindful that a system that locks people in place from generation to generation will produce an eruption when bread prices rise as they did before the French Revolution. People storm the gates of government when they have nothing to eat.

Keep in mind, that the close parallels between liberty and equality, as the ideologues define them, should not hide their differences. Equality emphasizes sameness; liberty emphasizes distinctiveness. The tension between liberty and equality – between sameness and distinctiveness – is an eternal tension. How much sameness and how much distinctiveness does society want to tolerate?

Also notice the definitions of liberty, law, and equality used by ideologues in political debates line up in the sense that one view of freedom carries over to the other definitions. Negative freedom and negative laws of the "do not" variety have their counterpart in a type of equality defined as "equal protection." It is Lady Liberty setting ground rules for her children. Positive freedom and positive law of the "do" variety have their counterpart in the definition of equality as "equal opportunity." Lady Liberty treats her children differently to draw out their individual talents. Without even a little leap, it should be clear by now that libertarians and conservatives will favor equal protection and liberals tend to side with equal opportunity.

Formally, "Equal protection" means everyone receives fair treatment under the law. This is an ancient concept. In the wilderness of Sinai, the Israelites received four types of law that capture the essence of equal protection:

1. Thou shalt neither vex a stranger, nor oppress him; for ye were strangers in a strange land.
2. Thou shalt not raise a false report: put not thine hand with the wicked to be an unrighteous witness.
3. Thou shalt not follow the multitude to do evil; neither shall thou speak in a cause to decline after many to wrest judgment.
4. Neither shall thy countenance a poor man in his cause.[6]

In every commandment, fairness cries out. Treat all people fairly before the law, whether they are citizens or strangers. Testify to the truth. Do not follow the crowd; follow your conscience. Do not favor the poor simply because they are poor. In the modern vernacular, equal protection requires the state to focus on fair processes instead of fair outcomes; it assures that justice is blind.

Equal protection does not lead to equal outcomes. People differ in abilities, upbringing, skills, social position, and luck. These differences make life vibrant for the winners, painful for the losers. But unfair outcomes are hard to accept if society relegates your kind to the back of the bus as Big Bill Broonzy summed up Jim Crow in three lines of lyrics:

---

[6] Exodus 22:21–23:10.

They says if you was white, should be all right If you was brown, stick around But as yours black, m-mm brother, git back git back git back[7]

It is this type of undeserved demeaning unfairness in society that liberals use to justify government righting past wrongs by intervening in society to promote equal opportunity. Besides, sometimes losses are beyond individual control. According to the American dream, anyone should have the chance to sit in the executive suite. The sins of the parents should not be passed on to their children. Nor should growing up in poverty or having a particular complexion hold a person back. Liberals have used government to make the game of life more even. Free education, especially higher education trained many immigrants, a few of whom became Nobel Prize winners. Excellence in elementary school, not background, was the criterion for entry into elite public colleges. Other programs such as public housing, food stamps, and early learning were intended to give people, especially the young, a decent start in life. When these welfare programs did not raise groups out of poverty, the push was for government to impose affirmative action. In the 1970s, government began to consider the number of African Americans and other minorities hired by companies or selected by colleges before awarding public contracts and funding.

Libertarians and conservatives warn that allowing government to single people out for aid would give the government too much power. Government officials would have to decide who is a black, who is white, who is Christian, who is Jewish, who is Latino, who is Spanish, who is a native American, and who is a recent immigrant. When government can decide who can enter, it can also decide who cannot. The image of lines, one going to the left, one going to the right run by officials either in jackboots or in wing tips, is too frightful to allow such power.

---

[7] Big Bill Broonzy. Black, Brown, and White. https://www.google.com/search?q=big+bill+broonzy+they+says+lyrics&rlz=1C1GCEA_enUS976US976&ei=njMSZOueLNqt5NoPg4mSwAY&oq=big+bill+broonzy+they+says+&gs_lcp=Cgxnd3Mtd2l6LXNlcnAQARgAMgUIIRCgATIFCCEQqwIyBQghEKsCOgoIABBHENYEELADOgcIABCwAxBDOg0IABDkAhDWBBCwAxgBOgwILhDIAxCwAxBDGAI6DwguENQCEMgDELADEEMYAjoFCAAQgAQ6BQguEIAEOggILhCABBDUAjoGCAAQFhAeOggIABAWEB4QCjoFCAAQhgMGCAghEBYQHhAdSgQIQRgAUOQGWKIWYKZCaAFwAXgAgAFziAGAGx5IBAzkuMpgBAKABAcgBEMAABAdoBBggBEAEYCdoBBggCEAEYCA&sclient=gws-wiz-serp. Accessed 30 April 2023.

1.3.1.4 Property

The meaning of the third core value "Property" adds another dimension to the ideological battles that poets have not yet connected with Lady Liberty but easily could. John Locke was more candid than Thomas Jefferson when it came to sloganeering. He said, "Liberty, Equality, and Property" instead of "Liberty, Equality, and the Pursuit of Happiness." Happiness is a vague goal beyond the reach of government, but property is a child of the law. The government can use the law to give title to a nation's possessions to whomever it wants. In the past, European law supported ruling classes by giving them complete control of large tracts of land forever. Since then, the law and property rights have become far fairer. As the market system grew, property became a commodity bought and sold instead of handed down. The landed aristocracy faded into fable as the middle class completed its domination of society. In Europe and America, conflicts over the distribution of property remain in a more disguised form. The issue is whether the poor and middle class get their fair share of national income.

Environmental concerns have also taken their place as a major political issue related to property rights, as humanity grows and spreads across the earth and people use the earth ever more intensively. Land, air, and water are becoming increasingly scarce. Except for Antarctica, a person, a group, an organization, or a nation now lays claim to every landmass. Increasingly, air above buildings, electronic airwaves, and deep seas are becoming property.

The dilemma today in America is not whether to parcel the earth but how to do it. Should people control some types of property in common? Should they leave swathes of nature untouched? What kind of development do Americans want: low density or high density, uniform or varied, temporary or permanent?

Answers to these questions do not simply hinge on efficiency or freedom. American soil is our inheritance and our bequest. Any proposal to change the mix of public and private property should address obligations and values commonly attached to property. Five ideas roughly describe these sentiments:

1. Guardianship – stewarding God's gifts (or Nature's gifts if you wish)
2. Partisanship – championing one's own cause
3. Fellowship – being part of a community
4. Entrepreneurship – maximizing the value of resources
5. Citizenship – assuring fair government representation

Libertarians and conservatives believe private property empowers owners by allowing them to plan for themselves, to reap the rewards of their efforts, and to accumulate property as a bequest to others, including those in need. They can establish private parks like Disneyworld open to the public and environmentally sound. As private property rights contract, libertarians and conservatives believe that the sense of personal identity contracts. People lose their ability to live in spaces where they can be candid and where they can become intimate with others. They lose the incentive to innovate because spies can steal their ideas. They become politically correct because Big Brother is watching them.

Liberals believe some government control is necessary for a healthful society. While private property is the key property right, it will not guarantee food for the starving or medicine for the dying, or national parks to protect nature from our own greed. Public property in many ways adds value to private property. Just visit America's great national parks. The sense of personal connection to nature raises the spirit and helps people see beyond themselves. The value of public spaces is not measured in dollars. That is one reason why towns plan public spaces. Large accumulations of private property also threaten liberty. A large corporation has easier access to government officials than a private citizen.

Liberals sometimes claim private property is pulling America apart, encouraging us to see others too as assets or liabilities. In an age where people bump into each other, they must restrain themselves, think socially, and act cordially. Ask a tenant in an apartment building if his family can use their apartment as they wish. Make noise and someone will complain. Put the garbage in the wrong pail and someone will send you a notice.

Liberals also warn private property makes people look inward. They try to push more of our wealth into smaller domains. Furnishing a house becomes a passion; food becomes a passion; trips outside the neighborhood become a passion. They are passions of exclusion. The rich have undue influence in private affairs and in influencing government decisions. Limits on private property holding help keep democracy healthy.

1.3.1.5 Security

Security is the fourth and last core value described here that ideologues fight over. Security depends on fair rules fairly applied to render speedy justice. Once again, the interpretation of this definition aligns with the others that each ideology supports. In keeping with her image as a lady of action who breaks up fights, libertarians and conservatives see Lady Liberty protecting Americans from physical harm, from oppression, from disorder in society, and from private citizens or government spying on each other. From a liberal's nurturing perspective, Lady Liberty symbolizes a social safety net that helps the helpless that aids people who suffer catastrophes beyond their control, who gives relief to the unemployed, to the homeless, to the broken family, and to the dispossessed.

America's social safety net, run by government, is a twentieth-century development. In the nineteenth century, poverty equated to a moral defect. Any industrious person should be able to support himself, according to thinkers then. If someone could not work and he was young, it was the responsibility of his family to care for him. Surely if his parents brought him into the world, they would be responsible for caring for him as long as they could. If the parents were no longer alive or could not care for him, he should turn to private charities. He should know his benefactor if possible and not depend on a public dole. As a result, eligibility standards were very restrictive and the method of support very paternal. A person had to demonstrate need; the payments were in services; the receivers had to work, if possible.

After the Great Depression of the twentieth century, public attitude shifted toward believing that poor people were victims of an unsteady economy. Families and communities were wiped out by the massive downturn in the economy. By the 1960s, social reformers claimed that welfare was a basic right in a just society. Means tests became unacceptable; cash replaced earmarked services; work was not necessary to receive aid. Job training and early learning programs were designed to help poor people out of long-term poverty. By contrast, libertarians and conservatives associated the welfare state with the breakdown of the family. Single-parent households were the root of poverty and crime.

1.3.2 Disaffection with America's Ideologies

The second decade into the twenty-first-century America has become an ideological cold war, color-coded in blue and red, a war fought with ideological tracts and political standoffs. Sometimes it flared into street battles in the name of freedom. Beneath the intellectual combat are passionate clashes of peoples separated by geography, culture, religion, and race – all of whom define themselves as American.

The brief summaries of different perspectives on the meaning of freedom, equality, property, and security – all core American values – identified flash points in the ideological struggles. Yet, the question remains unanswered: why has American politics become the equivalent of a holy war? More ominously, have groups formed that reject America's ideologies as hopelessly corrupt? Flash points do not have to translate into battle lines. One approach to understanding today's deep conflicts in American society is to find their historical roots. Although it is a reasonable approach, starting points become a problem. Many ideological differences are centuries old.

Again, I use as the starting point the end of World War II. I organized this section to highlight cultural and economic factors that may have led to a loss of faith in government and to the narrowing of perspectives that they may have caused. Next, I tackle the disruptive effect of technological change caused by the Coding Revolution.

1.3.2.1   Hubris: The Government's Belief It Had the Power to Eliminate Social Ills

I base my historical analysis on the assumption that we are still adjusting to the fallout from WWII. Paradoxically, After WWII, America saw itself most clearly as the "City on the Hill," the beacon of hope to the world, the nation which led the charge to restore freedom worldwide and produced a global victory for the allies over evil empires. American culture had its roots firmly in Judeo-Christian culture. The pathway to a good life was the Protestant Ethic. Successful people worked hard, saved, and were upright and diligent in upholding the golden rule to treat each other with respect. The experience of the Nazis made Americans ashamed that prejudice against Jews, blacks, and other minorities persisted. Civil Rights became a powerful national crusade.

Yet, in a short period of 80 years, America's self-image for many has morphed into a City in the Plain, like Sodom or Gomorrah, or perhaps a decaying Roman Empire enfeebled by its own people fighting each other. How did it happen? Many explanations are given – government hubris, government deception and paranoia, endemic racism and victimization, and loss of confidence in American goodness – none of them really provable but all reasonable. I am going to expand on these themes.

Government hubris after WWII is understandable, and so are the recriminations from vastly inflated expectations. During WWII, the federal government was able to marshal the nation's resources to conduct a global war. The public and intellectuals alike conceded that the federal government could reshape society for the good. By passing the Employment Act of 1946, the federal government took responsibility:

To foster and promote free competitive enterprise and the general welfare; conditions under which there will be afforded useful employment for those able, willing, and seeking to work; and to promote maximum employment, production, and purchasing power.[8]

During the war, the primary beneficiaries of federal activism were veterans. The GI Bill Servicemen's Readjustment Act of 1944 funded college tuition for veterans, which led to a surge in college attendance.[9] Veterans were eligible for VA and FHA loans that often required no down payment and very low interest rates.[10] In the 1950s, these government programs were highly successful. The generation of veterans who took advantage of the GI Bill became educated middle-class citizens.

Flushed with success, the federal government, under Lyndon Johnson, declared a War on Poverty. According to Johnson, America had the resources to cure and prevent people from living a degraded life. This time, however, the public didn't back the government wholeheartedly because it seemed like a handout to the undeserving. Veterans had served their country and deserved payback, while poor people were tinged with the moral failing of not improving themselves during prosperous times. The programs benefitted those out of work instead of the working poor. For example, eligibility for welfare programs was limited to women raising children alone. Critics still believe the programs caused a surge in out-of-wedlock births that still plague America because children raised without fathers at home were less likely to finish high school and more likely to commit crimes than children raised in two-parent households.[11]

Great Society programs seemed to coincide with race riots that shook America. The 1967 Detroit riot resembled a war zone.[12] Bill Clinton's administration pulled back from many of the programs treating them as misguided.[13]

Federal planning hubris was not confined to ending poverty. The federal government also began the postwar period believing that it could prevent recessions by using fiscal and monetary policies that John Maynard Keynes prescribed. When national demand for private goods was slowing down, the

---

[8] Wikipedia. Employment Act of 1946. https://en.wikipedia.org/wiki/Employment_Act_of_1946. Accessed 30 April 2023.

[9] Wikipedia. G.I. Bill. https://en.wikipedia.org/wiki/G.I._Bill. Accessed 30 April 2023.

[10] Wikipedia. V.A. Loan. https://en.wikipedia.org/wiki/VA_loan. Accessed 30 April 2023.

[11] Wikipedia. *The Negro Family: The Case for National Action*. https://en.wikipedia.org/wiki/The_Negro_Family:_The_Case_For_National_Action. Accessed 30 April 2023.

[12] Wikipedia. 1967 Detroit riot. https://en.wikipedia.org/wiki/1967_Detroit_riot. Accessed 30 April 2023.

[13] Wikipedia. War on Poverty. https://en.wikipedia.org/wiki/War_on_poverty. Accessed 30 April 2023.

government could cut taxes, raise federal spending, and lower interest rates to stimulate demand.

The program seemed to work well until the 1970s when unemployment and inflation increased at the same time. Slack demand was supposed to lower prices, but they were rising. Milton Friedman, a free-enterprise economist, led a counterrevolution against federal management of the economy. He believed the government was printing too much money, which was lowering its value, and the public began to build rising prices into their plans. The failures of the War on Poverty and Stagflation were capitalized on by Ronald Reagan who said in 1981 "government is not the solution to our problem; it is the problem."[14]

Then the 2008 financial meltdown occurred leading to the Great Recession. The causes are unclear and will be discussed later. Here, for simplicity, I focus on the opinion of banking experts who claimed banking deregulation was a primary cause of the banking panic. Deregulation was going on since the 1970s to allow American banks to compete for global customers. In this highly competitive market, banks took risks and pushed products that in retrospect look foolhardy and borderline criminal. Free markets began to be identified with exploitation. The Great Recession stimulated the Occupy Wall Street protest movement in 2011 aimed at checking greed and corruption of corporations and government.[15] The demonstrations were short-lived but contributed to questioning whether American democracy was being coopted by business interests. Arguably, Donald Trump's election was due, in part, to the clash between the interests of Main Street and Wall Street, the ordinary working people, and the elites that live on Park Avenue.[16]

Another paradoxical source of growing ideological alienation was America's push to end discrimination after WWII. America fought the racist Nazis. General Eisenhower forced German civilians to walk through the Buchenwald death camp after its liberation. Life Magazine published photographs of the contrast of ordinary Germans in their Sunday best walking by piles of corpses.[17] Although widespread prejudice existed in the United States, policymakers embarrassed by Jim Crow laws and other official policies that enforced

---

[14] Reagan, R., *Inaugural Address 1981.* https://www.reaganlibrary.gov/archives/speech/inaugural-address-1981. Accessed 30 April 2023.

[15] Wikipedia. Occupy Wall Street. https://en.wikipedia.org/wiki/Occupy_Wall_Street. Accessed 30 April 2023.

[16] Morris P. Fiorina, M.P. (2018), Is the Trump Election the Revenge of the White Working Class? Newsweek https://www.newsweek.com/trumps-election-revenge-white-working-class-781026. Accessed 30 April 2023.

[17] *What We Fought Against: Ohrdruf (2020).* Via The National WW II Museum, https://www.nationalww2museum.org/war/articles/ohrdruf-concentration-camp. Accessed 30 April 2023.

racism and anti-Semitism at home began to act. A series of federal laws were enacted to end official discrimination. The Civil Rights Act of 64 outlawed discrimination based on race, color, religion, sex, or national origin.[18] It was followed by the Voting Rights Act of 1965 that eliminated racial discrimination in voting practices. The Hart-Cellar Act ended national origins considerations in immigration.[19] It was followed by the Fair Housing Act of 1968 that aimed at ending discrimination in housing based on race, religion, or national origin.[20]

Ending official discrimination arguably led to an American victimization mentality, which eventually led to identity politics. Any group that felt oppressed wanted to have their rights protected and wanted payback for historical wrongs. Affirmative action by federal agencies, universities, and businesses that feared discrimination lawsuits had the effect of pushing white males to the back of the line for a wide range of opportunities. Commentators began to question whether the movement was fracturing society by pushing groups away from embracing common cultural values.[21]

A sense of paranoia seems to be gripping the media, government, and the public about enemies within. Even clothing has become a symbol of anti-American otherness. Make America Great Again (MAGA) hats became symbols of white racism. Burkas became symbols of Islamic fanaticism. Among anti-Israel groups, a kippah (skullcap) is a symbol of Israeli oppression of Arabs.

1.3.2.2 The Specter of the Military/Industrial Complex

Another cause of political and social division in America is the fallout from the Cold War that began shortly after WWII. It put America on permanent war footing, a condition at odds with freedom and democracy. During the War, America organized the centralized Office of Strategic Services (OSS), which later became the CIA, to decrypt enemy secret codes.[22] Fear of communism gripped Americans. Large chunks of Eastern Europe and Asia became communist. As mentioned before, Senator McCarthy searched for commu-

---

[18] Wikipedia. Civil Rights Act of 1964., https://en.wikipedia.org/wiki/Civil_Rights_Act_of_1964. Accessed 30 April 2023.

[19] Celler, E. Wikipedia. https://en.wikipedia.org/wiki/Emanuel_Celler. Accessed 30 April 2023.

[20] Wikipedia. Civil Rights Act of 1968. https://en.wikipedia.org/wiki/Civil_Rights_Act_of_1968. Accessed 30 April 2023.

[21] Wikipedia. Identity Politics. https://en.wikipedia.org/wiki/Identity_politics. Accessed 30 April 2023.

[22] Wikipedia. Office of Strategic Services. https://en.wikipedia.org/wiki/Office_of_Strategic_Services. Accessed 30 April 2023.

nists inside America. Notable economists such as Paul Samuelson contributed to the paranoia by supposedly documenting that the Soviet economy was overtaking us.[23] America searched for an authentic ideology that would counter the Marxian vision of a worker's paradise under communism. Perhaps the focus on ideology as a new political weapon became a weapon in the cultural wars.

A growing connection between defense contractors and the military led the departing President Eisenhower to warn of a growing threat to American democracy: the military/industrial complex.[24] Another theory articulated by Eisenhower in 1954 – the Domino Theory – led to America's military intervention in Southeast Asia.[25] America later became bogged down in the Vietnam War. The glorified military that saved the world in WWII was now vilified as a tool of Western capitalism by antiwar activists. War resistors became the targets of government surveillance. A sense of a massive internal struggle with supposed enemies within culminated in the Watergate break-in. After the Vietnam withdrawal, neoconservatives feared America was still too soft on communism.[26] Nonetheless, the public began to fear government disinformation and often viewed military intervention abroad as a product of American imperialism. People like Noam Chomsky, a world-renowned linguist, became a strong critic of the Vietnam War and American imperialism. He became a hero to anti-government groups.

1.3.2.3 Disillusionment with Material Progress

Another pillar of American faith that began to crack in the postwar period was the public's confident belief that material progress would cure all ills. It wasn't immediate. Veterans moved to Levittowns; low-cost tract houses built using building techniques perfected during the war.[27] The new [whites-only] suburbanites looked happy. It seemed to be a golden age, even if the threat of the Bomb was looming and more prosaically long commutes meant absentee

---

[23] Levy, D.M., Pearl, S.J. (2011), *Soviet growth and American Textbooks: An endogenous past, Journal of Economic Behavior and Organization.* Volume 78. Issues 1–2. pp. 110–125, https://www.sciencedirect.com/science/article/abs/pii/S0167268111000114. Accessed 30 April 2023.

[24] NPR Staff (2011), Ike's Warning of Military Expansion, 50 Years Later. NPR. https://www.npr.org/2011/01/17/132942244/ikes-warning-of-military-expansion-50-years-later. Accessed 30 April 2023.

[25] Wikipedia. Domino theory. https://en.wikipedia.org/wiki/Domino_theory. Accessed 30 April 2023.

[26] Wikipedia. Neoconservatism. https://en.wikipedia.org/wiki/Neoconservatism. Accessed 30 April 2023.

[27] Wikipedia. Levittown, https://en.wikipedia.org/wiki/Levittown, Accessed 30 April 2023, and Rosenberg, M. (2019). A History of the Levittown Housing Developments. ThoughtCo. https://www.thoughtco.com/levittown-long-island-1435787. Accessed 30 April 2023.

fathers and isolated mothers. Material progress was arguably a rationale for the War on Poverty.

Rachel Carson's Silent Spring started a global environmental movement in 1962 that challenged the religion of material progress.[28] While conservationists date back to the nineteenth century, Western nations, whether communist or capitalist, operated as if the earth could be converted into a giant factory. Huge dams were built to harness waterpower. Mining was a booming business. Pesticides were used almost wantonly to improve crop yields. Rachel Carson exposed the dangers of pesticides that were covered up by the chemical industry. It led to the banning of DDT.

Environmental protection became a competing religion to economic progress. The environmentalists painted a romantic view of nature that airbrushes survival of the fittest, tooth and claw struggles, into a Wordsworth, God-inspired tranquil landscape. The prime environmental commandment to humanity was to act like Noah and preserve all species, large and small. If anything, humanity was a spreading cancer that birth control could check. Nature was more than a Wordsworth or Thoreau refuge from the pressures of city life: it was God's way of letting humanity know the wonders of creation. If nature had its struggles, the hidden message was that humanity was put on earth to end the strife by tending God's Garden, not destroy it. Global warming and environmental pollution were sinful, and humanity would bear the punishment.[29]

Besides the environmentalists, others have barraged the public with similar messages that "more" doesn't bring happiness that technology – television or computers – contributes to isolating people. The cumulative effect was an erosion in America's sense of purpose in pursuing rising material standards of living.

1.3.2.4 The "Me" Generation: A Revolt Against Authority

Another attack on America's cultural stability grew out of the rise of the "Me" generation in the 1960s, so brilliantly described in Tom Wolfe's 1976 New York Magazine feature article.[30] He summed up that decade and the one afterward by a jingle coined by Shirley Polykoff, a Brooklyn native who was

---

[28] Wikipedia. Rachel Carson. https://en.wikipedia.org/wiki/Rachel_Carson. Accessed 30 April 2023.

[29] Nelson, R. (2010), *The New Holy Wars: Economic Religion vs. Environmental Religion*. Penn State University Press, PA.

[30] Wolfe, T. (2008), *The "Me" Decade and the Third Great Awakening*. New York Magazine. https://nymag.com/news/features/45938/. Accessed 30 April 2023.

just trying to sell a hair-coloring product: Clairol. Her slogan was "If I've only one life to live, let me live it as a blonde." Tom Wolfe just removed "blonde" and said people began filling in their own blank. A new generation was coming of age who lived for themselves. Hell with obligations to children, to community, to nation, to ancestors, to inherited culture. With one life to live, you did your own thing, no compromises. As a result, according to Wolfe, people became encased in their own self. The looked-for ecstasy instead of community. They had no time or interest in the political process except to say it was distant and corrupt. The "Dos and Don'ts" of rational religion didn't captivate their imagination. They wanted to experience Halleluiah. A career in business was committing oneself to wearing a gray flannel suit and stress-related illnesses like hemorrhoids. A jaded, wildly exaggerated description of American society? Yes, but it does resonate. For those who remember the 1950s and early 1960s, television projected a unified American culture epitomized by a popular television program, Father Knows Best, by images of President Eisenhower's smile, by the avuncular CBS News anchors Douglas Edwards and then Walter Cronkite. All of these images projected an ideal society rooted in "'Conscience," "Industry," "Success," "Civic mindedness," and "Antisensuality."'[31] They became phony fantasies for the "Me Generation."

Some of the "Me Generation" became hippies, a movement that popularized getting closer to nature and communal living at the expense of family connection.[32] The "Pill" introduced in 1960 was likely a catalyst technology for the sexual revolution that broke down sexual taboos.[33]

Another possible byproduct of the Me Generation is the Wolf of Wall Street mentality. Pump and dump stocks on an unwary public. Greed is good according to Gordon Gekko, the leading character in another Wall Street film. Australian Prime Minister Kevin Rudd in his speech, "The Children of Gordon Gekko" concerning the financial crisis of 2007–2010, stated "It is perhaps time now to admit that we did not learn the full lessons of the greed-is-good ideology. And today we are still cleaning up the mess of the twenty-first-century children of Gordon Gekko."[34]

---

[31] Lehmann-Haupt, C. (1991), *The Decline of a Class and a Country's Fortunes*. Books of the Times. New York Times. Section C. p. 21. https://www.nytimes.com/1991/01/17/books/books-of-the-times-the-decline-of-a-class-and-a-country-s-fortunes.html. Accessed 30 April 2023.

[32] Wikipedia. History of the hippie movement. https://en.wikipedia.org/wiki/History_of_the_hippie_movement. Accessed 30 April 2023.

[33] Wikipedia. Combined oral contraceptive pill., https://en.wikipedia.org/wiki/Combined_oral_contraceptive_pill. Accessed 30 April 2023.

[34] John Gapper, J. (2010), *Man in the News: Gordon Gekko*. Financial Times. https://www.ft.com/content/16b182a0-6506-11df-b648-00144feab49a. Accessed 30 April 2023.

The Me Generation mentality led to a counterrevolution by conservatives to uphold America's traditional, Christian values. In the1970s, the Christian Right organized to protect traditional family values.[35] In 2009, Tea Party organized to push back against government social engineering.[36] Their basic message was that making everyone happy by giving them money and praising their beliefs, however wanton, was tearing America apart. They wanted to refocus on what made America a holy nation – abstinence, hard work, self-improvement, and community attachment. Christianity, like it or not, was at the core of America's society. Those on the Left reacted by labeling them fascists. The militant Antifa (militant anti-Fascists) sprung up to defend the oppressed against the bigoted Christian Right.[37]

The murder of George Floyd by a white policeman symbolized for many that racism is still at the core of the American psyche despite so many efforts to outlaw it in government and other public institutions. Symbols of American pride – the American flag, the Founding Fathers, and its skyscrapers – became symbols of oppression. Once again, calls to "tear it down" that Americans heard in the 1960s and 1970s became commonplace.

All these possibilities suggest America's cultural wars are a product of largely unintended consequences of America's reactions to WWII. American hubris in its righteousness and progressiveness led to overreaching social and economic policies intended to transform the nation into a land of plenty for all eventually blew up causing hard feeling within society. Overdependence on material progress, overdone ego trips toward self-fulfillment, and pent up longings for revenge are all contributing to a fractured society.

Perhaps these vignettes also suggest America's "winner-takes-all" attitude that grew out of WWII and the successful war on communism has led to a zero-sum society mentality. Compromise became associated with pork barrel legislation or Vietnam body bag counts that produced new political evangelists who would have nothing to do with backroom, cozy deals. The rise of fundamentalist religion was a reaction to the rise of secular humanism as the dominant American philosophy in public life. The Gaia movement to save the forests, save the species, and save the planet produced a revolt against compromise with America's materialistic ethic.

---

[35] Wikipedia. Christian right. https://en.wikipedia.org/wiki/Christian_right. Accessed 30 April 2023.

[36] Wikipedia. Tea Party movement. https://en.wikipedia.org/wiki/Tea_Party_movement. Accessed 30 April 2023.

[37] Wikipedia. Antifa (United States). https://en.wikipedia.org/wiki/Antifa_(United_States). Accessed 30 April 2023.

1.3.3 Anomie in an Axial Age and Its Implications for Rational Reconciliation

Perhaps all these explanations for political dysfunction are wrong because they assume a logical cause and effect relationship. It may be that political turmoil is a byproduct of an irrational, superstitious reaction to a frightening world post WWII. The twentieth century had plenty of specters of radical fanatics: goose stepping Nazis; parades of tanks and troops in the Soviet Union and communist China; later on, South American revolutionaries in fatigues sporting shaggy beards; and later still, Islamic terrorists wearing Hijabs. At home, Americans feared Klansmen in white hoods and black power crusaders growing Afros and wrapped in Dashikis. Perhaps, those with like-minded fears used ideological arguments to articulate their feelings. If so, America is becoming an increasingly fearful society.

Americans haven't been honest in public discussions of their fears that America was becoming a multiethnic, multicultural Babel because they would have to express darker motives of losses and regrets and suffering and shame, from being helpless to preserve pure blood and breeding, from severing of links to family and culture, from an unrecognizable future where they don't belong. Cut loose from social moorings, they search for new ways to restore their security and sense of self. They begin to form groups for self-protection and take steps to fight back against a government that belittles their tribalism. Those steps may be hesitant at first and may never achieve the sure footing of a revolution. But sometimes, when the current order offers little hope, a stampede could occur. This mob may not even think of the people they trample or just excuse the maimed and dead as collateral damage. They may even say the trampled deserved their fate because they were blocking our way. The Trump/Clinton/Sanders presidential campaigns showed the markings of a society in the grips of a malaise hidden under the banner of ideological wars that carried over into the Biden administration. Victimization and revenge are replacing hope and progress in America's narrative.

Robert Ingersoll's nineteenth-century observations on superstition are worth repeating because they explain the irrational fixedness of a superstitious person:

> Superstition is the enemy of liberty.
> Superstition hardens the heart and softens the brain.
> Superstition disregards fact for fiction
> Superstition severs the link between cause and effect[38]

---

[38] Ingersoll, R.G. (1944), Superstition, In Ingersoll's Greatest Lectures Freethought Press Association. NY pp. 295–349.

If superstition sounds too strong for explaining America's ideological struggles, let me modify his view somewhat to make it sound less outlandish. A person forms a narrative about life to organize thoughts and give them meaning. Once someone has formed a personal narrative, he or she will tend to collect information that validates his story and either discount or discard information that contradicts it. The story line sometimes justifies personal fears and hates. For example, when a black person commits a violent crime, a prejudiced person reinforces his image of blacks as dangerous. An anti-Semite who sees an I-banker with a Jewish name convicted of financial fraud smirks and says, "I told you so about the Jews." Prejudice is a superstition – a belief based on distorted facts or fearful images of the "other" – because a very high percentage of African Americans are law-abiding, and the vast majority of Jews are honest in financial dealings. Narratives are necessary, but they do distort reality because they often have heroes and villains, a well-defined plot, and an accepted theme. Reality is full of surprises, shortsightedness, and a sense of existential drift that creates angst about the future.

By extension, mythical figures, marvelous events, dogmas, and ceremonies associated with religion, patriotism, or ethnic culture hold elements of truth and perhaps great insights into human nature but at the expense of filtering out contrary evidence. In international affairs one commonly hears Western and Islamic ideologues calling the other an evil empire while assuring the world they believe all people are basically good but misled into supporting corrupted values and ruthless leaders.

1.3.3.1 Filtered Reality

Filtering of information is likely to bolster an ideology, and it isn't hard to do because a "Zone of Indeterminacy" exists in explaining events. Each ideology can point to supporting data to explain current political and economic problems in its own way. Even an objective viewer of America's ideologies won't be able to reject them because events have many complex causes that are almost impossible to pin down. For example, I tried to present the causes of America's cultural and political clashes as objectively as I could. But is my analysis really objective? I can't prove it. Moreover, someone might assume that I believe the post-WWII political civility in the 1940s through the early 1960s was a normal period to be emulated. A longer view of history suggests it wasn't a normal period. Moving the starting point of my analysis back only a few years to the late 1930s would make the current political battles look historically familiar. After the economic downturn in 1937, America was splintering into hostile factions. Father Coughlin, a widely admired radio personality, was openly preaching anti-Jewish hate. The left feared "union-busting, red-baiting, and surging intolerance." Those on the right believed Franklin Roosevelt was ushering in state socialism.[39] In 2007, Jonah Goldberg published Liberal Fascism to connect progressive thought to Fascist ideology.[40]

This zone of indeterminacy has many causes:

Behavior Can't Be Turned Into Equations Academics have an interest in developing mathematical models of human behavior as if it followed a set of natural laws like planetary motion. They are in the process of tying genetics and epigenetic rules or inborn activation routines of the mind and mental algorithms together with other scientific laws to predict observed human behavior. Whether a reliable model of human behavior is realistic is open to question. It certainly is at odds with free will and moral behavior. At least in the near term, it seems reasonable to assume that behavior does not conform to known physical laws. As a result, a reasonable working hypothesis is that human behavior is often unpredictable. Human interactions among people at a given time and across time are almost impossible to understand with much confidence. Within this fog of uncertainty, many plausible explanations of human behavior are possible.

Empirical Analyses Are Faulty Many researchers recognize that they cannot predict behavior with mathematical precision, so they turn to statistical models to predict behavioral tendencies. The problem is that statistical models, as limited as they are in objective, perform poorly mainly due to their assumptions of an underlying stability of human behavior measured in the aggregate and that a causal chain can predict changes in aggregate behavior. For example, how do you model or test convincingly whether the Great Recession was the government's fault for not rescuing the financial system when it was about to collapse, or because the financial institutions expected a bailout based on recent history of government bailouts before Lehman Brothers collapsed, or because government deregulated the financial industry during the Clinton Administration that led to reckless behavior, or because the government forced financial institutions to offer mortgages in red-lined neighborhoods, or because private businesses started issuing new, risky securities and moving operations overseas to avoid regulation, or because a breakdown in moral

---

[39] Wall, W. (2016), *Why calls for 'unity' are not enough: Look at the 1930s and 1940s.* The Conversation. https://theconversation.com/why-calls-for-unity-are-not-enough-look-at-the-1930s-and-1940s-62405. Accessed 30 April 2023.

[40] Goldberg, J. (2008), *Liberal Fascism.* Doubleday. NY.

order occurred when home buyers and lenders became frenzied speculators? We don't have laboratory experiments to test for causality. The fact that statistical models have done poorly predicting economic downturns and abysmally in predicting financial panics is clear to anyone, ideologues included. Even more troubling, modelers presuppose that only things measurable are important. How do you model the effect of loss of moral moorings caused by irrational exuberance during the housing bubble or shame caused by seeing widespread defaults occurring and having done little to stop it? No wonder that an ideologue will reject any empirical evidence that doesn't fit his model. He or she can say sincerely, statistics lie.

Story Lines and Metaphors Are the Basic Tools for Trying to Understand History and Complex Events Despite uncertainty or because of it, people want to inject purpose and regularity into human events. Often, they force experiences to fit a story line but sometimes realize at some level that the events don't follow any script. Many narratives could describe the Great Recession and none of them neatly fit the facts, assuming we could agree on them, which is by no means clear. In general, story lines and metaphors are subject to cultural entropy because we live in an open, multicultural society. Narratives often conflict because people and groups see society differently[41]. They value elements of society differently. As events unfold, surprises occur that tend to weaken old story lines and metaphors. Cultural changes also undermine neat storylines. For example, the Jewish experience today in America is quite different than experience at the turn of the twentieth century. Jews now are far more integrated into society and hold Americanized beliefs that would seem foreign to their grandparents who saw America as a haven from oppression and a land of unlimited opportunities.

Proof Is Often Predicated on Belief Measurement of national or even political success is difficult. Is GDP or some other measure of national well-being the right measure for understanding the Great Recession, or is it unemployment, or discouraged workers? Perhaps the distribution of income or wealth among the population or among ethnic or racial groups is an important indicator of the effects of the Great Recession. Some would add environmental factors to the list that should be examined. The point is that whatever proof is offered, the other side may discount it because it doesn't fit the value system built into its story line. Ultimately, the key variables selected for quantifying a case depend on an underlying set of beliefs about what really is important for measuring, for example, economic performance.

---

[41] Auchincloss, Louis (1987). Recognizing Gaddis. New York Times. Available at https://www.nytimes.com/1987/11/15/magazine/recognizing-gaddis.html.

1.3.3.2   The Great Disruptor: The Coding Revolution

The possible explanations for political gridlock mentioned so far are is largely sociological – changes in norms perhaps stimulated by recent mass immigration of people with differing relationships with white, Christian Americans. This perspective largely ignored the effects of technology. Television, for example, was an enormous disruptor of the status quo when it became widespread. Its global reach and immediacy allowed ordinary Americans to see firsthand images of the TET offensive when the North Vietnamese invaded the South despite an enormous American military buildup, the My Lai massacre by American soldiers of Vietnamese villagers, a child on fire from a napalm explosion – all of which stimulated the antiwar movement. The image of Bull Connor, the white Commissioner of Public Safety in Birmingham Alabama who allowed Klansmen to beat Civil Rights protestors, led to public revulsion of segregation. The hippie counterculture lifestyle became glamorized by the huge, peaceful gathering at Woodstock.

Technological disruption is not new. In the late nineteenth and early twentieth centuries, the market system changed dramatically with the rise of the modern corporate giant. Interchangeable parts running on assembly lines led to mass production of uniform products at low prices. It also displaced workers – skilled and semiskilled – who produced with their own tools. Personal income rose but, at first, seemed like a Faustian bargain: more money in exchange for becoming an impersonal productive input on the assembly line unknown to top management.

National markets became more commonplace as a result of the industrial revolution that produced automobiles, planes, household appliances, and air conditioning to name a few. Families moved, communities thrived and wilted based on changes in national market conditions. Large investments in plant and equipment, dependence on suppliers, and huge financing needs made industries and employment vulnerable to sudden, unexpected changes in the market. Some of these changes were the result of companies trying to gain a competitive edge by bringing out new products, but some were the result of unanticipated supply and demand disruptions. People may have wanted to save for new cars, and if many did at the same time, and auto companies didn't realize it, production contracted and people were out of work, and so couldn't buy cars. If companies began to fail, lenders stopped lending to them and wanted their money back as soon as possible. Credit froze, banks could fail, and did during the Great Depression.

Liberals began their ascendancy during the Great Depression. They began to organize national programs to put people back to work because markets were national in scope. Government learned corporate management methods and began to operate like a corporation. During World War I, the War Industries Board managed the war effort by centralizing economic decision-making in Washington. The success of the effort in America showed liberals, at least, that government could manage social programs and regulate industry. The numbers show that American government grew rapidly during the twentieth century. Government spending grew rapidly in comparison to the private sector, from 6.55% in 1907 to 47.66% in 2020.[42] Libertarians saw the facts differently by noting that Germany had also centralized economic management during World War I. This allowed the Nazis to easily take control of the economy because it was already centralized.

As the twenty-first century unfolds, society will morph in unexpected ways because the Coding Revolution will keep pushing the boundaries of instantaneous interactive communication, virtual reality, genetic mapping, and snipping. This will raise basic challenges to America's ideologies. How does one define the rule of law and private property when money and documents can be transferred across the globe with a keystroke? What does freedom mean when everyone has a digital dossier that can disclose intimate personal information? Americans are aware the Internet has spawned social media, virtually limitless sources of news and fake news, and a circle of connections that has become global. All these digital-age effects are changing the narrative of what freedom means inside the virtual world that has surprising and disturbing dimensions. One consequence of the digital age is that extreme views gain a wide platform that can incite people to seek redress outside of the political and legal systems.

Financial panics can occur in days instead of extending over months. The hot wars are cyberwars that are global in reach. What is the meaning of human nature when genetic engineering can alter the basic elements of the body and mind?

As Professor Bernard Chazelle of Princeton University said, biologically based systems are best explained by physics plus history. It is not enough to develop a Lego version of a network to see how everything fits together.[43] It is also critical to know how the system evolved. Only then can we understand its operations, capabilities, and shortcomings. One of my goals is to provide a

---

[42] US Government Spending History from 1900. usgovernmentspending.com. Available at https://www.usgovernmentspending.com/past_spending. Accessed 30 April 2023.

[43] See, for example, YouTube. Why Biology is Different. Simons Institute, https://www.youtube.com/watch?v=780U3IBz21M. Accessed 30 April 2023.

history of the evolution of the Internet because understanding its structure and operations is still in its infancy.

1.4   A Strategy for Reconciliation

America's ideologies are not static and not as dogmatic as one would suppose from listening to talk radio and cable TV. They are living narratives that combine longings and rational justifications for those longings. Myth and mysticism associated with Lady Liberty and Uncle Sam, and perhaps new avatars turn abstractions into virtual reality. As you will see, the Coding Revolution like the industrial revolution will alter interpretation of core values such as the property right to privacy. On the positive side, the Coding Revolution offers enormous possibilities for improving life along many dimensions. Bolder dreams have the possibility of becoming reality. But unlike the industrial revolution, borders are becoming very porous, and national sovereignty is being weakened. Regulation in Europe can affect business practices in America. Tax havens are easy to find and easy to establish if you are rich enough or your corporation is large enough.

Ideologues will also continue to grapple with controlling the dark side of human nature that may wear different disguises as the centuries pass, but underneath is as familiar to ancient shepherds as it is to computer jockeys. Evil often expresses itself in extreme interpretations of virtues that are complementary – yin and yang. I picked four pairs of complementary virtues to help me explain the disastrous world wars and genocides and internal strife in the United States of the past century.

1. Power and obedience. The will to dominate and demand obedience from subject people is a top motivation for war.
2. Judgment and mercy. Excessive judgment leads to revenge. A classic case of the will for revenge was Germany wanting to get even after World War I. All mercy breaks down the rule of law, which can lead to crime because there are no consequences for breaking the law.
3. Control and trust. These two are somewhat similar to power and obedience but with less aggressiveness. There is a Russian saying that trust is good, but control is better. Trust is necessary because unexpected things happen, and you need to rely on people when you need them. Of course, naïve trust in elixirs and other miracle solutions has duped many people into bad medicines and bad investments. Control of one's life is good, but excessive control breaks up families, communities, and nations.

4. Honor and humility. Honor is often a visceral excuse for feuds and massacres. Excessive humility invites aggression.

The Coding Revolution will force America's ideologies to redefine their approaches for grappling with the dark side expressed in the digital world where people and governments can stalk you, gaslight you, impersonate you, and destroy your reputation. The flexible ideologues will search for answers even in competing ideologies.

My belief is that Religious Humanism and related methods of framing social problems that I offer can help ideologues update their narratives and find reasons and justifications for compromise and collaboration. As I mentioned, the narrative tools I use and combine in different ways to frame social issues fall into these categories:

- The "soulful" model – the soul has three levels: vital, conscious, and creative. Human needs range from necessities to rational planning to meaningful creative inspiration. The best policies account for all three levels and recognize the time frame extend farther as at the higher reaches of the soul.
- The Bell model: any government policy can affect the economic and technological structure of society, change its culture values, and transform the way government operates. Again, consistency and timing are challenges.
- The philosophical sources of Religious Humanism: wisdom the falls into four categories: rational/pragmatic, romantic, deist, and mystical. Each philosophical source continues to adapt to societal changes. They can be great new sources of wisdom for America's ideologies.
- Systems theory to analyze network effects of sudden disruptions and policy changes to tamp them down.

For now, my main point is that we are entering a new Axial Age like the old when the major religions and philosophies formed during a period of massive disruption between the sixth and ninth century BCE. Despite the broad ideological wars fought on battlegrounds socked-in by intellectual smog and fear produced by the loss of cultural moorings arguably created in part by the Coding Revolution, there is still a familiar way to tamp down ideological wars. It is not by crushing the enemy. Rationalists are on the wrong track when they ask someone what evidence will make him change his mind. The problem is that facts are not often king. Again, when people are committed to a story line, they are likely to screen data, selecting mainly the data that supports their view. This is especially true of people who have accepted an ideological model of society. Often, when the sense of "self" is at stake, people are more likely to double down on their beliefs instead of giving them up.

A better approach to changing is to let leaders of a political ideology grapple with features of their beliefs that feel uncomfortable and allow them to find ways for changing their opinions without having to admit mistakes. The key is not to expect to persuade a believer that your side is right. That almost never works, except perhaps with extremists who move from one edge of the political spectrum to the other as the communists did who became rabid Nazis. Implicitly, the most creative ideologues recognize that their ideology does not have all the answers and that their predictions have not proved very accurate. It is sometimes useful to coopt the ideas of others and make them your own. This flexibility rests on the belief that trial and error over time can yield core values such as personal freedom that virtually everyone will accept. It also rests on the belief that beyond these core values are other values that often conflict, and sometimes a reassessment of values is necessary to fit the times. But people have to come to terms with change in a way that doesn't demean their sense of self.

Plenty of examples of a "don't admit" ideological shift have occurred, but the evidence is circumstantial, and the motives not clear, even to the ideological shape shifter because people start to believe their own rhetoric. Arguably, the award for the most brazenly smooth and charming ideological shift in recent memory goes to Ronald Reagan. He explained his switch from being a New Deal democrat to a libertarian republican by famously saying, "I didn't leave the Democratic Party; the party left me." The democrats no longer were champions of middle-class values.[44]

Bill Clinton began his presidency in classical liberal fashion. He put forward a national health care plan; he pushed for "Don't ask, don't tell" that allowed gays and lesbians to serve openly in the military; he led the charge to raise minimum wages and smoking restrictions in public places. Whether it was for pragmatic reasons or a change in intellectual perspective, Clinton moved his ideological center from liberal to cautious liberal by adopting a middle way between pro-government liberalism and Reagan's anti-government conservatism by inclining "toward market solutions, not government bureaucracy, focused on economic growth, not economic redistribution, and dedicated to equality of opportunity, not equality of outcome." In this new role, he set time limits on welfare benefits and supported vouchers to the poor, both libertarian initiatives.[45]

---

[44] The 'Ol' Switcheroo: Ronald Reagan (1962) Time Magazine. https://content.time.com/time/specials/packages/article/0,28804,1894529_1894528_1894518,00.html

[45] Peter Beinart, The Rise of the New Left, Daily Beast, July 11, 2017, https://www.thedailybeast.com/the-rise-of-the-new-new-left. Accessed 30 April 2023.

George W. Bush is an especially interesting example because of his strong ideological and religious beliefs. During his first term in office, he stuck to the conservative agenda by slashing taxes and favoring less government oversight of private enterprise. During his second term, he ran huge deficits to fight the war in Iraq and approved a massive bailout of the financial industry.[46] (*Bush's Shifting* Ideology, by Michael Abramowitz and Dan Eggen, Washington Post Staff Writers, Saturday, September 20, 2008.)

My approach in this book is to reprise America's ideological story lines, identify disruptive trends in society exacerbated by the Coding Revolution, and offer new narrative pathways and narrative tools to help ideologues make their leap toward each other – a leap toward collaboration and cooperation.

I will not offer a grand plan for America. Instead, I will offer a few suggestions for policy reform to generate constructive dialogue. My belief is that rebuilding faith in government depends less on the scientific method for defining public policies and more on a broader sentient view of life. I do not believe, at least in the foreseeable future, that behavior can be turned into mathematical equations, or algorithms, or that measurements of performance can be precisely measured, or that cultural entropy can be reversed.

In some ways, the book exalts the spark of inspiration hidden in the imagination. This inspiration is an everyday affair. I believe we all try to anticipate what the future holds with only partial knowledge. We try to manage our future knowing full well that we cannot predict well, especially changes in tastes and technologies. Systems evolve to manage uncertainty, but I believe the driving force in human civilization rests mainly on fables turned into reality. Modern products may be useful and critical for well-being, but they typically started as figments of the imagination. This is also true of political ideologies; they will flourish if they continue to engage the imagination and produce tangible results that benefit America.

Bringing the challenges into focus will depend on proper distance from the subject and the will to overcome distortions caused by seeing the world through ideological lenses. My motto, which I created, is:

Don't look too far that you only see the horizon
Don't look too closely that you only see yourself.

---

[46] Froomkin, D. (2008), Bush Fatigue Hits Bush. Washington Post. https://busharchive.froomkin.com/BL2008092201223_pf.htm. Accessed 30 April 2023.

Part I

Respect: Uncovering the Wisdom of America's Ideologies

Abstract This section delves into America's three major ideologies and their articulation in response to specific historical crises. The story begins with news articles that racially profile delegates at the 2012 Republican and Democratic national conventions. The intent is to show that color rather than content has often dominated the public debate. Afterward, key items from the 2012 Republican and Democratic platforms are described and compared to the 2016 and 2020 platforms. Then the story shifts backward in time to explain where the ideas came from. Both party platforms have their origins in America's mainstream ideologies. They are described in detail by summarizing the thoughts of the grandees who formulated them. It turns out these ideologies developed in response to crises that have merit even now. This section ends with a warning. Disaffection with accepted ideologies sometimes leads to warring factions, which sometimes lead to a totalitarian takeover of government.

Descriptions of the delegates to the 2012 presidential conventions are a tipoff to the basis of political sentiments in America. Matt Katz, a staff reporter for the Philadelphia Inquirer reported:

> [A] study found that 2.1 percent of this year's GOP delegates are black. Republican activists see themselves as defenders of hard work and merit without regard to creed or color – their presidential nominee, after all, is a Mormon – and they recoil at Democrats' use of an affirmative-action system to pick some delegates based on race, ethnicity, and sexual orientation.
>
> [The] thousands who attended the festival [prior to the Democratic Convention] included gays, mixed-race families, and many African Americans.

A succession of black women took photos in front of an oversize picture of President Obama plastered on a truck sponsored by the National Jewish Democratic Council. Dozens lined up to spin a wheel for free regalia from the Human Rights Campaign, a gay-rights organization. Buttons proclaimed groups such as "Native Americans for Obama."[1]

Fast forward to the 2016 presidential conventions and nothing much has changed except for the stridency of the convention speakers. Race became an even bigger issue. Michelle Obama reminded America that she wakes up every morning in a house built by slaves. Republican delegates shouted USA, USA as if they were rooting for America to be great again. Half the democratic delegates were people of color and approximately 6% of republican delegates were of color with less than 1% black.[2]

The undercurrent of these descriptions easily spills over into a visceral picture of the "other side." It is not hard to imagine democrats thinking of republicans as "pale, male, and stale" as one commentator quipped, or older white people trying to hang onto the countryside after having being driven out of the cities.[3]

The message was the same in 2020. Robin Givhan, writing for the Washington Post wrote:

The roll call on opening day of the Republican National Convention was sleepy. Low energy. And sad. This American ritual, during which each state pledges its delegates to the winning candidate, was bereft of charm. It was technically stultifying. It was also devoid of Black people and sorely lacking in people of color. And it was a long way from exemplifying gender parity. In essence, it was White men in a room simplifying complex issues and repeatedly pledging their fealty to guns, fetuses and the importance of kneeling to pray and standing for the national anthem.[4]

---

[1] Katz M (2012) Party and its delegates paint picture of diversity. Philadelphia Inquirer. https://www. inquirer.com/philly/news/politics/presidential/20120904_Party_and_its_delegates_paint_picture_of_ diversity.html. Accessed 30 Apr 2023.

[2] Frostenson S (2016) Half of the democratic delegates were people of color. For Republicans, it was only 6%, Vox. https://www.vox.com/2016/7/29/12295830/republican-democratic-delegates-diversity-non-white. Accessed 30 Apr 2023.

[3] Phan A (2012) Pale, male, and stale: comparing diversity at the Republican convention to the Democratic convention. CAP Action. https://www.americanprogressaction.org/article/pale-male-and-stale-comparing-diversity-at-the-republican-convention-to-the-democratic-convention/. Accessed 30 Apr 2023.

[4] Givhan R (2020) The Democrats' roll call showed America's beauty and diversity. The Republicans' roll call … did not. The Washington Post. https://www.washingtonpost.com/lifestyle/style/roll-call-republican-convention/2020/08/24/e24451b2-e639-11ea-970a-64c73a1c2392_story.html. Accessed 30 Apr 2023.

Just listen to conservative radio talk show hosts, and their message is also very clear and confrontational. A typical monologue would sound like this: Democrats, especially the "progressive" ones, want to tear down America. They want to tax the rich, they want to end racism, they want reparations, all aimed at bringing down white male supremacy in the United States. Defunding the police and no bail – no jail, and open borders are conscious policies to destroy white-dominated American society. "Progressive" seems to be code for both non-whites and for brainwashed white college students.

What can come of this type of shouting match? What do both sides expect will happen? Do they expect the other side to see the errors of their ways, or were they rousing their base for the next round of political conflict? Did the base really represent the parties? Or were they hijacking them?

To me, the political struggles resemble a version of what I call a complexion complex, a new expression of racialism and tribalism that tore Europe apart and can tear America apart. Surely, racism exists on both sides of the political divide. Among the more forgiving Americans, the conflicts likely result from wounded dignity. Both sides feel that the other side is wronging them unfairly. Many Americans honestly believe they have right and facts on their side, but the other side won't recognize it.

I devote this section of the book to overcoming what economists call statistical discrimination. It is the belief that part of the conflict is that both sides truly do not understand each other, and if they did, at least part of the animosity will drain away. At a distance, it is easy to dismiss republican libertarians and conservatives as naysayers who support negative freedom, negative law, negative rights to property and security. It is easy to label liberal democrats just say "yes" to every government program, to social engineering, to positive freedom, to positive law, to positive rights to public property, to social safety nets. At a closer range, ideologues are not all gesturing in unison. All three American ideologies do differ on important social issues, but each ideology is not as rigid as one might suppose. Most of the great libertarian, conservative, and liberal ideological thinkers were far more nuanced than their opponents supposed. They did not abide by an ideological checklist. Many did not define their principles in a library or a classroom as an intellectual exercise. Their principles evolved as they struggled with challenges that threatened their views of life. Their insights have enriched Western culture. If their wisdom were taught in school, I suspect all Americans would better understand each other.

The ideological standard-bearers I chose to champion America's ideologies lived before the 2012 convention. All faced existential threats to Western civilization. They all experienced major wars or revolutions that overthrew great powers known for their wealth and power, and as centers of high culture, admired by other nations for their sophistication and intellectual achievements. Then, as if overnight, these great nations were upended. It was not simply a change in regime. It was as if society became inverted and perverted. The mob became the people's assembly, criminals became sheriffs, and land grabbed by force became liberated property. These wars shook accepted values and forced these champions to grasp why the temples of civilization collapsed.

These champions understood how economic poverty robbed good people of their dignity. All but one of the champions experienced the Great Depression. Those that did grappled with what caused it. Was it true that private enterprise left to its own devices was unstable or did government cause economic havoc? The answer to this question is crucial to define government's role in a modern economy. After the passage of decades, explanations of the Great Depression that had seemed settled no longer appeared adequate.

Anti-Semitism is another key to understanding the thinking of the champions who lived in Europe during the twentieth century. For them, the Jew was historically the stand-in for the alien, the outsider who threatens national culture. The Nazis blamed the Jews both for capitalist profiteering and for communist expropriation of property, and for infecting the Aryan people with their alien genes and alien ideas. Anti-Semitism exposes the dark side of human nature, the hidden hideous portrait of the soul of the hater who often appears in public well groomed and smiling benevolently. Many of these ideological groundbreakers of the twentieth century were Jewish or had Jewish colleagues, which made them sensitive to even the subtle gestures of the anti-Semite and realized how dangerous it is for haters to be in charge of a nation. It is a mistake to lump all the champions' reactions to anti-Semitism into a simple "well I'm against Jew haters." As you will see reactions to anti-Semitism by Jewish thinkers ranged from a rejection of all "tribal" thinking to proudly hyphenating their heritage.

Moving beyond the "complexion complex," these ideological giants also tackled the effects of technology on culture and government. One of the most subtle challenges they faced was whether scientific management, at the heart of corporate success, could be extended to the entire national economy in the form of socialism. Could a democratically elected governing body plan and organize the economy along rational lines that would eliminate waste and, more importantly, give the public their fair share of the nation's income? The twentieth-century experience shows that concentrated power in any form, whether by a king or a congress, could endanger freedom and democracy.

2

Libertarianism: Centralization Can Lead to Serfdom

Abstract Libertarians fear government authoritarianism. The best protection of individual freedom is to minimize the size of government control. That does not mean a night watchman state where the government only controls the legal system, judicial system, and military. I highlight the thinking of major libertarian thinkers who recognize that government has more roles to play but suggest methods for limiting use of arbitrary power by government. The major libertarians discussed are Frederick Hayek and Milton Friedman. Other notables are cited but more briefly. To see how libertarian thought has influenced American politics, the chapter ties Republican Presidential Platforms to libertarian thought.

2.1 Introduction

Libertarianism is the ideology with the smallest political base but with broad influence on the Republican Party. Because it has the most clearly formulated principles, it is the easiest to convey. For this narrative, the setting is the 2012 Republican Convention. Then the Tea Partiers were at their height of power in the Republican Party. They were a combination of ideologues that wanted to reduce the federal government's power. In demonstrations outside the convention, some dressed in colonial costumes to remind Americans of the how ordinary people rose up against the British in Boston and freed the colonists from government oppression. If my experience with libertarians is indicative, they were the least flamboyant members in that crowd. The libertarian movement gained a sizable following on college campuses in the 1970s. Frederick

V. Glass, *Humanizing the Digital Economy*, https://doi.org/10.1007/978-3-031-37507-1_2

Hayek and Milton Friedman, both libertarians, were replacing John Maynard Keynes as the faces of economics during that period. To contrast themselves with the straggly hippies, libertarian college students were well-kempt, often wearing pressed shirts and ties as signs of sobriety and rational thinking.

By 2012 and certainly by 2016, a clean-cut libertarian of the "70s" would naturally have a lot less hair, be a little red in the face, sport a paunch, and had also grown a more seasoned view of what it means to be a libertarian. It may surprise some that like other American ideologues, libertarians are not one unified, fundamentalist group answering in unison to a set of basic questions of political beliefs. It might also surprise you that major developers of libertarian thought did support government welfare programs and temporary government activism during major business downturns, and I will discuss them shortly. But for the most part, libertarians are the most reliable opponents of government, and within the Republican Party, the staunchest opponents of government planning, whether it is to standardize business practices, redistribute income and wealth, insure against loss, create jobs, or define proper social arrangements.

Libertarians "Just say no," to government doesn't mean that they are backward looking to the days of little villages because they learned from Adam Smith how stifling little villages were in eighteenth-century England. They are social revolutionaries in important respects. They do not oppose abortion, or same-sex marriage, or legalizing marijuana, or prostitution, or any seemingly outrageous lifestyle as long as it does not physically harm others. If you want to follow your fantasies in private, that's okay with libertarians.

If you look at the 2012 or 2016 libertarian party platforms and compare them with Republican platform, you will see many similarities.[1] In their view, as government grew, personal freedom was diminishing. Government was chipping away at private property rights by imposing price controls, wage controls, taxing profits, regulating use, and taxing inheritances. Libertarians like most Americans are environmentally conscious but don't want the government setting aside huge tracts of land, or dictating proper use of land, or deciding on the types of energy sources that should be promoted. They favor a free market in education, a free market in healthcare, and a free market in

---

[1] Libertarian Party Platform (2012). chrome-extension://efaidnbmnnnibpcajpcglclefindmkaj/https://2012election.procon.org/sourcefiles/libertarian-party-platform-2012.pdf. Accessed 30 April 2023. *Libertarian Party Platform,* (2016). chrome-extension://efaidnbmnnnibpcajpcglclefindmkaj/https://www.lp.org/wp-content/uploads/2018/04/Libertarian-Party-Platform-2016.pdf. Accessed 30 April 2023. Republican Party Platform (2012). https://www.presidency.ucsb.edu/documents/2012-republican-party-platform. Accessed 30 April 2023. *Republican Party Platform,* (2016) chrome-extension://efaidnbmnnnibpcajpcglclefindmkaj/https://prod-cdn-static.gop.com/media/documents/DRAFT_12_FINAL%5B1%5D-ben_1468872234.pdf. Accessed 30 April 2023.

retirement planning. Some favor laborers voluntarily organizing but not forcing everyone to join a union. If America truly believes in personal responsibility, people ought to plan their own education, their own health insurance, and their own retirement, not leave it to government planners. Even in the often-unstable financial markets, libertarians want minimum regulation and certainly no government bailouts. It may surprise you that libertarians are not big defense spenders. They want a military large enough to defend the nation and support a volunteer army but are against meddling in foreign affairs. They support free trade and open immigration as long as new arrivals are not a credible threat to national security or a burden on America's social welfare system.

Libertarians have put their stamp on the Republican Party's platforms, even if its stamp gets blurred by similar colored stamps of conservatives and left- of-center Republicans, called moderates by political observers. Because there is much overlap, I will limit the libertarian influence to government planning. As a result, the bulk of the Republican platform will appear as a conservative document in the next chapter, which discusses conservative thought.

The 2012 Republican platform begins with preambles that read like an ode to libertarianism. Up front, Republicans call themselves the party of maximum economic freedom. It is the party that celebrates entrepreneurship and innovation because they are the engines of growth, prosperity, and employment. To unleash the creative spirit, Republicans want to keep taxation, litigation, and regulation to a minimum. For too long, the 2012 preamble states America has let itself be managed by activist politicians – read Democrats – bureaucrats and experts who believe they know the way to manage the economy. These activists want to socially engineer society to their own specifications. They favor expanding entitlements and guarantees, creating new public programs, and expansive government bailouts. Democrats are the party of excessive taxation and regulation that impedes economic development. Their blueprint is failing the American people. It is time to believe in individual spirit again and get government out of the way. Little changed in the 2016 and 2020 preambles except to stress that America has agreed to unfair international trade arrangements that must be fixed.

In the libertarian mold, Republicans have a simple plan for getting America growing again: simplify the tax system, lower taxes, and reign in government spending and regulation. Taxes reduce a citizen's freedom. Those that are necessary should be simple, transparent, and flat, not like democratic proposals to tax the rich and promote class warfare. They want to eliminate double taxation on income and wealth. It is unfair for someone who has saved to pay taxes on interest or dividends earned from those savings. These types of taxes should be eliminated, and so should the death tax. Parents should have the right to bequeath their savings to their children without the government asking for a share.

Downsizing the federal government and keeping it out of the private sector were priorities. Massive funding of the housing market through the Federal Housing Authority (FHA), Fannie Mae, and Freddie Mac and forcing banks to lend to the "disadvantaged" led to the housing crisis in 2008, according to libertarians. When the market collapsed, taxpayers footed the bill for bailing out the nation. Libertarians knew a catastrophe was likely to happen because the government had replaced profit incentives based on prudent loans with profits based on dumping mortgages to government agencies and other unwary investors. Another sore point written into the libertarian platform was the Supreme Court's ruling allowing local government to seize a person's home or land, not for vital use but for transfer to private developers sets a terrible precedent for co-opting private property.

Republicans wanted to preserve federal deposit insurance but make sure banks hold enough reserves that insurance claims are a rare event but agreed with libertarians that the Dodd Frank bill aimed at reforming the financial sector was a regulatory nightmare of government overreach to fix every ill in the financial sector. It would have the unintentional effect of giving bureaucrats huge power and hurting small community banks that will be outside of its rescue plan for big banks.

Many libertarians agreed with other Republicans to support a federal-state-private partnership that would invest in the nation's infrastructure with the great emphasis on private initiative and block grants to states. By infrastructure, libertarians meant roads, bridges, tunnels, and ports – and other transport pathways and hubs. Not all mass transit should remain public, however. Republicans and libertarians wanted to privatize Amtrak because it is a money loser in public hands. Other projects such as urban renewal and other supposedly shovel-ready construction projects to boost production haven't worked and are wasteful.

Government should not pick winners and losers in the energy market. Republicans believe the federal government wasted billions on companies like Solyndra, a maker of solar panels that received a $536 million Department of Energy loan guarantee before declaring bankruptcy. According to Republicans, "experience has shown that the worst environmental degradation has occurred under government control." The EPA's expansive regulations impose billions of dollars on American businesses and consumers.

Both the 2012 and 2016 platforms go on to explain that massive expansion, centralization, and bureaucratization of entitlement programs have turned America into an entitlement society, with people asking what the government can do for them rather than what they can do for themselves. Libertarian Republicans believe Medicare and Medicaid are not sustainable financially and put the responsibility for healthcare on the wrong body. When approximately 80% of healthcare costs are related to lifestyle – smoking, obesity, substance abuse – far greater emphasis has to be put on personal responsibility instead of government guarantees. They want individuals to buy insurance policies instead of expecting government to underwrite all medical treatments. Instead of relying on government to check the books of healthcare providers, the government should introduce genuine competition to get rid fraud and abuse. Only then will healthcare providers have the incentive to cut costs and offer targeted healthcare services. Under federally supported programs, healthcare providers try to maximize government payments per patient. In a competitive market, healthcare providers would have to let patients know the price of services up front instead of reading them on an insurance bill. Users of healthcare services would want to make sure they were not overpaying for services. They might shop around. As for retirement insurance, Republicans wanted to give younger workers responsibility for planning their own retirement.

This flashback to 2012 and 2016 with all its sloganeering gives an outsider almost a caricature of what it means to be a libertarian, but the basic policy prescriptions are accurate.

For a more nuanced understanding of libertarian support for the Republican platform, I will summarize the basic ideas of the most important shapers of this ideology. Before starting, however, I want to take a detour that compares textbook description of competitive markets with the libertarian view. This short comparison will make it much easier to understand that libertarian's approach economic policy from a different perspective than one might expect after taking a few economics courses in college.

The basic model taught in economics courses is static. The model analyzes how suppliers of goods react to market changes in the "short run" when some inputs into their production process are fixed in place and how the reaction differs from a "long-run" response when all inputs are flexible. The textbook model assumes firms are small and do not compete with each other directly because they can sell all they want at the going price. This model is static because it assumes even in the long run that technology and tastes are fixed. In this ideal market, both suppliers and demanders either have perfect knowledge of prices and product characteristics or, if there is uncertainty, it can be estimated from historical data and prices.

By contrast, libertarians focus on market dynamics. Key psychological features drive economic growth: power, discovery, novelty, and a bit of uncertainty. Power is the will to control people and the environment. In a modern economy, power accrues to those with wealth. They can hire people to run their households or buy yachts and mansions. They set standards for living that others dream of emulating. Discovery is the need to produce something new and meaningful that allows a person to feel their life is worth living. Novelty is the need for newness, for new products and new services that grip the imagination. Finally, uncertainty expresses the need for surprise. People do not want to live a programmed life. They want the adventure of solving life's puzzles and overcoming unexpected challenges. Each of these psychological needs works against a stagnant society. Status, achievement, novelty, and uncertainty push them to want more and better products and services and discover new ways of living well.

Anticipation of peoples' needs is a crucial faculty of the libertarian "person." Those who do it well earn profits if they own a business or a high salary if they work for a business. In other words, extraordinary monetary gains are the reward for being sensitive to how the economy is changing. Old products and services often fade, replaced by new ones. Joseph Schumpeter, an economist from Austria who emigrated to America, called this process creative destruction. Firms earn extraordinary profits for a while but are often replaced by new firms with new sets of products.

Unlike the textbook firm that doesn't feel competition because it can sell all it wants at the going price, the libertarian entrepreneur is in a survival of the fittest struggle with other firms. Those firms that find the right balance of competing and cooperating with each other will win, at least temporarily, the competitive struggle against rivals. This is a war without firearms, but it is a war. Some people get displaced, but in the "long run," society is better off. The economy will grow and offer an increasing variety of products.

Greed is an important motivation, and profits are an important measure of success, but libertarians really believe the market is an agent for self-development, moral growth, and a test bed for creative ideas. People learn what they really value when they have to voluntarily pay for what they purchase. To succeed in a market, you need to build trust with clients, and to be trustworthy, you must be true to yourself and to those you are dealing with. Long-term survival in a market requires trying out new ideas and developing new products and services. In the interplay of market forces, power is directed toward progress – more and better goods and services, higher per capita incomes, and most importantly growing awareness of the ability to shape one's own life, even if the end product is never finished and rarely visualized.

This chapter's focus is on the libertarian's view of government's role. The main takeaway is that government should be incentive compatible with the profit-oriented market economy. When it gets too large and operates in a command-and-control mode, not only does the economy suffer, but people also suffer the loss of freedom and security.

The chapter is organized by major shapers of libertarian thought with important secondary characters making their appearance. Frederick Hayek and Milton Friedman are the grandees I have chosen to showcase. For freedom's self-development power, I'll discuss Ayn Rand, a secondary but important character in this narrative. The wrap-up section revisits the Republican platform and compares it to libertarian thought.

2.2   Friedrich Hayek: The Road to Serfdom

Friedrich Hayek was an Austrian of noble descent who lived through all the twentieth century's existential threats. He is the ideal spokesman for another basic libertarian theme associated with classical liberalism: the dangers of centralizing power in government. He experienced the political instability and inflation in Austria after World War I, the ensuing Great Depression, and the rise of the totalitarian dictators in Russia, Germany, and Italy. His struggle with totalitarian regimes led him to believe in an important but limited role for government in private economic affairs.

Hayek was born in Vienna, fought in the Austro-Hungarian Army during World War I, attended the University of Vienna in the early 1920s, and experienced Austria's hyperinflation, which was 1426% per year at its highest in 1922. This hyperinflation wiped out his family's financial assets. The noted Austrian economist, Ludwig Von Mises, a Jew, gave him a job to work on legal and economic issues. Hayek saw anti-Semitism firsthand in Vienna. This cosmopolitan capital was also the home to the likes of Karl Lueger, a virulent anti-Semite who won Vienna's mayoral elections at the turn of the century by vilifying Jews. Hitler was a great admirer and student of Lueger's tactics. During much of the Great Depression, Hayek was teaching at the London School of Economics. He was unwilling to return to Austria after Anschluss, when Austria became part of Hitler's Reich in 1938. After World War II, he left for the United States and taught at the University of Chicago. A future colleague was Milton Friedman and Nobel Prize winner, a Jew from New Jersey, and another key developer of libertarian thought. Hayek, himself, was awarded the Nobel Prize in economics in 1974. He died in America in 1992.

From his studies, Hayek was keenly aware that in the 1880s, Otto von Bismarck, the Iron Chancellor, remembered most today as a militarist who believed the iron fist was the best way to solve political problems, was also a great social reformer. He shrewdly co-opted the agenda of social movements demanding welfare reform in Prussia by introducing old-age pensions, accident insurance, medical care, unemployment insurance, and the 8-hour working day. Prussia was hailed in Western Europe and America as an extremely progressive socialist state. His accomplishments suggested that a top-down approach to social reform based on pragmatic principles could boldly reform society to improve the lot of its people. A little understood downside was that the German government in effect controlled a huge portion of the German economy. It was not hard to go from socialism to totalitarianism in a period of crisis as Hayek witnessed firsthand with the rise of fascism and Nazism.

Hayek understood that fascism, communism, and Nazism all had socialism as a core tenet. They all appealed to uplifting the poor, to giving people across all income brackets a sense of meaning and connection that was somehow lost. Italian fascism and Nazism simply limited socialism to a defined set of people to tap into desires for national rejuvenation. Italian fascism defined the nation as Italian citizens, while the Nazis defined nation as the so-called Aryan race. Communism theoretically appealed to all workers but as we will see is very similar to fascism and Nazism in their approach to organizing society.

Hayek recognized all three regimes based on their legitimacy on ideologies that had great appeal to the outsider in society. Typically, these poor and disgruntled people with a sprinkling of well-educated unsuccessful professionals and academics were looking to band together in a common struggle to overturn their oppressors. All three regimes used slogans that raised the poor or oppressed to nobility. Not surprisingly, he noted that the Nazis and communists in Germany fought each other for the loyalty of this core group.

In his most famous book, *The Road to Serfdom,* published in 1944, Hayek's overriding desire was to warn Britain and other democracies that socialism is dangerous that it could undermine all the values a member of a free society cherishes but takes for granted. You might say his book was part of an anti-tyranny genre that grew up during the 1930s and 1940s. Famous novelists such as Huxley (*Brave New World*), Orwell (*Animal Farm* and *1984*), and Koestler (*Darkness at Noon*) warned about false utopian visions preached by pigs and leaders who grabbed power, crushed the opposition, set up corrupt ruling classes, and through it all believed their actions would be hailed by future generations as necessary to build a better society. Instead of being a novelist, Hayek was an economist with a stuffy Teutonic's writing style, and his focus wasn't on evil characters. Instead, of analyzing Hitler, Stalin, or Mussolini by name, he examined the evils of centralized planning and management, not exactly riveting subjects. His exposition may not be riveting, but his ideas are.

Hayek began by saying socialism was beguiling because workers and those in need felt they should get their fair share of the nation's output through democratic means. Central planning by elected officials instead of unelected corporate executives should produce socially desirable outputs from available resources and protect the environment as well. The invisible hand of the private sector was messy, corrupt, and lacked direction. The visible hand of government, in the right hands, was efficient and fair.

Unfortunately, Hayek said, countries that embraced socialism abandoned economic liberty and as a result weakened personal and political liberty. Socialists gave individualism a bad name by falsely identifying individualism with selfish egoism. In truth, he believed individualism sets people free. His firsthand experience led him to believe a socialist society is doomed to fail or morph into something far worse: a tyranny.

While socialism was a rising and seemingly fresh political movement in Europe, he identified another reason the public ceded control to an iron-fisted strong man. People were scared of something: lawlessness after World War I, the ineffectiveness of democracy to deal with hyperinflation and depression, and the looming threat of the Bolsheviks dominating all of Europe. Citizens were willing to embrace a savior who promised security and order at the expense of freedom. What sense does it make to talk about freedom when there is no bread on the table and elected politicians don't know what to do or are deadlocked in petty quarrels. Only a strong ruler could protect the nation from outside threats and settle old scores with former enemies.

Hayek built his case for limited government by examining socialism and its worst outgrowths: fascism, Nazism, and communism. He said unbridled socialism can and has led to totalitarian regimes, governments that control the military, the press, and the means of production. When this happens, Hayek deferred to Leon Trotsky, the communist revolutionary, to explain the likely result: "In a country where the sole employer is the state, opposition means death by starvation."[2] Actually, the Nazis were more proactive. They simply gassed their enemies.

Hayek didn't attack Hitler, Stalin, or Mussolini personally as monsters but as products of corrupt systems built on utopian socialism. He started his attack by examining what socialism really means and found it was at its core

---

[2] Hayek, F. (1944), *The Road to Serfdom.* University of Chicago Press, IL. p. 119.

an empty idea. Catch phrases such as social justice, greater equality, and security, reasons for economic reform,[3] had no real definition. None of these high-sounding phrases are measurable by a single scale of less and more. In actuality, no yardstick will ever exist because it would require a complete ethical code, agreed to by all, as the basis for ranking values needed for social choices.[4] Not having a social yardstick didn't stop leaders of socialist governments from justifying their actions by saying a particular policy or program will help achieve a "social goal," or a "common purpose," or improve "general welfare," and is in accord with "general interest." Logic wasn't their strong point. They leaned on emotional arguments and mystical visions of being the chosen to rouse the people.

Although Hayek realized logic wasn't the true selling point of socialism, he pressed on with his logical attacks on its slogans. For example, he asked, what do socialists mean by workers getting their fair share of the value of their output? Hayek said allowing a worker to have the whole of his product would favor workers in capital intensive industries who produce highly valuable products such as an automobile. If these types of workers should have their "fair share" reduced, then dividing output among workers across industries becomes a difficult issue.[5] Hayek wryly observed that divvying stops at a state's borders. Even the most diehard socialists believe a state's capital doesn't belong to humanity but to the nation. They are not willing to share capital with a foreigner.[6]

Hayek then shifted from attacking empty phrases to socialist economic theories. He said, socialists mistakenly believe scientific progress has produced important outcomes that favor democratic control of production and distribution of wealth. The logic goes that private enterprise tends toward monopoly because scientific management is much more efficient than disorganized markets that often duplicate efforts and waste resources. If monopoly works best, government should democratize industries to prevent a few unelected executives who run these companies from enriching themselves at the expense of workers and consumers. Because modern corporations operate on principles of scientific management, a government bureaucracy run by experts could do just as well without exploiting the public. Surely, a democracy will operate in the public good, much more so than self-serving businesspeople.

---

[3] Id., p. 32.
[4] Id., p. 57.
[5] Id., p. 111.
[6] Id., pp. 140–141.

Hayek's response was to say socialists oversell democracy, and the public is likely to be gulled into thinking that democracy is always a benign institution. He believed public control easily became corrupted, and even in the best of circumstances, it has functional limitations that make it a poor vehicle for improving the "common good." He began with the obvious: democracy is not geared well for central planning. It is an institution designed primarily to debate legal issues, not to plan an economy. Moreover, he said, democratic legislation need not conform to the rule of law.[7] He observed firsthand Germans and Italians voting in dictators who co-opted big swathes of the economy from private citizens.

Even legislators with good intentions often produce immoral results according to Hayek. For example, legislation aimed at helping a particular group because they were discriminated against or because they were disadvantaged in some way sets a precedent for allowing government officials to favor one group over another, which is a violation of the rule of law.[8] Taken to an extreme, as it was in Central Europe during his lifetime, individual rights and equal rights of minorities lost all significance.[9]

Hayek claimed people who abhor a political dictator as they did in Britain often clamor for a dictator in the economic field.[10] Even the best minds want to be free from material cares to focus on plain living and high thinking.[11] They don't want to be dirtied by a system where everything has its price, and they don't want to name their price. Instead, they implicitly want others to make their tough choices.[12] Even better, they wish tough choices were not necessary at all. Private enterprise forces them to make bitter choices that would not happen if a socialist system spread the wealth and allowed everyone to pursue his own interests.[13] In effect, this person resents the economic problem of scarcity. He wants it to go away and convince himself about the economic freedom available in a land of plenty.[14] He doesn't realize that making economic choices is a basic exercise of that extends to other freedoms. Any meaningful choice carries the risk of being wrong and responsibility to accept the consequences.[15]

---

[7] Id., p. 82.
[8] Id., p. 83.
[9] Id., p. 87.
[10] Id., p. 88.
[11] Id., p. 89.
[12] Id., p. 97.
[13] Id., p. 97.
[14] Id., p. 98.
[15] Id., p. 100.

Hayek said, another common objection to private enterprise is that competition is blind.[16] It doesn't measure a person's true worth, which of course it does not. But competition has an important feature in common with the rule of law: they are both blind to a particular person's felt worth. It is this impersonality that characterizes a free society. You are not judged by your pedigree but by your actions and contributions. Hayek went on to stress that the choice between socialism and private enterprise is between two starkly different views of society. Socialism theoretically offers a system where everybody gets what he deserves according to some absolute universal standard of what is right instead of one determined by accident or luck. In practice, it is a system where a few determine who is to get what. By contrast, private enterprise depends on the ability and enterprise of those who compete.[17] The record of private enterprise was clear to Hayek. The fact that opportunities open to the poor are more restricted than those open to the rich does not make it any less true that a poor person is much freer than a person with more material comfort in a different type of society.[18]

Many people, according to Hayek, don't realize money offers us the widest choice for enjoying the fruits of our efforts.[19] Naturally, lack of money restricts what you can do, and many have come to hate these restrictions,[20] but, in fact, according to Hayek, money is one of the greatest instruments of freedom invented by man. Money opens an astounding range of choices to the poor man – a range greater than a rich man a few decades ago.[21]

He warned that when rewards are not economic, when they are instead public distinctions, positions of power, better housing, better food, and opportunities for travel or education bestowed by government, the rewards are not chosen but received.[22] Complete economic control gives government officials almost unlimited power over society.[23] Compare this threat to any in a private economy. Even in the best of worlds, freedom is very limited. Few have many meaningful choices for an occupation in a private economy, but at least they have some choice,[24] not so in the Soviet Union or Nazi Germany.

---

[16] Id., p. 101.
[17] Id., p. 101.
[18] Id., p. 102.
[19] Id., p. 89.
[20] Id., p. 89.
[21] Id., p. 90.
[22] Id., p. 90.
[23] Id., p. 93.
[24] Id., p. 94.

Science, with its beguiling images of crystalline simplicity and beauty, doesn't carry over to social organization. Scientific advance doesn't mean government officials have the potential to plan and control more efficiently. In fact, the opposite is true according to Hayek. A few cannot absorb the vast complexity of modern society. As a result, their plans will have to simplify economic problems greatly. The outcomes will be incredibly clumsy, primitive, with limited scope. A centrally planned society like the Soviet Union would not be able to produce the kaleidoscopic variety of a competitive economy.[25] Fewer products would inevitably cut job opportunities.[26] Job qualifications would become objective and uniform. Strength of desire would account for little. Special arrangements to test unusual job candidates would not be allowed – unless someone is a party member. Diversity of human capacities works against a plan designed for everyone to fit a slot.[27]

Socialists tend to believe their trump card is to use experts and scientific management tools to avoid waste, according to Hayek. He countered that experts also impose their own values on society. For starters, they believe scientific organization of society is possible.[28] They endorse a conscious approach to organizing society and are aesthetically in love with the clean lines of a blueprint.[29] In the socialist worldview, engineers and scientists have the false distinction of being leaders in the march toward a better world[30] because history is supposedly obedient to scientific laws, which they are not.[31]

Unfortunately, a cadre of experts who worship science won't account for trade-offs beyond their knowledge and expertise.[32] They will overvalue the importance of their specialties[33] and, if I might add to Hayek's argument, the effectiveness of their theories and tools. Experts have notable successes in limited fields, but Hayek pointed out that extreme technical excellence in a particular field such as the Soviet Union's early triumphs is space exploration, which happened after publication of Hayek's book in 1944, is a sure sign of misdirection of resources.[34]

---

[25] Id., p. 50.
[26] Id., p. 95.
[27] Id., p. 96.
[28] Id., p. 189.
[29] Id., p. 190.
[30] Id., p. 191.
[31] Id., p. 197.
[32] Id., p. 53.
[33] Id., p. 55.
[34] Id., p. 54.

Socialists further justify their claims that socialism works best organizing production and distributing wealth. They offer two basic reasons for government control, according to Hayek. The first is that because private enterprise tends toward monopoly, a government takeover or control is inevitable. Hayek offered a counter argument. He said the recent rise of monopolies in Britain resulted from the deliberate collaboration between organized capital and labor.[35] The second reason given for government control was that protection is necessary to allow new technologies to come online.[36] When he was writing *The Road to* Serfdom, British socialists were lamenting that if the British auto industry were a monopoly, it could supply better and cheaper cars than the United States. He wasn't sure this was true, but even if it had some truth, it could limit future progress. It would be a sacrifice of liberty for immediate gain;[37] moreover, he strongly believed technological progress is not incubated by government; it depends on personal liberty.[38]

In Hayek's view, socialists imagine a highly competent executive team developing plans to make the state powerful to its enemies and compassionate to its citizens. What socialists missed in Hayek's opinion was the dangerous type that rises to power in a socialist state. When the state controls everything, the only power worth having is to share the exercise of power.[39] The people at the top fought their way to power in Germany, Italy, Spain, and Russia by murdering their competitors.[40] He gave three reasons explain why a strong group with fairly homogenous vision will form from the worst elements. First, the more educated have diverse views. Second, it is easiest to gain support from the gullible who accept ready-made systems. Third, it is easiest to agree on a negative program – hatred of an enemy, a Jew, for example – rather than on a positive program.[41]

Once government controls more than a certain portion of the whole, its effects dominate the system leading to the fall of democracy.[42] For example, Hayek pointed out the German government in 1928 controlled an estimated 53% of national income.[43] With that type of reach, Hayek observed, it wasn't hard for Hitler to take control of the economy. The opportunity for a strong-

---

[35] Id., p. 199.
[36] Id., p. 50.
[37] Id., pp. 51–52.
[38] Id., p. 52.
[39] Id., p. 152.
[40] Id., p. 157.
[41] Id., p. 138.
[42] Id., p. 61.
[43] Id., p. 61.

man takeover rests on the inability of a socialist democratic government to manage a large economy. Hayek outlined the stages leading to government paralysis: elected officials will not be able to decide on a comprehensive plan because of political deadlock. To move ahead, legislators will break up the plan into parts. By doing so, they are admitting a unified design is beyond their reach.[44] Delegation to experts is one way out but that simply shifts the battle from the legislature to bureaucracies that vie for resources and power.[45] Eventually, the public demands reform. The easy way out is to hand over control to a Leader with sole responsibility for planning,[46] or to a small minority because they will be able to agree among themselves on an issue.[47]

Now in power, the ones in charge appointed by the Leader will produce a comprehensive plan and assure the public it will be carried out. The Plan becomes the law of the land. Anyone who doesn't do his part is potentially an enemy of the state. The rule of law cannot survive because there are no set legal standards of behavior only planning targets, and these can change if the plan is failing, and a new course of action is necessary.[48] No one is safe in this environment because ends justify means, and the ends may not be known to even a high ranking official, and of course, the ends can change.[49]

When the Plan is supreme, ruthlessness becomes a virtue. The appointed leaders will admit to stamping on individual rights but admit no moral failing because their goals and their plan for society, a plan designed to feed, employ, and defend society, are way above the puny and "selfish" interests of an individual.[50] In effect, they want the "people" to regard Plan as theirs, for their benefit alone.[51] The leaders will use propaganda to persuade the people and if that doesn't work, secret police will keep the "people" in line.[52]

Propaganda in a totalitarian state has a vicious edge.[53] The Leader wants to justify his worthiness by attacking the old order. He embraces prejudices he shares with many of his fellows and amplifies them and glories in them.

---

[44] Id., p. 64.
[45] Id., p. 67.
[46] Id., p. 67.
[47] Id., p. 69.
[48] Id., p. 73.
[49] Id., p. 147.
[50] Id., p. 149.
[51] Id., p. 153.
[52] Id., p. 153.
[53] Id., p. 154.

Eventually, these prejudices become systematized into core values of a society built on hate.[54]

Every thought, every desire, must support the Plan. Totalitarians hate science for science's sake or art for art's sake.[55] The word "truth" ceases to have its old meaning.[56] Nazis defined morality and truth on racial terms. What benefited the German people was right and good. They made no distinction between society and the state, between private and public.[57]

Hating the Jew as a demonic enemy drew wild applause from Germans. Having a scapegoat for all the setbacks the German people had experienced its defeat in World War I allowed German to vent their anger and fears on a target. The communists relied more on capitalists as the enemy, although Jews were prominent in that class as well. The ultimate objective of the Plan was not measured in tons of output or numbers of cannon; it was a Messianic vision of a new Eden, and this blissful age would require great sacrifice to win an apocalyptic struggle against the hated enemy.

In Russia, after its defeat in World War I, the Bolsheviks explained a great conflict was underway for supremacy between the proletariat and the bourgeoisie. The Nazis framed the great struggle as a fight to the death between the Jews and the Aryans. Both offered visions of a Messianic Age – an Aryan Paradise or Worker's Paradise – that would occur in the distant future, but only if the people fought for it.

Members of the anointed group were the vanguard of a new civilization, its chosen people, even if they seem like the lowest rung of society. The Aryans were part of an organic unity, a master race, or in the case of the proletarians, a part of the inevitable march of civilization toward ceding economic control to workers. Believers had to work selflessly for the whole, each according to his needs for the communists and each according to his offspring for the Nazis who planned to give birth to a pure Aryan nation.

It was not enough to produce messianic visions. Both had plans to reach the Messianic Age. Communists ended private property and instituted a 5-year plan. The underlying belief was that in a society with socialized property human, behavior would change. They would no longer exploit each other; they would have enough food, clothing, and other necessities to be freed from want. As a result, they would become part of a happy, carefree proletariat. The Nazis also put all basic industries under government control.

---

[54] Id., p. 156.
[55] Id., p. 162.
[56] Id., p. 163.
[57] Id., p. 187.

All resources necessary were to be marshaled for the apocalyptic struggle, but in Hitler's case it wasn't against property owners; it was against inferior races that were corrupting the Aryan nation. Once the Aryan's were purged of these genetic threats to their purity, Hitler believed that the purified Aryan nation would live like a happy, carefree tribe as in olden days.

In the march to the Messianic Age, some must lead; they were the head of the body. Hitler was billed as the modern-day Aryan warrior. Stalin, whose name meant steel, was the ideal rugged proletarian. It should be clear that looks didn't matter because neither leader looked the part. The part went to the survivor who beat his way to the top.

Hayek's defense of a free society had no marching bands playing in the background, no fiery speeches, and no phalanxes of men in uniform. In comparison to this bold imagery of fascists and communists, the libertarian agenda seems almost old-fashioned and naïve. People should go about their business of building a satisfying life. As drab as this advice might sound, this is the road to freedom, according to Hayek. He said in the real world there are no utopias. Life is a series of often messy trade-offs that require tough decisions best left to the private citizen. He expected decisions will follow fuzzy patterns because people are alike but not the same.

Hayek believed morality had its roots in self-interest of an enlightened variety, a type that leads to peaceful and productive exchanges and expands a person's interests beyond self. His profile of a responsible person is someone who is a producer of goods, services, and a provider who supports his children and others whom he cares for. The basic example of Hayek's meaning of moral behavior growing from self-interest is the traditional marketplace. Self-interested trades leave both sides better off, and often people cooperate to produce and deliver goods because these relationships are profitable.

Over time, free exercise of human ingenuity enables men to satisfy ever widening range of desires, and in the process, probably no class did not benefit.[58] Personal ambition led to speedy progress on a wide range of fronts.[59] The historical lesson was clear to Hayek. The prime objective of government was to oversee that the spontaneous forces of society being guided by common law and that it should resort as little as possible to coercion.[60] A good society creates a system that encourages competition instead of accepting institutions.[61] Hayek believed whenever competition could be created or nurtured, it is a better way of guiding individual effort than any other.[62]

---

[58] Id., p. 14.
[59] Id., p. 15.
[60] Id., p. 15.
[61] Id., p. 15.
[62] Id., p. 36.

Fostering fair competition requires a carefully thought-out legal system, according to Hayek. A system based on anticompetitive rules can have grave defects.[63] For example, price controls hurt coordination.[64] The pricing system should remain the province of the private sector.

A key market system imperative is the widespread availability of private property. The danger of transferring property to the state is that it puts it in a position to decide all incomes.[65] Private property is the most important guarantee of freedom not only for those who own property but scarcely less for those who don't because private property disperses control.[66] According to Hayek, inequality is more readily borne when it is not imposed.[67] When the state controls industries, a failing industry could trigger a government overthrow even when state management was not at fault. The point is that the government becomes a focal point for venting popular frustrations.

Hayek firmly believed in the negative view of freedom and law – protection from mainly physical harm. These laws were an outgrowth of common law, a set of laws that evolved from historical cases that settled disputes. These laws represented the wisdom of past ages which could not be reinvented according to design by a set of planners. They are laws of the "do not" variety. Hayek and other libertarians feared government trying to be a facilitator there to help people use their freedom wisely. This attitude turned government into loco parentis, a substitute authority for the family, telling people what to do. In this role of helper, government passes administrative laws designed to tell people what to do as opposed to traditional common law that tells people what they cannot do.

Yet Hayek was not for laissez-faire, where the government's functions are limited to running a night watchman's state – running the legal system, police force, and military.[68] He agreed these functions should be government's primary objective – to establish and maintain the rule of law and not give men with arbitrary power to maintain order. This does require government to run a fair and competent police force and court system. Government should also build a military to protect a nation against external threats, but not make it so large that it threatens personal freedom. However, Hayek was not opposed to government upholding minimum standards where markets failed, but he was very cautious in using government power. He wanted people to realize

---

[63] Id., p. 36.
[64] Id., p. 37.
[65] Id., p. 103.
[66] Id., pp. 103–104.
[67] Id., p. 106.
[68] Id., p. 15.

government intervention leads to regulations, to co-opting resources directly through taxes and government spending, and ultimately to government officials having power over the public.

If government is necessary, Hayek gave a blueprint for government action that was surprisingly flexible given the animosity toward government among many libertarians today. His basic advice to policymakers was to design programs that encourage competition instead of accepting that particular institutions should do the job.[69]

He distinguished between two types of security that the government should underwrite. The first is to prevent physical hardship such as falling below a minimum standard of living. When a society has reached a given level of wealth, Hayek believed it should guarantee that no one falls below the minimum. It is unlikely to endanger freedom.[70] He even felt, the state should protect individuals against common hazards of life when their uncertainty makes it likely that only a few individuals can make adequate provisions.[71] He was also a supporter of government combating general fluctuations in economic activity as long as it doesn't try to replace the market. He felt that modern democracies cannot bear a substantial lowering of standard of living in peacetime or a prolonged stationary economy.[72] He believed the ultimate countercyclical tool may simply be monetary policy,[73] a theme that that later earned Milton Friedman a Nobel Prize According to Hayek, only very special circumstances required absolute security such as to protect a judge's complete independence.[74]

However, government policies are insidious when designed to protect individuals or groups against loss of income.[75] A person who loses his fortune because of a new invention is tragic, especially if he worked hard and had great skill. However, protecting his income will require funds taken from someone else.[76] Rather than picking a person to protect, the real danger is that government will grant security piecemeal to this group or that, with the result that those left out become more insecure. This makes the demand for security more urgent.[77] The flip side of government judging undeserved loss is to judge

---

[69] Id., p. 15.
[70] Id., p. 120.
[71] Id., p. 120.
[72] Id., p. 210.
[73] Id., p. 121.
[74] Id., p. 119–120.
[75] Id., p. 122.
[76] Id., pp. 122–123.
[77] Id., p. 123.

when unmerited gain requires a giveback to society. To judge the merits of a case against a set of winners, the government would have to determine what they did, what they foresaw, and what their intentions were. Decisions on a supposedly just giveback will affect private behavior. It will affect what job a person takes, how hard the person works, and what types of risks to take. In general, people lose their incentive to do their best.[78]

If the government decides to promote security indirectly by fixing wages and prices, changes in market conditions must have some other outlet for expression. Hayek suggested employment and production will fluctuate wildly because employers can only hire or fire workers or raise or lower production to adjust when market conditions change.[79] In general, the more we try to provide full security by interfering in the market system, the greater insecurity becomes.[80] Yet some security is essential if freedom is to be preserved.

Most are willing to bear the risk of freedom as long as the risk is not too great. But nothing is more fatal than extolling security at the expense of freedom.[81] This was Hayek's warning to Britain and America in the 1940s that it could happen in democratic societies if the public is not careful. A welfare state can erode the message that people should be free to run their own lives. Although he may have exaggerated the threat, his basic premises hold a good deal of truth.

2.3   Milton Friedman: Free to Choose

Hayek's fears growing out of European tyrannies that were destroyed decades ago may read like a melodrama filled with corrupt unnamed characters that seem distant, drawn from a film-noire, who are interesting more so for their cloak and dagger intrigues than for their relevance for modern political policy. Well, that opinion is not correct. In Technicolor America of the 1950s and 1960s, where daylight was a given, and most people were smiling and definitely well-fed, libertarian thought continued to evolve and eventually became a powerful force during the Reagan administration. And the leader of that resurgence was none other than a diminutive, bald, smiley Jew from New Jersey: Milton Friedman.[82] Arguably, more than Hayek, he was the great

---

[78] Id., p. 124.

[79] Id., p. 129.

[80] Id., p. 130.

[81] Id., p. 133.

[82] This section is based on information from Friedman, M. (1962), *Capitalism and Freedom*, University of Chicago Press, IL; and Friedman, M. and R. *Free to Choose* (1980) Harcourt, Brace, and Jovanovich, NY.

twentieth century developer of pragmatic libertarian thought, applying libertarian principles to reform government programs. Perhaps, the tag pragmatic is a misleading description of him. Friedman was more like a horticulturist or better yet, a seminator of government policies that were original and inventive and that opened new paths for carrying out policy objectives many libertarians rejected as statist. As with other visionaries, some of his proposals did not work well, but they added a new dimension to policymaking: trying to develop programs based on stimulating market incentives that produce social welfare gains.

Even among libertarians he could surprise. Friedman believed government had an important role to play in enhancing a person's ability to build a satisfying life, but not in the usual way of doling out benefits in exchange for following rules defining what a person can or cannot do. Instead, he wanted government to jumpstart competition in fields normally controlled by government such as public education. He was the developer of school vouchers that allowed parents to pick schools and pay for them instead of relying on government to provide public education. He wanted to privatize the administration of social security, Medicare, and Medicaid to give people more choices in the type of social insurance they could buy. A simple mantra can sum up his advice to government policymakers: aim at complementing or stimulating market forces by keeping government policies simple, rule-based, impersonal, universal in coverage, with benefits and responsibilities that align with private markets.

From a strictly pragmatic perspective, he said government is organized in a way that would make it an inefficient provider of services. A bicameral legislator and majority voting are not conducive for rapid response, product innovation, or even effective management oversight. Because a democratic government treats voters alike, government services will have a gray mediocre look and taste. Like Hayek, he believed decentralization, especially small profit centers, works best in a complex, rapidly changing environment.

Also, like Hayek, he recognized libertarians faced their toughest challenge trying to define a stable framework for financial markets. Historically, financial panics turned economic downturns into sharp recessions and depressions as people drew their money out of the system and sat on it. The basic problem was that money and other IOUs were promises to pay backed by shaky assets that couldn't be unloaded during a panic to pay off lenders. His creative solution was for the government to adopt a rule-based monetary policy targeted at a specified growth in money supply. During financial panics, that meant the government would have to pump money into the system to offset money being drawn out of it by panicky investors. At the time of his recommendation, he examined alternatives such as targeting the money supply to keep overall prices stable but thought the target was too hard to achieve. Since his recommendation, credit cards and all sorts of new financial instruments have made it harder to define money. Perhaps Friedman would have changed his basic rule; he certainly would not have started adding a growing list of exceptions to prop his rule up.

Friedman also tackled another historical financial problem that created international dislocations was fixed exchange rates among currencies. Sometimes a nation felt its currency should be valued at a certain level to gain national prestige. Mispriced currencies could produce far more than international trade dislocations. They could also lead to a loss of freedom. In his view, many countries have protected their exchange rates using direct controls on foreign exchange. Friedman observed this route gave government tremendous power over trade and was often associated with authoritarian governments.

Other less intrusive methods to reduce trade deficits, for example, also proved ineffective or destabilizing according to Friedman. Traditionally, governments held foreign reserves to hold off temporary runs on their currencies. The problem is that currency traders know these reserves will run out and could speculate on an eventual devaluation of a nation's currency, producing a currency crisis. George Soros was known as the "Man who broke the Bank of England" by betting $10 billion in 1992 that the pound would have to be devalued. Another path was to force domestic prices down to make the nation's currency look more attractive to foreign buyers of domestic products. The problem with this approach is that domestic prices and wages don't adjust quickly to changing market conditions. It takes years of accepting unemployment to convince producers and workers to lower their prices. Friedman suggested a simple alternative: let a nation's exchange rate with other currencies float to levels defined by international trade in currencies. It would end speculative bubbles in a nation's currency. It would allow domestic prices and wage levels to remain fixed but still keep products competitive because the nation's currency would be worth less, effectively lowering the price of domestic goods and raising the price of foreign goods.

Keeping it simple, rule-based, and consistent with market incentives led Friedman to recommend a negative tax as a replacement for a confusing variety of paternalistic social welfare programs such as public housing and food stamps. Basically, the idea was to give poor people money instead of services allowing them to choose what was best for them. As they earned income, let them keep a percentage until they were actual taxpayers. He favored a flat tax as a replacement for the highly complex federal income tax that, at least on paper, looked like a means of taxing the rich and creating class divisions.

As for fiscal policy to stabilize or grow the economy, his reading of history was that it didn't work. Policymakers who pushed pet projects often used as an excuse that the spending would cut unemployment or prop up a long-term decline in the economic activity in some part of the nation, the rust belt, the heartland, or some other colorful part of the country. The result was growing and more volatile government spending that increased uncertainty in the market. Spending through borrowing hurts private investment unless people are indifferent between holding money and bonds, which generally doesn't happen except in cases of financial panic or the fear that interest rates have nowhere to go but up, so people will hold cash until bond interest rates go up to normal levels.

Friedman was never one to let ideology get in the way of good sense. He was a great believer in markets, but he also believed government should step in to prevent panic. He supported government work projects during the Great Depression to give the nation hope that government would protect them. Nonetheless, he feared sustained government control because government has the most potential of any segment of society to exert monopoly control over people's lives. He ranked governments by their oppressiveness. Using a simple categorization, he said communism and fascism were the most oppressive regimes because they controlled the military, press, and industry. Dictatorships were less oppressive because they controlled the military and press but often left production and trade in private hands. Western democracies were least oppressive because the press and production were largely in private hands, and the public had some influence over government policies.

2.4   Other Contributors

The next few contributors to libertarian thought are academics without the public panache of Friedman who was a great debater and enjoyed taking on the opposition. Perhaps in private, they were great raconteurs, but it doesn't show in their theoretical discussions. They added important insights into the limitations of democratic political bargaining, justifications for government control over legal objectives, and constitutional arrangements. Admittedly these are dry but necessary topics for getting a better sense of libertarian thinking.

Buchanan and Tullock are first up. They applied economic analysis to voting rules and vote trading within democracies in their book *Calculus of*

Consent.[83] In a brief discussion, they describe that cultural clashes among groups raise the cost of democratic decision-making. Unyielding factions will have little interest in trading political benefits, when it is "us against them." Political deadlocks will occur frequently, and oppressive coalitions are likely to develop, leading perhaps to civil war.[84] The Arab Spring is an example of the failure of democracy because of clashing tribal and religious differences. On a much lower intensity level, Ideological struggles in America have led to political gridlock. America's politics in the twenty-first century is following this pattern so far.

Buchanan and Tullock did not pursue this line of analysis. Instead, they assumed a society where people have different interests but expect to be treated fairly by the political system and when collective action is necessary do it in a way that is most efficient. Voting rules trade off collective decision-making costs against the fear of being harmed by unfavorable outcomes. Majority rule is simply an expedient for being able to act on most political issues. On very important issues such as ratifying treaties, a two-thirds majority is necessary in America.

Vote trading in congress can improve policy when interest groups have strong preferences. Both sides can gain by voting for the other's policy proposal. Buchanan and Tullock stressed that even with vote trading government will never approach the flexibility of the marketplace. Political decisions and their costs and benefits are collective. The individuals reaping government benefits such as improved roads may not be the ones bearing the costs.

Voting strategies will come into play that don't work in a competitive market where you have to take it or leave it option at the market price. Instead, political bargainers will try to hide their selfish intentions by suggesting their policies will help society by creating jobs and caring for the unfortunate. The strongest interest groups will co-opt the legislative agenda, putting their requests ahead of others.

Theodore Lowi, a noted political scientist, said that since the Franklin Roosevelt Administration, especially, interest groups look to government as a source of funding and protection. The acceptance of long stretches of deficit spending by the public allows government to grow into a huge shapeless mass with an increasing number of groups seeking justice through government action.[85]

---

[83] James M. Buchanan, J.M. and Tullock, G. (1974), *The Calculus Of Consent* (1974) Ann Arbor Paperbacks Michigan.

[84] This is a mild extension of their descriptions of factions on pp. 115–116.

[85] Lowi, T.J. (1969), *The End of Liberalism, preface.* W. W. Norton. NY.

Extending economic analysis to the law, leads to another libertarian developer: Richard Posner, a legal expert who claimed the law should aim at producing efficient markets.[86] In the traditional marketplace, traders must have the right to use and transfer private property with the least impediments because holders of property will have the most incentives to sell when others value their property more or invest to boost the future value of their holdings. Property rights need not remain frozen for all time to give holders assurance of potential gains. Following Friedman's observation, Posner agreed that private property rights change with conditions. Rights in a rural area are more expansive than in an urban setting where people are packed together. No matter the setting, however, Posner still said the legal objective remains the same: the law should spur voluntary and efficient trade.

Posner cited many examples of how a legal system outlaws forced trades. Illegally taking your car for a joy ride is punishable by law because the car thief should have paid for the privilege of using it, and if he didn't, he should pay a stiff fine. Along similar lines, eminent domain, the government appropriating private property for other uses is an involuntary trade that should be avoided, even if the government attempts to compensate the property holder because the fair market value of the taking to the property holder is likely higher than its supposedly fair market value. Any type of government regulation should be viewed as a taking, to be avoided, if at all possible.

He also stressed the limitations of relying on market forces to right wrongs caused by breaking the law. Jail time was necessary for criminal acts because it communicates that someone cannot pay in dollars for hurting or killing another. Notions of fairness and sacredness of human life trump efficiency as social objectives. Wrongful death has no market value. The legal system does not place a price on the loss of life. Someone who unintentionally kills another may pay fines for pain and suffering or for loss of future earnings but not for the death itself.

Robert Nozick, a philosopher, made the case to justify why libertarians favor a democratic government that has ultimate control over the law, military, and police and yet are against all other government social services.[87] He said humans have basic rights that a collective should not take away. It is inadmissible to sacrifice a person for the greater good or to take away property from a person for the greater good. A legal system and a police force are necessary to guarantee inalienable rights to all members of a state. Although state

---

[86] See Richard A. Posner, R.A. (1977), *Economic Analysis of The Law*. Little Brown and Company, NY. For further information on Posner's views, see Posner, R.A. (1981), *The Economics of Justice*. Harvard University Press, MA.

[87] Nozick, R. (1974), *Anarchy, State, and Utopia*. Basic Books, NY.

borders are typically the product of war, Nozick says a monopoly of policing power would evolve even if all people were of good will because a society cannot survive when police forces compete. As if by an invisible hand, people realize the benefits of uniform rules and objective enforcement. When government goes beyond setting and enforcing the rules of the game, the political actors have a vision of a pattern for the distribution of benefits and costs that they would like society to adopt. Inevitably, some groups will gain, others will suffer. Critically, as Hayek said, the basis of this redistribution has no objective standard and gives government officials power over people's lives.

Now that the economists, political scientists, and lawyers have had their say, it is time to introduce a much more colorful character, a famous libertarian author who developed her own libertarian ethics. Her name is Ayn Rand, a Russian émigré from the Soviet Union, of Jewish origin. A bit of sociological history, compliments of Jean-Paul Sartre, may help explain her penchant for worshipping a superman who rebels against conventions that try to mold him into a Babbitt character, who does what others expect him to do.

In the *Anti-Semite and the Jew*, Sartre explained that modern anti-Semitism was really an unreasoning passion, sometimes justified by so-called theoretical propositions.[88] He believed, and I think justly, that passion dominates life. The objects of passion, according to Sartre, were women, glory, power, and money, with "women only" being a bit outdated. Anti-Semites had a passion for economic security, for guaranteed status, for knowing future generations will be better models of themselves. The anti-Semite hated the Jew as an alien who threatened his security. He believed he was a foot soldier in the struggle against the Jewish menace but was never at risk because the Jews were unarmed. He was willing to accept evil for the greater good, if the evil would rid society of the Jew.

Sartre said one type of Jewish reaction to anti-Semitism was to fall back on the Rights of Man, to champion individual rights in the face of tribalism, to champion reason over passion as the means to settle disputes, to champion the rule of law over the weak protections of democracy that could be easily co-opted by hordes of anti-Semites. Prices, profits, and money were liberators because they didn't have a face; they were universal instruments of payments and rewards measured objectively in markets. Von Mises, Friedman, Posner, and Nozick were all Jewish.

---

[88] Sartre, J.P. (1944), *Anti-Semite and Jew*, Schocken Books, NY, chrome-extension://efaidnbmnnnibpca jpcglclefindmkaj/https://abahlali.org/files/Jean-Paul_Sartre_Anti-Semite_and_Jew_An_Exploration_ of_the_Etiology_of_Hate__1995.pdf. Accessed 30 April 2023.

In my opinion, Ayn Rand, also represents this Jewish response to anti-Semitism, even as she rejected her Jewishness. Starting with her name; it was originally Alisa Rosenbaum. Ayn has an ambiguous meaning; it may be a contraction of several Hebrew words, one meaning "eye" another meaning "nothingness." Even her last name "Rand" suggests a typewriter brand, Remington Rand. Using the "eye" definition, her name seems like shorthand for one who writes what she sees. Whatever her true motivations for discarding her birth name, her response to anti-Semitism contributes greatly to the history of libertarian thought because she re-centered the ethical focus of private enterprise from greed to creativity. Adam Smith and his intellectual offspring believed self-interest, a euphemism for greed, was the prime mover of markets. It was only the beneficial results of market behavior that morally justified private enterprise because traders had to satisfy each other's needs. Joseph Schumpeter believed in the market not because of ethical behavior but because of its dynamism, its creative destruction. New products and processes would overturn monopolies that greedy businessmen built. Hayek doesn't really say if greed is the prime motivator of people in a free society. Rand took a different tack. She said a truly human's prime motivation is to be creative and reap the benefits of this creativity. It is creativity that gives birth to markets and destroys monopoly and this creative force is what makes people human. Private enterprise is the most ethical system imaginable because it unleashes individual creativity by freeing the reasoning person from social harnesses, from tribal barriers.[89]

Rand longed for an atomistic society without traditional ties. She was much blunter than Hayek in condemning any government social enterprise. Any politician who supported welfare programs was a merchant of false hopes, a peddler of quack cures, and a huckster who curried and cuckolded the public. Her Creator Man opposed religion because it rests on nonnegotiable, irrational dogmas, belief in miracles or God were unacceptable because they take away from the dignity of man's capacity to be self-sustaining using intellect and reason. If she were alive today, her heroes would include Bezos, Gates, Page, and especially Elon Musk, the driving force behind a whole series of new companies including Tesla and Space X. They are all creators of new industries, mavericks who realized the potential of new technologies to transform society. In the Schumpeterian mold, they replaced the Rockefellers, Fords, and DuPonts as the leaders of American industry.

---

[89] See, for example, Ayn Rand, A. (1961), *For the New Intellectual*. Random House, NY.

2.5   The Republican Platform Reconsidered

Putting together the sentiments and ideas of Hayek, Friedman, Buchanan, and Tullock, Posner, Nozick, and Rand explain a libertarian's political platform. Libertarians believe government's tendency is to control an increasing share of the economy directly by expanding social and military programs and indirectly through taxation policies and regulations of private industry. One explanation for government growth is the public's desire for simple and bold solutions to current economic and political problems. Another motivation is that politicians are themselves self-seeking. They, like many others, want to control their destiny, to say their lives had meaning, and to be remembered as making a difference to future generations. Gaining votes is the ticket to power. Special interests can deliver votes and campaign funds. Hiring media specialists can gauge public opinion and deliver targeted messages to attract voters. Election campaign organizations turn out the vote.

This doesn't have to be an insidious process with money passing under the table or money being used to gull the public. Again, Buchanan and Tullock said vote trading within Congress can potentially direct resources to those most in need. However, libertarians believe the political market is likely to be co-opted by special interests. Whoever wants government influence – ethnic groups, social groups, or corporations – will invest in political influence, and it will keep growing as long as the investment pays off. Often the public is uneasy with special interest legislation, but when government programs are marketed, they seem fair individually.

As Friedman pointed out, social groups begin with the beguiling proposition of taking a few dollars away from many to support needy few. Political blocks often appeal to the interests of the nation or to salve the public conscience by righting past wrongs in society. "Jobs, jobs, jobs" is the mantra used by corporations to protect themselves from competition and gain government contracts and bailouts. Some African Americans will talk about Jim Crow or some women about living in a cultural cage to push legislation and government programs to eliminate discriminatory policies and repair the damage caused by historical discrimination through affirmative action or quotas. Once groups form to influence government, it is necessary to form groups to protect one's interests, so political influence can be either an offensive or defensive maneuver. Google, Amazon, Microsoft, and other large online presences learned they needed Washington influence after being accused of monopolizing the Internet. As a result, the big platforms spent $55 million in 2021, a 27% increase from spending in 2020. They are the biggest spenders on lobbying of any industry. The size and growth of this outlay suggests that the platforms feel that government may sharply limit their online activities.[90]

When the federal government launches sweeping programs, libertarians warned that the public often sees only the visible good and not the hidden harm or unintended side effects. For example, in 2022, California's Air Resources Board ruled that by 2035, all new cars and light trucks will produce zero emission.[91] Few would argue with the aim of the ruling. Everyone wants clean air. Libertarians would object to this politically imposed solution because of so many unknowns. Right now, the (not so) rare earths used in EV batteries come from China. Domestic mining has its own environmental issues. Recycling batteries is another environmental concern. Then there will be a need for an enormous increase in charging stations. Home charging will likely occur at night when there is no local source of solar energy. Will that require longer transmission lines to carry solar power across the country? Charging on the road takes 20–30 min. Is this an acceptable delay for travelers? Who will pay and how much to subsidize low-income people who cannot afford expensive electric vehicles? These problems are likely solvable in the long term. Libertarians would prefer to rely on profit-oriented markets to solve the clean air problem. Instead of imposing a ban on internal combustion vehicles, impose a carbon tax. Instead of disadvantaging domestic producers of cars, impose tariffs that make the production of electric vehicles and their components based on true costs instead of allowing foreign nations with lax environmental standards to gain an unfair edge.

Once a big program is in place, growth in special interests leads to funding creep and regulatory creep because no clear measure exists for deciding on their importance or performance. Those who didn't benefit at first want to catch up. With public acceptance of a social safety net, Medicare, for example, public dialogue shifts from promoting competition to fostering fair outcomes and social protection. Once a protective web is spun, regulation gives a false sense of security to the public, and the web is too complicated to change to accommodate new technology. Worse yet, a dense set of ambiguous regulations cultivate insincere social interactions because of the fear of being sued.

---

[90] Birnbaum, E. (2022), Tech spent big on lobbying last year. Politico. https://www.politico.com/newsletters/morning-tech/2022/01/24/tech-spent-big-on-lobbying-last-year-00001144#:~:text=TECH%20LOBBYING%20SURGE%20%E2%80%94%20Apple%2C%20Amazon,as%20defense%20and%20pharmaceuticals%2C%20for. Accessed 30 April 2023.

[91] California moves to accelerate to 100% new zero-emission vehicle sales by 2035. California Air Resources Board, Release Number 22–30, August 25, 2022. https://ww2.arb.ca.gov/news/california-moves-accelerate-100-new-zero-emission-vehicle-sales-2035. Accessed 30 April 2023.

Growth in government size and the complexity of regulations will also give bureaucrats undue control over private lives, even in America. For example, government control of health and welfare will lead to more control over private behavior, according to libertarians. If government is spending money, it will naturally want to control payments. It will decide when a procedure is necessary and at what price. If government is responsible for the health and welfare of its people, it is likely to pass laws dictating proper nutrition, proper weight targets, and proper exercise. It is likely that government will exercise a form of triage by setting guidelines for permitting operations. This is one of the great fears under Obama Care. Lavish social programs will also encourage legal and illegal immigration that will prove costly to American citizens.

Politicians recognize that democratic government is not designed like a corporation aimed at winning in the marketplace, but so what? Hayek warned that American liberals like socialists of yore believe they can approximate the administrative efficiency of corporations by hiring experts and asking them to run government agencies and subcontracting to the private sector. Libertarian theorists such as William Niskanen (Bureaucracy and Democratic Government) point out that a government bureaucrat wants status and power, which translates into bigger budgets and larger organizations. Government agencies will vie for resources, often by expanding their oversight into each other's turf. Conflicting regulations multiply. Government becomes a Kafkaesque labyrinth. An ordinary citizen has no idea when he is breaking the law, who to appeal to if indicted, and how much it will cost to fight his case.[92]

An alternative, favored by some libertarians, is to subcontract government services to the private sector. Other libertarians argue this logic also suffers from critical problems. Subcontracting has the downside of ceding daily control to organizations outside of government. As a result, politicians and government bureaucrats have little understanding of the policies and decisions of these private entities. Subcontracting is also a method for surreptitiously avoiding salary caps or official head count numbers. For example, America hired thousands of security forces at top dollar to operate in Iraq in the post-Saddam period.

In general, governments have no equivalent of a profit motive to reign in bad decisions. Few bureaucrats understand the workings of big, complex organizations, yet they feel they can make decisions for them on behalf of the public interest. When the decisions are wrong, bureaucrats don't need to declare bankruptcy, but companies like AT&T did. When the federal government runs a program through funding and regulations, bad outcomes cannot

---

[92] Niskanen, W.A. (1971), *Bureaucracy and Representative Government*. Aldine and Atherton. Wiley, NY

bankrupt the federal government. Mistakes can be hidden for decades without great consequences to public officials, whereas government programs developed and operated at the local level are at least subject to citizen overview on an ongoing basis.

Deficit spending is good, especially in periods where the economy is operating sluggishly makes some sense in theory, even to some libertarians, but like Friedman they oppose countercyclical fiscal policy for many reasons. Deficit spending becomes a habit, justified by injecting money and orders to offset spending shortfalls in the private sector. Slowing down or speeding up government programs such as public housing starts will lead to massive inefficiencies. If a government program is important, it should be completed. If it is a marginal program, it is unlikely to be "shovel ready" when needed. Often, temporary construction programs are wildly wasteful. For example, David Brooks, a New York Times editorialist, admitted that President Obama told him that he knew that the "shovel-ready project" propaganda he employed to pass the massive porkulus bill was a steaming load of bullcrap.[93] Eventually, countercyclical government spending will erode the public's confidence in the ability of the government to use taxpayer dollars responsibly.

Libertarians like Friedman warn that government is not a community and does not build communities, except in the sense of preventing crime. Other attempts at community building are doomed to fail. The reason is simple: government officials are far removed from the targets of their sympathy. Often the government is seen as a war on something such as poverty, much like a campaign mapped out at headquarters. It is as if victory is possible, and a new age of peace and prosperity will begin. Or social programs are called new deals or fair deals as if society is like a game where no one can lose the game. Both metaphors are wrong according to libertarians. Even in war, headquarter plans don't work; victories are mainly through personal initiative in the fog of war. And society is not a game where a reshuffle or change in rules will make everyone better off.

For example, Great Society programs didn't build inner city communities because they rested on the false premise that a paternal government can change a supposedly sick culture leading to poverty and crime. Instead of improving the lot of the poor, these programs created a sense of entitlement and worsened class conflict by making it seem the government was trying to

---

[93] Michelle Malkin, M. David Brooks (2010), D. Obama Told Me "Shovel Ready" Was a Crock … a Year Ago. https://www.unz.com/author/michelle-malkin//2010/10/16/david-brooks-obama-told-me-shovel-ready-was-a-crock-a-year-ago/. Accessed 30 April 2023.

gold-plate inner cities to keep blacks where they were. In general, programs to redistribute income and wealth are likely to lead to class conflicts.

Friedman didn't object to unionization, but other libertarians did because it allowed workers to confiscate private property from risk takers who put up capital only to see it expropriated by workers. These libertarians point to the weakest industries being unionized. They are against affirmative action – government saying who to hire and what proportions – because it co-opts the decision-making power of property owners thereby weakening the quality of output. More insidiously, government officials now have the power to decide who gets a job and who doesn't. Rand's contribution was to embody Schumpeterian economics in her devotion to a Creator Man. Her Atlas was chained by social conventions and government regulations. She wanted to free him. She would support gay and lesbian rights because they were between consenting individuals.

Environmental concerns – global warming, destruction of natural habitat, massive extinctions – are top political agenda items. Libertarians are quick to point out that governments have been a great source of environmental destruction. In 1948, the communist party released the "Stalinist Plan for the Transformation of Nature." It envisioned nature as a giant factory of resources that could be used in the struggle with capitalism. The United States built great cathedrals to technology, the nation's majestic dams.[94] The Endangered Species Act was used to protect the woodlands in the Pacific Northwest where the spotted owl lived. The policy didn't work. The spotted owl population went into a deep dive because the barrel owl appeared to replace it.[95] Some libertarians believe that environmentalists are tree-worshippers. They don't realize that property owners want to improve the value of their land.[96] Other republicans recognize that air and water and other public resources lack the features private property. Pollution taxes would internalize costs that spread to others. Detailed regulations to prevent environmental harm are likely to become oppressive in the hands of bureaucrats.

Internationally, libertarians are for nonintervention. The American military should not be used build nations and should not foster regime change unless America is threatened by an imminent attack. Libertarians oppose foreign aid as paternalistic; they point out rapidly developing nations did not rely on foreign aid to lift themselves out of poverty. Nations that succeed

---

[94] Robert H. Nelson, R.H. (2010), *The New Holy Wars: Economic Religion vs. Environmental Religion*. The Pennsylvania Press, PA, pp. 92–93.

[95] Id., p. 231.

[96] Libertarian Party on Environment. On the Issues. https://www.ontheissues.org/Celeb/Libertarian_Party_Environment.htm. Accessed 30 April 2023.

economically secure private property rights. They give people the incentive to draw themselves up from poverty. Of course, emergency relief for those who may die of starvation or disease is acceptable but needs to be monitored carefully for societal corruption.

Libertarians rank foreign threats: totalitarian regimes worst (control military, press, and means of production), dictators next (control military and press), and democratic movements ruled by religious fanatics (tyranny of the majority trumps rule of law) may actually be worse than dictatorship, but the democratic process does hold out hope that practical interests will trump mystical visions of a pure society. The basis for this ranking is to what extent a regime weakens private property rights preserved by a fair legal system. Using this standard, libertarians decided a communist-led democracy (Allende) is worse than a dictatorship (Pinochet). Some libertarians went so far as to suggest a foreign crisis is a perfect time for regime change. America should support freedom lovers but not send American troops.

To outsiders, libertarians seem dogmatic believers in the sacredness of private, voluntary trades. To some extent this is true because libertarians feel they are in a tough, long-term struggle for two reasons. It is hard to fight big government because well-funded special interests often win the battle. The main brake on government growth is the specter of government collapse, and this can be postponed for long stretches of time. In the meantime, fighting social programs appears mean spirited to the average voter.

Looking back, the thumbnail sketches of libertarian beliefs seen in the Libertarian and Republican Party platforms were accurate in their basics. To associate them with white middle class men is to demean their motivations and to discount their important message. Besides, the image is wrong. Many notable libertarians are black: Thomas Sowell, Walter E. Williams, and Larry Elder, to name a few. A libertarian from any background believes an individual is in the best position to chart his own course, not his parents, not his community, and certainly not government. No one else, especially an impersonal institution, can know himself the way he does or care about himself the way he does. When people have freedom under fair rules, fairly administered, libertarians say the historical record shows clearly that the freest nations are also the richest nations. They are the nations that have created the most new products and services, many of which have extended the life and comfort of a large portion of humanity. The amazing fact is that unimaginably complex and supple solutions to life's problems have emerged from people following their own self interests. Obvious but often unused examples are easy to find. Language keeps developing without central design. Moral behavior and codes of ethics keep evolving without conscious oversight by a governing body. Even much of a nation's legal code is not the product of a government legal committee. Instead, the law has evolved to settle disputes that cannot be settled privately.

A libertarian ranks highest market-based solutions to social problems because the market operates a positive sum game. Both buyers and sellers gain from trade. Firms compete for customers peacefully. Instead of blowing each other's' factories up to gain an edge in the market. Instead, they are forced into a peaceful struggle with weapons of war being replaced by price wars and the development of new products and services to gain an edge in the market. The market is preferable to government-based solutions to economic problems because a democratic government ideally treats all consumers equally. Not so the market, where a person who most wants a product is willing to pay more for it. In practice, democracy is a dangerous social engineering tool. Public elections occur once every several years, insulating politicians from voters. In practice, government favors organized groups that deliver voting blocks and campaign funds.

When government takes over delivery of services, it will likely hurt society, according to libertarians. At the broadest scale, the reason is simple: a democratic government is not designed to imitate an efficient corporation; its primary purpose was to set rules for binding people together by giving representatives the power to set rules for defining the limits of public action. Politicians will focus on blocks of voters instead of trying to satisfy individual customer needs. Although a corporation also doesn't typically individualize its product offerings, its decision-making is top-down instead of by majority vote. It can vary prices by market segment, whereas a government, out of the need for fairness, will typically offer services for free or uniformly to all citizens. Again, out of fairness, politicians and bureaucrats want to set standards for services. As a result, the services tend to be uniform, not tailored to customer needs. Because politicians can hide behind majority votes and subtle reasoning for supporting or vetoing a bill, the connection between public decisions and personal responsibility is often threadbare. Both politicians and bureaucrats can claim they were in the minority or only following rules. Worst of all – and this can be unintentional – government control of services gives politicians and bureaucrats control over private behavior that goes beyond the bounds of traditional law, which sets limits on behavior. Instead, government can tell an individual what he must do to be eligible for support instead of what he cannot do to stay out of jail. A large concentration of economic activity in government often leads to a loss of personal freedom and a loss of economic vitality. The economic sickness of Britain for many years after World War II was associated with the rise of socialism. Even setting aside Britain, most tyrannical governments controlled a large percentage of their nation's national income, whether the regime was democratically elected as in Nazi Germany or the result of a coup as in Soviet Russia.

The libertarian firmly believes that this seemingly harsh philosophy of relying on individual initiative to organize and drive society is actually the most liberating social arrangement that humanity has so far conceived. It honors the creative individual. It relies on them to find uncharted markets. Relying on individual spontaneity to organize and direct society seems risky, almost foolhardy, but the historical record is clear: states that base their future on the rule of law are by any measure the most prosperous, the most satisfied, and, for the most part, the most peaceful societies. These are the societies that produce the most inventions that have shaped modernity.

As Hayek pointed out, however, a rich society that is indifferent to its poor, to its outcasts, and to those who can't defend themselves will become a society divided. It becomes vulnerable to revolution or a power grab by fanatics because they can legitimately claim there is something rotten about a society that is cruel to its weakest members. Hayek warned, however, that helping the helpless should not justify guaranteeing everyone a lifestyle, and government officials should not have too much discretion in giving out favors. Support should follow rules and where possible, beneficiaries should pay back once on their feet.

Even more succinctly, a strict libertarian motto could be, "A society that denies its people freedom of action will know no happiness." Hayek would add, "A society that ignores its needy will not survive." Libertarians want to energize personal freedom to produce a Great Society that benefits all.

3

Conservatism: Cultural Dissolution Can Lead to Despotism

Abstract Similar to libertarians, conservatives fear massive overhauls of a nation's institutions, especially those leading to centralized government control. In part, they attribute the cultural dissolution in America to the federal takeover of health, education, and welfare. In addition to the centralizing threat, they fear the emerging identity politics that inspires groups to demand special consideration for past victimhood. They are even uneasy with the ideology of free markets. A market system erodes community, places a dollar value on human worth, promotes excessive consumption and gaudy displays, and leads to the bulldozing of neighborhoods in the name of profits. Conservatives want to raise ladies and gentlemen who have strong ties to family, community, and religion. I selected conservative champions – Burke, McCauley, De Tocqueville, Kirk, and Bogle – to show they are not against government services just wary of remote, centralized control and deficit spending. To see how conservative thought has influenced the Republican Presidential Platforms, I compare their planks with conservative thought.

3.1 Introduction

Now that you have a summary of the libertarian world view, this chapter focuses on conservative ideology. Before explaining its elements, I want to highlight how each ideology sees the individual in society. The libertarian sees the individual as a rational self-creator. The backdrop landscape is the techno-economic system. His inner growth is largely transactional, based on deals he makes with others.

81
V. Glass, *Humanizing the Digital Economy*, https://doi.org/10.1007/978-3-031-37507-1_3

The conservative ideology sees the individual as a product of culture. Culture sustains personal identity by offering a coherent aesthetic view and moral conception of self. It answers existential questions that confront people during their lives. These are recurring questions that cross generations. A vibrant culture depends on the continuity of traditions. A conservative learns how forbears lived meaningful lives and overcame predicaments. Family and community nourish self-development. Religion provides the compass. The backdrop landscape is of people working together like farmers building a barn or a city soup kitchen.

By contrast to libertarians, conservatives believe the good society is not a product of atomized self-seekers. Rather, it is the product of social evolution, building on the wisdom of the past, sometimes adapting it to address current problems. A conservative is not a Master of the Universe; instead, he or she is a homebody: a member of a family, community, and religious tradition.

In the next chapter, I will give the liberal's world view. For now, a liberal's sees an individual living in a mass society where its social structures – schools, healthcare systems, police – mold the person. Self-development depends on the structures in society. The government provides support and sets limits to acceptable personal and social behavior. The background landscape is the political and social institutions.

Because all three ideologies have different perspectives, they see societal change differently and react to changes at different speeds. Conservatives adapt to societal changes cautiously. Libertarians are more likely to make quick business decisions. They may support the same policies but for different reasons. For example, libertarians oppose big government social projects. Libertarians hate the paternalism of these programs. Conservatives feel they co-opt the services of communities and religious institutions. A libertarian sees no reason to outlaw gay marriage. Conservatives are moving in that direction, but many resist gay marriage because it goes against a long tradition of marriage as union designed to produce children who connect one generation and the next. It does not mean, however, that opposition is written in stone. Liberals would support gay marriage and look to breaking down institutional barriers that prevent them.

With this backdrop, let me shift the scene to the Republican national conventions. Among those white people at the 2012 and 2016 Republican national conventions, conservatives were the church goers, and some are Bible thumpers. To them, the American saga is a modern Exodus story, of oppressed people coming to a Promised Land where they could practice their religion openly and not have overseers who controlled them.

They are very fearful of the dark side of human nature. This is especially true in a world where a few fanatics can create widespread havoc. The

Constitution is so admired by them because it recognizes people are flawed and sinful if not guided to righteousness. Wealth is a temptation. Hard work teaches discipline. Communal attachments help a person think of "We" instead of "I."

Although the Constitution is a great example of conservative moral thinking, it is not a document that shapes a person's everyday affairs. In the main, the fallibility of man is kept in check by cultural norms. In the American tradition, good manners depend a great deal on self-restraint, of not showing off, of not wanting to win by pulling others down, and by gaining confidence and strength as a member of a community.

These traditions evolved slowly, and emerging from them were moral principles to make society workable, pleasant, and fulfilling. Managerial science may be great for organizing factories, but it is not the template for organizing a community or a nation. When it comes to deciding on social change, it requires wisdom, patience, and dialogue to refine the gifts of previous generations.

Conservatives will not split the difference or come to a pragmatic solution when the solution violates moral principles. They believe ideology with shallow roots in culture is often a dangerous, pallid excuse for escaping one's traditions and imitating others. A life built on abstractions is an inauthentic life that cuts someone off from childhood intimacies and behaviors and sometimes leads to ruptures with family and community.

Their ideal society raises gentlemen and ladies as opposed to egotistical self-seekers. Tea Obreht put it nicely by saying a small boy becomes a gentleman when he takes responsibility for others.[1] This person recognizes that a sense of self, of self-worth and personal well-being, depends on the reactions of others to your own actions and their view of you as a person.

Unlike the libertarian's ideal life focused on personal perfection, a conservative person hopes to raise a loyal son or daughter who contributes to the community, who becomes a statesman in government, and like an engaged and selfless university trustee, a person who wants the organization to succeed by operating effectively and morally.

Ladies and gentlemen are not out to maximize profits if it means cheating others, even if they don't realize they are being cheated, because the true measure of worth is not the bottom line. Instead, a life worth living depends on righteousness and refinement. A righteous person exhibits personal control focused on good deeds, kind words, and lofty aspirations for self and others. Refined people want to elevate their desires and cultivate good taste. Building

---

[1] Tea Obreht, T. (2011), *The Tiger's Wife*. Random House, NY, p. 371.

the good life is done through small projects and everyday activities raised spiritually. Customs serve as guides and ancient visions for inspiration.

A true conservative is a trusted inheritor who is committed to preserving and renewing culture and family heritage. In an open society, this obligation is especially heavy because it is so easy to float away and let the past fade into the distance. It requires a delicate balance of erecting fences to preserve one's inheritance while not walling off one group from another.

The education of an inheritor begins early by teaching a child where he comes from, who his ancestors were, and his religion. When an outsider wants to join or more generally when a life-changing decision is in the offing that affects the family and group heritage, the decision-makers should be sensitive to how his choice may alter the heritage he passes on. Ideally, the change will refresh his heritage by contributing to its long-term health. Starting close to home, the decision to marry should not be a simple, no-fault contract because it affects the future of two families and the group's long-term survival. Not surprisingly, a conservative wants a ceremonial marriage, announced to the whole group, and a sacred one that requires the bride and groom to offer gifts. The couple promises to protect each other forever and pledges to treat the union as sacred in the eyes of the community and, most of all, in the eyes of God.

Though many customs may be oppressive seen from a historical perspective, they are at least accepted as explainable within a particular culture and thought fair in the sense that no one felt singled out for unfair treatment.[2] Over time, seemingly hidebound rules can give way to newer ones if a culture supports personal dignity. For example, the descendants of the Puritans have moved away from the belief in God orders all human events to one where people are responsible for their own destiny. Living an ascetic life has given way to a comfortable but not ostentatious life.

England hundreds of years ago was a very class-conscious society that had little tolerance for religious sects like the Puritans. Yet over time an ethical code emerged from provincial moral customs that defined good character of a person, no matter a person's station in life or religious belief. When disputes occurred, an objective judge settled the case, and his decision rested on the resolution of previous disputes, and these resolutions were anchored in the group's ethical code, which itself was rooted in moral customs. From this process of objective decision-making arose the common law, which then reshaped the group's ethical code and moral behavior. This organic evolution of law, ethics, and morals is firmly connected to a group's culture that produced a fairer society. The benefits of fairness, especially of fair laws, extended to

---

[2] Peter Singer, P. (2011), *The Expanding Circle*. Revised Edition. Princeton University Press, NJ, p. 95.

strangers. As a result, equal treatment and respect for other groups evolved with the growth of common law because the same set of rules applied to the stranger as for the citizen.

Social evolution works best, according to conservatives when it is built on personal relationships, when you look and touch others in ways that alter their lives and your own. When people know each other, they are likely to rely on each other in times of need and work together, especially when a need cannot be met by acting alone. The most enduring groups are people who have similar backgrounds. Yet, just as a sense of family carries over to a sense of community, it is the community spirit of helping those in need that carries over into the larger society. One should not be surprised that the greatest patriots are conservative people by nature. Patriots support inherited institutions because they believe them to be effective and just.

Small is beautiful is a touchstone on conservative thought. A person radiates a spiritual breath of self that mixes with others. But this breath travels only so far. Distance and separation are barriers to developing a sense of empathy. As a result, a conservative is wary of big business. Even a firm like Wal-Mart that started out with the best intentions to give the consumer a good deal by keeping costs and margins down may lose its soul when it becomes too big. Anonymity is a destroyer. Sam Walton knew his workers; the current CEO cannot. Walton wanted to save his customers money so they could live better. Instead of Walmart being a living expression of a person, it is now a mission statement printed on the sides of a company box. As a disembodied corporate rule, keeping prices down justified pressing suppliers even into bankruptcy and buying products abroad from companies that operate sweatshops. This is not an indictment of Wal-Mart because it has brought down prices of goods. It is simply an observation on the effects of size and the resulting distance between executive and floor employee, between company and supplier, and between company and customer.[3] In the case of financial institutions, distance, anonymity, and a libertarian mind-set of maximizing personal gain, lead to corporate corruption.

The importance of empathy leads conservatives to want locally controlled government aimed at satisfying local community needs. This personal touch has limits even within the community. Conservatives don't want government intruding into private affairs. They frown on a local community shunting personal obligation to a government bureaucracy. It hardens hearts when government takes over because help is no longer a private affair. By extension, keeping government at arm's length has led conservatives to

---

[3] Fishman, C. (2006), *The Wal-Mart Effect*. Penguin Press, NY.

recommend the America should stay out of other nations' affairs, unless directly threatened.

Classical conservatives would never put in their lot with unyielding fundamentalists who see life as unchanging, who look for solutions in literal Biblical passages, who seek guidance from moral supermen. They do not support a policy based on race, blood, and soil. They support policies based on moral traditions that treat individuals with justice and humanity. The historical growth of fair play as a moral imperative is as close as conservatives get to moral absolutism. They are against the modern-day moral relativist of the libertarian stripe who defines his own set of moral beliefs and is judged by the consistency of his beliefs. To a conservative, a hypocrite violates community standards by saying he is for them but acting otherwise. To a moral relativist, a hypocrite is someone who says one thing, whatever it is, and does another. He has no common ties with others.

Conservatives are believers in the monotheistic Judeo-Christian God, a God of cause and effect who designed purpose into the cosmos with humanity as a crowning example. It was God who gave scientists the insight to find a unity to the universe. While some conservatives are creationists who reject the theory of evolution, many conservatives see religion as adding a moral dimension to science, and a mystical dimension in which science supplies the letters and notes to a cosmic poetry chanted by humanity – a musical libretto to the wonders of a universe that has laws and ultimate purpose.

It was Jews and Christians who eventually recognized that being created in the image of God meant that all people are sacred, and none should be a slave to another. It was Judeo-Christianity that believed in the rule of law, of treating the stranger and the citizen alike, of not favoring the rich or the poor in a dispute. It was Judeo-Christianity that pointed to evil as a destructive force in humanity and nature, and a concerted battle needs to be fought to bring out the better side of human nature, not by force alone but by kindness, not solely by imposition by a caring parent but by example of righteousness in action, of deeds that elevate humanity to sacred vessels.

Before I go any farther, does this description of a conservative sound fantastical? Undoubtedly yes to a die-hard democrat.

Pan back to the 2012 Republican convention and imagine asking a democrat to pick out a conservative. He might quip they all are, especially those cheering conventioneers wearing cowboy hats who can't wait to waive to the folks back home watching on TV, or he might point to Mitt Romney and say he is a typical conservative, a white male who looks undressed without a dark suit and has graying hair neatly in place, trim, with a patrician look that suggests he is comfortable with money and power – and how unlike he is from a real American you see on the street. The democrat, if he's expansive, would probably classify all the speakers as super-patriots and Bible thumpers who are all phonies because they wrap themselves in the flag and biblical text to hide their real intention: to keep the poor and non-whites down.

For starters, let's see if my description fits the 2012 Republican Party's platform at least echoes my description of a conservative.

The opening paragraph of the platform states:

> Prosperity is the product of self-discipline, work, savings, and investment by individual Americans, but it is not an end in itself. Prosperity provides the means by which individuals and families can maintain their independence from government, raise their children by their own values, practice their faith, and build communities of self-reliant neighbors. It is also the means by which the United States is able to assert global leadership. The vigor of our economy makes possible our military strength and is critical to our national security.[4]

In the preamble, the Republican platform calls for a restoration "of Jefferson's vision of a 'wise and frugal government.'" It is not right for future generations to inherit enormous national debt because the federal government spends a great deal more than it takes in. Republicans want federal spending to be absolutely necessary, more so if the government has to borrow to fund the program. They favor a balanced budget amendment because history suggests that federal legislators need a rule to curb overspending.

In the necessary column of government funding were continued tax deductions for "religious organizations, charities, and fraternal benevolent societies" because they foster "benevolence and patriotism."

The platform also calls for stimulating small business formation by cutting regulations and other barriers. They want to stimulate home ownership because it gives Americans "a decent place to live, a safe place to raise kids, a welcoming place to retire, … [a] quiet pride of those who work hard to shelter family and, in the process, create caring neighborhoods."[5] Conservatives are all for prudent regulation that promotes prudent investment and oppose federal funding of housing that encourages speculation and mortgage scams.

The platform was against activist courts that have expanded the definition of marriage. Instead, the public should decide how gay marriages and other forms of nontraditional marriages affect traditional family and community values.

The platform sought to promote American goods abroad and bargaining with other nations for fair treatment of American goods sold on foreign soil. The want legal immigrants who, like so many in the past, have contributed to

---

[4] Republican Platform (2012), p. 1.
[5] Id., p. 4.

America's prosperity. They want to encourage the world's innovators and inventors to come here.

Still not convinced. Rhetoric to win an election? Lofty phrases to protect self-interest?

Historical consistency is my next defense. The problem is that conservatism does not have a true starting point. One account of the evolution of America's conservative ideology could start with a history of the Puritans or the American Revolution, especially the Declaration of Independence, the Constitution, and the Federalist Papers. But in their time, even the Puritans were radicals who wanted to break free of English domination. Instead of following this track, I return to England, to Edmund Burke, a fierce opponent of the French Revolution.

3.2   Burke's Reflections on the French Revolution

Many conservatives believe he is the clearest, most colorful, most quotable (and most paraphrased in my case) spokesman for conservative sentiments. Burke was born in Dublin 1729 to middle-class parents and died in 1797. He was a member of parliament from 1765 to 1780. He was also a great supporter of the American Colonists demands for no taxation without representation in parliament and their belief that English liberty extends to American colonists by law and culture. Yet Burke detested the French revolutionaries because they sought to wipe away king and Catholic Church and replace them with a new regime built on abstract concepts of reason and freedom. Burke hated the idea of overthrowing an entire culture; it was wrong-headed and likely to cause great suffering as it did to the French people and to future generations sacrificed by revolutionaries bent on redesigning society according to their own master plan.

Burke's attack on the French Revolution is critically important for understanding a conservative's opposition to any revolutionary movement that claims it will usher in a new blissful society only by destroying a heritage that supposedly is built on plundering the people and enslaving them in superstition.

His criticisms of the French Revolution predict the damage Nazism and communism would inflict on the world. More subtly, conservatives also oppose any sweeping social change that threatens the traditions of a people, including programs with noble intentions such as America's Great Society programs.

Burke saw the French revolutionaries as fanatics who overturned laws, damaged commerce, impoverished the people, pillaged the church, and produced the Reign of Terror. He would have agreed with Julian Barnes's description of the French Revolution's desecration of the Church:

> They had taken crucifixes from the field and made an auto-de-fey of them. They had paraded asses and mules wearing the vestments of bishops. They had burnt prayer books and manual of instructions. They had forced priests into marriage and ordered French men and women to spit on the image of Christ ....[6]

Burke attacked the French Revolution's cause célèbre: liberty. In the *Reflections*,[7] Burke said sometimes upheavals are necessary to root out corruption, but in the main, change should occur gradually to fit the times. He asked, the rhetorical question, was the cry of liberty enough to justify the French Revolution? Liberty, what does it mean?

He answered, traditions give reality to every abstract principle. They are the product of the manners and principles of forebears. They are not defined as something wholly new; they are developed by analogy. Therefore, liberty is not a theoretical definition based on ideal philosophical principles. Liberty requires curbing passions, thwarting inclinations that would harm others.[8] Its definition emerges and evolves as conditions change. It is not static and defined in the abstract. It is wise to reject proposals for reform based on a priori principles detached from traditions.[9]

He goes on to say you can evaluate any definition of liberty only when you understand how it combines with government, with public force, with discipline and obedience of armies, with the collection and distribution of revenues public and private, with morality and religion, with the solidity of property, with peace and order, and with civil and social manners.

In government, liberty is not defined by a group of rulers on behalf of society. It gives them too much power to sweep away the social compact that does not fit the passions of the moment. In 1215, King John signed the Magna Carta that limited the king's power over the aristocracy and church. Afterward, government rule became more pluralistic. Over time, government was

---

[6] Barnes, J. (1966), *Cross Channel*. Knopf, NY, p. 51.

[7] Burke, E., *Reflections on The Revolution In France and The Rights Of Man* by Paine, T. (1961), Doubleday and Co., Garden City, NY.

[8] Id., p. 73.

[9] Id., p. 73.

becoming sensitive to a widening group of interests.[10] Burke went on to say that developing a totally new constitution gives a state unbounded power[11] and those who attempt to level society never equalize it.[12] Strict equality is at war with human nature.[13] People are not equal, except at the abstraction of basic humanity. Those who attempt to invert society by raising the lowly to rule will cause chaos.[14] Beneath lofty rhetoric lurk speculations and monstrous fictions.[15] Burke believed cries for revolution had a selfish origin: the lust for revenge.

The lust of the poor to confiscate or destroy property of a ruling class is understandable, but Burke warned that when the people destroy property there is no liberty.[16] Cutting the throats of the rich will not feed the poor. It is like burning the mills to make bread cheap.[17]

It might sound like Burke was a shill for the elite who wanted to preserve the status quo. Not so! Burke was also against entombing tradition. He said a state without means of change is without means of conservation. On the other hand, it needs solidity. In his words, no government can stand if it can be blown down with loose and indefinite accusations of misconduct. Progress rooted in tradition to him was a necessity because people will not look forward to posterity when they never look backward to their ancestors.

His prescription was that changes in government affairs should be done with due caution. A reformer should approach the faults of the state as to the wounds of a father, with pious awe and trembling solicitude. The proper attitude of a statesman is to search carefully and humbly for outmoded or corrupt practices. Statesmen should display and exercise moral competence, permanent reason, steady maxims of faith, and justice. They should uphold time-honored fundamental policies that are binding on authorities. English traditions suggested that government ought to confine itself to clearly public needs and leave other problems to be solved by private discretion. It takes time to recognize when a problem is best solved by the concerted action of government.[18]

---

[10] Acemoglu, D., and Robinson, J.A. (2012), *Why Nations Fail*. Chapter 7, *The Turning Point*, pp. 182–212. Crown Publishing, NY.

[11] Reflections, p. 58.

[12] Id., p. 61.

[13] Id., p. 62.

[14] Id., p. 69.

[15] Id., p. 49 and p. 76.

[16] Id., p. 65.

[17] Burke, E. (Author), Louis Bredvold (Editor), and Ross, R. (Editor) (1960). *The Philosophy of Edmund Burke: A Selection of His Speeches And Writings*. Ann Arbor Paperbacks, MI.

[18] See the Works of Edmund Burke. Available at https://books.google.com/books?id=x7l2XhB2RzwC&pg=PA278&lpg=PA278&dq=Burke+%22what+the+state+ought+to+take+upon+itself%22&source=bl

By this wise prejudice toward caution, he said we are taught to look in horror on those children of a country who rashly hack the aged parent in pieces and put them in the kettle of magicians, in hopes that by their poisonous weeds and wild incantations, they may regenerate the paternal constitution and renovate the father's life.[19] The state is a partnership between those who are living, those who are dead, and those who are to be born.[20] It is to the property of the citizen and not the demands of a creditor state that the first and original faith of civil society is pledged.[21] A nation is a moral essence, not a geographical arrangement, or a denomination of the nomenclature. It is the production of the human mind.[22] It is an extension of who people are.

Restraint works best under two conditions: government of the people led by statesmen who lead by their spirit, manners, and principles. They do not serve petty interests; they take the long view toward an image that forefathers and progeny could respect. Each has his own perspective, his own share of wisdom, and by exchanging ideas with supporters and opponents openly, in the spirit of fellowship they find common ground.

Burke was opposed to hypercritical analysis of government. He believed a nation's constitution does not have to be discussed in every detail or be the subject of altercations; it should also be enjoyed.[23] He was against democracy with no connection to history. It is dangerous because it suggests that all are law givers and potentially immune from punishment.[24] The state can be changed by floating fancies.[25] Democracy needs to be restrained[26] a sentiment that our Founders believed in that led to separation of government powers.

A good benchmark for progress from Burke's perspective is when we improve, we are never wholly new; in what we retain, we are never wholly obsolete. In this way we retain the principles of forefathers and are not guided by the superstition of antiquarianism as is a fundamentalist who wants the ancient regime to remain in place forever.[27]

Unlike in modern egalitarian societies, He was a believer in pedigree as a great binding force of moderation and measured reason. Any culture or any

&ots=ViuoMYJGTK&sig=QOmVIvbzj5ndYqQu9sQzlVABKxE&hl=en&sa=X&ved=0ahUKEwivnP
T2grXZAhVENd8KHZPTCfYQ6AEIKTAB#v=onepage&q=Burke%20%22what%20the%20
state%20ought%20to%20take%20upon%20itself%22&f=false. Crown Publishing, NY.

[19] Reflections, pp. 109–110.

[20] Id., p. 110.

[21] Id., p. 121.

[22] Philosophy, p. 50.

[23] Reflections, p. 105.

[24] Reflections, p. 107.

[25] Reflections, p. 108.

[26] Reflections, p. 109.

[27] Reflections, p. 46.

family should have a gallery of portraits, monumental inscriptions, records, evidences, and titles to mark the nobility of a people. Statesmen need not have identical opinions.[28] Many times, they will disagree, but the differences are those of gentlemen who respect each other and aim at being constructive. In honest debates everything ought to be open, but not indifferently to everyone. Burke believed that from a constructive struggle of discordant powers, a constitution emerges that draws out the humanity of the universe, renders choice deliberate, changes subject to compromise begets moderation, and produces even temperaments.[29]

In Burke's view the offspring of convention is law; it is built on honesty and justice.[30] Government is a contrivance of human wisdom to provide for human wants. Law and government are necessary because, according to Burke, the inclinations of men should frequently be thwarted to bring passions into subjection.

Burke pleaded his case that abstract rights cannot be divorced from methods of procuring them and administering them. Rights grow in a well-tended garden; they are not constructed by theorists. In Burke's words, when sophists, economists, and calculators have succeeded, the glory of Europe is extinguished forever.[31] Principles of mechanical philosophy can never embody love, veneration, admiration, and attachment. To make us love our country, our country must be loveable.[32] Our manners and our civilization depended for ages upon two principles: the spirit of the gentleman and the spirit of religion.[33] Beware of shortcuts to moral virtue.[34] Prejudices must be examined, but don't assume they are destitute of reason.[35]

Conservative thinking continues to evolve, perhaps too slowly for some, and it may sound as if it favors the well-healed and those in authority, but Burke's message has been on-target for many of the crucial challenges faced by modern society. One of the biggest was the threat of fascism, Nazism, and communism. Burke would have likened them to the French revolutionists. They had all the markings of fanatics from the start, the twisted imagery of a new beginning, a new utopia only possible after overthrowing the oppressive regime in power. Instead of focusing on individuals and communities, both

---

[28] Id., p. 46.
[29] Philosophy, p. 37.
[30] Id., p. 65.
[31] Reflections, p. 89.
[32] Id., p. 91.
[33] Id., p. 92.
[34] Id., p. 95.
[35] Id., p. 105.

fascism and Nazism worshipped an idealized collective "self." In the case of Nazism, this collective self was racial in origin. The communists plugged the workers' paradise.[36]

Start with Italian fascism, a case study in fantastical visions and rhetoric to see how well Burke understood revolutionary thinking. Mussolini wanted Italians to believe the Italian nation was really one big family, and like a family everyone belonged, everyone was taken care of, where no child was left behind. It was really a political religion. No realm of life is beyond politics; the state would protect moral values; it would shape the moral character of its people. If only the Italians believed, a utopia was possible. All it required was an aesthetic vision of a blissful society shaped along aesthetic lines, a society with no hard choices and certainly no conflicts. Burke would have scoffed at lumping together everyone as if they came from the same plowed field or from one herd of livestock.

He would also have attacked, as a page from the playbook of the French revolutionaries, the fascist attempt to suppress the supposedly small, mean-spirited individual will with the everlasting and all-knowing General Will. It would look strikingly similar to Burke that the fascists used a mass movement, grown in the streets, to overturn government, and rule it with an iron hand once in power. The fascist railing against messy, undirected democratic institutions would be all too familiar to Burke, and so would be the adoration of a distant, idealized past that bore no resemblance to a nation's culture. In Italy, the fascists did have their innovations. They elevated military organization and, with it, military morality as the pathway to strengthen the nation's resolve and point it toward glory – Roman glory. Il Duce, the leader, would lead the Italian nation like a caesar of old, toward a clean, orderly, and manly life. All the Italian people had to do was to worship him and follow his ways. To help Mussolini win the minds of the people, he had strong support of intellectuals who were fed up with liberal democracy and saw fascism as the next step in the evolution of society. Beware of intellectuals without moorings, Burke would have said.

Nazism would have outraged Burke even more than Italian fascism because of Hitler and company's fanatical attachment to pure Aryan blood. Burke was no antagonist to maintaining a good blood line, but even his belief in family lines would not have led him to murder others to preserve the purity of his own. Although he said Jews was a group apart that couldn't be assimilated into British society and that they were profit-seekers instead of loyal patriots,

---

[36] See Liberal Fascism pp. 2-4, p. 13 for twisted imagery ideas.

he still criticized the British army for oppressing defenseless Jews during the American Revolution.[37]

Burke would easily have heard echoes in the rabid Nazi messianic call to glory of the battle cries of the French revolutionists. The Nazis believed they were the chosen people doing God's work. Faced with an apocalyptic struggle with irredeemable enemies, mainly the Jews instead of French aristocracy, the Nazis felt morally compelled to wipe the Jews from German lands much like the Jews did to the Canaanites. Hitler, the false prophet with demon visions, looked to the East for his Promised Land, to Poland and the Ukraine, areas that should not be controlled by Slavic groups. In victory the Aryan Germans would become a pure people in a pure land. Christianity, a Judaic religion, had to be erased and replaced with a more authentic Teutonic religion much like the French revolutionists wanted to rid France of Catholicism. The Nazis instituted their own holidays (the Munich Putsch), their own temples, and their own Messiah. They pushed "back to nature" as authentic to the German character instead of the artificial imposition of the defeatist, honoring the meek, morality of the inferior Latin and Jewish races. As naturalists, the Nazis leaders were often vegetarians instituted animal rights laws and pushed Hitler Youth to exercise. Surely Burke favored a hearty constitution and healthful food, but he also believed traditional religious wisdom purified the soul. He would have felt horror at seeing millions of people sacrificed to an alien god.

Of the three totalitarian revolutions of the twentieth century, the one that most closely resembles the French revolution was the Russian revolution that ushered in communism. The similarities are striking. The Russian revolution sought to level society by overthrowing the Russian noble class and middle-class farmers, expropriating their stores of wealth and land, and giving it to the working class. Religion had to be abolished because it was supposedly the opium of the masses. Society would begin again, starting with a blank slate, and from there redesigned along scientific lines according to Marxist economic theory. A vast, new bureaucracy would run society headed by the vanguard of the communist organizers and intellectuals. They would gauge and reshape the General Will to conform to a communist paradise. A new man and a new society would emerge from redoing work relationships and reeducating the people to believe in redistributing the nation's wealth based on need – each according to his ability to each according to his need. The assumption was that human behavior was infinitely malleable given enough time and determination on the part of instructors; the ideal proletarian would become

[37] Stack Exchange (2005) Anti-Semitism and Edmund Burke. https://history.stackexchange.com/questions/20828/anti-semitism-and-edmund-burke. Crown Publishing, NY.

the symbol of worship in an atheistic society. Naturally, Burke would have asked, did Russia have to undergo a revolution and gulags that killed millions and the suppression of any hint of bourgeois culture to affect reform in society? His answer would undoubtedly be, No.

3.3   McCaulay's Belief in Cautious Government Experimentation

America is not about to experience a revolution; consider instead a much less obvious threat to American culture from a conservative's viewpoint: Great Society programs. They have the noble intention of upgrading the education, housing, training, and neighborhoods of people locked into an intergenerational cycle of poverty. To see why a conservative would be leery of these grand scale programs, let's look back at the policies of Thomas Macaulay a nineteenth-century British Whig, a liberal of the times, who, in retrospect is a standout in the Burkean tradition.

Two hotly debated issues in nineteenth-century Britain discussed were free elementary school education for the poor and a child's workday. Thomas Macaulay, a poet, a historian, and a Member of Parliament believed a successful public decision eventually would gain almost universal support if it were spiritually satisfying and made good economic sense.

Macaulay championed free education for the poor and reducing the 12-hour workday to 10 hours for the young. He defended his positions with a subtle mixture of caring and good business sense. Private enterprise, according to him, was not working well to educate the poor. Comparing England and Scotland to make his case, he said 150 years before, England was the richest country in the world and Scotland was one of the poorest. The English, at that time, naturally held the Scots in contempt, confusing material superiority for natural superiority. Fletcher of Saltoun, a Scottish nobleman, like the English, thought that there was something fundamentally wrong with the Scottish character. He despaired over his countrymen's ignorance, idleness, and lawlessness. His sad conclusion was that only harsh discipline, the stocks, and the lash, and forced labor could reclaim his country. The Scottish parliament thought otherwise. They decided to set up parochial schools for the poor, and, happily, the result was spectacular. In Macaulay's day, the English envied the Scot. Wherever he worked and whatever he studied, the Scot seemed to rise to the top in England. The cry became that the Scot was getting more than his share.

Why did the English fall behind in educating the poor? Macaulay believed it was a clear-cut case of public action in Scotland outstripping private enterprise in England. Unlike Scotland, England had relied on the market to educate the poor. Those among the poor who were willing to pay for their education could select teachers from the likes of footmen and peddlers who could barely write a letter without blundering. Their schools were without heat and air and the rooms were encrusted with filth. They had to learn without the aid of proper texts or tablets. Judging from the public records, many of the poor either chose not to pursue this crude imitation of an education or had learned almost nothing from their classes. Macaulay's proof was that virtually all convicts could not read or write and less than half the people registering for marriage licenses could not sign their names. The loss of productivity alone was probably immense, and this loss was not a personal loss but England's loss. Forgoing sugar, according to Macaulay, hurts one person only, but when neighbors cannot read, they could easily fall prey to rabble-rousers out of ignorance, which put all England at risk.[38]

Beyond appeals to England's good business sense and fear of crime, Macaulay also appealed to their conscience. People sunk in ignorance are not truly free. Could England deny children their freedom simply because they were poor? Macaulay did not want anyone doomed to obscurity because of their beginnings. If some child had enough talent, he "should rise to the highest dignities and attract the gaze of nations."[39]

He used a very similar line of argument to cut a child's workday from 12 hours to 10. According to Macaulay, when too much work "enfeeble[s] the body and pollute[s] the mind," the government must step in to protect the commonwealth. For a child especially, leisure was necessary for healthy growth. They needed time to rest, to exercise, to develop their minds. Without leisure they would lose those higher qualities that made England great.[40]

While he argued for social change through political action, he offered cautious recommendations. Government should experiment but not recklessly. In the case of child labor, he only wanted to cut a child's workday by 2 hours and then check the effects it would have on the earnings of poor families and the competitiveness of England's industries. With free education, he wanted to ensure that government officials did not use the money to buy votes or dictate a curriculum. Because he believed that the towns would have the most

---

[38] Young, G.M. *Macaulay: Prose and Poetry*. (1947) Harvard University Press. Speeches, Education, MA, pp. 789–791.

[39] Id., *Essays, Gladstone on Church and State*, p. 634.

[40] Id., Speeches, *The Ten Hours Bill* (1846).

commitment to quality education for their children, he wanted them to run the schools. He also expected the towns to contribute their own funds to ensure that they had a stake in the enterprise.

If Macaulay had to judge America's Great Society programs, I think he would find that many of them failed his basic tests of morality and effectiveness. He would have opposed any program for single mothers that gave poor women reasons to divorce or have children out of wedlock. He would have been against razing whole neighborhoods to put up antiseptically clean and soulless apartment projects that destroyed neighborhood communities and made people into strangers in their own buildings because of their huge size.

He would not have tried to experiment on a grand scale. Rather, he would have allowed states to become experimental laboratories, allowing them to try different approaches to solving the poverty cycle, including, perhaps, dropping many welfare benefits, which would force families and communities to take on the responsibility of solving their own problems.

3.4　De Tocqueville's Warning About the Pursuit of Wealth

Another luminary whose opinions are consistent with Burke's but focus more on ordinary, law-abiding citizens outside of government was De Tocqueville. In his landmark *Democracy in America*,[41] published in two volumes in 1835 and 1840, De Tocqueville warned that pursuit of wealth could break the bonds between private citizens leading them to cede their civic responsibilities to government administrators.[42] The public would demand uniform treatment from these officials as a matter of fairness because someone in New York ought to receive the same treatment as someone in Georgia. This process would lead to central government administration with government officials gaining the power to tell citizens what they could and could not do in a paternalistic way.

De Tocqueville feared pursuit of wealth as an important potentially divisive social force in America because equality of condition was widespread then. In a land where most people have the same wealth, the way to stand out is to be rich. He believed religion was the primary check on the egotistical pursuit of wealth. Christianity taught people to take a longer view of personal actions

---

[41] De Tocqueville, A., *Democracy in America* (1945). Vantage Books, NY.
[42] Dr. Aydiner C. (2017), *Democratic Despotism and Democracy's Drift: Tocqueville's Validity Today.* Beyond the Horizon. https://behorizon.org/democratic-despotism/. Accessed 30 April 2023.

because moral behavior and commitment to an active religious life led to rewards in heaven.[43]

One major religious commitment is to help the poor. God, for whatever reason, chooses people who are favored with special gifts. It is their religious obligation to uplift the poor and helpless, to lead and support the community. If we follow De Tocqueville's logic, he, like Macaulay, would oppose Great Society programs when they shunted personal obligations to the government. He also suggested that government social programs would enfeeble religious institutions by taking away their responsibilities, and by doing so marginalize them as a civilizing force in society. Although De Tocqueville focused on the importance of Christianity as the bulwark of American society, I believe he would have extended his views to all faiths if they had been important in early American society.

3.5   The Supporting Cast in This Portrayal

The next conservative featured is an American born in the twentieth century, someone much less known than William F. Buckley or Russell Kirk (who will make an appearance in the wrap-up chapter to this section). His name is John Bogle, the founder of the Vanguard funds. Bogle did not believe that self-interest and free markets alone are capable of building trust in a modern society. He wanted to bring back the notion of professionalism, stewardship, built on an ethical oath and an outlook to use special skills in the public's interest. Stewardship seemed to disappear during the period leading up to the Great Recession when brokers and agents treated investors as marks with pockets waiting to be picked.[44] According to Bogle, a society that worships the bottom line will encourage traders to push aside professional standards of conduct to pump up the annual bonus. In the end, society suffers because markets cannot be sustained without a reliable relationship between buyers and sellers.[45]

Along similar lines David Brooks, an editorial writer for the New York Times, believes the argument over the size of government may be misplaced. According to him, liberals and libertarians have atomized society by raising a free-standing individual to heroic levels and substituted material benefits as a measure from other desirables such as friendship and community that are necessary to lead a fulfilling life. Public policy should support nurturing

---

[43] See De Tocqueville, Volume 1, Chapter 17 and Volume 2, Chapter 6.

[44] Bogle, J.C. (2011), *Don't Count on It* (2011) xvi. John Wiley and Sons, NY.

[45] Id., p. 157.

networks within society that impress on the public the meaning of social obligation and community. Government officials should lead by example by displaying good character, respect for culture, and above all moral behavior. It should filter down through government policies.[46]

3.6   Back to Policy

A good way to predict a conservative's outlook is to understand he has a holistic view of society. Science and spirit, individual and community, business practices, and ethical beliefs are all part of a soulful unity. The motive force of a good society is raising ladies and gentlemen who glory in tradition, connect to community, and gaze into a future from a standpoint built from honoring the past. Whatever a conservative's religion or ethnic background, he or she believes in the essentials of the Protestant ethic – work hard, be frugal, aim at improving self and society. God wants better plows, better music, better houses, and better clothes to robe his creation in wealth. This is a crown of His glory (Ingersoll). Whatever a person's background, conservatives support strong family and community because from them a person gains security, develops a sense of responsibility, learns to identify with others as a larger group entity, and gains hope that together they can do God's will.

In business, the concept of "lady and gentleman" translates into a professional code of ethics. A professional has no use creative accounting and razzle-dazzle models to give others a false sense of security. Proper business culture reduces the likelihood of passive boards of directors and greedy executives exploiting corporations. A professional thinks long term and does not demand immediate gratification in profits or stock market gains.

In public affairs, a conservative' ideal is the statesman: a leader who rises above public opinion polls and special interests and looks to renew and reinvigorate society. He is also cautious, knowing that he doesn't have all the answers, and for him to alter private arrangements would require solid evidence and careful experimentation. A proper statesman is not a glory seeker. He is someone who embodies the community's virtues. His public decisions are an outgrowth of his personal beliefs and conduct. A conservative rejects the idea that a public official's personal conduct should be kept private because it supposedly does not affect performance in office. Conservatives believe personality and moral uprightness cannot be compartmentalized. For example, a balanced budget is important to a statesman not because it is the most

---

[46] Brooks, D. (2011), *The Social Animal*. Random House, NY.

efficient course of action but because it shows prudence, a necessary virtue to long-term health for society.

Civic responsibilities extend to private citizens. Conservatives honor patriotism but not the "my country right or wrong" variety. It is an expression of appreciation for gifts, unearned, gifts, bestowed by previous generations and other living now who have made America a wonderful place to live. Patriotism means giving back, earning the right to those gifts, and passing along gifts to fellow citizens and future generations.

They oppose any movement that wants to tear down society and remake it. Bold programs and bold visions that uproot traditions often feed on passion and action. They conjure myths of military glory. They seek to remold human nature from the top down with the movement's leaders in control. Conservatives oppose anyone who wants to use government to restore a lost purity – of tribe, nation, race, or class – who sees society as an organic unity that must be cared for and pruned by concerned leaders, and who tells use to envision a utopia and forget our petty needs for the sake of the larger whole.

Conservatives fear any group that wants to remake society violently, if necessary, to rid America of racism and exploitation. They see them corrupt revolutionaries who justify killing police, robbing banks, smashing, and grabbing loot from stores, setting fires, intimidating anyone who opposes them. They also fear evangelists, the born-again variety, who know to the true path to salvation, because they will impose their religious values on society for our personal benefit.

On the other hand, conservatives oppose any movement that defends the status quo at all costs. This holds true for any group that fights against cultural unraveling, when, as Tea Albrecht said, the fight is about your name, the places upon which your blood is anchored, the attachment of your name to some landmark or event that leads to nothing but hate, that feeds on hate, that leads to endless fighting, and that comes in waves and waves and seeks total destruction of the other.[47] The only good fight is to protect the innocent and have hope of finality.

Conservatives support religion as a powerful civilizing force. In America, religions are no longer magnets for extreme views. Instead, they counteract the desire for personal gain and fame at the expense of others. Some moral behaviors are not up for a vote. Conservative religious thought protected society against the progressive views of eugenics in the nineteenth and twentieth centuries aimed at sterilizing people designated as genetically unfit to reproduce. Britain freed the slaves for religious reasons. The Reverend Martin Luther King helped bring down the walls of prejudice. The Bible has much wisdom that should not be ignored in schools.

---

[47] Supra, Tea Obreht, p. 435.

Conservatives oppose large government because it destroys community and weakens civic virtue. When local governments have power, elected officials are answerable to people with familiar faces, many known by first name. Small government leaves room for other institutions to have a greater role in community affairs because the need to coordinate with large bureaucracy is not necessary. Federal takeovers of health and welfare services have weakened religious institutions, for example, because they are no longer the primary source of help to the needy.

Conservatives are spiritual environmentalists. Nature is God's design. By examining its majesty, humanity has an insight into God's wonders. Nature is a gift from God to humanity. In the Bible, God gave humanity dominion over nature, but that dominion was limited to tending His garden. Noah saved the animals from destruction. Humanity has no less obligation. A person who believes that the proper way to act is to act as if a Judge were watching is not likely to pollute. Those who pollute should bear the cost. They should pay for the cleanup. And just as important, they should bear the shame of corrupting God's creations.[48] Some conservatives would oppose a pollution tax because it reminds them of Church indulgences. One should not be able to pay to sin, or in this case to pollute the environment.

Looking outward, conservatives support tight borders and tight standards for accepting immigrants because they make a person realize that American citizenship is more than a business deal. It requires commitment to what they should see as an enchanted land of many types of people pulling together to keep America vibrant. Conservatives are wary of illegal cross-border movements with Mexico, for example, because it introduces a permanent but potentially transient and nonintegrated community into American society that flouted the law. Worse than a business deal of Mexicans coming for better pay, it seems like a land grab by Mexicans according to people like Samuel Huntington, a former professor at Harvard University.

Many conservatives believe mass migration is a threat when the newcomers come from a very different culture because they will likely dilute traditional American values, speak a different language, hold allegiance to different nations, but they are not racist. They want a measured inflow of immigrants so that America is not overwhelmed by new cultural practices that may break America into factions. People are all in the image of God, but men are different than women, and many world cultures are not entirely compatible with Western traditions. They want immigrants who show strong commitment to

---

[48] Pope, A. (2017), *We are Corrupting the Beauty of God's Creation.* https://www.scross.co.za/2017/02/pope-corrupting-beauty-gods-creation/. Accessed 30 April 2023.

their adopted nation by entering the country lawfully, showing their worth as a potential citizen during a trial period, and learning the basic principles of being American citizens.

Conservatives do not support nation-building abroad and do not reflexively believe democracy will lead to peace and prosperity in failed states. In the conservative tradition, a successful state evolves. The public eventually learns that openness within society encourages personal success. Warring groups must come to truly believe they are all better off if they work together than fight each other. This process, unfortunately, takes time. Often a burlesque of democracy actually produces worse outcomes than dictatorship because the ruling faction plunders the state as a dictator would but has little interest in providing government jobs and access to natural resources to other factions. A dictator would have more incentive to keep all groups happy.[49]

However, conservatives are wary but support regime change in threatening nations and dislike strong-man regimes and regimes controlled by revolutionary movements. In general, governments are unacceptable when they enflame public passions, when they denigrate individual choice (except in religious matters such as the right to life), when they exclude groups from government, and when they call for radical change in society. In general, however, conservatives want America to stay out of international battlegrounds because America is not the policeman of the world. American lives should not be sacrificed for vague abstractions such as promoting world democracy. But conservatives permit extraordinary measures during wartime subject to legal review during peacetime.

Looking back at the imagery of conservatives, allying themselves with libertarians is outwardly deceptive because it only applies to public policy. Conservatives see Lady Liberty as a nurturing mother who gives birth to new generations of free people, who protects them from oppression, and who looks to her children to renew the world using their minds and hands. This Lady Liberty thrives in a community; she does not seek public office. She's a homebody.

When conservatives look for imagery, they look to the heavens. Loyalty is like gravity that gives constellations shape and beauty. When freedom means every decision is a choice, whether it is to stay with family, or religion, or culture, people begin to float and society drifts away into nothingness like lone stars in deep space.

A simple motto based on the three Rs captures the conservative spirit: remembrance, righteousness, and renewal. All the rest is commentary.

---

[49] Pinker, S. (2011), *The Better Angels of Our Nature*. Viking Books, NY, p. 312.

4

Liberalism: Economic Instability and Exclusion Can Lead to Riots and Revolution

Abstract Liberals believe that centralized government can be an instrument for improving social justice. The popularity of liberalism in America can be traced to social disruptions caused by the rise of huge corporations, economic depressions, the persistence of racism, and most recently environmental concerns. Although liberals prefer market solutions, they believe that markets need an outside umpire to operate fairly. The liberal champions I chose are Keynes, Schelling, Minsky, Samuelson, Berle, and Means. Others referred to briefly are Bentham, J. S. Mill, T. H. Green, Hobhouse, Hartz, Rawls, and Downs. To see how liberal thought has influenced the Democratic Presidential Platforms, I compare their planks with liberal ideological thought.

4.1 Introduction

Now I turn to the 2012, the first of three Democratic national conventions I consider because arguably it is the most clear-cut example of liberalism in action. The delegates are of all shades; women are prominent; Obama is the president; multicultural and multicolor images are everywhere to drive home that America is a nation built by minorities.

Their faces have changed dramatically over the last century, but the liberal soul has remained the same. The poor, the oppressed, the blue-collar worker, and the ordinary citizen of modest means have been the Democratic political base since Franklin Roosevelt's presidency. Protecting the weak against the strong, the liberal message, has brought together many types who feel oppressed in society.

In Franklin Roosevelt's day, it was the party that helped unions organize, protected life savings by insuring bank deposits, instituted social security and unemployment relief to help the elderly and the needy. Since then, its protective umbrella has expanded among others to ethnic and racial groups, women, and Gays.

Liberals like declaring war: on poverty, on prejudice, on the rich, and on organized vested interests that use government for their own selfish ends. They are not averse to redistributing income when private sector payoffs seem unfair by reasonable standards. It is an ideology based on government that can fix systematic moral failings and repair economic flaws, often by restraining the power of private and public institutions and by defining policies to prevent financial panics and tamp down business cycles.

The 2012 Democratic Platform is a classic testament to liberal ideology. It starts out with a blast at the rich and powerful, "Our political system is under assault by those who believe that special interests should be able to buy whatever they want in our society, including our government." Wall Street has to live by the same rules as Main Street. No more bailouts for banks. No more "too big to fail." The wealthy should not be allowed to "maximize profits through layoffs and outsourcing." Bush's tax cuts for the rich have to be reversed. Tax breaks will end for companies that ship jobs overseas. Oil companies will be held to account for reckless actions that lead to loss of life and massive oil spills.

Then the platform addresses the needs of those who feel exploited. It goes on to say the Democratic Party will protect consumers from flimflam lenders and mortgage brokers who trick them into borrowing more than they can afford. Credit card companies must not be allowed to charge hidden fees. Workers should not have "to choose between their jobs and their safety."

The platform states that minorities will be able to draw on new resources to assure their health, safety, and education. The Democratic administration "established new Offices of Minority Health," and is "helping state Medicaid programs fund home and community-based services." It is "committed to ending racial, ethnic, and religious profiling." The government under Obama has "invested more than $2.5 billion in savings from reforming our student loan system to strengthen our nation's Historically Black Colleges and Universities, Hispanic-Serving Institutions, Tribal Colleges and Universities, Alaska, Hawaiian Native Institutions, Asian American and Pacific Islander Institutions, and other Minority Serving Institutions."

Women will have access to birth control coverage. Democrats are steadfast in their support for Roe v. Wade giving women the right to an abortion. They are "committed to ensuring full equality for women by reaffirming support for the Equal Rights Amendment, recommit to enforcing Title IX, support the Paycheck Fairness Act, and will urge ratification of the Convention on the Elimination of All Forms of Discrimination Against Women."

As for marriage and family, Democrats support "marriage equality and support the movement to secure equal treatment under law for same-sex couples." To keep families intact, they support "Child Tax Credit and Earned Income Tax Credit. Parents and caregivers – regardless of gender – need more flexibility and support in the workplace." Democrats "support passing the Healthy Families Act, broadening the Family and Medical Leave Act, and partnering with states to move toward paid leave."

The platform states that the elderly need a defined benefits to plan for retirement. Toward that end, Democrats will "block Republican efforts to subject Americans' guaranteed retirement income to the whims of the stock market through privatization."

If anything, the 2016 party platform had become even more focused on minority rights, and clean energy targets and global warming threats became central issues. It outlined a strategy to prevent global warming by committing to a clean energy economy. Prominent proposals included cutting energy waste, investment in public transportation, taxing pollutants, increasing fuel economy standards for vehicles, promoting electric vehicles, and regulating hydraulic fracturing.[1] The 2020 platform was more of the same.

Behind the colorful imagery at the 2012 democratic convention is a portrait of an American as a citizen. This portrait resembles to some extent a libertarian's that an individual should create his own future and that of a conservative who pictures people seeking personal connections to define themselves, but the liberal's true essence is a citizen who finds honor and purpose in being a member of a great democracy that works toward ending inequality, ending exploitation of the weak, rooting out racism, protecting Americans from catastrophes beyond their control, and pitching in together to improve the lot of all who live here.

From a more philosophic standpoint, the platform is a liberal's case study for promoting positive liberty – enabling people to realize their capabilities by altering the terms of exchanges in society by uplifting groups pushed down unfairly. Even competent adults are vulnerable to forces beyond their control, catastrophic illness, an economic depression, and prejudice in housing and employment. Nudging society toward promoting personal excellence requires a judicious use of government influence. Liberals pride themselves on

---

[1] Supra Democratic Platform, 2016, pp. 24–25.

understanding historical trends and adapting their strategy to preserve and advance human dignity.

The historical record shows the adaptability of liberalism to address pressing social problems. Centuries before, back in England, the birthplace of liberalism. Then liberals fought for equal rights against king and nobility when they ruled Britain. Like libertarians today, English liberals in the mold of Adam Smith, the icon of free traders, wanted government to get out of the way. They wanted to rescind laws that tied peasants to the land, that regulated the price of labor, which defined the job a tradesman could have, that set the terms of his apprenticeship, and that limited anyone's ability to move from town to town. Then liberals favored a minimalist government, a cop keeping order on the trading floor, to paraphrase Thomas Carlyle.

In the eighteenth-century America, liberals supported liberty, equality, and opportunity as the basis of a good society.[2] In a land where farmers were property holders and laborers aspired to be property holders, liberals opposed central government. Open lands and rapidly developing markets gave people all the opportunity they wanted.

This giddy connection between freedom and markets didn't last long. Many, even in the South, were uneasy with the flourishing market for slaves. It was hard to reconcile a belief that human nature was unchanging and universal with the idea that certain humans were property. As large-scale corporations started to dominate industry, a working class started to develop that ate away at the image of the soon-to-be prosperous family. In the 1880s, one-sixth of all children under the age of 16 worked.[3] They worked on farms and in textile mills often alongside their parents and had little opportunity to become educated. In factory towns and cities, women worked 9-hour shifts without a break for lunch, often locked inside, without adequate toilet facilities. Some died tragically. One-hundred-forty-six young people died when a fire broke out at the Triangle Shirtwaist Factory in Manhattan on March 25, 1911.

In the early 1900s, it became apparent to liberals that big business owners like the aristocrats of the Old World were blocking human development by treating workers as chattel. The great migration from town to city caused by industrialization was producing a new type of social ill: being alone in a crowd. Newly arrived city dwellers had weak ties to other city dwellers. Religions were losing their drawing power, and religious institutions were being overwhelmed with the number of charity cases.

[2] Hartz, L. (1953), *The Liberal Tradition in America.* Harcourt Brace, NY p. 292.

[3] Zinn, H. (1999), *A People's History of The United States.* Harper Collins, NY p. 267.

As the twentieth century rolled on, liberals realized government needed to step in to support the helpless and needy, even if poverty was a sign of moral failing. They began to see government as an active agent to assure liberty, equality, and opportunity in America by protecting the weak against the strong.

Classical economists like Adam Smith tied personal freedom to owning property. In large corporations this connection broke. Managers did not own the corporation's property. Stockholders were passive investors with virtually no say in running the corporation. Unskilled workers were just another resource like machinery. Organizers of giant trusts like Standard Oil and U.S. Steel linked businesses together to control markets. Their power extended like an octopus's tentacles into the heart of the democratic process, threatening to strangle democracy itself by controlling politicians. Liberals sought to limit their power. Lloyd, a writer for the Atlantic, wrote in 1881:

> The Standard has done everything with the Pennsylvania legislature, except refine it. In 1876 its organization was brought before Congress and referred to a committee. A prominent member of the Standard, not a member of Congress, conducted the farce of inquiry from behind the seat of the chairman.[4]

Teddy Roosevelt's administration began a period of aggressive trust busting. Most notably, the Supreme Court ruled that a breakup of Standard Oil of New Jersey was necessary to maintain freedom in commerce. When a breakup seemed infeasible, the government sought to regulate the practices of giant utilities such as AT&T. In effect, the federal government began to regulate key industries instead of allowing corporations to regulate government. Eventually, the focus of antitrust actions was to improve economic efficiency by breaking up bloated companies that overpriced their products. Liberal thought never lost its distaste for large concentrations of economic power even if they were economically efficient or regulated by government.

With strong liberal support, the federal government began to balance the power between labor and management by passing worker's compensation legislation that made employers financially responsible for workplace accidents instead of placing the burden on the injured employee or a government dole. In 1916, the federal government outlawed child labor used to produce goods for interstate commerce.

During Franklin Roosevelt's administration, the federal government allowed unions to organize giving the wage earner power to negotiate with

---

[4]Lloyd, H.D. (1881), *Story of a Great Monopoly*. Atlantic Monthly. https://ehistory.osu.edu/exhibitions/1912/trusts/lloyd_article. Accessed 30 April 2023.

management on more even terms. His New Deal legislation also constructed a social safety net to protect ordinary people from catastrophes not of their own making. The government instituted deposit insurance to protect savings deposits in the event of a bank failure. Unemployment insurance gave people money to live on when they lost their jobs. Social security insurance gave the elderly money when they could no longer work.

Outside the factory, private property was also a means for oppressing minorities. As late as the 1940s, a legally acceptable practice in America was to put restrictive a covenant into a deed saying this land can't be sold to blacks, Jews, and Irish. Liberals fought for equal rights after World War II. How could America continue to allow racial segregation and voting restrictions after it had fought fascism and Nazism because of their oppressive racial laws? How could America support freeing colonial lands while America practiced a form of colonialism at home?

Liberals began looking at outcomes in society at large for violations of America's promise to its people and adjusted the federal law to make the outcomes seem fairer, more efficient, and more stable. One dangerous crack in the market system became clearly exposed in the twentieth century and still has no clear solution. Economists dryly called it myopic rationalism – short-sightedness. People trying to protect themselves from one class of market uncertainties produced other classes. Economists claimed that economic downturns occurred when people stopped spending to protect their economic future. When enough people did this, consumption declined and as a result production declined, and people lost their jobs. Something like a self-fulfilling prophecy.

Financial panics were a feature of a market-driven society. Psychology played a key role in the unraveling of the economy. It started with a sudden shock such as a major bankruptcy, which shook the public's confidence in the business sector. Unease sometimes led to a run on the banking system. The biggest one happened in the early 1930s when people rushed to banks to withdraw their funds after the stock market tanked. It happened again when a herd of investors panicked in 2008 leading to a stampede to withdraw their funds from financial institutions. Panic selling caused the Great Recession. Call it what you like, myopia or panic, liberals believe the government needs to step in to steady the economy by spending when private individuals don't and shoring up financial institutions when they are in danger of collapse. In retrospect, liberals believe that prompt and determined public action would have prevented the Great Depression and Great Recession. Government had the obligation to regulate financial markets to prevent financial panics from occurring.

This obligation extended to protect Americans from downturns in the economy that threatened common financing practices that would have been prudent in normal times. For example, installment buying and widespread use of borrowing took off in the early twentieth century. Like modern supply chains, installment buying works well when economic conditions are stable. People didn't have to wait to buy a house or a car. They would pay them off out of their paychecks. But when a downturn in the economy left many unemployed, defaults became widespread, magnifying the downturn in business.

Fixed loan rates are another example of trying to stabilize expectations of lenders and borrowers. But when market conditions turn sour, loans at high fixed rates can't be paid, resulting in a rash of bankruptcies. Requiring pension funds to invest only in AAA bonds makes sense in normal times to promote conservative investing but turns out to reinforce a financial panic when bonds are being downgraded across the market. Pension funds had to unload downgraded debt, contributing to widespread panic selling. Bankruptcy laws that work well in normal times can freeze markets in general downturns.

The sanctity of private property is an extremely important American value. However, when private property leads to exploitation, the rights of property owners have to be cut back. Liberals supported unionization as a fair means to counter the power of corporations. Eventually, organized labor was successful in setting wage scales and defining working conditions and other working arrangements. Liberals recognized a key downside of protecting workers and consumers was economic inflexibility. When wages and labor hours don't adjust during a general business downturn, employers will lay off workers to cut costs, leading to unemployment. Unemployment could become protracted if people were unwilling to move from a depressed part of the country to a booming part.

In recent elections, liberals have called for higher taxes for the rich, especially the ultrarich. According to Fast Company, CEO salaries are now 324 times the median worker's pay.[5] Burrough and Helyar, the authors of Barbarians at the Gate, said that self-interested CEOs were cashing in by expropriating corporate assets either by encouraging a leveraged buyout or giving themselves stock options.[6] Even the great innovators like Bezos and Musk, would likely plough new markets if tax rates increased.

[5] Rainey, C. (2022), The age of "greedflation" is here: See how obscene CEO-to-worker pay ratios are right now. Fast Company. https://www.fastcompany.com/90770163/the-age-of-greedflation-is-here-see-how-obscene-ceo-to-worker-pay-ratios-are-right-now. Accessed 30 April 2023.

[6] Burrough, B. and Helyar, J. (1989), *Barbarians at the Gate*. Harper and Row, NY.

Not every government program has a long list of debits and credits that need to be balanced. Sometimes one federal program can solve several problems at once. In 1944, the federal government went beyond protecting the oppressed to showing its gratitude for war veterans. It passed the G.I. Bill, which gave returning veterans money, healthcare benefits, tuition, and living expenses for college, employment counseling, and low interest loans for mortgages.[7] In 1948, it accounted for 15% of the federal budget. It was a tremendous success. It prevented unemployment after the war, trained a large segment of the labor force, and stimulated demand for education and housing, which boosted the economy.

Still later, in the 1960s, liberals shifted their philosophical focus from helping the distressed out of necessity or pity to declaring entitlements that accrue to a citizen without having to earn them. Each person has a right to live decently and with dignity regardless of merit. Another major sociological change in liberalism came about during the 1960s, championing multiculturalism. Until then, liberals represented ethnic minorities who bought into WASP culture as the ideal for American society. Arguably, they used to measure themselves against the WASP image of being tall, blond-haired, blue-eyed people dressed in understated, richly tailored clothing, going to the club, having a cocktail, and taking for granted they were in control. Many authors such as Philip Roth and Toni Morrison told stories of people who wanted to be WASPs but couldn't be WASPs but who hated their own and wound up living false and hollow lives.

Then a cultural revolution began spearheaded by liberal activists. Minorities and ethnic groups came out of the closet. Suddenly black became beautiful, and Jews wore skullcaps outdoors. The Puerto Rican Day Parade in New York City, which started in 1958, grew tremendously in popularity. Liberals pushed immigration from Third World countries. The ethnic American was born, and beyond that liberals didn't want anyone even burdened by cultural identity if they wanted to go their own way.

The record of liberal activism should not make anyone think liberals are starry-eyed about the beneficence of government. Looking at the historical record, they had the same fears of big government as conservatives and libertarians but chose to push ahead and experiment instead of waiting for the market imperfections and social prejudices to fade away. For example, the Pure Food and Drug Act of 1906 banned contaminated food from the marketplace. Before that people had to buy different brands or go to different local stores to test the purity of the products they bought. As a result of

---

[7] Freeman, J. (2012), American Empire: 1945–2000. Penguin, NY p. 33.

market imperfections, children died from tainted milk; many sickened and died from spoiled meat.

Liberals did fear government paternalism could dampen personal initiative and weaken family and community values. For example, in 1996, President Clinton signed legislation requiring people on welfare to work that began after receiving 2 years of assistance. The justification was the work requirement would break the cycle of poverty that lingered across generations. They feared regulating industry because it drew the rich closer to government.

Liberals feared a growing government bureaucracy. As a result, liberals kept trying to review and refine their programs by using the same management tools used in private industry to monitor and control performance. For example, President Obama said, we live in an Information Age, but the last government reorganization happened in an age of black-and-white TV.[8]

Liberals admit that government's share of Gross Domestic Product has grown substantially during the twentieth century. However, it does not mean it will continue or that government programs will never die. They cite a litany of examples to support their case. In the 1970s, the government tried price controls and then discarded them when they failed to stem inflation. The government regulated banks as a result of the Great Depression, deregulated them to a large extent in the 1980s, and began re-regulating them after the Great Recession. The airline industry was deregulated. AT&T was broken up. Great Society programs were downscaled when they failed to produce results. Social experiments have symbolic value. Sometimes it is better for the government to do something than do nothing.

They will also admit that government regulations have expanded dramatically but for a very good reason. Society has become massive and dense. In the classical economic model, groups are at best individuals with common buying habits – market segments. In modern society, building a new highway or urban renewal pits individuals as groups with common interests against the policymakers proposing the public work. Liberals recognize that group interests are a fact of life that must be addressed fairly and efficiently.

While liberals believe that vested interests, especially those representing big business, will use government for their own benefit, over the long sweep of history, legislators have worked to right the wrongs in society. Many elected officials have taken a wider, longer, and much more unbiased view of society than any individual or community. Franklin Roosevelt was from a patrician

---

[8] Kamensky, J. (2020), Evolution of Efforts to Reorganize the Government, IBM Center for the Business of Government. https://www.businessofgovernment.org/blog/evolution-efforts-reorganize-government. Accessed 30 April 2023.

family but championed the common people. Statesmen like him are in good position to fix structural flaws in society.

Government has also been an engine for innovation, invention, and discovery. Government research and funding led to the development of the Internet, then allowed access to its network to private users, then turned the network over to the private sector, and from there the World Wide Web took off. The Defense Advanced Research Project Agency (DARPA) sponsored contests aimed at developing automated vehicles.

All of the examples suggest government activism can improve the structure, relationships, and personal behavior in society for the better. Government-sponsored education and healthcare, rules to improve working conditions, and funds to promote science and scientific management are public building blocks for human betterment. Hallmarks of the liberal creed are flexibility and open mindedness. Sometimes the market is the solution; sometimes the government is the solution; sometimes it is a collaborative private/public solution.

Liberals like Tea Partiers see America's Constitution as a modern-day ecumenical Bible that gives government purpose and direction. The Bill of Rights, for example, extracts the highest ideals contained in holy books without ascribing them to a chosen people or a chosen religion. But in contrast to Tea Partiers, liberals believe the Constitution is a living document that needs to be reinterpreted to fit the times. In modern society, an expansive view of the constitution can become an instrument for economic and social liberation.

Looking back at the twentieth century, a case can be made that liberalism saved private enterprise and democracy when socialists, communists, and fascist movements were gaining in popularity as the wave of the future. Teddy Roosevelt, a president with strong conservative and imperialist leanings, felt it necessary to clip the power of Robber Barons because the public felt they were running America as if it were their own corporation. Wilson showed government could effectively marshal the economy to fight a world war without permanently commandeering it. The Great Depression reinforced the notion that private enterprise is beset by periodic manias and panics and that the public needed welfare protection for people thrown out of work through no fault of their own. Franklin Roosevelt's administration kept experimenting with bold new programs to put people to work. Whether the programs were successful or not, they gave people hope that prosperity was just around the corner.

After the Nazis defeat, liberals pressed even harder to once and for all tear up Jim Crow laws and break down more subtle forms of prejudice, the Gentlemen's Agreements that excluded African Americans, Jews, and other ethnic minorities from the best schools and choice jobs in industry and government and from genteel communities and hotels. Liberals wanted anyone who fought for his country to gain benefits as a partial payback for their sacrifices. Later, liberals focused on silent environmental killers: pesticides in the fields, asbestos in the home, a variety of dangerous workplace conditions, air and water pollution, and most recently, global warming. Most recently, liberals fought for open and proud expression of ethnic identity, Gay pride, and equal rights extended to all groups.

So where did liberalism come from? How did develop historically? As I mentioned, liberalism is not a homegrown ideology. Arguably, its founders were ancient Greeks who thought government was a positive force for promoting the common good.[9] The liberal tradition crosses many academic and national boundaries. British liberals such as Jeremy Bentham, John Stuart Mill, T. H. Green, and L. T. Hobhouse, -- all from Great Britain – greatly influenced the likes of John Dewey, Louis Hartz, and Anthony Downs, all Americans. With the exception of Downs and perhaps Mill, they are political philosophers, sociologists, and educators. With the exception of Downs and Hartz, the others lived in the nineteenth century. But when the discussion shifted to myopic rationalism, I was dealing with twentieth-century perspectives formulated by liberal economists. They were the intellectual innovators of liberalism and offer great insights into modern social and economic problems.

I have chosen John Maynard Keynes, a British economist, as the main champion of modern liberalism because many of the cracks in society open during sharp recessions and deep, prolonged depressions. His most famous expression is "In the long run we are all dead" also intrigues me. What it means is up for debate. In a few paragraphs, I will give the standard account of its meaning that is related to market myopia and price rigidities. I will point Keynes's less well-known writings to suggest he recognized a Darwinist streak in private enterprise. The market is a place of fierce struggle. Only the fittest survive until a new species of competitor appears armed with a new organizational structure or new goods and services. Like in the jungle, old and young businesses often fail, and many lose their jobs. The market is held in high esteem because this competitive struggle has raised standards of living immeasurably. But the losses are particular to individuals and recovery is time-sensitive to people running out of resources. Keynes's expression captures the idea that society and individuals need some protection from the ravages of the marketplace.

---

[9] Green, T.H. (1964), Political Theory. Croft Classics. NY p. 80.

He is also an interesting character study from a moral perspective. He might be called a classic liberal hypocrite. He thought that Jews were money lovers who corrupted European civilization by spreading their addiction to the gentiles; yet, he had Jewish friends.[10] More importantly, he wanted to save Jews from Nazism and supported Zionism after World War II.[11]

Keynes's reaction to Jews is symptomatic of an underlying human sympathy toward others that Adam Smith attributed to putting oneself in others' shoes. It is this dispassionate objective eye that allows even the prejudiced to act with honor. In my estimation, it ties directly to Keynes's far-seeing view of economics that made him a giant of the twentieth century.

Beside Keynes, I've added three supporting American economists who were liberal: Paul Samuelson, Thomas Schelling, and Hyman Minsky. They are followed by a brief introduction to the works of a lawyer, Adolf Berle, and an economist, Gardiner Means, who examined changes in private property rights caused by the rise of the modern corporation. Other economists make cameo appearances. John Rawls, an American philosopher, is the final champion in this series. He justifies redistributing income from rich to poor because of unfair outcomes that inevitably happen in an open, competitive society.

4.2   Keynes: In the Long Run We Are All Dead

In 1926, Keynes had already dismissed Marxian Socialism as a wonder of "how a doctrine so illogical and dull can have exercised so powerful and enduring an influence over the minds of men."[12] He couldn't imagine how government control of industry could work well when many government services were so inefficient and wasteful, but yet, a private sector free for all wasn't optimal either because of imperfections in competition and its survival of the fittest mentality that left little hope for those unable to compete.

His masterwork, the General Theory of Employment, Interest, and Money, published in 1936 gave a comprehensive justification for government intervention to lift economies out of the Great Depression. In it, he argued that the economics profession spawned characters like Pangloss from Candide. Despite repeated financial crises and massive economic downturns,

---

[10] Anand Chandavarkar, A. (2000), Was Keynes Anti-Semitic? Economic and Political Weekly. Vol. 35, No. 19, at pp. 1619–1624. https://www.jstor.org/stable/4409262. Accessed 30 April 2023.

[11] Ungar-Sargon, B. (2013), On John Maynard Keynes' 130th Birthday. Tablet. https://www.tabletmag.com/sections/news/articles/on-john-maynard-keynes-130th-birthday. Accessed 30 April 2023.

[12] John Maynard Keynes, J.M. (2004), *The End of Laissez Faire: The Economic Consequences of The Peace*, (Originally published in 1926) Prometheus Books. Buffalo, NY.

economists kept saying we live in the best of all worlds. Recessions are temporary and mild.[13] He pointed out that business doesn't operate the way economic models suggest. Prices and especially wages don't adjust to changes in market conditions.[14] The supposedly most efficient market, the stock market, has a dubious effect on economic efficiency. It allows companies to raise large sums, but it makes businessmen focus on daily stock price movements instead of long-term, real market developments.[15] Financial markets lead to speculation. Investors try to guess what others believe are good investments instead of focusing on long-term, fundamental analysis.[16] He also attributed the break between objective information and stock investment strategy to the separation of ownership and management in large corporations.[17] The true worth of these firms was not known to an investor in common stocks.

He pointed out that business is highly psychological and built on expectations and perceived risks. No one really can predict beyond a short period, yet businesspeople invest in factories and other long-term investments. Often buyers and sellers don't understand each other, especially in the aggregate. People may want to save more but businessmen see this as an immediate drop in demand. Even if the businesspeople knew about the change in spending habits, it is not clear when the consumers will spend the saved money.

Debt is fixed in dollars; wages are set in dollars. Neither is allowed to change with overall price movements. The results are defaults and unemployment. In depressed times, companies feel they have enough plant capacity and holders of money want to sit on it instead of risking a loan in bad times.

Keynes believed that the economy was self-correcting but took an unacceptably long time. He thought that frictions and barriers, thought inimical by classical economists, actually helped prevent the economy from experiencing wild swings. He believed that very flexible prices for all commodities would produce wild gyrations in prices. Practical limits to investment and disinvestment in plant and equipment placed a ceiling on booms and a floor on busts. In depressions, he did believe the rich would eventually want to build mansions and pyramids to employ the poor, but why wait for them to act?

Instead, Keynes recommended the government spend during a depression and pump money into the economy, though he believed this was a less effective policy instrument. He likened government spending to digging for gold,

---

[13] Keynes, J.M. (1965), *The General Theory of Employment, Interest, And Money* 6–7 (1965) Harbinger, Harcourt Brace, NY. pp. 6–7.

[14] Id., p. 8.

[15] Id., pp. 154–155.

[16] Id., pp. 155–156.

[17] Id., Chapter 12.

a potentially useless endeavor on its own similar to burying money and digging it up, and yet this seemingly wasteful economic activity puts people back to work and has them spending on other goods. Of course, Keynes preferred government spending to be as efficient as possible, but the point is that government inefficiency can be an efficient strategy in a larger context.

4.3   Samuelson: The Fallacy of Composition

Keynes became the intellectual giant of the economics profession especially in the first two decades after World War II. A great popularizer of Keynes's thought during this postwar period was the Nobel Prize winner Paul Samuelson. In his Principles of Economics, Samuelson picked up on Keynes's famous quote, "In the long run we are all dead."[18] Samuelson focused on near-term government policy to offset business cycles. Samuelson, like Keynes stressed the importance of using fiscal policy – government spending and tax policies – to curb unsustainable booms and business downturns. In depressions, especially, Samuelson used Keynes's notion of a liquidity trap to suggest that pumping money into the economy will only wind up in the public's pockets unspent because interest rates were too low to invest profitably in bonds, and investment in real assets was a very risky proposition when many assets lay idle.[19] Instead, government spending would be a source of direct demand for idle goods and services, and because the demand for one good led to the demand for the materials needed to produce the good, a dollar of government spending would expand economic activity by a multiple amount. Similarly, tax reductions could induce the public to spend more.

Samuelson also popularized Keynes's Fallacy of Composition (originally fallacy of thrift). Rational individual behavior can produce disastrous results for the nation. The desire to save more by an individual may be prudent in the long term but suppose everyone decided to save more because they fear economic instability. The result would be a decline in total demand, a buildup in inventories, a decline in production, and ultimately a recession.

---

[18] Samuelson, P.A. (1948). *Economics: An Introductory Analysis*. McGraw-Hill, NY.
[19] Id., Chapter 15, p. 207 especially.

4.4 Schelling: Not My Job

Another important disciple of Keynes was another Nobel Prize winner, Thomas Schelling. In his book *Micromotives and Macrobehavior*, Schelling explored the fallacy of composition across a variety of social systems and examined long-term effects. His examples are fun to read, but their meanings have wide implications for social policy. Here are three of Schelling's examples followed by a fourth of my own:

Seating in Church: Suppose a pastor asks questions of congregants seated in the first two rows of his church and people don't like to be called on. To avoid potential embarrassment, congregants fill the back pews first. Suppose when all are seated, the first two rows are empty. The pastor questions people in rows three and four. Everyone is worse off because they are all farther back than they want and the unlucky latecomers in rows three and four get pressed into service by the pastor. The easy solution to the problem is to cordon off last two rows.[20]

Picking up a fallen mattress on a highway: Without the driver knowing it, a mattress he is transporting slides off the roof of his car. Thankfully, no one behind the car was hurt. Typical of commuters, they will gawk a bit, traffic jam builds, and certainly no one is willing to get out of the car to pick it up. A simple solution is to have a highway policeman pick up the mattress.[21]

Preferring majority status: A person is looking to relocate to a new neighborhood. He is not overtly prejudiced but does prefer to live where his ethnic or racial group is in the majority. He is willing to accept let's say a 3:1 of his group as his neighbors. In other words, he is willing to mix to some extent but doesn't want to feel like a stranger. This social preference will actually lead to segregated communities.[22] Here the solution to the problem is by no means clear.

Love and Marriage: Suppose two people fall in love at college. They are from different backgrounds. It turns out one of them is from a religious group that is dying out. In the next generation, it will become even harder for people of the endangered religion to meet each other. After a tipping point, the likely long-term result is the disappearance of the religious group.[23] Again, it is not clear how government policy can help.

---

[20] Schelling, T.C. (1978) *Micromotives and Macrobehavior*. W. W. Norton and Co, NY pp. 11–12.

[21] Id., p. 125.

[22] Id., p. 140.

[23] Based on Id., p. 35.

Schelling's line of reasoning is that a society has many systems, the economic system being only one of them. Most of these systems are open or at least very porous. Within them, individual behavior is often myopic. As a result, self-serving behavior may not lead to satisfactory results.[24]

In some cases, according to Schelling, government intervention is clearly superior to private behavior. Installing traffic lights is one example, or, as mentioned, having a highway policeman remove a fallen mattress. Other interventions are possible but require a great deal more government finesse. For example, builders expect an increase in demand for housing, but it turns out they were off in their estimate of when the demand will pick up. This mistiming will lead to a decline in construction as builders work off excess inventory. The result could produce a downturn in the economy as a whole. The issue is how to improve market information to improve industry planning. Another example: Suppose people decide they only want one or two children. If they prefer male children, America could wind up with many unmarried males in the next generation as is the case in China now. Government incentives could equalize the gender mix.

4.5   Minsky: Speculative Excesses

The last disciple of Keynes I will mention is Hyman Minsky, an American economist whose reputation shot up after his death. Minsky focused on Keynes's notion of animal spirits to produce a model of financial panics. Keynes believed irrational exuberance and pessimism were part of human nature and when unchecked create economic and political instability. Government policy was for Keynes a key for building public confidence against wild swings in the economy. It was an antidote to animal spirits that are too optimistic in boom times and too pessimistic in bust times.

Hyman Minsky elaborated on Keynes to produce his model of speculative bubbles. Minsky believed financial investors, especially small ones, are largely ignorant of market fundamentals, and so invest mainly on emotion and hearsay. They are prone to a herd mentality, following friends or supposed experts like sheep to slaughter. He links innovations to a psychological cycle that begins with euphoria, then prudency, on to sobering fear, finally to collapse:

An innovation occurs or a general sustained improvement in business conditions; or a push for deregulation opens new opportunities.

---

[24] Id., p. 25.

Prudent investing gives way to speculative investing on asset prices (can pay interest, not principle), to Ponzi schemes (can't pay interest, bet on asset appreciation).

Real conditions become less favorable than expected.

Financial distress leading to panic, causing a major downturn in the economy.[25]

Following Minsky's line of argument, the speculative bubble in mortgages before the 2008 real estate collapse is a perfect example of his psychological cycle. Lax lending practices were the stimulant. People rushed to buy houses because they did not need a down payment. It was like buying a house for nothing. Free. Housing prices began to rise rapidly as demand surged. Then, sober people who held back jumped into the market to buy houses before they became too expensive. Eventually, the buying frenzy eased, prices started to moderate. People holding huge mortgages without the means to pay them began to get nervous. When housing prices dipped, defaults blossomed, and the panic was on. Interestingly, Keynes mentioned in a footnote that a mortgage was like an option to buy.[26]

These four economists – Keynes, Samuelson, Schelling, and Minsky – highlight systematic weaknesses in purely private behavior. They were greatly influenced by the hardships caused by panics leading to the Great Depression in the 1930s. While they all believed private enterprise is the best approach to running a modern society and opposed socialism, they did believe government had a major role in shoring up private enterprise when cracks appeared.

4.6 Berle and Means: Separation of Ownership and Management

Two other liberal thinkers, Adolf Berle and Gardiner Means, largely forgotten by the general public, took aim at concentrations of corporate power from a new perspective. Instead of tagging corporate exploitation to industrialists like Henry Ford or financiers like J.P. Morgan, they warned the public that huge organizations were a public threat because of their organizational design. In 1932, prior to Keynes's General Theory, Berle and Means published *The Modern Corporation and Private Property*.[27] They noted the modern govern-

---

[25] Charles P. Kindleberger, C.P., and Aliber, R. (2005), *Manias, Panics, and Crashes: A History of Financial Crashes*, 5th Edition, Chapter 2, pp. 24–37. John Wiley and Sons, NY.

[26] Keynes, *General Theory*, p. 241.

[27] Berle, A., and Means, G. (1932), *The Modern Corporation and Private Property*. Transaction Publishers, NJ.

ment broke the connection between ownership and management by making the modern corporation a legal entity. Because stockholders were typically passive investors and held relatively small shares of total stocks outstanding, corporate managers effectively controlled the corporations and could potentially use its resources for their own benefit. They suggested extending voting rights to all shareholders and improved accountability of corporate managers. Making sure top management represents the interests of stockholders, employees, and customers is an active agenda item for liberals.

4.7   Rawls: Fairness

John Rawls, the last champion discussed here came of age after World War II and published his major work, *A Theory of Justice,* in 1971.[28] His contribution to liberal thought rests on a highly theoretical model, a thought experiment, used to justify redistributing income and wealth to the least well off in society. It is an interesting exercise because it is a sophisticated example of using axioms and theories built on highly rational analysis to justify a sentiment that society ought to help the poor and helpless.

He built his model on a long history of highly rational arguments drawn from philosophy, economics, and political theory to justify government programs to improve the lot of people at the bottom of society. He like other philosopher who were defenders of equal rights against the oppressive rule of kings adopted an image of man living in the wilds who lived free, who by his very nature had inalienable rights to life, liberty, and the pursuit of happiness, and these should carry over into a just society. When the common man began to demand equal rights and a voice in government, he agreed with political theorists who claimed majority rule improved social welfare because each citizen had an equal claim on society. When majorities seemed threatening, the justification for limiting their power was to treat others as you would treat yourself, that fair rules must have universal applicability and could not be overturned by a majority.

His next step in the progression relied on economics. The original justification for helping the poor and helpless was that it paid off in real terms over the long run. Educated people, for example, were more productive workers and more informed voters. When Rawls was developing his ideas, America had declared war on poverty. People had a right to a decent standard of living no matter their ability to earn a living. Rawls developed a theory of fairness to

---

[28] Rawls, J. (1971), *A Theory of Justice.* Belknap Press, MA.

justify funneling money, assets, and support services to the poor. His theory developed the idea that the transfer was a right built from an implicit social contract.

Rawls said, imagine setting up American society but not knowing if you were white or black, stupid, or smart, blessed with a supportive family or the product of a broken home. In this situation, a reasonable person might say that any unearned benefit was a common good of society and that these common should be shared with the least well off.

One could also imagine this almost disembodied man also imagining a society that operates like a fair game producing payoffs that are wildly out of proportion to a person's actual contribution to society – a lottery winner, for example, or a hedge fund manager. It would seem reasonable to say before the game began that excess winnings will be redistributed to those who have incurred large losses.

Intuitively, it is a reasonable argument. Many times, someone reaped huge rewards for entering a market a hair faster than the competition. Founders of online businesses have become billionaires overnight without having produced a really innovative product. A person out of work because of a depression or disabled through no fault of his own may suffer a catastrophic loss in lifestyle. Rawls said if we could only imagine a fair society that produces extreme outcomes and that we could potentially be a great loser in this game, we would opt for a society that would provide for the losers by transferring wealth from rich to poor. This justification has nothing to do with payoff to society. Instead, it is an obligation of society to limit extreme losses in society. His book helped justify Great Society legislation aimed at caring for those who could not support themselves.

4.8   The Liberal Mindset

Liberals are not opposed to accommodating power blocks as long as the results redress a social ill. Often, the least well off are spread out, or isolated, or lack the resources to organize effectively. Lacking power, they get shunted aside by society. Liberals supported government help to industrial workers unionize who struggled for a fair wage and freedom in the marketplace to be honored by employers as an equal. African Americans needed a powerful presence in white society that would end racism in the workplace, in local government, a presence that would raise African Americans out of being a permanent, identifiable underclass. African Americans needed to become a power block to end the psychological claustrophobia of being in a ghetto, the rage of being penned in and told to stay in your place, the alienation from white society that led to crime, out-of-wedlock children, and escapism through drugs. For similar reasons, liberals oppose unlimited campaign contributions because the rich gain undue access to government that could lead to corruption and cronyism.

In the Greek Eudaemonic tradition, the government's role is to nurture happiness. Government has an obligation to maximize social welfare by offsetting the ill effects of myopic behavior of individuals, by breaking oppressive power blocks or regulating them so that they don't exploit the public, and by correcting the unintended consequences of an open market and society when the results lead to a permanent underclass. Government should nurture the helpless and enable all Americans to make the best of themselves.

Experimenting with new roles for government is necessary as private behavior and technology changes. Liberals believe in the absolute necessity of treating everyone fairly before the law. But they also favor the notion of government promoting positive freedom: uplifting the fallen, righting past wrongs, and using government policies to change the way we view each other and treat each other.

Government has a role to play in shaping the economic structure of society: regulation and anti-recession policies, government social programs, and environmental laws are good for America. Government has a role in community building at home, if done with respect for the sensitivities of the target group. Even affirmative action may make sense to integrate groups into society. In general, rules for hiring and firing have helped make the labor market and workplace more efficient and equitable.

Small, personal government that fosters civic responsibility is a worthy goal when it doesn't lead to local cronyism and discrimination against minorities. Modern realities point to the need for government on a national scale. Markets cross state boundaries and often national boundaries. Uniform national legal and administrative rules are necessary to make trading reliable and uncomplicated. Beyond trading efficiencies, national policy is necessary to protect America's natural resources. Pollution from power-generating plants in one part of the country wafts over state borders. As products became more complex and exotic chemicals were used to produce products, the government stepped in to protect consumers and workers alike.

A small, local government would not have the authority or expertise to protect the public from economic problems that were growing in scale. An alternative was a new type of organization: the government bureaucracy. Usually the butt of jokes, government bureaucrats are a cadre of professionals hired through civil service exams who are given the authority and training to become experts in consumer protection. These bureaucracies can be centralized or decentralized depending on their task. The continuing challenge is to make each bureaucrat a morally responsible professional, sensitive to the public's changing needs and wary of those who would try to use them to exploit the public.

Environmentalism is at the frontier of liberal thought. Protecting the oppressed has expanded from humans to nature. Nature, plants, and animals of all types have rights because they have intrinsic value that can't be monetized. Humanity's extravagant consumption of the earth's resources must be curbed quickly if humanity wants to avoid environmental collapse. Liberals point to studies about the loss of biodiversity and global warming. Liberals favor sweeping proposals to check nature's destruction. They would use all the tools available to the federal government to impose behavior patterns that assure the sustainability of our ecosystem.

Abroad, liberals stand for using government influence to assure fair play whether in war or peace. Liberals favor promoting democratic institutions because they support private property rights and personal freedom. Wars, unfortunately, continue to break out as is the case with Russia and Ukraine. After World War I, Keynes said that victorious nations should consider the consequences of the peace. The victor's aim should be to revitalize the defeated, not crush them so they never rise again. The victors should promote dignity and self-sufficiency and bear down on what he would call Jew-baiting. During peacetime, America should coordinate its policies with other nations to promote fair dealing and prevent economic downturns and crises. They will champion world standards for labor practices, for accounting practices, and for environmental regulations.

Liberals have little to say about religion it in private affairs, but they are against organized religion in public places. They believe religious positions are often nonnegotiable; therefore, they are likely to lead to repressive government policies. The Constitution replaces the Bible as the framer of American morality and government powers. As opposed to some religions, liberals are also for genetic engineering to reduce suffering, prolong life, and improve the quality of life.

In the spirit of Reinhold Niebuhr, a simple motto for the liberal could be, "Freedom thrives when people know when to act alone, know when to act together, and know the difference."

5

Assessment: Common Goals Different Narratives

Abstract This wrap-up chapter stresses the wide overlap in psychological needs of ideologues and suggests common ground is there. The key takeaways are as follows: they all believe democratic institutions are important, they all believe that a unifying national culture counts, and they all believe in the importance of personal motivation to succeed in life as crucial for societal health. They are like religious denominations of a common religion. Small differences in interpretation of core beliefs can lead to large differences in policies and practices. Nonetheless, there is room for reconciliation when all of them have the same basic vocabulary and reference texts.

5.1 Introduction

Daniel Bell, a noted sociologist, published two provocative books that have shaped my ideology narratives: *The End of Ideology* (1960) and *The Cultural Contradictions of Capitalism* (1978).[1] He distinguished philosophy from ideology. Philosophy attempts to understand life; ideology translates ideas into action. It offers a set of principles and a particular perspective for analyzing social problems and solving them.

I wanted to show that America's ideologies are like denominations embedded in a larger philosophical framework with common beliefs:

---

[1] Bell, D. (2000, originally, 1961), *The End of Ideology*. Harvard University Press, MA, and Bell, D., *The Cultural Contradictions of Capitalism* (1978), (originally, 1976) Basic Books, NY.

V. Glass, *Humanizing the Digital Economy*, https://doi.org/10.1007/978-3-031-37507-1_5

They all believe institutions count. Governments that are democratic, pluralistic, support the rule of law and property rights, and defend personal freedom outperform dictatorial or one-party regimes by almost any measure.

They all believe that culture counts. Cultures that honor family values, hart work, righteousness, community giving, and thinking in generations outperform by almost any measure those that do not.

They all believe in the importance of personal motivation to succeed in life. Societies that reward creativity, collaboration, flexibility in the face of change outperform societies characterized by rigid hierarchies or groupthink.

Like religious denominations of an Abrahamic religion, small differences in interpretation of basic beliefs lead to large differences in policies and practices. Nonetheless, there is room for reconciliation when all of them have the same basic vocabulary and reference texts.

The perspectives I chose to illustrate the differences between America's three ideologies are also from Bell. I said that libertarians believe private enterprise will solve most social problems. Conservatives believe that many social problems stem from narrow, egotistical demands that rip families apart and tear down communities. Liberals believe political solutions to social conflict are necessary in a mass society because the political arena can balance a variety of group interests that seek social change.

As one might expect, people are likely to choose an ideology inherited from parents or which best fits their current interests. As a result, not everyone who subscribes to an ideology has the same motivation. This diversity makes America's ideologies flexible and adaptable to some extent.

Bell also distinguished between parochial and universal ideologies. Parochial ones justify the aims of a particular group, whether it is a business group or ethnic group. A classic example is "What is good for General Motors is Good for America." Universal ideologies want to shape the American way of life. America's ideologies fall into the universal category. All three want to see Americans live better. In the past, that vague expression "live better" translated into increased material wealth, but not completely. Other values come into play such as family values and respect for others and mature into a person that others can respect. More recently, environmental issues are front and center.

Because they promote a grand cause that will enhance Americans and all humanity, America's ideologies point to the wisdom of their own heroes. They also subscribe to mythological figures that make their ideas seem real, touchable, and visual. I used Lady Liberty as the incarnation of the American spirit.

Turning back to the images from the 2012, Republican and Democratic conventions – the people, the candidates, the speeches, and platforms – point to an ideological divide that seems to show in the faces of the conventioneers. On the surface, the Republicans look like a unified group of white people and the democrats far more diverse in gender and color. To some extent, the stereotypes are true. Republicans and democrats clearly have different ideological agendas, so different in recent decades that anything proposed by one side is rejected out of hand by the other. Republicans seem to reject any social program proposed by Democrats, and Democrats haven't seen a social program they did not like. The gulf is there. For a variety of reasons, even the moderates in both parties cannot seem to join hands.

The whole thrust of my descriptions of America's ideologies was to get beyond stereotypes, to show that each ideology has a legitimate point of view grounded in one or more historical crises, articulated by spokespeople who fall into the brilliant category. From a historical perspective, the political divisions seen at the conventions are not new, not the product of racism, although it could be a factor, and not because of selfishness, also a possible factor.

Rather than emphasizing differences, I tried to show America's ideologies have much in common. They have similar but not the same values. One should expect that a society built on freedom would spawn competing ideologies that would stress and interpret those values differently. Republicans gravitate toward ideologies that support their lifestyle. They want government to protect private property and family values. Democrats are more likely to feel marginalized by an oppressive majority, pictured as the white middle class. They want an activist government to give them a fair deal.

Digging a bit deeper into what each ideology stands for, the reasons for the name calling and intellectual jibes that picture Republicans, for example, as father figures who keep their children in line with a strap,[2] lose their force. It should be clear that Hayek and Friedman, the libertarians, and Burke and McCauley – the conservatives – could accommodate social welfare programs. Keynes and Samuelson relied mainly on private enterprise for a vibrant economy while promoting government policies to stabilize the economy. These shapers of America's ideologies had much common ground for working together because they all realized that private behavior produces unintended social problems and government behavior can sometimes fix social problems but may also create unintended harm. Turning ideologies into story lines was my way to bring out the humanity of America's ideologies. I wanted to show that their ways of thinking, and their passions are very familiar to all of us. Here I reprise the three ideological mindsets with a great deal of sympathy.

---

[2] Lakoff, G. (2006), *Whose Freedom?* Picador, Farrar, Straus, and Giroux, Macmillan, NY

5.2   The Conservative Mindset

Start with the conservatives, although the word itself is sometimes a code word for inflexibility, the conservative story line should suggest otherwise. It is better to think of a conservative's visions and decisions undergoing countless little revisions as events unfold, to paraphrase T. S. Eliot, and yet a conservative's basic attitudes toward self and society hardly change in essence across the ages. In some respects, the conservative attitude almost seems fit for a simpler age. It rests on as Burke said, the strength of the little platoon of people comfortable with their group. Even among the most cosmopolitan people remains a strong desire for belonging. Most people label themselves by birth, by gender, by religion, by college, by profession, and by pronoun so that they are part of some type of community.

Of all the ideologues, a conservative is perhaps most sensitive to anomie, wary of change, spiritually lonely in a mass society, a person who wants to uphold traditions and pass them along, who wants to maintain the integrity of place and people, who knows he must accommodate change but not to the point that the world becomes alien. He is someone more prone to believe in duty than the pursuit of happiness; he is against a consumer society that measures worth in dollars and treats people as customers instead of counterparts. He opposes trickle-down economics if it enriches people who haven't earned it, and he opposes trickle-down welfare programs that destroy family and community. He opposes extensions of the law and government programs that are beyond their competencies to operate effectively because, when stretched they lose their integrity, and stretched too much, they lose the trust of the people. As government tries to serve more and more needs, people never learn to stand on their own.

In my poetic state of mind, a simple poem sums up the weary hope of the conservative for better government:

> Tired of political queries and economic theories
>   Of pitchers and catchers
>   Of statisticians and econometricians
>   Of associations and commissions
>   Orders and reconsiderations
>   To implement and vacate
>   To simplify and unify
>   Another rule to fix the old
>   With its own interpretations and modifications
>   Where are the wise men who don't read from teleprompters?

Who don't have all their hair and perfect teeth?
It's time.

Russell Kirk, the great twentieth century's encyclopedic summarizer of conservative thought, finally makes an appearance here to show how the conservative attitude has evolved into a coherent ideological worldview that other
ideologues should see in themselves. His insights are somewhat disguised
because I choose to present his conservative view from a Jewish perspective to
avoid the accusation that conservatives are from the patrician class. Like Tevye
in Fiddler on the Roof, a conservative fears impulsive actions that have permanent consequences but also knows the world is changing and that he must
change too to not be left behind. It is this uneasy struggle to turn change into
renewal that opens paths for ideologues to work together.[3]

Conservative ideology has Judeo-Christian roots. Its narrative follows a
basic biblical story line that begins with a cosmic view of creation and rapidly
narrows to portraits of individuals, both good and evil, often drawn from a
composite of characters that mark the founders of a civilization. Then the
vista expands to encompass the formation of a people from a mixed multitude. A momentous event, the gathering at Sinai, marks their covenant with
future generations, a covenant that defines them as a people seeking renewal
and redemption through righteousness and faith. The saga ends with a glimpse
of a Messianic Age in which all humanity lives at a higher level of existence
freed from sin and evil. This is also the American story.

This is a conservative's universe: permeated by a God who created the universe, stamped it with laws that apply to nature and humanity. Laws that
apply to the physical universe are for humanity to discover and to use for
tending God's Garden and cultivating new products and ideas. But God
wanted more than scientists; he wanted a partner, a "Thou." Humanity was
created to give existence meaning and purpose to the physical universe by
mastering its laws and using them to become a counterpart to God. The creative spirit required humans to have a soul that is a blend of aggressive self-
serving passions and receptive, caring passions for others. Humanity's eternal
challenge is to channel the destructive urges toward creative uses.

The religious spirit pushes humanity to uncover values that will elevate
humanity to higher levels of dignity. Over time, Western societies realized
that justice, private property, freedom, and peaceful order are core values of a
righteous society. They may change their external features to fit the times, but
they are recognizable across the ages. Other cultures have also groped toward

---

[3] Kirk, R. (1985), *The Conservative Mind: From Burke to Eliot*. Regenery Publishing, Washington D.C.

understanding these eternal values. As a result, each world culture has many similarities but has its own unique history and expressions that taken in isolation may seem an offspring of a superstitious imagination but meets needs in its own ways.

From a Jewish perspective, the label "conservative" has the wrong image. It suggests someone who is tired, who wants to conserve energy, or, even worse, who wants to hibernate. The true label is People of the Covenant. A covenant is a binding oath, which in ancient times, the powerful (usually a chief) said he would protect a weak group on condition that they remain loyal. God's covenant with the Jewish people was not negotiated. In this sense it is one-sided, and yet the benefits were tilted toward them. It was not a trade and not exploitative. The covenant often remained in effect even when the Jewish people had lapses in judgment.

Covenants are more common than one would suppose. There are implicit and explicit covenants with family, community, religion, and nation. People wrongly believe they are free standing individuals who will make their own way in the world, an outlook that borders on being self-absorbed and exploitative of others. Family loyalty should not be based on a cost-benefit analysis – giving back, although it does play a part. A conservative would frown on someone who walked away from helping even a bad parent in need. A Jewish conservative expects Israel to help Jews in the diaspora. They wouldn't expect Israel to help all people in need. Patriotism to America and to Israel is based on a personal narrative linked to each nation. Jewish American or American Jew, which is the noun (essence) and which is the adjective (particularity)? or is a Jew just citizen of the world. A virtuous person is someone who accepts the burdens of history and the challenges of passing on heritage. It is a covenant instead of a two-sided contract (see Sandel What Money Can't Buy).

As People of the Covenant, conservatives are obligated to raise righteous people, "menches," who would fit the English idea of ladies and gentlemen. By birth or circumstance, some people gain more wisdom than others. They are the ones who should become leaders of the community because others can learn from them. They are part of the Jewish covenant to nurture each other, honor the past, and produce offspring that will honor the Jewish people.

In an open, moral society, these ideas accord with conservative thought. Ladies and gentlemen, people of culture and spiritual goals, feel the obligation to improve society, to elevate it in ever widening circles: from family to community to nation. They will think in generations, honoring the wisdom of their ancestors and bestowing their own wisdom on future generations, building ties that bind people together in a common culture, with a common purpose: to redeem the world.

A great fear is to turn into people who leave their heritage at the front door. They want to keep their image of a platoon intact even as they labor to channel new wealth, new forms of property, and new opportunities into a spiritual undertaking that redeems and renews our basic humanity.

In business a cultured person honors professional standards of business behavior. In the legislature and executive branches of government, a cultured person aspires to be a statesman. Whether in business or government, they have a common obligation to those who they represent. They have a duty to improve the lot of those who trust them. If change is necessary, it should not aim at tearing down the old order but by serving wider interests.

A statesman has a covenant with society to uphold customs, laws, private property, balance of power, and many more methods that restrain passions and encourage reflection on social problems. He or she does not worship reason as the sole method of solving social problems is dangerous. Science is a powerful tool for uncovering physical laws, but to treat humans as scientific objects and to apply mathematical exactitude as if it will predict or alter behavior are at odds with human nature. A statesman should examine trends but needs the intuition to know when the public is ready to change and accept changes that may affect culture.

Government activism is sometimes necessary to protect individual rights and encourage or enable moral training that aims at discipline and creativity. However, government should not take responsibility for what people should do for themselves.

Conservatives, as the label suggests, are more cautious than the other ideologues. Exploration requires prudence because a change in rules can have great consequences for society. Adopting no-fault divorce, for example, may have championed individual rights but likely led to a jump in divorce rates, the devaluation of the family unit, the impoverishment of single parent families, and the neglect of children.

Usually, a good guide to rule changes is consistency with the past because a great deal of wisdom is embedded in habits and precedents. Loyalty to the past is an expression of piety to forebears for bestowing on this generation reliable guides for future actions. Change for change's sake or to fit a predetermined plan, especially a theoretical one of economists and philosophers, put humanity at great risk. Proceeding cautiously is best done with experiments in local communities and depends crucially on moral training and deep appreciation for a nation's culture. Administration by a distant government is likely to be oppressive even while it produces inefficient and mediocre services.

Experience suggests to conservatives that legislators should be wary of entitlements for the poor, middle class subsidies, and any form of corporate welfare. Opportunities, chance, and culture itself all produce inequalities of wealth and station. These inequalities, if not imposed, stimulate those at the bottom to learn from those at the top instead of envying them. Those at the top should give back voluntarily because their gains are often outsized.

A conservative's uneasy ally in his revolt against the Leviathan is the libertarian because they both believe in decentralization and private initiative and, more often than not, the most creative programs for privatizing and deregulating come from libertarian economists. The libertarian gives hope that the creative spirit endures, that it can be relied on to raise living standards without government support. But a conservative will never accept the libertarian's worship of the individual as a type of superman who creates himself and measures life by his own accomplishments.

5.3   The Libertarian Mindset

Using Jews in America again as the focus group, let me turn to the libertarians. Most libertarians do not think of themselves as supermen. More often they have felt government oppression and societal discrimination. Again, the label, in this case, "libertarianism" gets in the way of its visceral meaning. In its outward form, it rhymes with antiquarianism, of frontiersmen with muskets defending their homes, an image that doesn't work well in a metropolis or even a suburb. Perhaps a better label is the Party of the Self Creators, people who band together to protect their rights to make their own way in the world. They will resist any tyrannical power whether it is a king, a democratic majority turned into a herd as it was in Nazi Germany, or democratic majority of "do gooders" who want to use government to remake society in their own images.

Kirk would have agreed with Sartre premise that many Jews wanted to escape from being outsiders by promoting the idea of universal man – a person who beneath all the outward appearances was a sacred individual worthy of respect. Many Jews wanted to become Americans. They were willing to wipe away all the traditions that made them second-class citizens, aliens in a foreign land even if their families lived in a country for many generations. Jews eagerly accepted America's secular religion that held liberty, equality, and opportunity as sacred values derived from reason, from a distillation of the great legal codes of modern, open societies that venerate the dignity of man. They and many immigrants from communist countries and other oppressive regimes are afraid of government, even when it tries to be benevolent will become oppressive. Ayn Rand, the grand dame of libertarianism, came from this type of background. She wanted people to be left alone, to melt into society from the government's perspective, to be allowed to make their own way. Libertarians long for a government peopled by anti-establishment champions:

> They oppose liberals and progressives
>> Because they turn parades into grand marches
>> Because they designate a patron of the people
>> Because they tell us where to stand and how to step

Libertarianism is a secular religion of self-realization. "Free to choose" is the sacred utterance. The act of choosing is much more than a way to gain satisfaction or learn the art of the deal. Choosing clarifies what is of value, what really matters. The act of choice is an act of becoming. Choices determine what someone wants to be even if the picture is never clear. Free trade of value for value informs the players. It generates information about self, about others, and through open discussion and haggling, new ideas, new forms or cooperation, and new products and services emerge. Not surprisingly, libertarians validate their beliefs by adopting free market theories and the rule of law and the essential need for private property to explain their emotional aversion to government. Most of their policy prescriptions for downsizing government line up with conservatives but not all of them. They support gay rights, legalizing marijuana, and other seemingly countercultural because they do not physically harm others. They believe in private actions under fair laws because open societies are just, efficient, and vibrant – seedbeds of creativity.

Hayek, a Christian, is an important counterpoint to the Rand-like libertarianism popular in America. Much like Burke, he understood the importance of tradition, especially society's moral obligation to help the helpless. But Hayek rejected the label conservative because he felt conservatives were liberals in slow motion. He was too analytical not to recognize the political dangers of too much power in the hands of a few even in a land like America with strong democratic traditions. Eventually, those traditions weaken as people get used to government for their necessities. The public becomes passive when they subcontract government decisions to experts and managers.

5.4   The Liberal Mindset

Although Jews became prominent libertarians, the bulk of American Jews have traditionally been members of the Democratic Party, the Party of the Oppressed. In America, the federal government was a liberating force. It helped people in distress rather than putting them under stress. Jews allied themselves with liberal democrats and fought to protect the poor, the helpless, and the underdog by using federal power to lift the worst off in society to a level of dignity that conscience demands. "Never again," became a Jewish slogan that carried over into politics. Never again should anyone be an alien in their homeland. From their perspective, a liberal's universal unit is the group: Jews, blacks, women, gays, and Hispanics – not platoons, not individuals, but oppressed people that deserved protection. A liberal realizes that he, himself, needs protection from his own shortsightedness and tendency to want to control others. Social security, for example, is a recognition that people often don't save enough for retirement and yet expect others to support them if they are destitute. It is a human failing that government can correct.

Liberalism also had another personal attraction. In line with libertarians, liberals held to a secular religion, one where freedom, equality, and opportunity were self-evident, ethical values that cut across all cultures. These values were absolutely essential for self-actualization in a humane society. Paradoxically, many liberal Jews found liberalism as a way to shed their label as a group apart even as they fought for the rights of other groups. They found liberal ethics and politics in America as a natural progression toward an ecumenical land devoted to leading the world toward righteousness. Covenant gave ways to the Constitution, which became their universal Bible; Washington D.C. became their New Jerusalem, and Lady Liberty evoked a unified spirit of sanctity. Within this nation of nations, where all groups are chosen, many liberal Jews wanted to meld into an American nation – out of the many, one – with the label Jew as a place of origin, not a destination.

Liberals, as you might expect, have their own profile of a statesman and proper government:

In the name of the public, never again
    To exploitation and depredation
    To shameful concession and silent collaboration
    Faithful always to sympathy and responsibility
    The binding forces of a Great Society

Liberals see government policies as a secular expression of religious teachings to lift up the poor and oppressed and to moralize power. They turn to economic and political theories to justify their beliefs in government activism. Like a big corporation, government can marshal great resources to deliver services to the entire nation. Government effectiveness depends on leaders with vision and flair and self-motivated employees. The federal government, especially, can look beyond special interests and look way beyond the next quarterly financial report and really find flaws and design improvements that will improve society. They aim to eliminate exploitation by the powerful; to eliminate myopic behavior that causes financial panics; to strike deals that benefit society that could not be accomplished privately like ending child labor, limiting working hours; and to end prejudice by making work rules and voting rights fair for everyone.

5.5   An American Mindset Reconsidered

These brief summaries and the previous chapters highlight the importance of inner makeup common to all ideologues – a common sense of fragility, a common need to explain cataclysmic upheavals and periods of unease. Each ideological narrative starts with very similar moral premises but applies them differently because their composers interpreted the events from their own perspective. Libertarianism's self-supporting individual regained his vividness as a counter to fascism's noble savage and communism's worker. Conservatism's principled gentleman was a wonderful contrast to goose-stepping troops marching across Europe, threatening to wipe out historical traditions, especially religion. Liberalism evoked the good man down on his luck selling apples on street corners during the Great Depression to raise the banner of a caring government that must intervene to help those in desperate need.

In some respects, the central characters in all three American ideologies are all from the same family but grew apart in their formative years. In some respects, it is a family saga of children who left their homeland for a new beginning in a foreign land. Underneath it all, ideologues have common ancestry and hold many of the same values. The differences between libertarians, liberals, and conservatives are nuanced, narrative shadings, about human nature, traditions, and the effectiveness of collective action, especially by government. Their separate journeys through history explain most of the differences.

Oppression by governments in the Old World led to the individualism of libertarians. Understandably, libertarians want the government to shrink in strength and disappear from sight. Self-development is their path to a fulfilling life. Spontaneous creation is their blueprint for society. Self-seeking, profit-motivated participants in markets will form decentralized systems and informal rules that are highly efficient and flexible for delivering products and services. More than that, private enterprise turns self-seeking into a social good. In the search for profits, market participants need the freedom to act creatively to boost profits. Markets produce a kaleidoscope of products, services, and connections that could not be anticipated and certainly not designed in a laboratory. This system self-corrects as winners in the marketplace gain resources at the expense of losers.

Conservatives see different images when they picture man in society because they have witnessed the horrors of mob rule that overturn society and try to remake it according to some fantastical image. They recognize the powerful drive of self-seeking but want to raise ladies and gentlemen who define themselves on Hillel's precept: "If I am not for myself, who will be; if I'm only for myself, what am I; if not now, when?" To them, life at its core is a religious undertaking aimed at redeeming humanity. Conservatives look more to the soul of the nation than to its systems or physical operations. They focus on culture, on familiar, healthy habits and rituals that build trust, a critical quality for any market or government to operate with public support. Conservatives are wary of worshipping reason. A rational approach devoid of any appreciation of history can break down any standard of truth, beauty, or excellence because all human values evolve through trial and error over many generations. The ideal government is a town council, where private citizens know their elected officials and have the potential to win a seat if they run for office. Small is beautiful because it promotes civic virtue.

Liberals have experienced the disasters caused by human frailties that are systematic and produce great harm if not checked by a "Good Shepherd." People are self-centered, which makes them myopic. They often do what seems right but with a narrow frame of reference. They save too much and cause an economic depression; they want to protect their ethnic or racial heritage, which leads unintentionally to systematic prejudice against outsiders. Liberals believe government can be that Good Shepherd that can protect society from itself. Liberals believe market failures happen with regularity and cause irreparable damage. Like doctors, they see no reason not to examine the economy, look for weaknesses and breakdowns, and figure out ways to make the system operate better, quickly. Liberals believe they have identified system failures associated with concentrations of market power, lack of markets to serve rural people living in remote areas and poor people, and market instabilities associated with psychological factors, especially in highly liquid markets, which on the surface appear to be highly efficient markets. Liberals believe in scientific management of the economy without requiring direct control of large portions of the private sector. Their view is similar to using thrusters on a rocket occasionally to keep it on its course.

Not surprisingly, each defines the meaning of liberty, equality, and property differently though they believe in their essences. Each ideology has been ascendant at different times. From the middle of the Great Depression to the early 1970s, liberalism, as defined by John Maynard Keynes, ruled academia and public policy. The government tinkered with markets and other social systems in an attempt to make America into a Great Society. From the 1970s through the Great Recession, Libertarians held sway in academia and gained much government support. Regulations were dropped; social welfare programs were cut back; and it seemed that society was the better for it. Then the Great Recession jolted society. A form of neo-Keynesianism is resurging. Conservatives have not made much headway in academic institutions in recent decades but have gained ground in politics, and lately, because of the Great Recession, people like John Bogel have raised the issue of professional standards again.

The main takeaway from this summary is perhaps best captured by a loosely interpreted proverb[4]:

Do not disdain any of these believers
  Each has learned a truth by trial
  Each has experiences to share
  And for that, each has its place under the sun

---

[4] Ethics of the Fathers: Chapter Four, Verse 3, Ben Azzai. https://www.chabad.org/library/article_cdo/aid/2032/jewish/Chapter-Four.htm. Accessed 30 April 2023

6

Radicalism: from Babel to Sodom

Abstract While Americans have much in common, that raises the question, why have they become so hostile to each other? A general sense of victimization lies at the heart of America's divisions. European history before World War II has much to say about the dangers of victimization. According to the philosopher Hannah Arendt, a spiritual disease began to spread in the late nineteenth century ending with the rise of Nazism. Worship of the individual, the gentlemen, and the statesmen was failing as ideals. Religion had lost its voice. Tribalism emerged as a national ideal with roots in a fantastical past. Although Peter Drucker, an economist, was skeptical that an upsurge in primitivism led to the rise of Nazism, he also believed that the rise of communism, fascism, and Nazism were the result of widespread loss of confidence in capitalism and democracy. Europe's idealized image of America began to shatter when the Great Depression hit. His warning was that loss of confidence in ideologies that honor America's core values can lead to totalitarianism. By contrast, the King-led nonviolent civil rights crusade created internal discord but ultimately sought to reinforce America's core values of freedom and equality.

6.1 Introduction: American Victimization

While Americans have much in common, that raises the question, why have they become so hostile to each other? This chapter is a prelude to the next section that describes why the very premises of all three ideologies are being questioned by Americans.

A general sense of victimization lies at the heart of America's divisions. Groups on the right and left politically believe they are being exploited

V. Glass, *Humanizing the Digital Economy*, https://doi.org/10.1007/978-3-031-37507-1_6

systematically by a powerful group controlled by an elite cabal that seeks to dominate them. This is not a new phenomenon in America. In the late 1800s, American farmers believed they were being manipulated by bankers, railroads, and corporations. [1]

The victims and victimizers changed by the 1960s, but the sense of alienation and anger remained the force fracturing American unity. Saul Alinsky's *Rules for Radicals* contains short sketches of alienated groups on the left and right of the political spectrum.[2] While they may seem cartoonish, they capture the alienation in society that occurred then that led some to seek change in the streets instead of in the chambers of Congress.

According to Alinsky, radical leftists lost faith in the American system because it was not delivering the American dream of equality and justice but just the opposite; it was destroying it. Young Americans were dying in Vietnam without the hope of victory or a sense that their sacrifice was liberating people from communist oppression. At home, prejudice and poverty persisted. Blacks, Chicano, and Puerto Rican and the migrant workers were part of a permanent underclass.[3] After Rachel Carson's expose of DDT in 1962, they worried that our water was contaminated by excrement, insecticides, and detergents. Information pollution poured out of the Pentagon. The Pentagon kept reporting that within the next 6 months the war would be "won."[4] Corporations did not recognize that they were beneficiaries of government subsidies and contracts, and that meant they had social responsibilities beyond the bottom line.[5] Radical change was necessary, according to the extreme left. While Alinsky favored organized struggle to change the system from within, other groups wanted to tear it down or blow it up.

These attacks on American society produced a strong reaction that gave rise to radicals on the right, according to Alinsky. The middle-class white Americans, especially blue-collar workers felt threatened from all sides. Inflation, unemployment in a slumping economy, high taxes, insufficient savings for retirement, and not enough health protection made them feel vulnerable. On top of that, they feared non-whites moving into their neighborhoods, depressing property values, and increasing crime. And they hated how the

---

[1] See, for example, Friedman, M., and Schwartz, A. (1993, originally published 1963), *A Monetary History of the United States*: 1867–1960. Princeton University Press, NJ. pp. 116–119.

[2] Alinsky, S. (1971) *Rules for Radicals* (1971) Random House, NY. chrome-extension://efaidnbmnnnibp cajpcglclefindmkaj/https://chisineu.files.wordpress.com/2014/02/saul-alinsky-rules-for-radicals-1989. pdf. Accessed 30 April 2023.

[3] Id., p. 9.

[4] Id., p. 190.

[5] Id., p. 194.

government was using their tax dollars to pay for a vast variety of massive public programs. Colleges were waiving admission requirements and giving special financial aid for the poor. Where were their rights? They wanted to know. In reaction, they became defenders of the "American" faith. They cried for law and order, and many were seduced by George Wallace, the John Birch Society, and the Red-menace perennials.[6]

The basic tactic used by populists to reform society is to pressure government to act on their behalf. Without mob tactics, they believe government won't act because of political paralysis brought on by dueling parties or a secret pact within government to keep the power elite intact.

Since Donald Trump's presidential bid, the label populist is normally pinned on his supporters. CNN and other left-leaning media outlets describe them as white males who are trying to hold onto power in a nation that increasingly is non-white and gender neutral. In turn, Trump supporters see Wall Street, the Beltway, the Media, or the liberal professors who are replaying the 60s counterculture to tear down America. But the label populist also holds for Sanders's supporters who have never met a rich, white person they can trust. Both sides label each other un-American, which leaves little room for negotiation, let alone compromise. So, both sides dig in and refuse to hear what the other side is saying. Instead, they mainly listen to media sites that feed their anxieties and anger.

Reminiscent of the nationwide demonstrations after the Kent State student killings by the national guard in 1970 or the killing of James Powell by the police in Harlem in 1964, another single event, the murder of George Floyd by a white policeman triggered demonstrations and Antifa riots across the country. Defund the police became a rallying cry. Tear down symbols of historical racism in public squares. The Unite to Right rally in Charlottesville pitted white supremacist groups who did not want Confederate monuments removed against counter protesters. That led to the death of Heather Heyer and injuries to dozens of others. Armed people dressed in uniforms have become commonplace media images. The January 6 riot at the Capitol after President Trump's election loss was labeled an insurrection by many democrats. The other side claimed the riot was preventable if the democrats had allowed the national guard to protect the Capitol.

Who can you trust to know what really happened? According to a 2022 Gallup poll, only

---

[6] Id., p. 187.

34%, Americans' trust in the mass media to report the news "fully, accurately and fairly" is essentially unchanged from last year and just two points higher than the lowest that Gallup has recorded, in 2016 during the presidential campaign. [7]

The trustworthiness of government is about the same. According to a 2022 Gallup poll, 54 percent of the public distrusts the federal government. In this environment, populists on both sides are unlikely to believe that the government and courts will produce justice. In other words, people are losing trust in America's basic institutions.

6.2   The European Breakdown

European history before World War II has much to say about the threats to democracy posed by a general loss of confidence in government and public ideologies. According to the philosopher Hannah Arendt, a spiritual disease began to spread in the late nineteenth century in Germany ending with the rise of Nazism.[8] Societies across Europe were in turmoil. In Germany, social and political dislocations were severe after Germans laid down their arms in 1918 and agreed to harsh terms that included huge reparations to the allies for damages. At the end of 1918, the Kaiser abdicated and fled to the Netherlands and German nobility lost their class privileges. Germany replaced its constitutional monarch with a liberal democratic government and was almost immediately challenged by communist groups within Germany.

These revolts were suppressed, but the social unrest simmered. An outward indicator of internal conflicts is economic instability created by political instability. One of the provisions of the Armistice was that Germany had to pay huge reparations to the allies for "causing" the war. This heavy burden was unmanageable. In response, Germany financed this debt by printing money. Inflation accelerated starting in 1920. By the end of 1923, a wheelbarrow of money could only buy a newspaper. Food riots broke out. In 1924, the debt burden was reduced by the allies. Germany then introduced a new currency backed by the dollar. Hyperinflation ended and Germany experienced prosperity for a few years. Then America, the symbol of liberal, democratic capitalism, plunged into a massive and prolonged depression that spread to Europe. Society began to fracture with massive unemployment. The Weimar

---

[7] Benan, M. (2022), America's Trust in Media Remains Near Record Low. Gallup. https://news.gallup.com/poll/403166/americans-trust-media-remains-near-record-low.aspx. Accessed 30 April 2023.

[8] Arendt, H. (1976), *The Origins of Totalitarianism*. Harcourt Inc. NY.

government's structure proved fatal to democracy. Extremist party representation, notably the communists and Nazis, grew in the legislature.

Germany like other European countries was a state in turmoil. Dislocations once again created factions within society. Those at the bottom or those displaced wanted redress by seizing control of government policy. Many Europeans became outsiders after national boundaries were redrawn. A great sense of pessimism gripped Europe. People of similar ethnicity wanted to huddle together. Clannishness grew. Fear of the other grew. They wanted to feel like chosen people and get even with oppressors that held them down. The rise of factions broke the moral center of society that relied on all people within the state as citizens. They sought an ideology that would fit their legendary figures and mythical stories.

Hannah Arendt claimed that all ideologies have totalitarian elements because they claim to know the mysteries of the historical process.[9] They order facts and filter others to prove their ideology correct. She classified secular ideologies into two categories: economic and racial.[10] Their policies followed their own versions of the laws of nature that drive the historical process. In the economics category were capitalism and communism. Capitalism's law of nature – the Invisible Hand – failed to prevent depressions. Communism failed in its promise to make workers free from want. Race struggle was a prominent ideology in the 19th and early twentieth century. In England, it became the White Man's burden to civilize savage societies[11]. Philosophers like Gobineau believed societies crumble because of racial mixing.[12] Pure blood and native soil replaced abstractions such as liberty and equality as the goal of society. The Nazis could easily claim equality was the biggest myth. People are not born equal, families are not equal, and cultures are not equal. Darwinism suggested survival of the fittest. Many people across the globe believed in eugenics as the pathway to raising humanity to supermen. The Nazis used government to conduct a massive racial cleansing program. Their legendary figure to support their Darwinist ideology was the Aryan.

Nazi racialism appealed to frightened members of society. Germans of "Aryan" descent wanted to belong to a secure and nurturing society at any price, including the sacrifice of personal freedom. They wanted "aliens" out – out of power, out of the country, and later out of existence. The new tribalism became a holy image. Laws did not define rights and obligations; right became

---

[9] Id., p. 470.

[10] Id., p. 159.

[11] Id., pp. 164–165.

[12] Id., p. 172. See also, Gobineau, *Selected Political Writings: Roots of the Right* (1969); general editor: Steiner, G. Harper and Row, NY.

what is good for the German people. Sacrifice for the Aryan cause gave life meaning, not an extra car or bigger house. The Aryan experiment meant that Germans were part of a tribe. Like a tribe, they needed to cooperate as a unit. "We" replaced "I" as the basic human value. The Aryan experiment would take decades or even centuries to accomplish, so people had to think in generations if they were true Aryans.

The Nazis could point to the unworkability of democracy in Germany and in the former Austria-Hungary as examples. Parties create confusion and turmoil.[13] Germany needed a party above parties: the Nazi Party, and it was not a party that represented a particular economic interest.[14] It was a movement to build a pure Aryan race by whatever methods needed. This appealed to the downtrodden who could claim superiority just by being members of the Aryan race. Like any fanatical movement, any deviation in thought or action could become a crime against the movement. The police did not discover crimes; they just arrested categories of people. Everyone could become a police agent, so no one dared to say anything against the regime. A Nazi had the obligation to police his family and neighbors. [15]

One of the strongest support groups for the Nazis was intellectuals because they embraced great theories and scientific processes. Laws were constantly changing and should change to suit the new and better understanding of human destiny. Rights to life, liberty, and property for everyone did not accord with the new vision of the golden-haired Aryan.

In this poisonous environment, the Jews became the mortal enemies because they supposedly also believed in racial purity and were chosen by God. The Nazis claimed they were the ones who created communism, and a Jew was responsible for the humiliating Armistice. They were a perfect target because they had lost their function as financiers in Europe and were rapidly disintegrating as a group due to intermarriage and secularism. In other words, they didn't have a power center to oppose the Nazis.

Peter Drucker[16] disagreed with Arendt on many points but not on the effects of societal pessimism, alienation, and loss of faith in ideology. Marxism was failing in Russia; capitalism was failing in Western Europe and the United States; democracy was failing as more and more countries in Europe opted for dictatorships; and religion had long since failed to galvanize and uplift the

---

[13] Id., p. 312.

[14] Id., p. 313.

[15] Id., pp. 341–346.

[16] Peter F. Drucker, P.F. (1995, originally published 1939), *The End of Economic Man: The Origins of Totalitarianism*. Transaction Publishers, NJ.

public.[17] The image of economic man (capitalist) seemed antique; progress seemed farcical because science was inherently destructive in the hands of humans. Massive states seemed ungovernable. Not surprising, protection of minorities equally seemed farcical when millions were desperate to pay for food and shelter. The gentleman was replaced by a beggar as the symbol of society. Hitler's genius was to raise the poor to the status of Aryans, put everyone to work whether the outcome was efficient or not, and move away from status based on income by taxing the richer segments of society. Big businesses were controlled to assure they fit the Nazi criteria, one of which was to outlaw Jews and other undesirables from working for them.

Ironically, Drucker was skeptical that an upsurge in primitivism led to the rise of Nazism. In his view, it was a loss of rational vision in how to achieve a Great Society. He said that the rise of communism, fascism, and Nazism was the result of widespread loss of confidence in capitalism and democracy. America's Depression shocked Europe.[18] It was the land of opportunity where anyone could become a millionaire.[19] Europeans bought into that image, and now it was gone, like America being a haven for the poor and oppressed until it shut its borders to immigration in the 1920s.

He didn't believe that Nazism triumphed because it appealed to primitive barbarity, or capitalists protecting themselves from socialism, or because of fined-tuned propaganda. He pointed out, for example, that the media constantly ridiculed Hitler and Mussolini.[20] Rather, these totalitarian ideologies rose despite the public not believing their promises. In Germany, according to Drucker, many people did not believe in Germanic gods, the Nordic perfect man, the corporate state, or the heroic family.

Germans just did not believe the old order was working. What they believed was a series of negatives: repudiation of the past, of conservatism, of liberalism, of socialism, of capitalism, of communism, and of religion. They did not even take racial antisemitism seriously.[21] The old order was breaking down from within. They were willing to accept magical solutions by mystical leaders because they lived in a world governed by irrational forces and inhabited by demons. At first, the Church supported Franco, Mussolini, and Hitler as bulwarks holding back hordes of communist pagans who threatened to destroy Christianity.

---

[17] Id., p. xv.
[18] Id., p. 44.
[19] Id., p. 42.
[20] Id., p. 8.
[21] Id., pp. 238–241.

Looking back on the 1960s and 1970s in America, Drucker saw racists, white and black, like stormtroopers, extremists who thought that "no" was a positive policy: no to business as usual, no to politics as usual.[22] They had to be overturned. They had great compassion for the weak and wanted society to raise them up or America would burn down. The COVID pandemic spawned new groups of extremists who believe either America is corrupt or groups within society are poisoning her. Both extremes want a secure and nurturing society that rights past wrongs and upends a corrupt power structure that has lost the faith of the people. The only difference is the victims and perpetrators differ on the Right and the Left.

Both Drucker and Arendt suggest that long-standing hatreds and distrusts among ethnic groups and differing historical mythologies and mystical visions of the future play crucial roles in understanding the current American Agonistes. In the next section, I will suggest that the Digital Revolution has created a growing online society. Many entrepreneurs, self-promoters, evangelists, and fanatics have an interest in promoting extremist views and foreign interference in America's affairs. Protecting America from these types of online threats and attacks has concentrated enormous power in government security agencies. America's palace guard could also be a danger to American society.

6.3   The American Challenge

This loss of confidence in traditional values described here help explain America's Balkanization into uncompromising factions. The images of fear, pessimism, and revenge described in Germany and to a much lesser extent in America sharply contrast with the King-led nonviolent civil rights crusade that created internal discord but ultimately sought to perfect the implementation of America's core values. King's genius was to appeal to the conscience of America. In the 1960s, people believed in the Constitution's preamble that all men are created equal. By 2016, equality became a code word for tearing down or taking away.

The challenge of how to formulate policies that will bind the nation is the subject of the last section of the book. This will require a change in public consciousness that will restore "equality" to its proper meaning and galvanize society to work together. For now, I will focus on the disruptive forces created by the Coding Revolution.

---

[22] Id., xxxi.

Part II

Coding Crisis – Existential Threats to Core Values and Human Nature

Abstract Respect usually does not lead to active collaboration. A more likely trigger is a national crisis. That happened briefly after 9/11. However, the more recent turmoil in the United States is associated with populism, nativism, and other movements that turn Americans against each other. This section focuses on a technological disruption that magnifies these divisions. The main disruptor is what I call the Coding Revolution. I believe it is a major cause for America's ideological battles. The Coding Revolution is not a sharp crisis like 9/11. It has been building up for decades. I suggest the Coding Revolution is weakening core values: privacy, private property, and the rule of law. It is also changing human nature itself, assumed relatively unchangeable by all three mainstream ideologies. The section chapter headings are chosen to highlight the disruptive effect of the Coding Revolution on privacy, personal security, the functioning of markets, and effectiveness of democracy. The chapter headings encapsulate the topics covered: cyberspace capitalism, digital overexposure, stealth security, and designer eugenics.

I hope I convinced you that libertarians, conservatives, and liberals are not crazy, closed–minded provincials who just can't see the light of truth. If I did my job well, you might say they are all worthy of respect, after all they do agree on basic American values: to treat individuals with dignity, to afford them basic rights to life, liberty, privacy, security, property, pursuit of happiness, and democratic participation in government. Ideologues clash because they sincerely differ on how to achieve these values.

And yet, you may still believe they don't have the answers you are looking for. The 2016 Presidential race suggests that America's ideologies are in trouble. Donald Trump and Bernie Sanders embodied a deep dissatisfaction with government gridlock caused by legislators voting along party lines, spouting the same tired reasons why the other side is destroying America. Old-style populist and nativist anger surfaced. Sanders and Trump ran on the premise that interest groups have captured government. Sanders pointed fingers at the rich, Trump at media moguls. Both wanted to protect American workers from unfair foreign competition. They differed in their solutions to domestic problems. Sanders focused on leveling society by taxing the rich and extending social welfare programs such as free college education. Trump focused instead on cutting regulations that were killing jobs, Obamacare, high corporate tax rates, and undocumented aliens flooding across the Mexican border. While Sanders wanted to protect most illegal immigrants, Trump vowed to deport those with criminal records and build a wall on the Mexican border to keep out illegals. His core constituency is working class whites who are facing the prospect of becoming a minority who already believe America is discriminating against them.

I am going to suggest that the political turmoil seen in the 2016 presidential election is a product of a tectonic shift in American society caused by a Digital Revolution that began decades ago. The loss of middle-class jobs traces back to digital computer code riding on fiber optics that connect America at little cost to the rest of the world. Not surprising, new worldwide supply chains based on sophisticated communications networks funnel jobs to low-paying countries like India. Robots run by programs are replacing thousands of blue-collar workers. Machine learning is likely to allow software to replace more educated workers. "Bricks to clicks," is the epitaph of traditional box stores that have died because of online shopping.

Virtual products are replacing real products. Electronic copies are almost costless to make and can be shipped worldwide with a mouse click. Many services have no explicit price because an implicit barter exchange has arisen: "free services" for information. Legitimate website owners and search companies appropriate any content they can grab as long as it boosts website hits and with-it advertising revenue. Massive amounts of data are being mined for their marketing value.

The standard model for competition used by economists assumes spontaneously formed open and distinct markets. Now, large platforms such as Amazon set market rules, monitor trading activities for a vast array of goods and services, and judge which products and traders can use its platform. Amazon sets prices for trading on its platform. In the process of managing its platform, Amazon collects and analyzes an enormous amount of data. In return, Amazon has become a low-cost, low-profit margin online colossus that has lowered the cost of buying goods, delivering parcels to your door quickly. Yet many feel uncomfortable that Amazon and other huge platforms threaten to dominate markets and limit innovation.[1]

Privacy is under attack because of massive, real-time data collection. Mouse clicks and call records build a picture of you – your purchase patterns, your political opinions, your religious affiliations, your friends, and business relationships. It is as if each new piece of information is like a pixel that makes your image come into focus and with enough of them collected over time produces a personal digital video of you – all this without reading your emails or listening to your phone conversations. Retailers, health care providers, lenders, employers, and other institutions will buy data to target customers and screen job applicants.

This is a very tempting milieu for cyber pirates to steal and distribute movies, books, and music. In cyber world, a few hackers can bring down a nation's financial system, communications system, transportation system, power system, and perhaps use a nation's own defense systems against itself. In the virtual world of cloud computing, cloud transportation, and cloud storage, critical personal, corporate, and government information can cross borders with a few keystrokes. Such ease makes the meaning of private property and the rule of law shaky because virtual property is no longer tied to a particular nation.

Even when a network withstands outside attacks, its performance can degrade by unilateral decisions within the networked community. In the communications system, for example, equipment providers such as Apple, telecommunication networks, website owners, and content providers are all fighting for the customer. In this environment, uniform network standards are difficult to develop for improving the resiliency and quality of network performance. As a result, firms are often not able to deliver the types of services requested by their customers, most notably privacy and security.

Private enterprise may also be a casualty of the Digital Revolution that has morphed in ways the intellectual descendants of Adam Smith are still trying to understand. Didn't fast communications help create the 2008 financial crisis? Didn't it allow holders of financial assets to do the equivalent of a run on a bank at lightning speed?

Democracy itself may be at risk because of the Digital Revolution. The Internet was supposed to bolster democracy by expanding the channels of communications on public affairs from a few controlled by television networks to a wide range of information sources accessible through a browser.

---

[1] Lina M. Khan, "Amazon Antitrust Paradox, 126 Yale Law J. 710–779 (2017).

Arguably, the short relatively factual news accounts of the major broadcast television networks – CBS, NBC, and ABC – have been replaced by a confusing blend of entertainment, snooping, biased facts, and fake or misleading stories. CNN, Fox New, and Genesis Communications Systems (the host for Alex Jones) seem to report on different worlds. It appears that intense competition for viewership has turned politicians like Donald Trump into bankable online personalities. Exaggeration seems to sell. Inside stories about politicians get more space than political issues. The politicos themselves have resorted to gutter talk. "Crooked Hilary," "lock her up," "Trump's small hands," "Fake news," "Deep state," and "Witch hunt" have coarsened political discussion and perhaps damaged the civility needed for democratic dialogue.

Governments know the risks of open virtual borders and are attempting to protect national security by employing armies of cyber warriors attached to the FBI, CIA, NSA, the military, and even the Post Office. America's intelligence agencies are using cyber techniques to monitor worldwide communications. Because of its policing power, these agencies can potentially monitor every voice call we make, every text message or email we send, every movement we make inside the home if we have Wi-Fi, and outside the home via Global Position System data. All this gets drawn into a huge government database, which can be used to single out any person or group for secret investigation.

This monitoring extends to other nations and is raising questions about America's digital attacks on other nation's sovereignty. Massive gathering of information along with covert actions increasingly has turned the upper layers of intelligence agencies into the equivalent of a palace guard ready to defend the nation's government and people, sometimes without congressional approval, sometimes without abiding by the law. This palace guard has gathered to itself enormous power. Although it is a present danger to our core values, not having them on constant alert may also give terrorists and rogue nations an unacceptable first strike ability to attack us with bombs or with software viruses. Without cyber warriors, private companies may not be up to the challenges of withstanding cyber-attacks aimed at stealing valuable military and industrial designs.

Another type of coding, genetic coding, is threatening the very integrity of life. What will core values mean if the human condition enters a reality only partially explored by science fiction writers? Sequencing techniques, big-data tools, and other scientific breakthroughs are accelerating the development of artificial life and hybrid life, part organic and part not. In effect, man is becoming a creator god that can transcend biology and transform ecology. Designer eugenics is already having a positive effect on humanity and holds great promise. Genetically altered crops are already helping to feed the poor. Genetic engineering is on the cusp of preventing disease, extending life, and improving general well-being. As with any paradigm-changing breakthrough, however, designer eugenics poses a challenge to the integrity of what it means to be a human being. In the wrong hands, the new science of designer eugenics could desacralize and perhaps destroy creation.

The first step in grappling with both the digital and genetic revolutions, which I will call the Coding Revolution, is to define its characteristics, its language, and its means of communication. My claim is that the Coding Revolution has altered the axis of civilization. Old truths and core values have lost their bedrock feel without solid replacements. Like the Axial Age centuries ago that produced new religions worldwide and philosophical insights, the great uncertainties we face can lead to enormous creativity, to new visions of humanity and nature.

Inevitably, America's ideologies will extend their principles and story lines to explain the benefits and threats of the Coding Revolution and suggest coherent policies to extract the best it has to offer. They may begin by recognizing they are themselves codes: easily understandable to their followers but an alien language to their detractors. Ideologues will eventually have to step out of the past and fully accept the implications that a few actors with bad intentions, or good intentions but are ignorant or shortsighted, can disrupt the lives of millions and perhaps bring down civilization itself. These actors are not elected officials, although they could be, they are not generals or religious leaders, although they could be rather, they are likely to be invisible actors, seemingly normal people who live next door. Even now, an ordinary person using an ordinary laptop with certain access codes has the potential to bring down major corporations or governments. None of the three ideologies have convincing policies for preparing and reacting to unexpected catastrophes that could start next door.

To sharpen the challenge, I examine four emerging trends: cyberspace capitalism, digital overexposure, stealth security, and designer eugenics. As you will see, the underlying political divisions associated with them predate the Coding Revolution but have become much more troubling because of it. Our challenge is to develop policies to limit the downsides caused by the Coding Revolution without destroying its benefits.

Besides challenging core values, the technological threats described in all six chapters also have common subthemes related to how ordinary human behavior is changing in uncomfortable ways. An ordinary citizen has difficulty distinguishing real emails from phishing attacks, feels angst when providing personal data online, and doesn't know if the government or a thief is stalking their digital footprints.

Institutions have become associated with a metric obsession – measuring performance by numbers, whether in dollars or throughput. They rely on numbers to quantify integrity, professionalism, and spiritual togetherness, and by doing so, break down societal trust in supplying truthful data.

The obsession with scientific answers, paradoxically, is making civilization susceptible to catastrophic events no one can predict. People increasingly rely on experts to help them; and experts are often self-serving and have an incentive to overstate their expertise to boost their importance.

At the core of this new and potentially unstable digital world is a web of interconnected systems largely without central control and yet they have powerful control over everyday life. Seemingly isolated network breakdowns such the burnout of a generator in one location can cascade and turn out the lights thousands of miles away or the crash of a Global Positioning System can ground fleets of passenger jets. People are now preparing for massive breakdowns in vital services as if they are regular events. Anyone on the East Coast that experienced Hurricane Sandy knows how quickly home-generators were selling, and now many homes have them as a basic selling feature.

This brief introduction is meant to scare anyone, even the most rock-solid ideologue into saying, "okay, I've got your point, now what." This "now what" reaction is my more positive goal that I explore in the book's third and final section. I want to supply America's ideologues with reasons to open up to alternatives and perhaps cooperate across ideological lines when joint efforts are necessary to solve a problem. I am not asking anyone to concede their viewpoint, only to recognize their ideology is not a complete plan, only a perspective on how to solve problems. To use a financial analogy, no true American would want to withhold information from others to "short" American society, allowing it to crash, just to show the public his ideological vision was right all along.

Expanding vision is not an easy task. People don't say, okay I need a bit of retraining. Instead, this section is meant as a teaser for ideologues to get more comfortable with the likely effects of technological change and see how it affects their traditional beliefs. Perhaps then, a new constructive American dialogue will take off.

Most of all, I am challenging Americans, readers of this book, to become champions, pathfinders who can find new ways that extend current ideological thinking to address new realities, path makers when an ideology needs to grow in new directions not considered before, and path tenders who keep alive the wisdom of older champions.

7

Cyberspace Capitalism, Part 1: Introduction to the Online Economy and Its Fragilities

Abstract The chapter begins with a description of the basic features of the online economy, but the main line of investigation is to examine instabilities in the financial market created by the Digital Revolution. A key example is financial market meltdown in 2008. The case is made that the Digital Revolution led to giant financial institutions that were too big to fail. It also produced new financial instruments that even sophisticated traders did not understand well. Coupled with new trading techniques, lack of oversight, and a herd mentality that could form overnight because of instant wire transfers, the Digital Revolution helped produce the 2008 crash.

7.1 Introduction

The first example of the enormous effects of the Coding Revolution on American civilization is cyberspace capitalism. It began with the Digital Revolution in the 1960s. Mainframe computers connected to dumb terminals began to transform the workspace. In telecommunications networks, telephone companies began introducing digital switches. From there, the cost of collecting, processing, and transporting data began to fall rapidly. The reach of these networks expanded rapidly when fiber replaced copper wiring. Global communication began to take off with the laying of underseas fiber cables that connected major cities around the globe.

Two facts summarize the magnitude of the Digital Revolution. Between 1956 and 2015, computer performance has increased a 1 trillion-fold.[1] In the 1980s, telephone companies were transitioning to digital transport of traffic. Their typical backbone transmission links were DS1s and DS3s and then OC1s and OC3s. A Digital Signal 1 cable (DS1) had the capacity to handle 1.54 megabits of data per second. An Optical Carrier 3 (OC3) could carry 155 megabits per second. Today a home connection is often faster than an OC3.

One of the first casualties of the Digital Revolution was the offshoring of manufacturing. Underseas fiber-optic cables connected America to other nations. This allowed American companies to monitor overseas businesses in real time. Firms no longer had to cluster in a tight geographical space to work together. Containerships, a major breakthrough in oceanic transport, reduced the cost enormously. Before 1960, costs of international transoceanic shipments for most commodities were easily 15% of retail value containerization lowered cost to 1%.[2]

Together, fast communications and low-cost shipping allowed major American companies to tap into low-cost talent overseas. As a result, America began to lose manufacturing jobs and other related jobs such as call centers to places like India and China. Even during the Great Recession "many U.S.-based companies were shifting the balance of their workforces overseas. Ford, for example, reported in 1992 that 53 percent of its employees worked in the U.S. and Canada. By 2009, its North American workforce (by then Ford had expanded to Mexico) made up only 37 percent of total payroll. With 53 percent of big U.S. firms implementing offshoring strategies, 'there is no job security now,'" said Lauren Asplen of the IUE-CWA, an electrical-workers union.[3] More recently, the list of companies that do the most overseas manufacturing are Apple, IBM, Nike, Cisco, and Walmart.[4]

American consumers benefitted from globalization. They saw the price of manufactured goods and other online services drop markedly in price. The net result was probably good in the long term for the American and global economy, but in the short term, many American blue-collar workers lost their

[1] McCarthy, P. (2017), Infographic: The Growth of Computer Processing Power. Recoil FFGRID. https://www.offgridweb.com/preparation/infographic-the-growth-of-computer-processing-power/. Accessed 30 April 2023.

[2] Delong, J.B. (2022), *Slouching Towards Utopia: An Economic History of The Twentieth Century*. Basic Books, NY p. 466.

[3] The Week Staff (2015) Where America's jobs went. The Week. https://theweek.com/articles/486362/where-americas-jobs-went. Accessed 30 April 2023.

[4] ITI. Which Five Companies Do the Most Overseas Manufacturing. https://itimanufacturing.com/five-companies-overseas-manufacturing/. Accessed 30 April 2023.

jobs, and once great manufacturing cities like Detroit became part of the rust belt.

I qualified the long-term benefit because there are many hidden and not-so-hidden costs associated with the outflow of manufacturing jobs from the United States. Overseas outsourcing is likely to result in a loss of intellectual property and know-how to foreign countries that may even be threats to America. From an environmental perspective, America is shipping jobs to countries with lower pollution standards gives polluting companies abroad an unfair trade advantage.[5] Globalization transfers control over American well-being and regulatory control to foreign nations. As we will see in the Stealth Security chapter, is it more cost-effective to have gun-boat diplomacy or be self-sufficient for essential services even when they are more costly to produce in the United States.

The COVID pandemic highlighted another shift in demand for labor and location of businesses that may create long-term dislocations. The Digital Revolution caused many businesses to shift from working in the office to working online. To the extent that this is a permanent shift in work activities, office building may become less economically useful. Workers may look for homes in less expensive exurban areas. Home communications and reliable electricity supply will become more important than before.

Online business became a real option with the introduction of packet technology into the communications network in the late 1990s. It ushered in what I call true cyberspace capitalism. Packet technology replaced digital transmissions of bit streams that required dedicated paths from originator to destination. Packet technology contained bundles of information with an origination label and a destination label. It could travel from source to destination over many possible paths. Packet technology reduced the need for centralized switching technology. As a result, the world's communication networks opened up and interconnected. Packet technology became the basis for the Internet.

Even though information and communication technology accounted for only 7% of the economy in 2014,[6] it is obvious that the shift in trade to the Internet has transformed the American economy. In reality, cyberspace capitalism covers much more than the Internet. Networks that transport Internet traffic also support private broadband networks, for example, those used by financial houses for trading securities. They also support hybrid network services that are private but have access to the Internet. Connected to these networks are huge server farms, large clusters of computers integrated to provide

[5] Zhou, Y.M. (2017), When some U.S. firms move production overseas, they also offshore pollution. M Ross Businessimpact. https://businessimpact.umich.edu/when-some-us-firms-move-production-overseas-they-also-offshore-their-pollution/. Accessed 30 April 2023.
[6] Gordon, p. 441.

"cloud," or more common terms, "remote" data collection, storage, and processing. Smartphones, other customer equipment and network servers are the brains of cyberspace directing inquiries and receiving answers from person to person, from person to machine, from machine to machine.

Cyberspace capitalism extends to any industry that relies on connecting to equipment such as a cell phone and online trading and advertising for a significant source of its business. Many of the services traded are informational and virtual: online books and videos, application software to aid consumers and producers, slick interfaces to make applications easy to use, and remote shared data storage and processing to reduce computer hardware costs and insure against disasters that occur in a specific location. Tools and techniques for digital trading and pattern recognition are developing rapidly. Expressions such as "machine learning" herald another transformation in the marketplace: the loss of the personal touch in favor of algorithms to solve problems. Increasingly, markets are becoming global and mobile. An American citizen with a smartphone can buy service from an American provider, download applications from a provider in another country, and buy products in still another country. When a company's primary assets are software applications, it can shift its nationality at little cost. Blurring of frontiers and national responsibility are weakening a nation's ability to regulate and tax these Digital Age companies and end users. New virtual currencies such as Bitcoins even threaten a nation's monopoly over legal tender.

Not to oversell the change in trading behavior, virtualization of property is not new, but cyberspace has accelerated its pace enormously and extended it in undreamed directions. An example of pre-Internet virtualization is the financial market. The dollar itself was once backed by gold then silver then became backed by nothing but the good faith of the nation in 1971. In a few decades after the World Wide Web opened for business, money used in transactions changed from currency and checks to computer bits. Corporate shares, once stock certificates, are simply line items in computer accounts. Trading, once done by market makers on trading floors, has disappeared. Direct trading has become the norm. Digital transactions typically happen without supervision by an outside authority such as a stock exchange or government regulator. Traders have become disembodied text messages, digital voices, and, more often than not, one machine communicating with another without human intervention. Gains and losses that could pile as high as a mountain show up on a screen as a few debits or credits to an account. In this virtual world, anyone can imagine himself a master of the universe. With a keystroke a financial gamer can move millions, sometimes billions of dollars from one country to another. No one seems to be watching carefully, not the boss and not the regulator. It is a heady sense of freedom that knows no borders.

Starting with the Internet, as the most obvious example of the growth in cyberspace capitalism, this medium has changed how capitalism works on many levels. As recently as the 1990s, market data for any industry were hard to come by and expensive to gather. Companies like Procter & Gamble conducted surveys, organized focus groups, conducted telephone interviews, and monitored sales and turnover rates – all in the quest to collect scarce and often sketchy information. Then massive amounts of Internet data and text became over the Internet, which led companies like Google, Amazon, and Facebook – companies that did not exist before 1990 – to quantify market patterns down to an individual's behavior in order to customize services.

One unintended result is a massive assault on privacy. Supermarkets know what you buy. Anyone who signs up with a utility company for a rebate in exchange for allowing the company to cut power during peak periods should recognize the utility's employees can predict when a customer is not at home. Automobile companies track vehicles in order to respond quickly when an accident has occurred; automobiles, themselves, have guidance systems to assist drivers. In the past, real estate investors read obituaries for potential fire sales. Now they can get a head start by finding out who has contacted a funeral home over the Internet.

Web platforms such as Google and Facebook, data brokers, and other parties that transact online record sensitive information, feed data-mining groups, and sell the data to other organizations. On certain streets and in many stores, a person's image is recorded on video cameras. Although all this sketchy data may produce an inaccurate profile, a company that develops a profile may find that a 30% success rate in anticipating a person's purchases has a good payoff. The profit motive has been pushing companies to fine-tune their personal profiles. As they become more accurate, they could allow a stranger to watch you accurately almost all the time without your knowledge unless fair ground rules for electronic surveillance develop or enough companies find it profitable to encrypt transmissions for customers. None of these fixes are foolproof, especially when the cyber world is morphing so rapidly.

Faster is better when it comes to drawing out market trends and reacting to them. Humans are slow calculators and have glacial reaction times compared to a computer algorithm. Not surprising, decision-makers have delegated decision-making to "quants" that develop computer algorithms to search for profitable market changes, sometimes at the nanosecond level and then react to them.

Like any system, cyber markets have their own unique vulnerabilities. Sudden flocking, called correlation of behavior in economics-speak, occurs in a flash. It can cause a web posting to "go viral." It can cause sudden network congestion at nodes where bandwidth isn't available. More ominously, traders trying to unload securities can clog the financial system as they did during the financial meltdown in 2008 and then the economy came crashing down. Hackers have broken into websites and stole credit card information, injected viruses into the Internet targeted at what they consider offensive corporations. Insiders have downloaded the equivalent of a company's intellectual storehouse and peddled it to competitors.

The implications of virtualization are being learned in real time, but the fixes are by no means apparent. Using the news and entertainment industries as an example, Internet pirates steal and distribute copyrighted material with little risk. Attacks no longer require daring, just access to codes or a digital copying machine as simple as a camera. The entertainment industries are losing huge sums to pirates that have used algorithms for downloading and sharing data.

In a virtual world, bright lines between stealing, borrowings, sharing, and altering have been blown into bytes. Google can summarize a news article, gain advertising revenue, and not share it with the news agency. Equipment manufacturers that want to sell boxes for copying content and websites to look the other way if pirates use their products to steal content.

Cyberspace challenges keep morphing with technological changes. From an end user's perspective, the Internet used to be a linkup of personal computers connected to websites. That perception is changing rapidly as end users start to use cloud computing and storage to save and process large quantities of data, including such necessities as virtual photo albums. Sensitive private information gets mingled in cloud storage facilities.

Industries are resorting to private virtual networks for speed and security, for communicating and sharing information and trading goods and services. A variety of hybrid networks have emerged that often use the same physical facilities and often have portals onto each other. For example, an Internet service provider's service bundles typically include a cable offering, which is nothing more than a private channel to guarantee quality of service and to limit hacking. Like other users of cyberspace, financial firms are petrified of cyberattacks of hackers stealing sensitive financial information, of insiders putting a company's vital information on a thumb drive and selling it elsewhere. They too buy virtual private networks that are walled off from the Internet.

7.2   Prelude to the 2008 Financial Panic: Revolutions in Data Processing and Communications

A great threat to the cyber economy is the Black Swan event, an unknowable market change that spreads rapidly like a seismic shock that takes down the system.[7] Sticking with the financial industry, the collapse of Lehman Brothers precipitated a financial freeze that led to the Great Recession. It became predictable only after the fact when hindsight allows analysts to piece together a narrative that may or may not be the whole story. Libertarians, conservatives, and liberals continue to debate the cause of the Great Recession. It may be impossible to know whether it was the Fed's low interest rate policy, or the push for banks to issue mortgage to risky customers, or the sale of new risky asset-back securities that weren't well understood, or the rise of an unregulated shadow banking system, or a culture of greed that took hold of Americans, or the failure of the Fed to rescue Lehman, or some combination of these and other effects such as international banking conditions.[8]

The financial meltdown in 2008 is an extreme example of a lightning speed chain reaction of what can happen in cyberspace. A thumbnail history of the Great Recession will help highlight changes in the marketplace that make Black Swan events an increasing threat. After World War II, the financial industry began to operate in a global market. By the 1970s, Europe and Japan had recovered their economic might and had developed large multinational banking institutions that competed with American financial institutions to become the financier of national governments and multinational corporations. Nations, such as the Cayman Islands, allowed bankers to park money with no questions asked. American banks pushed to have the same flexibility and reach as foreign banks. The American banks wanted to become one-stop-shopping financial institution for big worldwide entities. In the 1980s, both republicans and democrats with the support of many economists decided the banks needed more freedom to operate.[9] Gradually, the controls put in place during the 1930s to protect American banks from financial runs were discontinued, not because of any conspiracy between the banks and government but

---

[7] Taleb, N.N. (2010), *Black Swan: The Impact of the Highly Improbable*, 2nd Ed., Random House, NY.

[8] See, for example, *The Financial Crisis Inquiry Report (2011)*, issued by the Financial Crisis Inquiry Commission, chrome-extension://efaidnbmnnnibpcajpcglclefindmkaj/https://www.govinfo.gov/content/pkg/GPO-FCIC/pdf/GPO-FCIC.pdf. Accessed 30 April 2023.

[9] Calomiris, C.W. (2009) *U.S. Bank Deregulation In Historical Perspective*. Cambridge University Press, UK.

because the fears of depression had faded, and American banks seemed to be operating internationally with a government mandated handicap.

The Digital Revolution changed corporate culture in ways that depersonalized trades and justified to many that greed is good. Start with investment banks. Before 1970, they would underwrite trade stocks and bonds. They were partnerships that in-house resembled a club or experts who brought in family members or other fraternity prospects that would be mentored in-house. If they fit in, they became partners. Their clients knew them. Trust and integrity were very valuable assets for keeping clients. By the 1990s, the Digital Revolution turned these institutions into massive corporations that made most of their money through computerized trades. The big new financial instrument was the financial option to buy or sell a security, developed by Black and Scholes and refined by Merton. College-trained experts could use computers to price these securities, meaning there was less of a need to mentor experts in house.[10]

Computerization lowered the cost of trading. The time to distribute new security offerings declined from days to hours. In 1968 and 1969, investment houses were having difficulty keeping up with orders to buy or sell securities. The introduction of the mainframe computer and later time-share services and later minicomputers lowered the cost of trading and increased their speed.

Rapid declines in processing and communications costs allowed investment banks to expand into new geographical markets requiring heavy investment in plants and equipment. These developments required a large infusion of cash and more employees to handle online trades. The Securities and Exchange Commission reacted in 1970 by allowing investment banks to issue shares and become publicly traded. In 1975, the Securities and Exchange Commission ended fixed fees per trade on the New York Stock Exchange to allow customers to benefit from lower trading costs.[11]

Traditional commercial and other depository banks also sought to expand as financial markets grew. Banking regulations were holding them back. The McFadden Act of 1927 forbade nationally chartered banks from owning and operating banks across state lines.[12] Government regulations imposed a ceiling on deposit interest rates and zero interest rate on checking accounts.

---

[10] Alan Morrison, A., and Wilhelm, J. (2008), The Demise of Investment Banking Partnerships: Theory and Evidence. Journal Of Finance 63, pp. 311–350.

[11] NYSE Was Revolutionized by SEC Abolition of Fixed Commissions. The Washington Post. https://www.washingtonpost.com/archive/business/1985/07/21/nyse-was-revolutionized-by-sec-abolition-of-fixed-commissions/8726b8b1-8013-4bcf-aad8-776fcc65f417/. Accessed 30 April 2023.

[12] Liberto, D. (2020), Interstate Banking, Investopedia. https://www.investopedia.com/terms/i/interstate-banking.asp. Accessed 30 April 2023.

Foreign banks began expanding in the United States in the 1960s and 1970s. They were not subject to the one-state restrictions. They could acquire domestic banks, but American banks could not acquire foreign banks. Domestic investment banks were offering money market funds with no interest limitation and allowed customers to write checks on their accounts.[13] The 1970s also saw a run up in inflation, which forced banks to offer "free gifts" to entice customers to keep their funds in banks. Pressure grew to liberalize banking regulation, which began in the 1980s. Banks could offer money market accounts. Bank holding companies could operate across state lines. In the 1990s, federal legislation sanctioned nationwide banks.

Computerization encouraged a movement away from personalized banking to using credit scores and other quantitative measures of credit worthiness such as a salary stub and income tax return.

Another cultural change that is important as a backdrop to the Great Recession is the slow shift from paper financial transactions to online transactions that occurred after the World Wide Web became popular. Banks and other financial institutions gave customers financial incentives to promote online banking. Major financial institutions traded online. People became accustomed to anonymous trades in ever-evolving investment opportunities, perhaps starting with money market accounts.

The shift from paying for something by withdrawing cash from a wallet feels different than paying by credit card. Studies show that people spend more money when using credit cards than with cash. Psychologically, withdrawing cash from a wallet makes people think twice about spending money.[14]

There was no reason to assume that traders who see numbers on a screen are any different. They were taking on more risks because the money is disembodied from reality. In 1995, one trader, Nick Leeson, drove Barings Bank into bankruptcy by losing $1.3 billion of the bank's money on unauthorized trades. Barings Bank had been in existence since 1762.[15]

Use of credit cards and online trades highlight the development of a new transmission product for financial institutions – the electronic funds transfer. In the 1980s, a financial institution could sweep funds from one account to another in real time. This new method of shifting funds led to "hot money,"

---

[13] Bowden, E.V. (1980), Revolution In Banking. Robert F. Dame Publishers, IN.

[14] Hurd, E., and Konsko, L., (2022), Does Using a Credit Card Make You Spend More Money? Nerdwallet.   https://www.nerdwallet.com/article/credit-cards/credit-cards-make-you-spend--more#:~:text=It's%20a%20normal%20feeling.,with%20value%20attached%20to%20it. Accessed 30 April 2023.

[15] Kenton, W. (2022), Who is Nick Leeson? Investopedia. https://www.investopedia.com/terms/n/nick-leeson.asp. Accessed 30 April 2023.

huge funds shifted within minutes from a troubled financial institution to a healthy one. When an online system connects thousands of financial institutions, a panic withdrawal from one financial institution can cascade rapidly into a financial meltdown.

7.3   New Complex Financial Instruments Misunderstood

A revolution was also occurring in financial economic theory supported by computing power and cheap data transmission accelerated the development of new financial instruments and with it new financial strategies that depended on debt financing. Long-Term Capital Management (LCTM) was at the center of this revolution. Founded in 1993 by sophisticated investors including two future Nobel Prize winners, the company borrowed large amounts of money to exploit slight yield differences in bonds of different maturities. Because it wasn't a bank or a mutual fund, but something new, a hedge fund, it was able to operate without oversight by a government regulatory agency. Financial crises in East Asia and Russia pushed LTCM's return into the red, and without much of an equity cushion, the company's stock went into freefall in 1997. The Federal Reserve organized a bailout in 1998 to prevent a financial crisis, and it worked. Thirteen private banks funded the rescue. Interestingly, the first investment bank to fall later in 2007 was Bear Stearns, which declined to participate in the rescue effort. Lehman Brothers was also one of the smallest contributors to the rescue package.

While LTCM should have served as a grave warning that the evolving financial system was fragile, it was just a blip because the rescue was a success. During the late 1990s through 2005, interest rates in America stayed low by historical standards. Investors still remembered vividly the high yields in the 1980s. Private banks and financial institutions looked at the higher yields on Fannie Mae mortgage-backed securities and wanted to get into the game, and so they did by developing their own mortgage-backed securities and other types of collateral debt obligations. Financial institutions put these assets and liabilities in the books of what are known as shadow banking institutions. These institutions borrowed large sums overnight to invest in long-term mortgage-backed securities without oversight from a bank regulatory agency.

Financial institutions were able to create a worldwide market for these new collateralized instruments because communication bandwidth availability exploded, starting in the 1990s. Twenty-four-hour trading became the norm.

Sophisticated buyers and sellers could communicate directly, bypassing organized exchanges. Screens flashed market data continuously. In real time – almost surreal time – $billions changed hands in a blink. Programmed, high-frequency trading took off as financial houses of all types wanted to catch changes in market trends as quickly as possible. Each institution tried to predict everyone else's behavior. In this hair-trigger trading pit, a rumor or a glitch in a program could start prices tumbling or soaring for no apparent fundamental reason related to actual business conditions.

Despite the failure of Long-Term Capital Management (LTCM),[16] financial theory took on the appearance of a science. Models began appearing in academic journals during the 1960s and 1970s outlining portfolio theory, option theory, and cost of capital theory. From then on, all sorts of financial assets developed based on objectively valuing risk and return tradeoffs. With the growth of the broadband communications system, market reach expanded worldwide and allowed for a high degree of customization for the benefit of market niche investors.

Two of the many types of financial instruments developed were collateralized debt obligations (CDOs) and credit default swaps (CDSs). They are closely linked to the 2008 financial collapse. The making of a mortgage-backed CDO begins with a bundle of mortgages originated by say a mortgage company. The mortgage company sells its mortgages to a bank, which in turn sells them to a shadow bank that borrowed overnight funds to purchasing them, and then packaged them as long-term CDOs. Variations on CDOs developed. One type bundled IOUs of different safety by defining which of a class of CDOs first absorbs mortgage default losses. The quality categories are called tranches. The AAA-rated tranche has the first claim to the cash flow from the underlying mortgages. The lowest rated tranche is akin to an equity tranche, which receives the remaining return after paying off the higher-rated tranches. In theory, the highest-rated bonds yielded a lower rate than the equity tranche because it has the senior claim on the cash flow from the underlying mortgages. The equity tranche is the first to absorb mortgage defaults. In exchange, the equity tranche stands to earn the highest return if defaults don't exceed a certain percentage of the bundled mortgages backing the CDOs.

A CDS is a tradable insurance policy on a security. In our example, a CDO originator could buy a CDS for a bundle of mortgages to make them all

---

[16] LCTM's computer models recommended that it hold Russian bonds that were in default. LCTM racked up huge losses and was in danger of defaulting on its own loans. The US government orchestrated a bailout. See Hayes A. (2021), What was Long-Term Capital Management (LTCM) and What Happened? Investopedia. https://www.investopedia.com/terms/l/longtermcapital.asp. Accessed 30 April 2023.

AAA-rated. The CDS can then be traded among investors. In effect, a third-party investor may buy a CDS, hoping the CDO originator defaults, which would mean for a small purchase price of the CDS, the buyer gets a full payoff on the insurance policy. This is almost the equivalent of allowing me to buy an insurance policy on my neighbor, a practice governments' outlaw to prevent intentional "accidents" from happening.

The two new security categories sold well, and by implication they added net value to the marketplace otherwise no one would hold them. On paper, they made mortgages very liquid assets, giving investors added incentive to invest in the real estate market because they could trade mortgage-backed securities, especially the ones with an insurance guarantee. The actual bundle of CDOs sold could be customized to buyers' needs, an added plus for the new securities.

The originator and holders of mortgages, which historically were banks, could sell them to outside investors, thereby spreading the risk of holding mortgages to a large investment community. Many of the buyers were financial institutions in Europe and other Western-style nations. Once the cash from the sale came in, the bank could issue more loans and earn more fees. The fees expanded from simply mortgage origination to CDO and CDS originator fees for their services.

7.4   Lack of Oversight

Business picked up so quickly that originators of CDOs and CDSs were hungry for new mortgages so that they could sell more asset-backed securities and insurance. No one really looked too carefully at the underlying quality of the mortgages because widespread defaults were rare, and this was proved by fancy statistical models called value at risk (VaR) models that proved mortgage-backed securities were safe. Never mind that these rating agencies were consultants to the originators, the models made everyone comfortable…at least for a time.

Government was also. Congress passed the Community Reinvestment Act (1977). It requires the Federal Reserve and other banking regulators to encourage institutions to meet the credit needs of communities where they do business.[17] The intention was to eliminate redlining of communities considered to be high risk borrowers.

Besides using faulty models to judge the riskiness of these securities, external controls were weak for other reasons. Rating agencies are paid by issuing companies to develop ratings and could lose business if didn't play along.

[17] Community Reinvestment Act. Board of Governors of the Federal Reserve System, https://www.federalreserve.gov/consumerscommunities/cra_about.htm. Accessed 30 April 2023.

Even the square players didn't fare well because the rating agencies were using the same models that the financial institutions were using to judge the security of CDO and CDS offerings. The record of government regulators is also abysmal. If management did not know what was going on in their companies, it is not surprising that a regulatory agency would even know where to look for the rogue operations and probably couldn't recognize them if they tried. Rapid changes in markets and the introduction of many new types of securities based on obscure financial theories are not a comfortable environment for the traditional auditor. Worse still, big corporations were becoming sophisticated regulatory arbitragers. They parked money where American regulators didn't see it, and if they did see it, couldn't get at it.

With more money flowing into the mortgage market, housing prices began to rise. Mortgage originators such as Countrywide perfected the NINJA mortgage – no down payment, no job, and no assets – to pump more mortgages into the system. They sold these toxic mortgages to shadow banks that turned them into mortgage-backed debt of supposedly different quality grades and sold a large percentage of them to big investors such as pension funds and international investors. A speculative bubble in the housing market began to form in the United States. People were buying houses to flip them, and banks were lending because they could resell the houses at a profit in cases where the borrower defaulted. Most sensed the market was rising on bad vapors but stuck with it, assuming they could get out before everyone else. Some investors, the big ones, run by supposedly sophisticated investors, held onto mortgage-backed securities because an insurance market based on the CDS had developed to insure these securities in case of default. Eventually the bubble burst when the demand for housing slowed and the insurers like AIG went into default.

7.5   The Crash

The financial collapse began with the shadow banking system. The most well-known one was a division of Lehman Brothers that collapsed spectacularly. Lehman's troubles began when it could no longer raise funds by borrowing money overnight using mortgage-backed securities as collateral. Once this happened, a run began on Lehman and other shadow banks because no one wanted to lend them money, and the first lenders to get paid back would avoid having their assets frozen by a bankruptcy court. A classic financial panic ensued, of the type Keynes described and analyzed. Liquidity dried up, spending dropped precipitously as businesses and households tried to deleverage, that is, pay off as much debt as possible. The government stepped in to prevent a financial meltdown. However, the government has had to purchase bad debt and offer fiscal stimulus programs such as funding shovel-ready building projects, which are likely to be low-return investments, loaded with waste because if a project made sense in normal times, it should have been undertaken. Waiting for a recession to fund public roads, for example, is not a good long-term policy.

7.6   Hindsight

In retrospect, it is clear that savvy players in these markets were wrong, bet the house, and lost it for a while, until bailed out to some extent by the government. Why? Let's start without relying on blind greed as the explanation. Instead, let's begin with the problem of complexity: product complexity, accounting complexity, and legal complexity. Then we'll move on to instabilities caused by instantaneous and anonymous trading. The final message is that super-rational, hair-trigger, super-efficient markets – the economic ideal – are not ideal. Markets are supposed to meet human needs by understanding human frailties and prejudices. Transparency in dealings builds trust, and even then, it takes time for both sides to become comfortable with each other. Not surprisingly, a shocked realization that assets being traded had a hefty amount of junk in them would create a stampede of panicked selling, freezing financial flows, and ultimately causing markets to implode. Eventually cyberspace capitalism will adapt ground rules that will humanize the virtual marketplace. The big question is whether the main source for humanization will come from profit motivated solutions or government intervention.

Starting with the complexity problem, in a typical textbook example of a well-functioning market, the product is uniform, say wheat, and both the buyer and seller can judge its quality. Only a few decades ago, financial securities were not terribly complex. You could buy stocks or bonds, and a few sophisticated traders bought and sold shorter-term debt instruments. Unlike wheat, the future payoffs from these securities were in doubt, so investors asked experts for advice. What about a CDO and a CDS? Does the buyer of a CDO really know the quality of the underlying mortgages and the probability that the particular mortgages backing a group of CDOs will be paid back? Does a holder of a CDS know the probability that Lehman Brothers will default on its CDOs? In hindsight, the investors had no clue what was backing the new securities they were holding or knew what they were holding and tried to get rid of the toxic securities as fast as they could shovel them out the door but were too slow to unload them during the crisis. Few realized – including the "experts" – the effects of a worldwide bank run would make all the models and theories useless because when an underwriter of CDS's such as AIG defaults, the market has no bottom. Everyone loses a bundle.

Accounting rules associated with CDOs and CDSs were often baffling even to sophisticated buyers and sellers. The CEO of AIG had no idea how much exposure these securities had to its insurance company. They were booked during the boom at market values that were wildly optimistic in retrospect. When the bust occurred, the accounting profession wanted them booked at their long-term values, whatever that meant, instead of at their distressed prices during the financial meltdown.

The damage from out-of-control employees magnifies in cyber world because agents can place bets large enough to threaten the viability of even the biggest financial institution. Bonuses and stock options in the financial industry are based on trading winnings. It is like feeding money to a person with a betting habit. The bets will only get bigger. Worse yet, leveraging the bet is a standard practice to multiply the payoff, and this strategy pays off spectacularly in good times, but an unexpected downturn in business can leave the firm unable to pay its debts.

Legal terms and conditions also helped cause a run on the shadow banking system and then on the rest of the financial institutions. Mutual funds that were holders of the AAA tranche CDOs had a legal obligation to unload them when they were rated as riskier assets, causing an acceleration of the selloff. Bankruptcy laws require assets to be frozen if a financial institution in fact declared bankruptcy. To protect its own financial viability, lenders to these institutions asked for immediate repayment of loans and stopped lending new funds to them. This is the classic run on a bank done by sophisticated financial institutions to other sophisticated financial institutions. It happened so quickly because transactions were electronic, done instantaneously in cyberspace.

As in past financial bubbles, a herd mentality developed where everyone, at first, thought they couldn't lose in the market and then thought they would be wiped out if they didn't cash in their assets immediately. The Federal Reserve and Treasury stepped in to prevent a bank run turning into a wholesale financial panic that could have brought down many financial institutions, but the Fed did let Lehman go under, which started the panic in the first place.

7.7 A Retrospective on Crashes in the Digital World

The financial collapse during the Great Depression of the 1930s would look like it was occurring in slow motion by today's standards. In the United States, it began with a run on a New York City bank, inconveniently named the Bank of the United States, in 1930. Between 1930 and 1933, bank failures spread to regional and smaller banks. By contrast, had the Fed not stepped in after the Lehman collapse in 2007, the worldwide banking system could have frozen and crashed within a few days. This is the new reality in cyberspace.

Hair-trigger transactions in seemingly highly efficient global financial market produce financial instability. Agents of shareholders within the banking industry, especially top managers and traders, can bring down the financial system with a keystroke, and it is unclear that international cooperation is up to the task of instituting rules to prevent crises for a variety of reasons. The least obvious problem is that rules become quickly outdated in the face of technological change. All sorts of complex securities are being developed that don't fall into a neat category, and their quality is very hard to evaluate, even by experts. The other problems are more of the usual sort: political battles and turf wars among regulatory agencies and the old beggar-thy-neighbor Cayman Island approach of looking at what benefits the home country and be damned about everyone else.

Making the world safe from financial collapse will require a complete revaluation of financial laws, and for this to be successful, a clear understanding of how the financial system works in cyberspace is absolutely crucial. Yet economists, other types of financial practitioners, and political philosophers have few solid answers. Gaming the system has become a profitable way for some businesses and some nations to pile up wealth by shorting the rest of the players. A place like the Cayman Islands where anything goes adds a layer of dirty dealing that debases the entire world market.

Trust among traders has always been critical for keeping financial markets going. Few will buy from someone they don't trust, especially if the product they are selling is hard to evaluate. A few basic conditions need to be held to assure honest trading. Both sides must have skin in the game, equivalent to the risks they are taking. It is also a great help if both sides are honest, but even an honest person becomes even more trustworthy if he stands to lose if he doesn't deliver what he said he would. In specialized cases, organized exchanges such as the New York Stock Exchange form to assure buyers and sellers that the market follows defined practices and penalties for violating exchange rules. Organized exchanges typically trade uniform commodities or securities. Government regulations including uniform accounting practices and legal recourse can build confidence in the marketplace. Notice, the shadow banking system collapsed, not the New York Stock Exchange. It may be that organized exchanges are a partial solution to the problem of trading anonymously through informal channels.

Economic theories of financial markets need an overhaul because as Alan Shiller, a recent Nobel Prize winner, and others have pointed out, stock price movements do not follow a pattern of a cool, rational investor. In recent decades, market traders have relied on economic theories, models, and empirical studies as an alternative means to build trust in the market. In the financial markets, for example, economists developed theories of investing based on a few commonsensical ideas. The value of investment depends on the future inflows of cash it generates. Investors expect higher returns for taking on more risk. The risk of a company is primarily associated with the business it is in. The value of an option to buy or sell an investment sometime in the future has value that increases with the length of the option, the variability of the price of the underlying investment, and the probability that the underlying business defaults. All these theories assume rational investors valued financial assets at their intrinsic value, that is, the earning power of the underlying assets producing real goods and services. The story line went that the gambler and the foolish speculator would lose their stake because savvy traders would take advantage of them. In the process, prices would move toward intrinsic values defined by the earning power of a firm's assets.

7.8   A Need for New Models

The problem with all these nice, rational theories is that they don't work; they don't track financial market movements well. Prices for disembodied products and abstract securities lack solid grounding in concrete, intrinsic values. Speculators can drive a market for a long time. Expectations can easily be herded and led in the wrong direction. In other words, the rational man, so important to economists, really has an irrational streak. Without a realistic view of behavior, economic theories have fatal flaws that crop up in unexpected ways. In mass markets, where a trader can become anonymous or when big trades occur occasionally, a breach of trust can pay off. This has occurred often in financial markets where the counterparty is nothing more than an account number.

Real conditions are often masked by clever announcements to engender excitement. Creative accounting rules make it difficult to understand the value of an offer. Big traders try to game their trades to eke out gains. Speculators with little information sometimes dominate the market and drag the rational traders along, forcing them to shift from evaluating true business conditions to learning what the speculators will do next. Even the so-called super-rationalists, the quants, try to anticipate what other modelers will do, which can destabilize the market. As a result of these and other behavioral quirks, markets don't clear, don't send accurate signals. Everyone operates in a speculative fog and, often for the sake of safety, follow the other flashlights they see, whether they are moving in the right direction or not. Economic theory is at a loss to explain critical instabilities in financial markets because they don't account for the importance of intuition and tipping points that turn a herd of investors from bulling forward to scattering in panic.

High interconnectivity, a feature of supposedly efficient markets in cyber-space, actually can create chaotic turmoil if something goes wrong in some parts of this communications web. Most obviously, high interconnectivity creates the medium for rule evasion. If you have a problem in America, ship your funds to the Cayman Islands. A virtual marketplace that operates continuously with many relying on programmed trading algorithms fosters a herd mentality that can form for no apparent reason and yet cause a financial panic. Scott Peterson's WSJ article, "Regulator Moves on Trading," describes how "runaway trading algorithms" wreak market havoc. He noted that a computer glitch caused Knight Capital Group Inc. to lose $461 M after faulty trading software caused a mistaken $7B buy in stocks in an hour of trading. Federal commodity regulators want to rein in high-speed training but are not sure of the consequences of more regulation. These regulators believe rules should push a large chunk of derivative trades onto electronic platforms. In another WSJ article co-authored by Scott Peterson, "Nasdaq in Fresh Market Failure," the authors report a technical glitch knocked Nasdaq trading out for 3 hours and paralyzed trading for "a broad swath of the market." According to the authors, this meltdown highlighted the fragility of electronic markets. Electronic markets are here to stay, but it is apparent the policymakers and private players are groping to offset machine-made volatility but haven't found solid answers yet.

Old market-based methods of incenting traders and top executives to act more like owners blew up in everyone's face, especially with the growth of online trading. In the early 1970s, a big issue was how to give top executives incentives to make them act like entrepreneurs. The answer was stock option bonuses. If the business did well, the stock option would rise in value. In the cyber world, huge financial institutions developed to cater to multinational corporations and sophisticated international investors. The problems with stock options became magnified in this environment of financial giants. Executive pay was also linked to size of organization, which incents poor managerial behavior. For example, hedge fund fees encourage growth in asset base at the expense of fund performance.

In practice, stock option bonuses led to an excessive focus on short-term gain because of benefits to agents (corporate executives), not to stockholders (principals). The top executives had little skin in the game. They didn't have to put up money to take risks. They would gain, however, if their bets paid off.

Receiving stock options encouraged risk taking by top management because those bets are with other people's money, the stockholders, and the lenders. A top executive often receives a big payoff even when fired, the so-called golden parachute. In effect, stock option compensation is a prime example of encouraging inappropriate risk taking – losses limited by the value of options. It is the equivalent of paying a top executive to churn out short-term profits even at the expense of the firm's long-term prospects. Joseph Stiglitz calls it a paying for piece work, a failed and discontinued practice except with upper management.[18]

The worldwide cyber market for financial securities leveraged these bets into $billion-dollar gambles. At the same time, internal controls had not caught up with the rapidly changing market for new types of securities and trading patterns. At Lehman and elsewhere, one side of a company didn't know what the other was doing – bond traders sell bonds, while other parts of the company bet against the holders of the bonds. This happened at Goldman Sachs, for example. AIG's top management claimed it did not know the risks they were shouldering in the CDS market.

Financial institutions became highly leveraged and huge as they vied to become financial supermarkets and boutiques all under the same roof. Then they bet big on developing new products and entering new markets without adequate controls. Management controls are not up to the task of protecting society from its own lightning-fast excessive reactions to events. Trust, the keystone for a well-functioning market, depreciates in milliseconds when a market threat is perceived. A critical issue is whether huge institutions are efficient or whether they are enormous because of mistaken strategy supported by expectations of government bailouts.

All of these misguided incentives and irrational passions became aligned in the recent financial bubble. A mistaken axiom of competition is that removing trading frictions improves the market because it drives transaction costs down. Now consider the effects of software-driven trading on financial markets. In stretches, cyber arbitragers did lower transaction costs, but at what cost? Remember the sudden drops in stock prices that are unexplainable except that they were produced by trading algorithms that somehow aligned into a rapid selloff of stocks.

Frank Knight, a notable economist who authored a book on risk and uncertainty in 1917, had much to say that could help the economics profession rethink their models. He recognized that economics is both an art and a science. For it to operate like other scientific fields, the subjects being tested

---

[18] Stiglitz, J.E. (2010) Freefall. W.W. Norton, N.Y. p. 151.

for behavioral or physical reactions must have a core stability that can be tested in isolation. An example may be a crop yield or the meat yield under a set of controlled conditions that are measurable such as soil conditions or feedstock. Economics begins to resemble more of an art when tight experiments are not feasible, which is for most economic phenomenon. Here statistics come into play.

From his perspective, the economics profession was and still is infatuated with statistical modeling. He and many future economists recognized its limitations. But many economists still believed that clever modeling would overcome their flaws. What are these flaws? Statistics works well when historical data are a reliable guide to the future. This is true of the height and weight of animals in the wild. It is also true of human life expectancy and morbidity after adjusting for improvements in medicine and cleanliness. Statistical models generally fail when they involve predicting consumer behavior or technological change. In both cases, history is not a reliable guide to the future. A simple historical example should prove the case. After many years of experts debating regulatory reform for communications networks, the government passed the 1996 Telecommunications Act. It had one line that referred to the Internet. Could you have predicted 10 years ago the trendy products, services, websites, apps, and platforms that people flock to now?

Another problem with using statistical analysis is to predict individual behavior as opposed to aggregate behavior. An insurance company can predict reliably what percent of people aged 75 will die in a year. The prediction falls off dramatically if the insurance company tries to predict if a particular person will die. As you will see, during the period leading up to the Great Recession, participants in financial markets were trying to predict if an individual company or a package of mortgages would fail.

A third important problem with statistical modeling is that there is a herding instinct among modelers. When a new technique appears, there is a rush to use it because it opens new possibilities for modeling. This happened in the 1980s with new techniques that modeled yes/no categories – the probability that someone will default on a loan. This type of technique flocking led to similar risk assessments across the financial industry. If the models are faulty, which they are, they introduce a systematic myopia into financial analysis that could lead to panic when they fail.

Statistical modeling may help decision-making to some extent because people need to anticipate change, but it is far from a cure all. These econometric models also do not align well with much of microeconomic theory – the theory of individual demanders and suppliers. The basic theoretical microeconomics model rests on the assumption that everyone has perfect information, which means you do not need statistics to understand trading behavior. Economists justify the perfect information assumption because they want to use the simplest model to predict market outcomes. A classic prediction is that when the price of a good rises, people will cut back their demand for it. This prediction makes sense for many trades, but there are many where it does not. For example, during a housing bubble, when people see the prices of houses rising rapidly, they may decide to buy before they are priced out of the market. When a company offers to pay a very high interest rate to attract funds, it may do the opposite. It may be a signal that the firm is in trouble.

Charles Kindleberger added texture to Knight's realistic descriptions of how markets operate.[19]Kindleberger said rational behavior is the basis of economic science, but what do we mean by it? Is it simply consistent behavior based on facts known by the decision-maker? Using this definition, is it irrational to buy a house when prices are rising because of speculation by other purchasers?

Another assumption made by economists is that the costs of transactions are zero. This assumption together with perfect information implies no need for firms to exist. If you want to produce something, you can organize production on the spot. But firms do exist because of the costs of organizing and managing production. And are zero transaction costs for trading even healthy in a digital world? It could stimulate a panic because bad news spreads rapidly and traders need to respond rapidly to survive.

The standard competitive model found in textbooks predicts that profits will disappear because excess profits encourage firms to enter the market, which drives down prices and profits. The opposite is true if an industry has negative returns. Firms will exit the industry causing prices and profits to rise. Only monopoly power is the basis for persistent profits. A powerful firm raises prices competitive levels by cutting back production.

Profits are unlikely to exist in a static world unless a monopoly has control of an industry. Economic theory assumes no technological change and perfect foresight. One justification for these simplifications was that it allowed economists to focus on how markets allocate resources through the pricing mechanism. Another reason is that technological change is often a surprise that cannot be predicted from historical data. The inability to deal with predicting under what circumstances technological change will occur leaves economists silent about the future dynamics of the economy because technological change reshapes old markets and opens new ones in ways that are not predictable using historical data.

---

[19] See Kindleberger and Aliber, Chapter 1, pp. 1–23.

Knight makes the case that profits are the payoff for business success in uncertain markets where behavioral and technological changes are hard to gauge. This type of probabilistic outcome is not insurable because business mortality rates that are particular to companies in new industries are too difficult to measure. Then the question becomes, what is a fair profit? Answer: it depends on circumstances. If the profit is simply because one company beating others to the market and gains patent protection, is this fair? Should financing contribute to profits, or should it be the underlying business alone? In recent decades, top management compensation packages have skyrocketed, while the income of mid-level workers is stagnant. Is that fair? This is called the principal/agent problem. Top management may be looking out for themselves instead of the interests of stockholders and other employees.

Policymakers rely on economic theory to shape markets and stabilize the economy. To the extent that economic models are faulty, it leads to ineffective and sometimes counterproductive government policies. There are claims that the government caused the real estate bubble leading to the Great Recession by pegging market interest rates too low and made homebuying too lax. These policies encouraged speculative real estate spending that was not sustainable. There is even debate about which economic theory worked to lessen the economic downturn. The monetarists claim that stabilizing financial markets did the job. The Keynesians point to government deficit spending as the effective policy.

Besides the goal of improving economic performance, policymakers have to consider which segments of the population gain from a policy and which potentially lose. During the Great Recession, the debate was over Wall Street being bailed out at the expense of Main Street. Surely, the immediate effects of the bailout could be quantified. But predictive power falls off rapidly as the planning horizon lengthens. Did the bailout of major financial institutions make them dependent on government for help in a crisis, or were they once burned, twice shy about future risky financial practices?

The principal/agent problem applies to government as well as big corporations, and so too is the bad effects of monopoly power when used to exclude competition or different voices. Policymakers have relied on political power for personal gain and prestige. Government bureaucrats have an interest in building their own empires. Will the financial crisis justify onerous financial regulations?

Most of the discussion so far is on economic theory and policy in isolation. I have followed Daniel Bell's view of America's civilization as being comprised of three sectors with different aims and time horizons: techno-economic, cultural, and polity. I claimed libertarians stress the techno-economic, conservatives, the cultural, and liberals, the polity. I want to show that a broader view of social problems is necessary. For example, digital transactions are impersonal; expanding markets uproot family members and weaken community. Government support programs can lead to overreliance on government help, whether it is a bank bailout of a welfare program.

That brings me to the art of economics and government policymaking. An artist learns techniques used by different schools. This allows an artist to adopt and adapt techniques from different schools to produce an arresting design or narrative. In addition, a great work of art requires inspiration. It is the basis for a good business deal and good government policy. A businessperson or policymaker needs to pick out the important elements of the environment to develop a picture and narrative of how society is changing. Good decision-making requires an artist's touch. The artistry needs to fit the times. Sometimes techno-economic issues are at center stage, sometimes, cultural or political. Each of America's ideologies has a somewhat different perspective that can work together to produce a kaleidoscope of approaches for solving pressing social problems.

7.9   Ideological Perspectives Need to Change

Returning to my theme, my basic premise is that the Coding Revolution created new, huge, but sometimes very fragile markets that could break down in ways that are almost impossible to predict. Yet, the only prescription libertarians have is that markets are decentralized and can absorb unexpected shocks. Eventually, rules of behavior will emerge to make the market more stable. Unfortunately, the rules of the game are very hard to set internationally. Worse yet, the products keep changing and will change in unexpected ways. Conservatives rely on a culture of professionalism to prevent antisocial behavior. But how do you get investors to look at the long-term, at fundamentals, and bear shame and financial loss for self-serving, hurtful actions? Are claw backs enough? Conservatives are hard pressed to describe how this professionalism would develop in a fast-pace anonymous market. The very dynamics of the new cyber marketplaces suggests that liberals do not have a compelling strategy for government oversight that will prevent future crises that very likely will bunch up. Pick any rule, say the size of the firm regulated, once the limit is announced, firms will split into smaller units and work as pieces of a mini network, all supposedly disconnected but in practice acting as a unit.

As recently as 2007, before the collapse, all three ideologies actually supported a light regulatory touch. Both the Clinton and Bush administrations actively disassembled financial regulations. Both administrations wanted

America's financial institutions to be free to compete against their international rivals. Besides, both administrations believed the private sector was developing securities to insure against financial failure, and the government had an effective arsenal of weapons to keep the economy on course in case the private sector faltered. I have built a case to suggest technological change is making these markets more susceptible to panics and traditional regulations and standard methods of international cooperation are probably not up to the challenge of restoring stability.

Perhaps everyone has been beguiled by a false belief that very efficient markets with low transaction costs are a desirable ideal. The record suggests they produce market instability. Prices can gyrate; markets can freeze. Low margin operations push buyers and sellers to leverage themselves with debt to boost profitability. In good times this works. In a downturn, high leverage creates seller panics.

Traders and policymakers have not come to grips with the reality that social behavior can become irrational, and no one – academics, bureaucrats, or lawmakers – knows how to keep behavior predictable enough and allow markets to function effectively and at the same time allow enough room for creativity. For example, policymakers want to split traditional banking from investment banking. But how can you do this in a market where financial products keep morphing, where, for example, a credit card replaces money as the medium of exchange? Should credit card companies be considered banks?

Effective policies both within corporations and government will depend on accurate signaling and feedback mechanisms. Perhaps a trigger to government intervention should have been the rapid rise in asset prices as opposed to monitoring traditional measures of inflation such as the consumer price index. Perhaps top management needs to have much stronger controls on the size of bets and betting patterns after a trader has lost money. The list could go on and on.

But even here, the issue is not clear-cut. The spectacular rise of online (over-the-top) competitors such as Netflix, Amazon, and Google are a surprise. I will examine them in more detail in the next chapter. For now, it is enough to say they are already vertically integrated. They are leaders in programming and distribution that allows them direct contact with customers (AT&T Pretrial Brief, p. 1 and p. 3). How are they affecting economic performance, cultural cohesion, and political action?

Another major issue is that online platforms allow traders to become anonymous. To what extent is this a risk to a well-functioning marketplace? A basic premise of an ongoing market is that building trust depends on knowing the people one trades with or having an intermediary such as a bank that keeps records and assures that transactions are completed and recorded properly.

Other types of markets depend on anonymity to remain untraceable. The market for illegal goods is an example, but so is the market for smuggling news, people, and assets out of oppressive nations that suppress economic and more basic individual freedom. The Digital Age has produced two platforms that greatly expand the power to remain anonymous: the Dark Web and blockchain technology.

The clear web is an online site indexed by search engines such as Google. Sitting below the clear web is a Deep Web that is not indexed for a variety of reasons. One reason is that public access is blocked legitimately. Corporate proprietary data and public health records fall into this category. In the depths of the Deep Web is the Dark Web, a network of sites concealed from the public sometimes for legitimate reasons and sometimes to deal in illegal activities. Special search engines both anonymize the sender and anonymize the transmission path of a query. In the Dark Web, people can buy illegal drugs, stolen credit cards and IDs, false IDs, false passports, counterfeit money, money laundering, illicit drugs, guns, and malware to penetrate or bring down legitimate websites – and other marketable illegal activities.

Bitcoin is the most famous online money used to trade anonymously, but there are others. They all use blockchain technology. It is similar to a database. It records transactions in time-stamped blocks that are distributed to everyone using a particular service. Each person using the service has an anonymized passkey similar to a password. No one else knows it. There are no intermediaries. The block chain database verifies that a legitimate passkey was used to trade a particular product. In effect, trust is embedded in the system, not in the person. Or is it as secure as the descriptions of blockchains suggest? Griffin and Shams suggest that a supposedly currency-backed token, "Tether," was associated with manipulating the price of Bitcoins. In other words, no central bank controls currency exchange.

Absorbing the lessons from cyberspace capitalism and turning those into realistic story lines that academics can later turn into equations have only just begun. As with any new frontier, it is a marketplace with many unknown dangers but alluring, nonetheless. We have to become like a new member of Alcoholic Anonymous and fess up to how much we don't know about our own knowledge and behavior and those of others.

8

Cyberspace Capitalism Part 2: The Rise of Platforms and Antitrust Policies

Abstract Large platforms are replacing traditional marketplaces. Microsoft, Amazon, Apple, Google, and Facebook are the object of extensive research and antitrust policy proceedings. Three basic questions frame the investigation in this chapter: (1) Why have they maintained for decades such a large presence in the online economy? (2) Are they shaping markets in ways that exploit customers and competitors? (3) Are they shaping politics to fit their own needs? This chapter gives an overview of how the online economy works and highlights the failures of government policy caused by a lack of understanding of its underlying technology.

8.1 Introduction

So far, I have defined cyberspace capitalism as an online economy comprised of companies communicating through broadband networks. In the previous chapter, I highlighted offshoring, and the 2008 financial meltdown affected the bricks-and-mortar economy. The message is that cyberspace capitalism is likely reducing the cost of goods and services at the expense of making markets more volatile and more vulnerable to global competition.

Here the focus shifts to the functioning of the online economy itself. The main focus is on the rise of online platforms like Amazon and Google. The basic issues are whether they have market power, if so, have they abused it,

179
V. Glass, *Humanizing the Digital Economy*, https://doi.org/10.1007/978-3-031-37507-1_8

and if so, how should government intervene to fix the problem.[1] The next chapter will tackle a third feature of the online economy: digital exposure, the loss of privacy, and media bias from a user's perspective.

Platforms like other big corporations have an ambiguous image in the American imagination and public policy. Giants like AT&T, Standard Oil, U.S. Steel, General Motors, and DuPont were symbols of American power before the digital revolution. The auto companies, in particular, were not only a symbol of, but also major contributors to, America's ability to mass produce trucks and tanks during World War II. They gave America a decisive logistical advantage over Nazi Germany, which relied much more heavily on skilled workers to produce war machines.[2]

Yet, Americans also have been (and continue to be) fearful that large corporations could be a menace to society by controlling essential services and government policy. Progressives called for government to rein in huge corporations as early as the late nineteenth century. The Sherman Act was the first legislative act. It prohibited corporations from forming business trusts where members worked together to boost profits.[3] In response to the Sherman Act, there was an increase in mergers in order to evade the legal prohibition on coordinated activity. The government responded by passing the Clayton Act in 1914 to prohibit unfair business practices that would hurt the public, including prohibiting mergers that may substantially lessen competition or tend to create a monopoly.[4]

A parallel strategy to tame corporate behavior was to regulate companies considered to be natural monopolies. AT&T, for example, agreed to federal regulation in exchange for a monopoly on telephone service. Many academic articles have critiqued the government's effectiveness in "domesticating" big business. To this day, there is no clearcut conclusion.

In the early twentieth century, the rule of reason was the basic method for identifying anticompetitive behavior. Using the reasonability test, price fixing, and secret price agreements among competitors was harmful, while price fixing of retail prices was acceptable as a marketing tool if the industry seemed competitive. This "I know it when I see it" approach did not set clear rules of

---

[1] Parts of the introduction and the following sections – Pricing and Product Differences, Cultural and Structural Differences, Edge and Applications Origins, and Suggestions – are largely taken verbatim from Victor Glass and Timothy Tardiff (2023) Analyzing Competition in the Online Economy. Antitrust Bulletin. Volume 68, Issue 2. Please refer to it for more details.

[2] YouTube (2022) How the Americans Outproduced Everyone Else in WW2 War Factories. Timeline. https://www.youtube.com/watch?v=wp3wQhDpQG8. Accessed 25 August 2022.

[3] In particular, Section 1 prohibits conspiracies, the primary example being price fixing, and Section 2 prohibits anticompetitive monopolization or attempts to monopolize.

[4] Clayton Act, Section 7 (15 U.S.C.).

competitive behavior because people see the same event differently. In the 1960s, the push was to make the rule of reason more precise by tying it to the economic theory of imperfect competition. At first, the focus was on maintaining a competitive marketplace by prohibiting business practices that impeded new firms from creating, enhancing, and extending markets. Basically, this translated into protecting small businesses. In the 1970s and 1980s, the focus changed to protecting consumers. The assumption was that competition, whether from small or large companies, lowered prices, increased supply, and pushed competitors to innovate in order to survive (Viscusi, Harrington, and Sappington, p. 96).

Setting clear rules that identified impermissible market behavior fell to the Federal Trade Commission and Department of Justice. They issued guideline papers that described market practices that would cause them to file an antitrust lawsuit. An examination of the guidelines shows they focused on identifying specific product lines and supply chains where firms could potentially exert harmful market power. Two recent examples illustrate when the government would intervene. The government attempted to block the merger of U.S. Sugar Corporation and Imperial Sugar, two companies offering similar products. The lawsuit failed.[5]

Another, much more publicized, antitrust suit that failed was against the merger of AT&T and Time Warner. The government feared that AT&T would control content and distribution of content, which would hurt competition in the cable TV business. The merger went through, and it was a financial disaster for AT&T.[6]

Repeated failures raised concerns that the consumer welfare standard, until recently, enjoyed a broad consensus for over half a century;[7] politicians on both sides of the aisle now believed this approach has led to underenforcement of antitrust laws – insufficient prohibition of anticompetitive behavior and mergers. There is great concern now on the emergence of huge platforms such as Amazon, Apple, Google, Facebook, and Microsoft because they appear

---

[5] Polk, D. (2022) Three recent merger enforcement decisions signal challenges for US antitrust agencies. https://www.davispolk.com/insights/client-update/three-recent-merger-enforcement-decisions-signal-challenges-us-antitrust. Accessed 30 April 2023.

[6] Stewart, JB. (2022) Was This $100 Billion Deal the Worst Merger Ever? New York Times. https://www.nytimes.com/2022/11/19/business/media/att-time-warner-deal.html. Accessed 30 April 2023. Or, Glass, V. (2022) *Culture Clash and the Failure of the AT&T/Time Warner Merger*, Rutgers Business Review. Vol. 6, No. 3, pp. 350–365.

[7] See, for example, Hovenkamp, H. Antitrust in 2018: The Meaning of Consumer Welfare Now. Wharton Public Policy Initiative Issue Briefs. P. 58. https://repository.upenn.edu/pennwhartonppi/58. Accessed 30 April 2023. In evaluating actual or potential (e.g., a proposed merger) alleged anticompetitive actions, the consumer welfare standard analyzes whether the action reduces output and/or increases prices (broadly defined), with the emphasis on the latter.

to dominate the online economy.[8] Like old wine in new bottles, the public's reaction is both heady and fearful. American companies dominate the world's online economy but are they safe? No one knows for sure, but many people have strong opinions.

Two basic questions have troubled economists: Why have the platforms grown so large, and why do they have such staying power?

The ongoing disagreements among economists and lawyers highlight that the use of economic theory to identify anticompetitive behavior in the online economy is problematic because the workings of the online economy are not well understood by economists. There have been some insights on the definition and operations of platforms of different sizes and with different objectives. But the identification of data clustering and flows related to product clustering and information production needs a great deal of investigation. The relationships between data, information, and innovation are weakly understood. The influence of corporate cultural factors on mergers is not well understood. Sometimes a merger can encourage anticompetitive behavior, sometimes innovation. Sometimes it can produce cultural clashes within an organization. The cultural issue becomes even more complex when a merger promotes both innovation and the abuse of market power.

The rest of the chapter summarizes the sources of difficulty facing policy-makers. To understand the issues, I look at the online economy from an economist's perspective and then from an engineer's perspective. Afterward is a brief history of the online economy's evolution followed by a discussion of policy challenges.

8.2   The Economist's Perspective

Typically, an economist examines the structure of a market, the behavior of the participants, and the overall performance of the market. Here I look at the differences between the bricks-and-mortar economy and the online economy.

---

[8] That the existence of such large firms has resulted in historically high levels of industry concentration is a controversial issue. For instance, Portuese reports that industry concentration barely changed between 2002 and 2017. Portuese, A. (2022) Five False Claims Underscore the Case Against the Senate's Leading Antitrust Bills. Information Technology & Innovation Foundation. https://itif.org/publications/2022/04/04/five-false-claims-underscore-case-against-senate-antitrust-bills/. Accessed 30 April 2023. Further, even if concentration has increased, prices could be lower as a result of more efficient firms with scale and scope economies serving greater proportions of consumers. Crandall, RW. and Hazlett, TW (2022). Antitrust in a Digital Era: A Skeptical Perspective. Center for the Study of the Administrative State. George Mason University. Working Paper 22–19. https://administrativestate.gmu.edu/wp-content/uploads/2022/10/Crandall_Hazlett_22-19.pdf. Accessed 30 April 2023.

8.2.1 Product/Pricing Differences

The online economy is different than the bricks-and-mortar economy because many products are fluid – they are rearrangements of bit streams. In this milieu, the big payoffs are in introducing new services and opening new markets that can yield temporarily large profits. A big tech company will try to identify complementary products that will draw customers to its platform. It may set up gateways and rules to shape its internal markets to exact rents from its users. Data processed into useful information is the key competitive weapon to gain a competitive advantage and a major source of revenue from advertising and preferencing products.

Online pricing strategies do not conform to traditional economic theory of the firm. Many services are "free" in exchange for data that can be marketed. When prices are charged, they are sometimes levied on one side of the market. An example is free credit cards to consumers with vendors paying the credit card charge when it accepts credit card payment from its customers. Therefore, price/cost margins on one side of the market are a deceptive measure of market power. Traditional economics suggests that a company with market power would have higher margins than a similar firm with a similar cost structure in a competitive market. Extremely low or negative profit margins on the "free" side of a transaction may be mistaken for predatory pricing. Recent research on two-sided markets explains this pricing strategy by pointing out the price levels on each side of the market depend on the price sensitivity of demand for a particular product. In the case of credit cards, the customer for them is very sensitive to credit card fees; therefore, the credit card companies bury their charges in the price of goods sold.

8.2.2 Cultural Differences/Structural Differences

Superficially, the online and bricks-and-mortar economies look alike. Both economies include firms that deal directly with their own customers and platforms, such as newspapers, that connect users with advertisers. Fundamentally, both facilitate the interaction between suppliers and demanders of products and services. Differences are also readily apparent starting with organizational form and culture.

The bricks-and-mortar economy that economists have analyzed for decades is populated by firms operating within supply chains. A firm is the equivalent of a closed network in which a firm's capabilities are managed within the organization to produce a specific type of product or a related group of products.

A firm's internal culture evolves over time in order to limit transaction costs. Firms are part of a supply chain based on contractual relations to produce a final product through stages of production managed by different firm types, perhaps with different cultures. For instance, upstream companies that produce raw materials often develop cultures that differ from those of retail firms. Conglomerates that offer a range of dissimilar products sometimes form where a staff function, such as managing finances, can reduce costs while allowing each product line to operate independently.

Online platforms, over which many types of buyers and sellers transact, are multisided markets. These platforms are relatively open organizations with a core expertise managed internally, which encourage many types of outside product and service suppliers to use the platform. Sometimes, these agents have contractual relations with the platform owner, sometimes not. Most agents are known as complementors because they augment the services or performance of the platform. Sometimes, they emerge as competitive threats such as when Netscape used Microsoft's platform to launch its browser, which could divert business from Microsoft. In order to achieve coordination of complementors and limit what it considers abuse, the platform owner sets rules for connecting agents and monitor performance by collecting transaction data. The rules defined by a platform to control its ecosystem can foreclose opportunities to innovators when, for example, a platform with a large presence in a particular market has exclusive agreements with original equipment manufacturers that effectively block new browsers and operating systems from entering its ecosystem.

The online economy is also altering the physical characteristics of the overall economy and the services offered to the public. End user devices such as smartphones and laptops and broadband networks connect traders, which reduce the need for physical wholesale and retail outlets for displaying and stocking products. Broadband transmission eliminates travel costs to search for products and services. Low-cost broadband connections extend market reach for products and services from local to global in some cases.

At first glance, lower transmission and transaction costs should favor ease of entry by small firms. Other influences, such as ensuring product reliability and protecting personal information, may offset low entry costs. For instance, large platforms like Amazon assure customers that they will monitor platform seller behavior and have high standards of security for personal information. In comparison, small, anonymous online sellers that sell directly to customers could be risky propositions. As a result, the virtual nature of the online economy can favor large, established platforms that can offer a wide variety of services to many types of buyers and sellers – something like virtual shopping malls or virtual social event locations.

Many online products are digital by nature. They are combinations of data bits instead of raw materials, which can substantially shorten product life cycles. For instance, 500 h of video is uploaded per minute to YouTube.[9] Because of short product life cycles, platform competition often focuses on new markets instead of deepening penetration in existing markets. Large platforms are also likely to emerge because digital content is reproducible without cost, which gives a large platform a cost advantage if there are upfront costs of introducing a new product. Algorithms that reduce search costs encourage global market penetration. Peer review has added customers to the marketing process, which in the past was virtually absent in the bricks-and-mortar economy. Widespread tracking of enormous data flows has allowed online platforms to improve the efficiency of targeted marketing but also raise privacy and data security issues.

Privacy and security become important concerns because online platforms can profile accurately users of their services. For instance, there has been concern that Amazon could charge uncompetitively high prices to agents selling products and services on its platform or purchase new companies at an uncompetitively low prices because of insider information.[10] This will also be discussed later in the chapter.

Much of antitrust policy focuses on whether a company has the power to set prices above competitive levels for inputs and outputs. In the online economy, inputs are mainly software and data instead of physical raw material or products, and many outputs are associated with search and digital content, which are often free. Advertising becomes a major source of revenue in the online economy in addition to or even perhaps instead of the sales price of commodities. As a result, many services can be offered at very low (even free) prices, which is not a feature of traditional markets.[11]

Because of the enormous amount of data flows into platforms from browsers, search engines, and platform trading, large online platforms can profile potential customers accurately to advertisers. This informational advantage

---

[9] OBERLO, *10 YouTube Statistics*, https://www.oberlo.com/blog/youtube-statistics#:~:text=500%20hours%20of%20video%20are,uploaded%20every%20day%20to%20YouTube. Accessed 30 April 2023.

[10] [27]Lyons, K. (2021) Amazon charges sellers' fees that are high enough to offset losses from Prime, a new report says. The VERGE. https://www.theverge.com/2021/12/3/22813872/amazon-profit-small-business-fees-sellers-prime. Accessed 30 April 2023. Mitchell, S. (2021) Amazon's Toll Road. Institute for Local Self-Reliance. ILSR. https://ilsr.org/amazons-toll-road/. Accessed 30 April 2023.

[11] That is to say, consumers pay for a product with a combination of a monetary price and the cost of their attention to (or perhaps annoyance with) the ads. Brandenburger, A. and Nalebuff, B. (2021) Sell/Buy Bundling. Fall Antitrust Chronicle pp. 9–14.

has raised market power concerns for advertising and marketing. For instance, Google has been accused of biasing purchase searches to favor paid advertisers and charging advertisers uncompetitively high fees.

Despite some common features, not all online platforms are alike. Google and Facebook rely mainly on advertising as the sources of revenue. Apple mainly sells devices such as smartphones, as well as its own and third-party apps for those devices. Amazon specializes mainly in being an online shopping mall. Platforms have not always been successful competing for the core services of other platforms. For instance, Google failed to enter the social media market with Google +.[12] More examples are discussed below.

On the other hand, once Amazon pioneered cloud computing, Google and Microsoft jumped in to compete and did so successfully, perhaps because all major platforms have huge server farms to store and process data. Despite these differences, four common basic supply-side elements are sources of online business success: data, software, hardware, and broadband networks. Demand side specialization such as search or online trading also strongly influences success. Whether these common elements also facilitate potentially anticompetitive and perhaps antisocial behavior is an important and challenging consideration in determining whether new competition policies are needed.

Data has been viewed as an essential competitive input. To determine whether and when it is raises a number of issues. First, data is not a uniform commodity. Translating data points into alphabetic letters illustrates the point. The data points have value in context. Letters can be combined into a huge variety of words, and words into a huge variety of sentences, and sentences into paragraphs, and paragraphs into story lines with some storylines that are newsworthy and immediate, and others targeted for libraries. Second, data's value differs depending on the audience (industry) and its durability. Third, clusters of data like research papers have value because they may identify new products and services. A company that collects and processes data is like a researcher that sometimes wastes time and resources looking for the kernel of inspiration. This could justify losing money on many products to find the data that will unlock a new, profitable market.

A second consideration is that large platforms monetize data differently. Apple mainly generates revenue from hardware and apps. Google and Facebook generate the bulk of their revenue from advertising. Google runs an auction where winners pay Google for priority placement in searches.

---

[12] Fox, C. (2019) Google shuts failed social network Google+. BBC News. https://www.bbc.com/news/technology-47771927. Accessed 30 April 2023.

Similarly, Facebook relies on digital display ads for most of its revenue. Amazon, by contrast, uses data to improve product searches on its website.

None of these platforms claim to sell data, but they offer data to customers looking to advertise. Google offers advertisers data to encourage them to bid for search placement and helps companies bid more effectively. Amazon shares data with co-brands such as Starbucks, OfficeMax, Verizon Wireless, T-Mobile, and Sprint.[13]

Third, large platforms may face conflicting regulations, e.g., mandates to maintain customer privacy and data security, but at the same time open the flow of data to potential competitors. Facebook and Apple have imposed privacy screens that could be interpreted as erecting barriers to competition.

A fourth issue is the extent of overlap in their data collection, especially in real time. Large platforms and broadband carriers all have access to similar data. Under what unique circumstances do data translate into market power under multihoming of data?

8.3　The Engineer's Perspective

From an engineering perspective, the online economy has three basic components: edge equipment that connect to a network, a transmission network, and services provided over the network. I begin with a description of the Internet (the transmission network) followed by the equipment that is attached to it and the platforms that offer applications used in the online economy.

8.3.1　Network

The Internet operates using a technological layering of functions strategy. Table 8.1 summarizes in a matrix a simplified view of the Internet's physical design and services based on the open system interconnection model of the Internet. The columns identify three basic service categories: content and search services, data as a service, and desired transmission functionality. The rows define the Internet's transmission layering (Kurose and Ross 2017) and

---

[13] Martisiute, L. (2020) Does Amazon Sell Your Personal Information? DeleteMe. https://joindeleteme.com/blog/does-amazon-sell-your-personal-information/. Accessed 30 April 2023.

Table 8.1 The matrix approach's view of the online economy

Online services		Digital content and search as services	Data as a service	Edge and network equipment functionalities as services including quality of service (QoS), reliability, privacy, and security
O	Application layer	Email, web, file transfer, streaming multimedia, Internet telephony	Digital profiles based on web browsing, purchases, emails, use of apps such as driving directions	Smartphone, laptop, and PC settings
S	Transport layer	Best effort transmission protocols (UDP and TCP) and addresses (IP)	Data packet origin and destination, deep packet inspection of content	Congestion management, routing
Class of service (not yet available) to distinguish time-sensitive streams from those that are not
MPLS and metro ethernet for virtual private lines and QoS
Border Gateway and Authentication Controls security and other management services
I	Network layer	Physical connection using physical address known as MAC addresses	Routing information	Gateways or bridge devices that connect networks
Physical private line services. Guarantees may include no jitter, no congestion, few dropped packets
	Server farm functionalities	Content delivery networks that store, for example, video content close to customers	Cloud data processing centers to enable cloud computing APIs for applications development	Content delivery networks improve QoS and customer experience. Gateway controllers that store information to offer authentication, security, and other management services

Taken from Glass, V. (2019). The Net Neutrality Debate is Outdated: Time for a Wider View, Review of Network Economics, De Gruyter, vol. 18(4), pp. 243–276 physical network elements associated with content delivery networks (CDNs) and cloud computing.[14]

Even this complicated table is still a narrow snapshot of the current online economy. Each layer is morphing, sometimes in unpredictable ways. For instance, the next-generation broadband network will embed much more intelligence than previous versions. The original Internet was a dumb network. It simply shipped packets of data from an origin point to a final destination. The packets themselves contained the shipping information. The network simply reads the forwarding address and routed it to its destination.

AT&T and other internet service providers (ISPs) are now deploying software defined network (SDN) programming for transmission. This software can coordinate and control traffic at all layers of the Internet simultaneously. With a few keystrokes, an ISP can build virtual storage machines, virtual pathways, and virtual security and privacy controls.

This flexibility will make it easier for ISPs to offer bundled services that include fast lanes and special pricing for favored services as T-Mobile did even when the FCC's 2015 Order prohibited such arrangements.[15] Moreover, SDN will give landline and wireless carriers the ability to compete with other networks such as electric utility networks to connect smart devices, smart grids, and smart cities and eventually develop datasets that will allow them to compete with dominant application-layer platforms. The enormous potential databases that 5G will connect to autonomous vehicles is an example. Excluding edge devices such as smartphones from the net neutrality debate[16] no longer seems reasonable because they are gateways to the Internet and offer proprietary suites of services.

Holding to the Table 8.1 view seen as a simplification of the online economy's characteristics, it still highlights the complexity of the regulatory challenge. Lehr et al. point out that key Internet functionalities can span several network layers. For instance, regarding the ability to call 911 in an emergency,

---

[14] The table does not include access to utility poles and rights of way that are critical for broadband competition. It also does not distinguish explicitly between landline and wireless networks and open and closed platforms.

[15] Federal Communications Commission (2015) *In the Matter of Protecting and Promoting the Open Internet*, GN Docket No. 14–28 Report and Order on Remand, Declaratory Ruling, and Order Adopted: February 26, 2015. Released: March 12, 2015, file:///C:/Users/vglass.BUSINESS/Downloads/FCC-15-24A1%20(2).pdf. Accessed 30 April 2023.

[16] Federal Communications Commission (2010) In the Matter of Preserving the Open Internet Broadband Industry. *Practices,* GN Docket No. 09–191; WC Docket No. 07–52 Report and Order. Adopted: December 21, 2010. Released: December 23, 2010, p. 50

how can that need be fulfilled? A user might use a traditional landline phone, or a cell phone, or perhaps an app in the not-too-distant future.[17]

Some security problems may arise at one layer but only be detectable or correctable at higher layers. For instance, attacks on the inter-domain routing protocols of the Internet can cause packets to be misdelivered. The best approach to detection is to provide tools to the communicating end-nodes so that they can independently confirm they are talking to the correct counterparts. Therefore, it may take cross-layer coordination.[18] It also highlights that cross-layer effects also make it more difficult to identify the source of a network failure or security breach.

The application layer has evolved into a series of distinct market categories. BEREC (2016) distinguishes among over-the-top (OTT) service platforms that may point to unequal regulatory treatment, which regulators should correct. There are services that are close substitutes for telco voice service such as voice over Internet protocol (VoIP). Others are similar but not identical such as WhatsApp, an instant messaging service, and other over the top services that do not compete with an ISP's core services. In the "other" category is a wide variety of services including entertainment, social networking, and web browsing.[19]

8.3.2   Edge and Applications

Returning to the platforms, which operate at the application layer, platforms like Microsoft, Google, and Apple developed operating system platforms (OSPs) that control communication and processing of edge devices such as PCs and laptops that plug into the broadband transmission network. For instance, the Windows OSP controls the hardware and software that run on it. An application such as a web browser that operates using an operating system can itself be a platform that operates at a higher layer than the operating system. According to PC Magazine:

> Web browsers accept third-party plug-ins, and the browser application becomes a platform to interface with. Any software can be defined as a platform if it

---

[17] Lehr, W. Clark, D. Bauer, S. and Claffy, KC (2019) *Regulation when platforms are layered*, p. 28 *TPRC47*, 2019, Research Conference on Communications, Information and Internet Policy.

Available at SSRN: https://ssrn.com/abstract=3427499 or https://doi.org/10.2139/ssrn.3427499. Accessed 30 April 2023.

[18] Id., p. 29.

[19] Peitz, M. and Valletti, T. (2015). *Reassessing competition concerns in electronic communications markets*, Telecommunications Policy 39(2015):896–912.

provides programming interfaces (APIs), which are a set of rules and codes that applications are written to interact with. Social media networks such as Facebook and Twitter provide APIs and are thus called "social media platforms.[20]

While an operating system can work without a browser, a browser cannot operate without an operating system. Once in place, a browser can be a complement or substitute for operating system features because the software libraries that produce an operating system can be used to develop a browser. For instance, Microsoft integrated its Windows operating system with its Internet Explorer browser.[21] Bundling software applications is a general feature of the digital economy, which makes defining a market difficult and, therefore, defining anticompetitive behavior.

The broadband transmission network of networks includes the hardware, transmission software, and protocols to ship data to the right destination and an applications layer – or the human to computer layer where interactions occur between callers and called and suppliers and demanders. The major service platforms generate revenues and profits at the application layer.[22]

The OECD defines three categories for online platforms that show the overlap between digital service and operating systems platforms. The first definition defines a service platform as "a digital service that facilitates interactions between two or more distinct but interdependent sets of users (whether firms or individuals) who interact through the service via the Internet."[23] The report then distinguishes a platform from a platform ecosystem, which has features of both engineering and service platforms:

[A] Platform is distinct from a digital ecosystem, which is a broader concept that can include online platforms. Digital ecosystems are combinations of interoperating applications, operating systems, platforms, business models and/or hardware, and not all components of the ecosystem must be owned by the same entity. In fact, a digital ecosystem may involve thousands of different businesses.[24]

---

[20] PC Magazine Encyclopedia Platform. https://www.pcmag.com/encyclopedia/term/platform. Accessed 30 April 2023.

[21] United States v. Microsoft Corporation (2001) 253 F.3d 34 (2001), https://www.law.berkeley.edu/files/US_v_Microsoft3.pdf. Accessed 30 April 2023.

[22] Imperva, *OSI Model*, https://www.imperva.com/learn/application-security/osi-model/#:~:text=OSI%20is%20a%20generic%2C%20protocol,to%20enable%20any%20data%20communication. Accessed 30 April 2023.

[23] OECD, *An Introduction to Online Platforms and their Role in the Digital Transformation,* (2019), https://read.oecd-ilibrary.org/science-and-technology/an-introduction-to-online-platforms-and-their-role-in-the-digital-transformation_53e5f593-en#page1. Accessed 30 April 2023.

[24] *Id.* at 224.

Data flows of different varieties link the ecosystem together. These ecosystems have varying degrees of openness toward competitors. For instance, the payment solution for digital ecosystems is separated behind closed gateways.[25]

Typically, platforms are the product of a modular programming strategy, with modules communicating through interfaces. These modules can be assembled to provide a variety of services, which can lead to economies of scope produced by technology. APIs are interfaces that connect outside agents with the platform. As described in greater detail in the next section, the openness of APIs has an effect on the ability of agents (complementors) to develop products and services for the platform.

8.4   The Evolution of the Online Economy: Operating Systems, Search Engines, and Cloud Computing

The Internet was barely mentioned in the 1996 Telecommunications Act. Amazon began selling books in 1994; Google incorporated in 1998; and Facebook was launched in 2004.[26] Those are the splashy, surprising changes in the online economy that remind everyone that predicting the course of the online economy is challenging, to say the least.

8.4.1   Origins

This section describes how competition in the online economy emerged before these events, how companies once dominant fell, how startups rose to dominance, and how incumbents reacted to their rise. This brief history review has three objectives: (1) to describe in Schumpeterian terms how the online economy evolves through a process of creative destruction,[27] (2) to examine the role of corporate culture in this process, and (3) to highlight recurring competitive (anticompetitive) strategies used by incumbents, which are especially instructive for antitrust policy.

The online economy has its origins in the digital revolution. Hardware has evolved from mainframe computers to personal computers (PC), to laptops,

---

[25] *Id.* at 22.

[26] First, H. (2022*) The Internet of Change: Foreword to the Symposium on the Google and Facebook Cases*, 67 Antitrust Bulletin. 3.

[27] Schumpeter, JA. (3rd ed. 1942). Capitalism, Socialism, and Democracy. Harper Torchbooks, NY. pp. 31–32.

to tablets, to mobile devices, to smart wearables. Apple, Tandy, Commodore, and Atari brought personal computing into the home and educational system in the 1970s. IBM sold mainframe services to commercial customers. Top management at IBM realized, however, that the PC market was growing quickly and perhaps would find a place in business offices but did not know its market potential. To avoid IBM's complex product development bureaucracy, the CEO, Frank Cary, set up a special task force in 1981 to produce an IBM PC.[28] This group rolled out its PC in August 1981. By 1984, IBM's PC was the market leader.[29]

IBM followed a modular approach to speed up the introduction of its PC. Instead of modifying its own in-house hardware and software, IBM outsourced production of its PCs.[30] The outsourcing included an operating system and a processor. Tiny Microsoft won the contract for the operating system and Intel won the processor contract. Soon afterward, Microsoft and Intel (often called Wintel) took control of the PC business and became corporate powerhouses.[31] In August 1983, the special PC unit within IBM was reassigned to a division within IBM. It was now ensnared in IBM's bureaucracy, a move from which it never recovered. The PC business was eventually sold to Lenovo in 2004.[32] An important takeaway from an economist's perspective is that the traditional supply chain for building products was replaced by a market for complementary components that plugged together to produce a product, in this case, a personal computer. Therefore, the component producers emerged as major players (with the potential for anticompetitive practices leading to antitrust investigations). In this case Microsoft and Intel, the component producers, teamed up to assume the leading position in the PC market.[33]

[28] Cortada, JW. (2021) How the IBM PC Won, then Lost, the Personal Computer Market. IEEE Spectrum. https://spectrum.ieee.org/how-the-ibm-pc-won-then-lost-the-personal-computer-market. Accessed 1 May 2023.

[29] Dufresne, S. (2017) The IBM PC that Broke IBM. https://hackaday.com/2017/12/11/the-ibm-pc-that-broke-ibm/. Accessed 1 May 2023.

[30] IBM (2017) The IBM PC's Debut. https://www.ibm.com/ibm/history/exhibits/pc25/pc25_intro.html. Accessed 1 May 2023.

[31] Tilley, A. (2017) The End of Wintel: How the Most Powerful Alliance in Tech History is Falling Apart. FORBES. https://www.forbes.com/sites/aarontilley/2017/03/10/microsoft-intel-divorce/?sh=13b68341285f. Accessed 1 May 2023.

[32] Dufresne, *supra* note 288.

[33] Casadeus-Masanell, R., Nalebuff, B., and Yoffie, D. (2008) Competing Complements. https://www.hbs.edu/ris/Publication Files/09-009.pdf. Accessed 1 May 2023.

8.4.2   Microsoft

Microsoft's operating system, Windows, gave it a substantial initial advantage in the market for software for PCs. Windows, like other operating systems, manages a PC's hardware, runs programs without conflicts, manages files, and provides security. Microsoft was vying for a new type of market – business workers without strong programming skills. The company introduced Microsoft Office in 1990, which included Word, Excel, and PowerPoint as an interoperable package of applications (apps).[34] Novell, which owned a competing word processing software package, WordPerfect, claimed that Microsoft made it difficult for WordPerfect to use the Windows API to link and sell its software on a PC that used the Windows operating system. Connection to the API is crucial because it allows apps to speak to each other and to other services.[35] APIs are contained in API gateways, which contain a set of common tasks that run across APIs.[36] Novell lost its case, but the idea that a company controls a major operating system continues. The same issue of limiting APIs to competitors was again considered in the Microsoft antitrust case.[37]

Operating systems are also components of products that complement or substitute for Windows-based PC applications. Besides Windows, the major operating systems include Apple iOS and Mac OS. Linux-based ones are available.[38] Mobile platforms such as Google and Apple have been accused of barring apps or copying apps.[39] The incentives to shape the market are there because Apple, for example, generates a large portion of its revenues from apps.

Large OSs also have long-term relationships with hardware producers, which explains why there are so few of them. This is not surprising because customers much prefer to use an industry standard OS to ensure file exchanges

---

[34] Leonhard, W. (2014) 25 Years of Microsoft Office Roadkill. INFOWORLD. In Pictures: 25 years of Microsoft Office roadkill - Slideshow - PC World Australia (idg.com.au). Accessed 1 May 2023.

[35] IBM Technology. API vs. SDK: What's the Difference? https://www.youtube.com/watch?v=kG-fLp9BTRo. Accessed 1 May 2023.

[36] RedHat. What does an API gateway do?, https://www.redhat.com/en/topics/api/what-does-an-api-gateway-do. Accessed 1 May 2023.

[37] *Microsoft*, 253 F.3d at 34.

[38] Software Testing Help, *10 Best Operating Systems for Laptops and Computers*, (2022), https://www.softwaretestinghelp.com/best-operating-systems/. Accessed 1 May 2023.

[39] Perez, S. (2021) Apple and Google Pressed in Antitrust Hearings on Whether App Stores Share Data with Product Development Teams. TECHCRUNCH. https://techcrunch.com/2021/04/21/apple-and-google-pressed-in-antitrust-hearing-on-whether-app-stores-share-data-with-product-development-teams/?guccounter=1&guce_referrer=aHR0cHM6Ly93d3cuZ29vZ2xlLmNvbS8&guce_referrer_sig=AQAAAEmPqQvpwhc-h6IdOLfHp6i3HGpGYQHDNAkU69-XQ20kDqaWC1OnFQqy6gwY3qABN-cKQwEwAjs71qz87KVdb5J__t5eUanEYz1LRlWH_SNDf84kZLvBKgIcVSYbv0Pe2VdfvG1G89TIGkaJKPSSyPuScR0tkrPgM-U9d9HSjlGv. Accessed 1 May 2023.

are in a compatible format. This decision is reinforced if the company is Microsoft, for example, because it has had staying power and reasonably good upgrades to its app selection for PCs and laptops.[40]

While the antitrust case associated with Microsoft's Internet Explorer showed that an incumbent can impede competition, i.e., bundling and market share dominance were the bases for the antitrust suit, the resulting advantage may not last very long. Internet Explorer (IE) was released with Windows 95. It was free to download and bundled with its operating system. Netscape Navigator had captured 80 percent of the browser market before that, but it was not free and was buggy. IE had superior features to Netscape and customer support. By 2001, IE captured 95 percent of the browser market. However, new entrants have three potential countervailing advantages: (1) they do not have a portfolio of products and services they want to protect, (2) they may not rely on proprietary software, and (3) they are not encumbered by an internal bureaucracy which slows innovation.

The case against Microsoft was settled in 2001. Part of the agreement was that Microsoft share its APIs with third parties.[41] Mozilla, later called Firefox, entered the market in 2002. In 2007, Apple released Safari, and Google's Chrome entered in 2010. IE lost market share rapidly. By 2018, its market share was down to 2–7%. Many reasons were cited for the failure, among them were tying the browser to older vintages of Microsoft's operating system, proprietary technology, and web developers having embraced Unix-based operating systems, which allowed them to develop products across open-sourced operating system.[42] Indeed, Microsoft faltered in new markets associated with the Internet and mobile phones.

The failure of Microsoft's Windows 10 mobile operating system produces a similar message of legacy product management myopia as barriers to innovation. This mobile operating system was a compressed version of its laptop operating system. Steve Ballmer could have adopted the Android system that is the basis of Google's mobile operating system but did not and could have provided adequate funding for a mobile operating system but chose to create a smartphone/iPod hybrid, which failed.[43]

---

[40] My Choice Software. Why Do So Many Companies Use Windows OS? https://www.mychoicesoftware.com/blogs/news/why-do-so-many-companies-use-windows-os. Accessed 1 May 2023.

[41] *Microsoft*, 253 F.3d at 34.

[42] Gant, G. (2018) How Microsoft Lost the Browser Wars. https://www.emergeinteractive.com/insights/detail/how-microsoft-lost-the-browser-wars/. Accessed 1 May 2023.

[43] Enderle, R. (2019) How Microsoft failed with Windows 10 Mobile. COMPUTERWORLD, 2019, https://www.computerworld.com/article/3336057/how-microsoft-failed-with-windows-10-mobile.html. Accessed 1 May 2023.

The growth in mobile usage was a major disruptor in the digital economy. New OSs for mobiles phones became great successes. Google's Android is a prime example. The market for OSs became segmented, and new market leaders emerged in mobile. Over the last decade, US market shares for operating systems for mobile devices have been stable with Apple's iOS's market share ranging between 50 percent and 60 percent and Android's around 40 percent.[44] For nonmobile devices, Windows and Mac OS provide the bulk of the operating systems, with Window's share falling from 80 percent to 60 percent and Mac OS's increasing from 15 percent to 25 percent.

The importance of apps in mobile operating systems leads to another important observation. Controllers of operating systems cannot produce all the apps demanded and cannot anticipate (and may not even have the expertise to anticipate) other killer apps. Facebook and TikTok are in that category. Apple will have them in its store competing with its own apps. Competing apps such as Netflix have outperformed apps such as Apple TV.[45] In the online search space, Google's Chrome dominates Microsoft's Bing.

8.4.3   Google

Google's evolution into multiple activities illustrates online dynamics. Google began as a search engine, realized the revenue potential of gathering data for advertising, and expanded its operations to maintain its hold on online search. Google's breakthrough algorithm was called PageRank. Other search engines such as AltaVista used keywords to identify relevant websites. This led to gaming of search by spammers who would load up a website with popular keywords. Google's PageRank looked beyond text words to links to a particular website to measure its true influence. Search, by itself, was not a moneymaker. Eventually, Google learned from a competitor, GoTo.com, how to generate revenue from advertising. Bill Gross, the founder of GoTo.com realized that legitimate websites would pay for top placement of a keyword. He also

---

[44] See, for example, StatCounter (2012) Operating System Market Share Worldwide: Aug. 2021 – Aug. 2022, https://gs.statcounter.com/os-market-share, or NET MARKETSHARE (2020) Operating System Market Share. https://netmarketshare.com/operating-system-market-share.aspx?options=%7B%22filte r%22%3A%7B%22%24and%22%3A5B%7B%22deviceType%22%3A%7B%22%24in%22%3A% 5B%22Desktop%2Flaptop%22%5D%7D%7D%5D%7D%2C%22dateLabel%22%3A%22Trend %22%2C%22attributes%22%3A%22share%22%2C%22group%22%3A%22platform%22%2C%22 sort%22%3A%7B%22share%22%3A-1%7D%2C%22id%22%3A%22platformsDesktop%22%2 C%22dateInterval%22%3A%22Monthly%22%2C%22dateStart%22%3A%222019-11%22%2C% 22dateEnd%22%3A%222020-10%22%2C%22segments%22%3A%22-1000%22%7D. Accessed 1 May 2023.

[45] *Id.*

pioneered the pricing strategy of advertisers paying per click. Google rolled out a self-service advertising product, AdWords, and later AdWords Select, an auction-based advertising product that struck gold.[46] Unlike Microsoft, Google continued to improve its search engine to keep ahead of competition.[47]

Google recognized that a mobile operating system could expand its search business beyond PCs and open up other opportunities. In 2005, Google bought Android Inc. for $50 million. In 2007, Google filed patents to protect its operating system and entered into a consortium that included T-Mobile and Sprint to launch the first commercially available smartphone.[48] From there it partnered with other device manufacturers.

Google makes money from its Android OS in three basic ways: (1) from its Play Store (apps, movies, and TV) that would not exist without Android, (2) from search fees, and (3) from Google Maps. Focusing on search, Google shares search profits with phone manufacturers such as Samsung for exclusive use of its search on their devices. Google Maps is also an important source of revenue growth that would not be as popular without Google controlling a mobile operating system.[49]

Google's search and mobile strategy explain why it continues to maintain its large presence in the online economy. As of 2020, Google

> controlled about 62% of mobile browsers, 69% of desktop browsers, and the operating systems on 71% of mobile devices in the world. 92% of internet searches go through Google and 73% of American adults use YouTube. Google runs code on approximately 85% of sites on the Web and inside as many as 94% of apps in the Play store. It collects data about users' every click, tap, query, and movement from all of those sources and more.[50]

Like Microsoft, not all of Google's forays into operating systems were successes. In 2009, Google planned to develop an operating system to compete in the PC market against Microsoft's Windows. The strategy was to tie its

---

[46] Oremus (2013) How Google won the Search wars. The Denver Post. https://www.denverpost.com/2013/10/15/how-google-won-the-search-wars/. Accessed 1 May 2023.

[47] Dandekar, N. (2017) How did Google surpass all other search engines? https://medium.com/@nikhilbd/how-did-google-surpass-all-the-other-search-engines-8a9fddc68631. Accessed 1 May 2023.

[48] Wikipedia. Android (operating system). https://en.wikipedia.org/wiki/Android_(operating_system). Accessed 1 May 2023.

[49] Franek, K. How Google Makes Money from Android: Business Model Explained. https://www.kamil-franek.com/how-google-makes-money-from-android/. Accessed 1 May 2023.

[50] Cyphers, B. (2020) Google Says it Doesn't 'Sell' Your Data. Here's How the Company Shares, Monetizes, and Exploits It. https://www.eff.org/deeplinks/2020/03/google-says-it-doesnt-sell-your-data-heres-how-company-shares-monetizes-and. Accessed 1 May 2023.

operating system to its Chrome web browser.[51] That venture failed because Windows remained the superior product.[52] Similarly, when it tried to organize a social media platform in 2011, it failed. It didn't draw enough users and app developers. Its Google + API was discontinued in 2019.[53] The takeaway from the two failures mentioned – a PC operating system and social media --is that it can be difficult for a platform to enter successfully the core territory of another major platform.

This brief summary of Google's business practices also suggests why it has a similar "antitrust profile" to that of Microsoft's in the 1990s. To carve out and protect its turf, Google entered into exclusive agreements with distributors of its Android operating system, with browsers that used its search engine and agreements prohibiting contract partners from dealing with competitors. Google embraced Android and, although it is based on open-source code, Google and placed restrictions on "forking"[54] its system and bundling its products.

8.4.4   Apple

Apple introduced the Macintosh in 1984. From there it produced a whole string of popular products in the fixed and mobile spaces. The most interesting difference with Google is its long-term practice of building an explicit walled garden around its ecosystem. Apple has its own operating system and exclusive software products such as Facetime, AirPlay, SharePlay, AirDrop, Continuity, iCloud, iMessage, Apple TV, etc. They are not available to consumers that shift to Android-based products.[55] From Apple's perspective, this walled garden is a quality-control strategy to ensure that its products work seamlessly together. However, potential competitors have viewed Apple's strategy to be a barrier to entry. For instance, Affinity Credit Union filed an antitrust suit against Apple Pay, claiming that Apple does not allow competitors to use its tap-to-pay feature, a feature that allows a customer to tap a

[51] Helft, M. & Vance, A. (2008) Google Plans a PC Operating System. The New York Times. https://www.nytimes.com/2009/07/08/technology/companies/08operate.html. Accessed 1 May 2023.

[52] Small Business Trends (2019) 14 Google Products that Failed – and What Your Business Can Learn. https://smallbiztrends.com/2019/12/product-release-and-failures.html. Accessed 1 May 2023.

[53] Wikipedia. Google +. https://en.wikipedia.org/wiki/Google%2B. Accessed 1 May 2023.

[54] Forking means using part of existing from a platform in this case code to produce competing software.

[55] Prince, S. (2021) Apple Ecosystem – the "Walled Garden." https://medium.com/geekculture/apple-ecosystem-the-walled-garden-9f07644367be. Accessed 1 May 2023.

phone against a terminal in a store to pay.[56] Perhaps learning from bad experiences supporting legacy systems, Apple is forcing its iPhone users to move up to its 5G operating system by the end of 2022.

8.4.5 Amazon

Amazon's founder Jeff Bezos's vision has been to become a market for many products at low prices, something like an online Walmart with greater range. To maintain its edge, Amazon has been a leader in logistics and warehousing innovation. Like Apple, Amazon has employed a walled garden strategy, but its wall is not as explicit. Amazon ties users of its platforms to price breaks for using its logistics, shipping, and warehousing resources. Third-party sellers on its platform can use Fulfillment by Amazon, whereby third-party sellers can ship inventory and pay for storage, weight handling, and pick-and-pack operations. Consumers can pay for Amazon Prime to waive shipping costs.[57]

Amazon has been accused of using its insider information to introduce its own private label products to compete with third-party products.[58] Preliminary evidence suggests that it introduces products to compete against successful products traded on its platform.[59]

8.4.6 Facebook

Facebook also illustrates the effects of first-mover, last-mover, and tipping point on competitive outcomes. Like Google, it was not the first entrant into its core market. In 1999, LiveJournal started as a blogging website that featured social networking. Friendster launched in 2002 and had 3 million users in a few months. In 2004, the year Facebook was launched, MySpace had one million users and by 2005, 25 million users. None of these social media platforms are still in business. Facebook rose to prominence because it marketed exclusivity (Harvard only) and trusted as a "safe space." The platform attracted

---

[56] Nayak, M. (2022) Apple Sued Over Apple Pay, Accused of Antitrust Violations. Bloomberg. https://www.bloomberg.com/news/articles/2022-07-18/apple-sued-over-apple-pay-accused-of-antitrust-violations. Accessed 1 May 2023.

[57] Liu, Q.& Zhu, F. (2018) Competing with Complementors: An Empirical Look at Amazon.com, 39 Journal of Strategic Management. 2618. https://onlinelibrary.wiley.com/doi/10.1002/smj.2932. Accessed 1 May 2023.

[58] *Id.* at 2624.

[59] *Id.* at 2635.

sophisticated developers who improved its features. Facebook developed a revenue model based on linking ads to specific, targeted users.[60]

Facebook had difficulty transitioning to accommodate users of mobile devices. As a result of Facebook's vulnerability to new mobile, social media outlets may have been a motivating factor for the purchase of Instagram. In 2010, Instagram was a startup company focusing on photo-sharing. By 2012, it had 13 employees when Facebook bought it for $1 billion. Was it a purchase to coopt the competition or to fill out a product line? That will be determined in court.[61] Was it a good deal? That depends on counterfactual information – what would it be valued without Facebook support? Whatever the case, its digital marketing and advertising generated $24 billion in 2020.[62] Many of the original employees were still with Facebook in 2020, which arguably suggests that Facebook and Instagram had complementary cultures.[63] Similarly, Facebook purchased WhatsApp, then a popular instant messaging app. Whether these acquisitions were to coopt potential rivals is the subject of the government's antitrust case against Facebook. The acquisitions may also suggest that like Microsoft, its embedded software systems and corporate culture may have limited Facebook's agility to enter a new market.[64]

By 2019, Facebook was running into market headwinds. Between 2017 and 2019, Facebook lost an estimated 15 million users. Children and young adults were migrating to Snapchat. Privacy breaches associated with the Cambridge Analytica scandal was also a factor.[65] TikTok has been making inroads into Facebook's social media domain and is taking advertising dollars with it. Its sweet spot is young adults.[66] Possible takeaways are that Facebook may be more vulnerable in its core product because its app is not tied to its

[60] Press, G. (2022) Why Facebook Triumphed Over All Other Social Networks. Forbes. https://www.forbes.com/sites/gilpress/2018/04/08/why-facebook-triumphed-over-all-other-social-networks/?sh=7a14334f6e91. Accessed 1 May 2023.

[61] Federal Trade Commission v. Facebook Inc. (2021) First Amended Complaint for Injunctive and Other Equitable Relief. https://www.ftc.gov/system/files/documents/cases/ecf_75-1_ftc_v_facebook_public_redacted_fac.pdf. Accessed 1 May 2023.

[62] Wise, J. (2022) How Much is Instagram Worth in 2022? Here's the Latest Data. https://earthweb.com/how-much-is-instagram-worth/. Accessed 1 May 2023.

[63] Hartmann, A. (2020) Instagram is celebrating its 10th birthday. A decade after launch, here's where its original 13 employees have ended up. Business Insider. https://www.businessinsider.com/instagram-first-13-employees-full-list-2020-4. Accessed 1 May 2023.

[64] *Facebook, supra* note 320, First Amended Complaint for Injunctive and Other Equitable Relief.

[65] Jagannathan, M. (2019) Why did Facebook lose an estimated 15 million users in the past two years? MarketWatch. https://www.marketwatch.com/story/why-did-facebook-lose-an-estimated-15-million-users-in-the-past-two-years-2019-03-07. Accessed 1 May 2023.

[66] Sweeny, M. (2022) The rise of TikTok: why Facebook is worried about the booming social app. The Guardian. https://www.theguardian.com/technology/2022/apr/09/rise-of-tiktok-why-facebook-is-worried-booming-social-app. Accessed 1 May 2023.

own operating system, and people look for new venues for social connections. Despite the market pressures, Facebook is still a huge platform with 2.9 billion active users in 2022 but only grew by 1.3 percent from July 2021 to July 2022. In the last reported quarter (April 2022 to July 2022), active users declined slightly.[67]

8.4.7 Cloud Computing

Cloud computing depends on massive server farms that allow users to access apps and use the processing power of the cloud to do the computing work done by apps on an edge device such as a PC. These server farms can reduce the need of some OS functions such as a directory that defines company policies and best practices for online use of its network.[68] Many of the major online platforms have very large server farms to manage their networks. In 2006, Amazon launched its Amazon Web Services (AWS). Google followed suit in the same year. Since then, many other companies offer cloud computing services.[69] Once again, the first successful company in the market, Amazon, has maintained its leadership in the cloud computing market. As of 2021, AWS has a 34% market share of leading cloud infrastructure service providers, while Google's share is 11%. Microsoft's Azure is in second place with a 21% market share.[70]

This brief summary suggests that an early successful innovator in a market often retains its leadership if it is committed to improving its products. But new technology opened new markets that allowed new companies to enter and lead. For instance, Google's Android was a new mobile operating system that quickly offered substantial competition to Apple's iOS. History also suggests that companies with innovative apps can draw substantial traffic away from established platforms. Major platforms do compete successfully against each other when the new market requires capabilities that are common to them all. Cloud computing is the best example.

---

[67] Dataportal (2022) Facebook Statistics and Trends. https://datareportal.com/essential-facebook-stats. Accessed 1 May 2023.

[68] Washington, S. (2023) Do We Need a Traditional Operating System? https://www.mindcentric.com/blog/do-we-need-a-traditional-operating-system. Accessed 1 May 2023.

[69] Foote, KD. (2021) A Brief History of Cloud Computing. DATAVERSITY. https://www.dataversity.net/brief-history-cloud-computing/. Accessed 1 May 2023.

[70] Richter, F. (2022) Amazon, Microsoft & Google Dominate Cloud Market. STATISTA. https://www.statista.com/chart/18819/worldwide-market-share-of-leading-cloud-infrastructure-service-providers/. Accessed 1 May 2023.

8.5   The Data Ecosystem Evolution and Privacy Concerns

A main concern of the public and policymakers is surveillance capitalism.[71] "Spymasters" like Google and Facebook use algorithms to analyze a vast array of data. They are by far the major players, but not the only ones. Credit card companies process transactions and market supposedly masked data, Internet service providers see the packet streams sent from edge devices to websites, and they market data. Nonetheless, Google, for example, logged more than $100 billion in search revenues (see below), while Mastercard and Amex and Envestment logged $400 million in revenues by selling customer data to hedge funds.[72]

Both in the United States and Europe, policymakers have been pushing to give customers more assurance of privacy. The major platforms have responded by strengthening privacy protection. In 2018, Facebook announced it would stop sharing personal data with people outside Facebook and cut down the amount of personal data that third-party app developers could collect.[73] By 2021, use of third-party cookies placed on a user's laptop or mobile device that send reports to an advertiser accessed on the Internet is rapidly declining. By 2022, all of the major web browsers will block them by default.[74] The loss of third-party cookies may reduce Facebook's and Google's advertising revenues, but perhaps not by much. For instance, Facebook quickly evaded Apple's new privacy rule by using Apple's accelerometer data, or information automatically recorded and sent to an app owner to adjust screen orientation as users move the phone around. This information combined with data from a

---

[71] Helm, B. (2020) Credit Card Companies are Tracking Shoppers Like Never Before: Inside the Next Phase of Surveillance Capitalism. Fast Company., https://www.fastcompany.com/90490923/credit-card-companies-are-tracking-shoppers-like-never-before-inside-the-next-phase-of-surveillance-capitalism. Accessed 1 May 2023.

[72] Cohan, P. (2018) Mastercard, Amex, and Envestment Profit from $400 M Business of Selling Transaction Data. Forbes. https://www.forbes.com/sites/petercohan/2018/07/22/mastercard-amex-and-envestnet-profit-from-400m-business-of-selling-transaction-data/?sh=664155a67722. Accessed 1 May 2023.

[73] Wagner, K. (2018) Facebook will Stop Sharing as Much of Your Personal Data with People outside Facebook. Vox. https://www.vox.com/2018/4/4/17199354/facebook-stop-sharing-data-outside-app. Accessed 1 May 2023.

[74] Rivero, N. (2021) The Digital Industry is Rewriting the Bargain at the Center of the Internet. Quartz. https://qz.com/2000490/the-death-of-third-party-cookies-will-reshape-digital-advertising/. Accessed 1 May 2023.

user that has opted in to being tracked by Facebook allows Facebook to identify any user's location.[75]

The open spigot of data flow collected through credit cards is also being closed. Companies are opting to switch from giving employees credit cards to single-use virtual payment cards known as burner cards.[76] Apple introduced its own Apple Card, a no number credit card that will not trace purchases. APIs such as Stripe have been developed to retain anonymity when transactions cross several financial institutions. Despite these advances tracking is still extensive, and with a bit of artificial intelligence, MIT professors were able to de-anonymize 90% of supposed anonymized transactions.[77]

8.6 Suggestions but No Solid Answers

Political compromise is possible because this is a new frontier in America's economy. Sources of potential monopoly power are at every level of the broadband network. Major ISPs that control the physical and logical transport layers can block traffic and shape it in ways that favor its own services to the detriment of competitors and the public in unacceptable ways.

When analyzing whether major application-layer platforms are (or have the potential) to anticompetitively exploit market power, one needs to understand the underlying engineering platforms that they ride on and the corporate culture that spawned a particular platform. This survey suggests that an innovative online strategy can lead to long-lasting market strength, through a combination of learning by doing and increases in platform connections. The innovation may be an app or a cluster of apps, but the surest way to secure market resilience is to control an operating system. Apple, Microsoft, and Google fall into this category. Amazon does not have an operating system but has pioneered a logistics strategy that is difficult to reproduce. Control of an operating system allows a platform to manage apps on its operating system and monitor the performance of competing apps. This has been a subject for investigation of Apple and Google. Facebook is the most vulnerable platform

---

[75] Ikeda, S. (2022) Facebook's Use of Alternate Location Tracking Methods to Circumvent Apple Privacy Protection Expands to Accelerometer Data. CPO Magazine. https://www.cpomagazine.com/data-privacy/facebooks-use-of-alternate-location-tracking-methods-to-circumvent-apple-privacy-protections-expands-to-accelerometer-data/. Accessed 1 May 2023.

[76] Osman, M. How to Get an Instant Virtual Debit Card for Your Business. Plate IQ, https://www.plateiq.com/blog/get-instant-virtual-debit-card-for-business. Accessed 1 May 2023.

[77] Helm, *supra* note 330.

because it does not have a unique technological advantage unless it successfully develops one for its Metaverse.[78]

Proper representation of price structures that produce a major share of a platform's revenue is important in evaluating whether prices are above competitive levels and the concomitant effect on consumer and producer surplus. For instance, investigations of Apple should focus on app price structures, while for Google, the primary focus should be on advertising price structures.

Each major platform has attempted to expand into another major platform's domain. Competition among platforms is most likely when the underlying technology is available to all of them. That is the case for cloud computing. While Amazon remains the market leader, its market share is in the 30 percent range. Because it is a new market opportunity, the large platforms are all finding cloud computing profitable. Business networking that operates with the open-source Linux operating system also appears competitive. In an economist's vernacular, these are examples of supply-side multihoming.

Each platform collects large amounts of data, but their data streams are not identical. While such data differential advantages could raise competitive issues if there were economies of scale in collecting and deploying data, Crandall and Hazlett[79] report that available research has not established this is the case. Further, any differential seems to be smaller when the data collection is through a search engine. Google recognizes that Amazon's internal search engine is a major competitor, which is the equivalent of data multihoming. Internet service providers and credit card companies are also potential sources of data. Interestingly, the push for privacy may lead to walled gardens filled with data. Facebook's reaction to make its platform more attractive to businesses is a first step to overcome privacy policies.

Protecting end user privacy is a major public policy issue with uncomfortable tradeoffs. For instance, stricter controls on cookie use and other tracking methods could be used as a pretext for foreclosing a competitor from critical data to compete, especially in the advertising market. Facebook has accused Apple of using this strategy.

Finally, successful mergers apparently require cultural compatibility between the merging companies. The AT&T/Time Warner merger is an

---

[78] Bajarin, T. (2022) The Four Major Players Battling To Own The Metaverse OS. FORBES. https://www.forbes.com/sites/timbajarin/2022/11/18/the-four-major-players-battling-to-own-the-metaverse-os/?sh=14180da31e60. Accessed 1 May 2023.

[79] Crandall & Hazlett, *supra* note 266.

example where cultural clashes destroyed the potential value of the merger.[80] In contrast, the Facebook/Instagram merger proved that cultural compatibility could produce extraordinary returns to the merged companies.

What does this all mean for competition policy such as vertical merger guidelines,[81] which identify presumptively anticompetitive action? What actions should the government take if a merger looks like it will lessen competition? Vertical merger analysis would benefit from a technology assessment that informs both regulators and companies considering a merger of potential increases in market power. Operating system control is the most likely competitive concern. Does the owner of the operating system foreclose agreements with equipment manufacturers and app placement on mobile phones, for example?

Cultural compatibility could be an important factor in whether a merger would adversely affect competition. In the case of the AT&T/Timer Warner merger, while the lengthy case required millions of dollars in government resources, not to mention those of AT&T and Time Warner, according to a recent article, the anticompetitive harms predicted by the government did not materialize before AT&T spun off it Time Warner assets.[82] The merger of Facebook and Instagram was another story. The two companies had similar cultures, which could be relevant in assessing whether a merger could lead to undue market power.

While accounting for the underlying technology when analyzing the potential competitive effects of vertical mergers is necessarily fact intensive, policies based on certain structural characteristics such as market capitalization and overreliance on prohibitions of certain actions based solely on such structural factors run the risk of inhibiting procompetitive innovation in this growing sector of the world's economy. Finding a practical regulatory strategy for shaping online competitive practices is a likely source of collaboration because Americans within all three ideological camps are both exhilarated and fearful of the emerging online global economy.

---

[80] Stewart, JB. (2022) Was This $100 Billion Merger the Worst Deal Ever? The New York Times. 2022, https://www.nytimes.com/2022/11/19/business/media/att-time-warner-deal.html Accessed 1 May 2023. Glass, V. (2021) Culture Clash and the Failure of the AT&T/Time Warner Merger, 6 RUTGERS BUS. REV. 350 (2021), https://rbr.business.rutgers.edu/article/culture-clash-and-failure-atttime-warner-merger. Accessed 1 May 2023.

[81] Vertical mergers are between two companies in the same industry but at different parts of the supply chain.

[82] Carlton, DW., Giozov, GV., Israel, MA., & Shampine, AL. (2021) A Retrospective Analysis of the AT&T/Time Warner Merger. https://papers.ssrn.com/sol3/papers.cfm?abstract_id=3911492. Accessed 1 May 2023.

9

Digital Overexposure

Abstract Invasion of privacy is an old problem: searching mail, tapping phones, photographs, surveillance. The Digital revolution has created the capability to develop digital profiles that expose intimate personal lives in detail. Digital storage, artificial intelligence, and nonstop real-time data gathering is invading personal privacy, manipulating behavior, and causing exaggerated news coverage. The Internet, which originally was a way to connect people for social good, now exacerbates social divisions and threatens the democratic process. One interesting paradox is that too much data causes people to filter it, which causes digital blindness to opposing ideas.

9.1 Introduction

Burkas and bikinis suggest that skin exposure is a matter of taste or religious conviction. In Western society outfits once seen as shocking or strange curiosities have become so commonplace that passersby hardly notice purple hair or ripped clothes. Compare street scenes or beach pictures now to the staid outfits of the 1930–1950s, or better yet early 1900s. Then, men wore suits and women wore dresses, and bathing suits hid sensitive body parts.

Whether staid or psychedelic, American society converts exposed beliefs and desires into useful information. Before the digital revolution, many types of data were hard to gather. Organizations paid to conduct surveys, organize focus groups, and gather publicly available data, usually from government sources. Religious institutions paid professionals to track how often people attended houses of worship, their religious affiliation, if any, and whether they were switching religions or intermarrying. Large corporations relied on in-house marketing experts to gather information and analyze sales patterns to understand what customers valued. Scientists like Masters and Johnson conducted special studies to expose intimate sexual behavior previously considered taboo.

Protection of privacy has a long legal record in the United States because people only want exposed what they voluntarily expose. They don't want anyone examining their mail, tapping their phones, taking sneak pictures, or recording private conversations. They certainly don't want personal information used to impersonate them whether the motive is to steal or just pretend.

9.2   Death of Privacy in the Digital Age

The digital revolution has added a new dimension for exercising one's taste for exposure and for the dramatic. Facebook and YouTube allow people to share with others and be noticed. With 2.2 billion Facebook users and 1.5 billion YouTube users, and billions of videos shared, it is hard to stand out in the crowd, the result being outrageous public exposure becomes widespread.

The digital revolution is allowing online companies to intrude on our privacy whether we like it or not because a transaction usually requires the exchange of personal information. The public only vaguely understands how intrusive the online economy can be. The rub is that the bulk of spying is done by profit-making companies that want to win your business. Google, for example, keeps your search history; video and other downloads, photos, and other information you stored in the cloud; and your location history if you have an Android phone. They are likely to have your personal identification information – at the very least, your email address. All of this information can help Google improve your Internet experience, but it also gives Google enough information to develop digital mosaics of you and can even turn it into a personal movie. Just think Google knows where you go: schools, churches, stores, and homes. It can easily predict your daily routine. It can track you even on vacation.

Perhaps even more troubling than being physically exposed is being psychologically exposed. Facebook knows your likes and dislikes. Amazon knows your purchase patterns. These large platforms are using data mining and artificial intelligence to know when a person is vulnerable to manipulation. Behavioral economists are beginning to learn that people have psychological vulnerabilities that can be exploited. They typically double down when they have invested in a particular opinion or lifestyle. They often overreact to new information. They are myopic and impulsive. These massive online platforms can learn how to frame the online experience to lead you in a certain direction toward a purchase or reinforce someone's political leanings.

Many realize the Internet has invaded their privacy but shrug it off as the cost of doing business online, until someone steals your identity or exposes your intimate life. Public figures are especially vulnerable to overexposure. Photographs and sound recordings have plagued politicians and movie stars for decades. The digital revolution has invaded their everyday lives in ways only imagined in dystopias like 1984. High-profile public figures face the equivalent of Jeremy Bentham's panopticon, which was designed to let prison guards spy constantly on criminals in their cells.

9.3   Exposés of Public Officials Have a Long History

An interesting article by Michael Jensen published in 1979, almost two decades before the Internet took off, suggests why the public likes to leer at public figures. Jensen wanted to debunk the idea that the press was a closed fraternity of liberals who distorted the news to serve their own political agenda.[1] He said the news is not bought for its informational value. Everyone knows that the ordinary citizen has no political influence. Instead, people bought subscriptions or tuned into televised news for its entertainment value. The news was drama unfolding as the days passed. Like any drama, it needed to build up. People were not interested to know that a government program was ill-designed or poorly run. They preferred stories of the clash of good and evil. The program failed because it was controlled by the secret societies like the Skull and Bones, or the Man, or the System. News reporters could sidestep accusations of personal bias against a public figure by simply interviewing sources that supported their bias.

Another Jensen observation was that the bible, grand morality plays, and most modern ethnic novels often use family life to represent society's values. He suggested that the public often misrepresents a nation for a super-sized family, a mistake because families have long-lasting connections that lend themselves to giving without an immediate payback. Lending money to a

---

[1] Michael C. Jensen (1979) *Toward a Theory of the Press*, ECONOMICS AND SOCIAL INSTITUTIONS, Karl Brunner, ed. Martinus Nijhoff Publishing Company, https://papers.ssrn.com/sol3/papers.cfm?abstract_id=94038. Accessed 1 May 2023.

sister without a legal document may be satisfying even if repayment is unlikely, but would a cabdriver trust a "fare" to pay him sometime in the future? Politicians who believe they are acting as loco parentis will have public support from liberals who believe it is proper to builds low-income housing to save the poor and will maintain public support even if the program fails. Contrast public housing with a housing developer who pocketed large profits building low-income housing. The builder has the image of an exploiter of the poor.

Jensen wraps up by saying politicians who don't support the news media become the media's target. Like any business, media companies want a low-cost supply of interesting stories. They will not tolerate someone like Trump who calls them fakers out to get him.

9.4   Exposure Is Now in Real Time

The digital age has sped up news transmission to real time. News people constantly need to refresh their content constantly with startling stories or continuing sagas. With so many outlets for news and opinions, there is little time to fact-check. Mistakes will happen often.

Digital overexposure has become the norm in politics. Every public moment of Trump and Hilary Clinton was documented during their campaigns. A few decades ago, the Soviet Union was notorious for slicing fallen leaders out of public photos. During Trump/Clinton campaigns, it was so easy for fringe groups to Photoshop and digitally edit their careers to make them both look like psychopathic liars and, in Hilary's case, a killer. The mainstream news media were a bit more subtle. They often did try to fact-check their stories, but the pace of news releases sacrificed in-depth analysis for the fast and quotable. And with blurring of news and entertainment, fact and opinion, news person and media star, the media shade events and their meaning to build and hold their audiences.

The media in the digital age has made politics into a late-breaking clash of good and evil that keeps public hungry for more salacious "facts." Each public faction eagerly waits for news that justifies its ideology and prejudices. It has all the makings of a religious war based on classic yellow journalism. Remember Stormy Daniels is the new "Remember the Maine" to democrats. Monica Lewinsky has her place on the Republican side.

Political apathy has been replaced by a taught struggle that leaves no side the time for reflection and compromise. A visit of a winning baseball team to the White House becomes a political issue. It is as if the players endorse

President Trump if they attend the awards ceremony. They forget that they are also honoring a democratic tradition.

9.5   The Digital Herding Effect

"Fake news" has become a call to the troops that the other side has once again tried to poison the public's mind. Instead of branding the mainstream news outlets, consider the fringe outlets that border on opinion described as fact. Should they be regulated or outlawed? What if the group is in another country? Should we presume that a foreign influence is bad? What if this foreign group is trying to push climate control instead of a political candidate? Does it make a difference? What if the source is a multinational corporation?

The focus on Trump and Clinton is meant as a clear-cut warning that privacy and objectivity are under attack from legitimate businesses trying to satisfy the public needs and from new type of thieves that operate in cyberspace. America's ideologues are struggling for answers without having a solid understanding of what the Internet is and how it is morphing. What policies, if any, should the government adopt to prevent digital overexposure?

During the Obama administration, the death of a black man by a white police officer in Ferguson, Missouri, touched off riots. A black man ambushed Dallas police rousing a law-and-order backlash. And a killing could be considered institutional assassination of minorities even in a city like Baltimore where the government and police are managed by African Americans. In a time when America is struggling to redefine itself as a multiracial and multi-ethnic society, instantaneous, worldwide communication induces destabilizing viral behavior. Angry people have plenty of opportunities to see what they want to see on social media.

Privacy is becoming a memory, sociability without personal contact is common, viral behavior can be induced, crowdsourcing can cause riots, and national boundaries have become like stakes in the ground that many don't even see. In a time when America is becoming a multiracial society, instantaneous, worldwide communication can induce a new brand of tribalism that could undermine democracy by pitting one group against the other.

The Internet of Things (IoT) is the next stage in product development. Feedback from appliances to manufacturers would improve product design and suggest new features. Smart energy grids will improve energy efficiency by monitoring usage and grid resilience by identifying the location of potential and actual outages. These benefits come at the expense of uncovering more and more of personal habits.

9.6   The Challenge of Protecting Against Digital Overexposure

Digital overexposure creates policy challenges not easily solved by America's ideologues. Personal information is not like other types of private property. You may voluntarily trade personal information for free online services, but you still have an interest in that data, especially if it is sold to a third party without your knowledge. A company or government can take photos or track someone or simply have a 24-hour camera on. To what extent is that an invasion of privacy? Employers want personal data to screen applicants; insurers want healthcare records and personal checkups as a condition for being insured. Everyone wants a one-way mirror for gazing out into the world, allowing them to see and not be seen; or they only want to be seen as they want others to see them.

How do you solve the types of exposure that make people believe they are being watched by the Invisible Man? Libertarians would say, let the market take care of the problem. Companies will encrypt personal information to protect customers; they will anonymize data; or they will even spoof packet addresses – all in the name of boosting profits. This assumes that the public understands the threat and has power to change the behavior of Google or Facebook or new Internet businesses looking for an edge in the digital marketplace. Liberals might pursue an aggressive legal strategy to protect privacy. But lawsuits are expensive, the damages are hard to gauge because even if your personal information is hacked, it is not clear that the hacker has caused you financial damage. It may happen 5 years from now, but the immediate damages are hard to quantify. Besides, lawyers build cases by filtering evidence to win cases. Their objective is not to uncover the facts. Liberals may turn to regulators of business practices, but government regulations would impose best practices on industry security practices that are quickly outdated, and slow-footed regulators would always be trying to catch up. Conservatives probably agree with libertarians and liberals to some extent but are likely to recommend a return to government censors who know pornography and digital exposure when they see it. In the digital age, this might be the product of data mining to find measures of the public's distaste for unwanted exposure, especially on social media platforms. Again, there will be a tradeoff between transparency and privacy. No simple solution exists.

9.7 Gauging Digital Exposure Is a Starting Point for Policy Reform

To understand the depths of the overexposure problem, a good starting place are three categories of personal data defined by the Federal Communications Commission (FCC). They are listed from most to least sensitive.[2]

1. Individually identifiable Customer Proprietary Network Information (CPNI) as defined in Section 222 (h).

   CPNI includes billing information and network routing information that could identify a customer. Examples of CPNI are the type of broadband service bought, customer premises equipment information, Internet protocol (IP) addresses, traffic statistics information, and application information. Application information can include websites visited or emails sent or received. CPNI also includes geolocation information. To harmonize old POTS privacy regulations with BIAS regulations, the order classifies both IP addresses and telephone numbers as CPNI.

2. Personally identifiable information (PII)

   PII includes any information reasonably linked or linkable to a device. Examples are Social Security Number, date of birth, mother's maiden name, and government identifiers such as a driver's license, physical address, email address, phone numbers, and other unique identifiers. Some PII categories are also CPNI categories.

3. Content of communications

   Content of communications includes "any part of the substance, purport, or meaning of a communication or any other part of a communication that is highly suggestive of the substance, purpose, or meaning of a communication." Examples of content include, but are not limited to, the "contents of emails; communications on social media; search terms; web site comments; items in shopping carts; inputs on web-based forms;

---

[2] Legal Information Institute. 47 U.S. Code Sec 222 – Privacy of customer information. Cornell Law School, https://www.law.cornell.edu/uscode/text/47/222. Accessed 1 May 2023.

and consumers' documents, photos, videos, books read, [and] movies." The list is not exhaustive.

One supposed fix is to anonymize personal data. The problem is that uncloaking anonymized personal data is commonplace. Even aggregating geographic and historical data can be unraveled by clever algorithms.

Besides ordinary personal communication data, "smart" homes and "smart" businesses will connect customer premises with electric utilities or other networks. This type of data flow will allow a network to gather information that will reveal, for example, when a person is at home or when he is vacationing. Outside the home, street-scene data are routinely gathered by businesses and government. This type of data was used to track down the Boston Marathon bombers.

With so much data flowing into databases, data mining is becoming increasingly sophisticated, thanks to advances in artificial intelligence (AI). Want to decide whether someone is credit-worthy, or healthy, or a thief? An AI program could be designed to answer these questions. The use of AI raises a host of issues: Has the designer built his prejudices into the program leading to statistical discrimination? Who is responsible if a driverless car is in an accident? Do these types of programs invade your privacy by offering personalized recommendations for online products?

Most policymakers support increased transparency in the gathering, use, and trading of digital data. A person should have a right to choose what type of data should be kept confidential by the online business. But that may differ from website to website. People don't understand what they are trading away. Besides, new uses for collected data may surprise everyone involved.

The meta-message is that privacy linked to self-identity has many facets: physical identity (genetic, health, appearance), intellectual identity (genetic, environment), emotional identity (psychological fitness), and spiritual identity (religion). Norms protect and promote self-identity as long as they promote social welfare, but what is social welfare? Economists limit it to enhancing wealth, ethicists to controlling sensitive data, lawyers to clearly defined damages to others, and politicians to efficient governance.

Privacy is selective and voluntary release of personal information and reasonable collection by others of one's personal information either through direct exchange or outside surveillance. Privacy is less defined than private property because the sale of personal data does not alienate it from you. Privacy is not absolute. Complete privacy can cover antisocial and other destructive behaviors. Yet, privacy requires a certain degree of security from outside information gathering because fears of identity theft, identity distortion, exposure, and misrepresentation can distort personal values. Digital pictures that capture whims may become damning clips, and stored data can become politically toxic such as Jewish registration as a nationality in pre-Nazi Europe.

Digital overexposure has created an unsettling, unfocused anxiety in American society. The public doesn't know what personal information they have been given up. They don't know how third parties will piece it together. The lack of digital education is similar to lack of understanding of other new technologies. For instance, like microwaves, are unseen digital bits hurting our psychological health? Are people Photoshopping our lives?

9.8 Digital Overexposure Threatens Democracy

The Internet is distorting the political process because of relentless media coverage of politicians and other public figures, real-time exposure that pressures the interviewed to react instead of think and any misspelled tweet, any ungrammatical phrase, any spot on a dress, or inappropriate tie become headline news. Ominously, new digital technology can change a person's expressions and words in real time in ways that can play to the prejudices of the target group. Common national values, once taken for granted such as the rule of law, may splinter into tribal values that disregard fairness for tribal unity and honor.

The Internet is in its infancy. New AI tools could potentially cause major social disruptions that we cannot predict. People are already reacting to digital overexposure by hiding and lying. Markets are using encryption, spoofing transmission routes, and virtual private networks (VPNs) to protect the integrity of transactions. Blockchain technology promises to return control of personal data to individuals. With blockchain technology a person will control his or her data with a personal key that must be used by corporations to unlock their personal data. At the same time, these new tools create a cover for bad behavior. Digital exposure may drive away many capable public servants who cannot stand the 24-hour scrutiny of his every word and every bodily function. Digital distortion could permanently make the public wary of any news item.

Digital overexposure is not simply an American issue. The world is being shaken by the new digital dimension that humankind has invented. As we saw with the financial system, the Coding Revolution has added complexity and volatility that has spread across the globe, and none of America's ideologies has a sure fix to the problem.

10

Palace Intrigues and Stealth Security: Uncomfortable Tradeoffs Between Liberty and Security

Abstract This chapter begins with rise of secret services during and after World War II. The premise is that like with other secret societies, a tribal mentality forms to protect members. Their use of cryptography and later digital algorithms for processing huge amounts of data gives them enormous power to spy on American citizens. The need for cybersecurity is extending government's reach deep into the hardware and software used by Internet providers and other communication providers. Government overreach is likely and not controlled well by government officials. Domestically, intelligence agencies can weaponize data – emails, voice conversations, and locational information – to bring down political rivals and enemies. The rise of cyberwarfare as a primary tool in international struggles threatens to undermine the trend toward global trade and scientific information sharing.

10.1 Introduction

A little decoding is useful as a starting point. A palace intrigue in America is a plot by intelligence agencies to bypass Congress and the President. "Stealth" is a stand-in for secrecy in identifying, capturing, and disposing of terrorist threats. It covers the use of secret agents or cybersecurity experts or agents manning joy sticks that guide drones to their bombing destinations. "Security" is protection from terrorists, whether inside America or from rogue nations. The title of the chapter should now be reasonably clear to an amateur code breaker. America has organized a palace guard of intelligence agencies to protect America from its enemies, but they may also be lethal to American liberty.

Internal dangers from America's intelligence agencies are of a different sort than seen in the private sector. Businesses may try to profile customers, but they can't access any databases they want. No such access barriers exist if the government perceives a threat to national security.

Both businesses and intelligence agencies breed antisocial types, but their profiles are very different. A self-absorbed trader at an investment bank is perhaps the most extreme example of what an intelligence agent is not. He is often a loner who sees his bosses and customers as statistics. He sees nothing wrong with ripping off the system because the outside world is an anonymous bunch of suckers who deserve what they get because they are also greedy takers. In a nation that looks up to Masters of the Universe, he wants to become one. He wants to trade up from living in Lefrak City, Queens, a respectable middle-class neighborhood, to living in the Dakota facing Central Park and hobnobbing with celebrities. The public imagines him with slicked-backed hair, wearing gold chains, riding down Fifth Avenue in a Maserati – a Gordon Gekko.

By comparison, rogue covert operators are part of a throwback culture that resembles a paranoid tribal mentality. They are bound together to fight an enemy that is almost pure evil and justify any outrage as necessary for American survival (p. 15). If a secret agent errs in judgment, other agents may cover it up because they fear loss of honor and ability to maneuver if exposed. Extreme measures are justified because terrorists will use anything, such as trucks, roadside bombs, bioweapons, or dirty bombs, to terrorize and kill Americans. Top brass of an agency may slough off an agent's illegal mistakes as collateral damage. In tense war zones, where success goes unrecognized by the public, where they see the world through their own culture, agents tend to treat each other's wins in the field, however modest, as great triumphs for the service. Although they live by an honor code to protect each other, they never know if a fellow spy is a double agent. As for the public, the once glamorous master spy, someone like James Bond, now looks like a break-in bungler like G. Gordon Liddy.

A secret army of spies is bound to limit access to what they are doing because what they do abroad and sometimes at home is illegal. The public feels uneasy relying on standard gatekeepers to govern the intelligence agencies in the public's interest. If the leaders of the intelligence agencies rise through the ranks, they have taken on the tribal culture as their own. If an outsider runs the agency, he doesn't really know its intricacies and culture, or even the breadth of its operations, which may be fragmented, and some covert activities past and present may be kept from the incoming chief.

Like other government bureaucracies, the upper levels of an intelligence agency serve a passing parade of elected officials. Human nature suggests that a bureau's leadership will see themselves as professionals with deep knowledge of their specialized area compared to the shallow knowledge of elected officials. Without much of a leap in logic, the leaders of a bureau will believe they know better than elected officials what is good for the country. They may attack covertly elected officials they see as dangers to the country or to their bureau.

Then there is competition among intelligence agencies and the military. They all have an incentive to hold back information for their agency's gain and fight any perceived encroachment on their turf. Few in government, however, want to combine them in one unified agency because they fear organizing a Gestapo. Oversight of the separate agencies by politically elected officials may not be effective because they are even further removed from operations than insiders. Worse yet, political officials may have their own agendas and use the intelligence agencies to further political objectives by spying on the opposition.

Gatekeeping becomes even more difficult when an enemy such as Al-Qaeda is not directly state sponsored. They don't respect physical borders and cyberspace makes state borders much more porous than ever. American intelligence agencies are now eavesdropping on Americans, allies, and other states for the sake of security. They want to download every communication in the world if such massive data gathering will improve America's security. They will err on the side caution without carefully weighing the cost of likely attacks and the harder to determine costs of invading the privacy of innocent people at home and abroad.

Realistically, gatekeepers can work on preventing over-reach by intelligence agencies, perhaps by offering a sobering view of the historical effectiveness of covert activities. Government can lessen the internal threat from these agencies by putting in more legal controls and announcing to the public the broad outlines of the intelligence agencies' operations. Nonetheless, this huge military intelligence complex, which may be necessary for American protection, is a new type of threat that could detonate American democracy in stressful times. Past presidents have used the secret services to topple foreign leaders and cripple or silence political enemies at home.

The ultimate focus here is going to be on cyber snooping and cyber-attacks on infrastructure. The coding revolution has made America's power grid, military command and control centers, and commercial information vulnerable to secret and swift attacks. Like the threat of a nuclear strike, a cyber-strike needs to be defended in minutes or hours – time frames not well suited for democratic discussion.

To look at them cybersecurity and cyber weaponry in isolation, however, is to miss how these covert policies fit into the broader development of a palace guard and a huge stealth security operation that was born in World War II and grew rapidly in size and reach during the Cold War. This long stretch illustrates the precedents that have led to the strategies and tactics used in cyber wars. My belief is that covert action had limited value during the Cold War, many times causing more harm than good. I do believe, however, that America's intelligence agencies have often been effective in defeating enemies on the battlefield using decrypted intelligence in World War II and recently to destroy Islamic terrorist organizations. However, recent information gathering is often heavy-handed and overdone as is typical of a government organization that draws in resources to fight against a threat that is hard to quantify by playing on the fears of the public. It is often difficult to tell whether the source of damaging leaks that are disrupting government is from America's own intelligence agencies off from abroad.

10.2   A Brief History of Covert Operations

So, when did America organize a permanent palace guard of spies?

Gary Wills, the historian, pinpoints the rise of the Imperial President and palace guard of spy agencies to the Manhattan Project, secretly funded by President Franklin Roosevelt to produce the atomic bomb.[1] According to Wills, this covert project became the prototype for a tectonic shift of government from operating as if peace in the world was the norm toward a permanent war footing where devastation could occur in a matter of hours. When Harry Truman assumed the presidency, he didn't even know the Manhattan Project existed, nor did most of Congress, and yet this was a huge undertaking costing billions of dollars. Once Truman was debriefed, he and others began to realize he had was in control of a weapon of mass destruction. After the Soviets had the bomb, a devastating attack could occur within hours, the time for a few Soviet bombers to pierce American air space. The president had to be prepared to act on his own if such an attack was underway. He had to have his finger on the bomb.

---

[1] Wills,G. (2010) Bomb Power, The Modern Presidency and The National Security State. Penguin Press, N.Y.

A new devastating war seemed imminent as communism advanced rapidly across Eastern Europe and China, sometimes by military coups. America had no idea when the next communist putsch would begin or where. Truman responded with his Truman Doctrine, which said that "Totalitarian regimes imposed on free people, by direct or indirect aggression, undermine the foundation of international peace *and hence the security of the United States.*" This policy set the precedent for fighting terrorism any place in the world.[2] It was a call to arms that didn't consider the size or imminence of the threat or its likely threat to the United States in particular. It puts America on war footing, ready for engagement anyplace in the world. America had to show the communists it could react fast and decisively to any threat. One outcome of this policy was that Truman sent troops to defend Korea without the approval of Congress.

Another much less publicized outcome of America feeling vulnerable was the buildup of a government wing devoted to covert actions aimed at killing key enemy targets and bringing down rogue governments, often by supplying money and other resources to an approved political faction within a country on America's watch list. Millions of secret files became classified. Weiner, a writer for the New York Times, documented that during the Stalin Era, the CIA opened clandestine prisons in Germany, Japan, and Panama and conducted a program of "overseas interrogations."[3]

Eisenhower was a generally successful overseer of targeted overseas assassinations and regime changes. He used the CIA to install the Shah on the Iranian throne. The CIA also successfully toppled the regime in Guatemala, funded anti-communist factions in Italy and Japan that came to power, but failed to overthrow the Syrian government in a botched coup attempt. Other botched and successful overthrows in South America, Africa, and the Far East produced the specter of the Ugly American throughout the developing world.

His other important strategy, which doesn't fall under the covert operations umbrella but is important for understanding current conflicts, is Eisenhower's deployment of tactical nuclear weapons in Western Europe. America did not have enough troops in Europe to protect its allies from a Soviet attack, so he believed tactical nuclear weapons would serve as an effective deterrent. It is perhaps reasonable to assume Iran wants nuclear weapons to deter an American attack on its sovereignty. Eisenhower ended his presidency with his famous farewell speech warning that "We must guard against the acquisition of unwarranted influence, whether sought or unsought, by the military

---

[2] Id., p. 72.

[3] Weiner, T. (2007) Legacy of Ashes: The History of The CIA. Doubleday, N.Y. p. 512.

industrial complex. The potential for the disastrous rise of misplaced power exists and will persist."[4]

During the Kennedy and Nixon administrations, the line separating domestic and foreign covert activities began to fade. John F. Kennedy had Allen Dulles, then the CIA chief, "step up coverage of Castro activities in the United States."[5] Richard Nixon used the "plumbers" led by a recently retired CIA officer, E. Howard Hunt, to plug security leaks, after Daniel Ellsberg released the Pentagon Papers.[6]

During the Reagan administration, "don't ask don't tell the president" became a policy tool for shielding Reagan from illegal covert activities. The Iran-Contra scandal involved CIA operatives who were illegally supporting Nicaraguan insurgents and shipping arms to Iran to gain the release of American hostages. The weapons were shipped without Reagan's explicit approval.[7]

This culture of "us against them" spread to unusual parts of society. American universities had a hand in American anticommunist policy and so did American corporations. Milton Friedman developed the strategy of economic "shock treatment" to tear down the socialist society that was forming in Chile under Allende and replace it with a free market society.[8] The University of Chicago trained a cadre of economists to agitate against planned economies, and some of these graduates eventually ruled or had great influence in Chile and Argentina. American multinational corporations became informal channels of intelligence. With the rise of specialized weapons makers, a section of the American economy found it profitable to sell weapons abroad. Subcontracted civilian armies such as Blackwater began maintaining security in war zones.

The movement from spies to gadgets had its inception during the Eisenhower administration. The Killian report stated America was learning little inside Russia from covert actions.[9] The report urged Eisenhower to tap science for intelligence gathering "to build spy planes and space satellites to soar over the Soviet Union and photograph its arsenals."

Unfortunately, American intelligence agencies did not know what was going on behind the Iron Curtain until it was practically rusted through. The CIA misled the public about a missile gap with the Soviet Union leading to a

---

[4] Id., p. 512.

[5] Id., p. 177.

[6] Id., p. 318.

[7] Id., pp. 403–405.

[8] Klein, N. (2007) The Shock Doctrine: The Rise of Disaster Capitalism. Henry Holt and Co. N.Y. p. 7.

[9] Weiner, supra note 346. p. 113.

rapid, expensive, and potentially dangerous buildup of nuclear armed missiles. Later, America was surprised when the Soviet Union fell.

Two major intelligence failures occurred after the fall of the Soviet Union: the 9/11 attack and the failure to find weapons of mass destruction (WMD) in Iraq, which was supposedly the justification for the 2003 American invasion. As for 9/11, the basic conclusion of a congressional report was a failure of imagination on the part of the CIA, FBI, and NSA to connect the dots. One glaring example was the flight training of many foreign national in the United States who showed little interest in learning how to land a plane.[10] The Senate Report on Iraqi WMD intelligence issued in July 2004 concluded that the intelligence community either overstated or misrepresented the information pointing to Iraq having a WMD program.[11] One will never know if the reason for the invasion was that the Bush administration decided to declare war on a gut reaction because it had lost confidence in the intelligence community's ability to deliver solid information.

The seeming ineptness of American intelligence agencies in the exposes I've cited is lopsided because they minimize America's success in cryptography. During World War II, Britain and America teamed up to break enemy battlefield codes. Bletchley Park, England, was the hub for Nazi code breaking. Military historians attribute Allies' successes in defeating the Nazi U-Boats in the Battle of the Atlantic, defeat of Rommel in North Africa, and critical intelligence for D-Day.[12] William Friedman led an American intelligence team that broke Japan's Purple cipher. Decoded messages gave Admiral Nimitz a detailed look at the Japanese plan of attack for the Battle of Midway. The defeat of the superior Japanese forces during this battle was the turning point of the Battle of the Pacific. An engaging book by Neal Stephenson, *Cryptonomicon*, builds a reasonably accurate story that the success of the allies during World War II depended heavily on decrypting Nazi and Japanese battlefield messages.[13]

A lone voice in the CIA, Henry Crumpton, did predict the dangers of Osama Bin Laden and did say that Iraq had nothing to do with the Twin Towers attack. He recommended a hit on Bin Laden's compound that was

---

[10] Wikipedia, Failure of Imagination. https://en.wikipedia.org/wiki/Failure_of_imagination. Accessed 1 May 2023.

[11] Wikipedia. Senate Report on Iraqi WMD Intelligence. https://en.wikipedia.org/wiki/Senate_Report_on_Iraqi_WMD_Intelligence. Accessed 1 May 2023.

[12] See, for example, Wikipedia. Bletchley Park. https://en.wikipedia.org/wiki/Bletchley_Park. Accessed 1 May 2023.

[13] Stephenson, N. (1999) Cryptonomicon, (1999) Avon, NY.

turned down by the Clinton administration as being too risky. Eventually, he took charge of the early War in Afghanistan and did win it.

Overall, the record suggests that covert intelligence can be effective, but the overall history is one of failure. It did not bring down the Soviet Union; it did create many enemies throughout the world in its bumbling attempts to overthrow communism. The CIA kept its eyes on military threats, so it overlooked the crumbling Soviet economy. Eventually, communism was going to implode without America's help.

10.3 The Security/Privacy Tradeoff

A very important question is how far is America willing to cede power to a palace guard to protect itself? The answer is by no means simple because the potential danger is hard to quantify. Are we willing to accept occasional car bombs in New York City in exchange for dismantling the palace guard? If we shrink the palace guard, will the attacks stop with car bombs or dirty bombs, or something worse?

Code breaking during World War II was a precursor to cyber-attacks and cyber-spying, the latest and most wide-ranging tools of America's spy agencies. From a historical perspective, it may have been the allies' greatest secret weapon during World War II. Allegedly, the United States and Israel used a virus call Stuxnet to sabotage Iranian nuclear plants. The virus attacked process control centers that regulated motor speed that drove the centrifuges used to enrich uranium. By varying the speed of the centrifuges, Stuxnet was able to damage them. The attack was bloodless, no bombs were dropped, and no collateral human damage was noted.

It is also likely that America's cyber-eavesdropping global network has averted terrorist attacks. Electronic surveillance was used effectively during the 2005 Iraq War. After the 9/11 attack, the Bush administration widened data collection using a "collect it all" policy. The PRISM data collection by the government covers voice, data, photo, and video communications here and in many other parts of the world.[14] Undoubtedly, "big data" searches did and will uncover more terrorist plots than a more targeted search. The "collect it all" approach will also produce more "false positives" – communications that look like those of terrorists but are not – leading to the surveillance of innocent citizens. The false positives need not be random. It could lead to the cyber equivalent of racial profiling to stop street crime and ethnic profiling to

---

[14] Wikipedia. PRISM. https://en.wikipedia.org/wiki/PRISM. Accessed 1 May 2023.

break up Islamic terrorist cells. The power of data mining will continue to grow as new techniques for analyzing language and messages and for analyzing facial expressions and voice patterns will give the government and private entities the ability to become an invisible Big Brother, constantly watching even one's most intimate actions.

Many people within the government and outside it such as the consultant had access to sensitive government files and could download them. Eric Snowden, a consultant, exposed PRISM and downloaded PRISM files illegally. Bradley Manning released military information to WikiLeaks, which released many of the files to the public. These exposures raise many questions about secret information in cyber space. Leaving aside the question of whether Snowden or Manning is a hero or traitor, the larger issue is cybersecurity. People can tap into sensitive databases. Unlike a private company, the government has the capability of gathering digital information from a wide variety of sources and integrating them, including such government tracking devices as E-ZPass. The government can require private businesses to hand over their encrypting and decrypting algorithms. In the government's case, a false profile could lead to a government investigation of innocent people. With PRISM, the issue is whether a smaller more targeted network, one under legal and congressional review, would do the job almost as well. What can America do to disperse monitoring power so that it isn't solely in the hands of government agencies? What are the tradeoffs? Again, the cost/benefit analysis of exchanging core values such as privacy for security is hard to measure.

The biggest issue is the power shift caused by permanent war footing in the cyber age. Like the arms race during the Cold War, America and other nations are developing cyber capabilities to knock down military networks and critical civilian infrastructure such as the electricity grid, financial systems, and hospitals. The Internet of Things, a smart cyber network that links machines to machines, computers to computers, across America and globally, is vulnerable to attack by foreign nations, thieves, and rogues.[15]

Other nations will point to America to justify their own cybersecurity and weaponry programs. China and Russia can point to us as eavesdropping on the world and disrupting other nations' infrastructure. Was Stuxnet the first cyber blast in a new type of war? Most likely.

A government committed to being permanently ready for war has tremendous potential power over citizens at odds with America's ideologies. Permanent crisis mode leads to coalitions whose members tend to forget

---

[15] Allison, G. (2017). Destined For War: Can America and China Escape Thucydides' Trap? Harper Collins. NY. pp. 163–167.

subtleties and avoid compromises in the face of overwhelming danger. It has led to the growth in executive power, a massive expansion of the military, and a massive increase in the size and scope of covert agencies. It has made breaking international and sometimes domestic law acceptable to prevent national disasters.

10.4   Security Restrictions on Private Enterprise

Permanent war footing has also changed government's terms of engagement with private industry. The US government has imposed a series of restrictions on telecommunication companies that make the government their virtual partners. Spencer E. Ante and Ryan Knutson reported that the government has used the merger approval process to gain a say over telecommunications companies' mergers.[16] To protect critical telecommunications infrastructure from cyber-attacks, national security agencies require multinational companies such as SoftBank, Sprint, T-Mobile, Verizon, and Vodafone and their major equipment suppliers such as Alcatel-Lucent and Ericsson to operate under security agreements. Recent merger documents require these companies to supply detailed network descriptions, including equipment design specifications. The government gets streamlined access to the networks and can require removal of certain equipment from a network. In the T-Mobile agreement, the carrier must inform the government when it uses a new equipment vendor. Fearing Chinese hacking, the government concluded the Chinese equipment company Huawei Technologies Co. and ZTE Corp. pose national security risks. When Japanese-owned Softbank took over Sprint, the government acquired the right to approve a director to Sprint's board, and Sprint was not allowed to use Chinese equipment to upgrade its network.

By 2022, the Federal Communications Commission issued an order to protect against national security threats. The order

> Prohibits authorization of all telecommunications and video surveillance
>   equipment produced by Huawei and ZTE (and that of their subsidiaries and
> affiliates);
>   Prohibits authorization of telecommunications equipment and video
>   .surveillance equipment produced by Hytera, Hikvision, and Dahua (and
> their respective subsidiaries or affiliates) until such time as the Commission
>   approves these entities' plans and measures that will to ensure the such

[16] Ante, SE. & Knutson, R. (2013) U.S. Tightens Grip on Telecom. The Wall Street Journal. https://www.wsj.com/articles/SB10001424127887324906304579037292831912078. Accessed 1 May 2023.

equipment will not be marketed and sold to for "the purpose of public safety, security of government facilities, physical surveillance of critical infrastructure, or other national security purpose"[17]

"The U.S. Department of Commerce's Bureau of Industry and Security (BIS) administers U.S. laws, regulations and policies governing the export and reexport of commodities, software, and technology (collectively "items") falling under the jurisdiction of the Export Administration Regulations (EAR). The primary goal of BIS is to advance national security, foreign policy, and economic objectives by ensuring an effective export control and treaty compliance system and promoting continued U.S. strategic technology leadership. BIS also enforces anti-boycott laws and coordinates with U.S. agencies and other countries on export control, nonproliferation and strategic trade issues." It uses export controls to "promote national security by limiting access to the most sensitive U.S. technology and weapons."[18]

The Biden Administration has introduced new restrictions on exports to China of advanced integrated circuits, certain computers, and related software, which is part of a larger strategy to limit China's military capabilities. There is also a restriction on "US person" activity in China to limit intellectual transfer of sensitive information. To secure the US chip's capability, Congress passed the Chips Act in 2022, which expands subsidies to support domestic chip manufacturing.[19]

10.5 Dangers to America's Democratic Process

Cyber eavesdropping is also undermining the democratic process. Was it Russian hackers or was it targeted leaks from campaign insiders, or American intelligence agencies that exposed the dirty side of the campaign and perhaps influenced the outcome of the Trump/Clinton presidential election? Someone inside the intelligence community may have leaked damaging information that led to General Flynn's resignation from Trump's cabinet. Targeted leaks can push personnel selection and government policy in desired directions.

---

[17] Federal Communications Commission (2023) FCC Amends Equipment Authorization Program. https://www.fcc.gov/document/fcc-amends-equipment-authorization-program. Accessed 1 May 2023.

[18] Overview of U.S. Export Control System, A Resource on Strategic Trade Management and Export Controls. https://2009-2017.state.gov/strategictrade/overview/index.htm. Accessed 1 May 2023.

[19] Dorsey and Whitney LLP (2022) Biden Administration Restricts U.S. Exports of Advanced Computing and Semiconductor Manufacturing Equipment, Software, and Technology to China. https://www.dorsey.com/newsresources/publications/client-alerts/2022/11/us-adds-strict-limits-on-technology-exports. Accessed 1 May 2023.

The Dreyfus Case in nineteenth-century France should be a warning about the dangers of career security agents with too much control. The General Staff of the French Army knew a spy was sending secret documents to Germany. They mistakenly fingered Alfred Dreyfus, an outsider in the army with Jewish and German connections as the perpetrator. The general staff concocted evidence to convict him and, even when they suspected he was innocent, continued to produce false documents to show they were right. They closed ranks and perhaps murdered those who would undue them. In the end, the Dreyfus Affair split France apart and discredited the army and its supporters at a time when unity in the face of the growing threat of German power was increasingly unnerving.

All this secrecy and spying are wearing away America's core values in obvious ways. A more subtle problem is its effect on the American psyche. People tend to exaggerate unknown dangers because there is little hard evidence to prevent the imagination from imagining all sorts of conspiracies. Partial leaks and exposes of American plots conjure dark images of America as a nation that wants to judge and police the world on its own terms and an America that is willing to invade any nation or the privacy of any individual, including its own citizens, to further the ends of its power elite.

Although Wiener's warnings mainly dealt with agents in the field and mainly with history prior to 9/11, they are still relevant today. Wittingly or not, America is breeding a super-patriot personality, someone who thinks he or she knows more than the public and is willing to sacrifice himself for an unknowing public. An intelligence agency's work often becomes politicized, used for winning elections or punishing political opponents and personal enemies. The plumbers in the Watergate break-in, the Iran-Contra operatives, and J. Edgar Hoover's secret files are scandalous examples of illegal use of spies by government officials. After 9/11, national identification cards were discussed but rejected. More ominously, the CIA received formal power to spy internally because hot pursuit of enemies such as Al-Qaeda knows no borders.[20]

10.6   Questionable International Intrigues

Covert operations abroad often lead to dealing with unscrupulous traitors in other countries looking for payoffs instead of disillusioned idealists. Normal operating procedures for effective spying depend on skirting or breaking

---

[20] Wiener, pp. 482–482.

foreign laws, even in democratic countries such as Italy where America funded anticommunist political parties. When the decision is to "fight fire with fire,"[21] almost any plan of attack is open for discussion. Almost anyone can be a source, even the devil himself, if the information is reliable. In 1994, Woolsey described "agent validation" as the quality of agents' information weighed against perfidy of conduct.[22] For instance, it may be okay to work with a known butcher to prevent a biological weapon attack. America takes a chance with eyes open. This is not terribly different from America's import of ex-Nazis to work on developing ICBMs, or hiding a Nazi, Klaus Barbie, known as the Butcher of Lyon, because he was useful for counterintelligence.

Buying foreign politicians, supporting foreign coups, and running guns to foreign rebels erode American values.[23] Unfortunately, history shows that covert action can never win a war, only forestall it. In the meantime, leaks and scandals expose America's disregard for national rights and human rights and its ineptness and impotence.[24] Screw-ups will occur that may threaten international peace such as the bombing of Chinese Embassy in Serbia, thought to be the military headquarters of the Serbian army. Inevitably, covert actions lead to retaliation. Assassinations abroad invite assassinations at home.[25]

America has to be on its guard not to allow intelligence agencies to become a secret army with secret alliances. It may become dependent on foreign security agencies for intelligence, and these other agencies can sell America out.

The digital revolution has added different types of agents who feel most comfortable behind a computer console. Armies of agents have access to private information that they could use to spy on their fellow citizens or download and sell to the enemy. There are agents who play God using a joystick to order a drone to fire at a target. What happens if one of them decides to assassinate a key official that starts a war? What happens if they are used in America to protect our borders? The genetic-engineering revolution in the hands of security agencies may have created the COVID-19 pandemic. Who becomes responsible if this is true?

America's three major ideologies have no easy answers to limits of palace guards because their storylines do not include a state of permanent war with enemies that operate in failed states and have the potential to disrupt American society with the threat of detonating weapons of mass destruction on American

---

[21] Id., p. 26.
[22] Id., p. 458.
[23] Id., p. 273.
[24] Id., pp. 293–294.
[25] Id., p. 187.

soil. Turning to Wiener again, he asked a few basic questions with no palatable answers:

> How do you manage a secret service that thrives through deception?
>> How do you operate a secret service in an open democracy?
>> How do you serve truth by lying?
>> How do you spread democracy by deceit?[26]

American ideologs should also be careful not to oversell threats to American democracy. Since 9/11, there have been no major attacks in the United States. Considering the massive scale of American eavesdropping, only scattered cases of abridged freedom have been registered in the United States and pursued in court. Al-Qaeda is in decline (though other terrorist groups are taking its place, e.g., ISIS). Presidential administrations have changed; the press remains vibrant, although arguably more fractious and politicized; and social networks continue to flourish. What would have happened if Al-Qaeda had been able to land "a second blow on par with 9/11."[27] Even before 9/11, President Carter's use of clandestine operations for human rights.[28]

Nonetheless, America must come to grips with the fact that no nation can be perfectly secure; others will not tolerate having no protection from an invulnerable state; they will ultimately use our own methods to undermine our security.

---

[26] Id., p. 501.

[27] Yoo, J. (2011) Ten Years Without an Attack, WSJ Opinion. https://www.wsj.com/articles/SB10001424053111904332804576538443334834166. Accessed 1 May 2023.

[28] Wiener, p. 357.

11

Designer Eugenics: The Nearsighted God

Abstract A brief history of genetic engineering shows how it has evolved. Selective breeding is giving way to genetic engineering. This new scientific approach treats genes as systems that can be manipulated in ways that threaten the integrity and sanctity of human life, and core ideological values become at risk because they lose definition. Genetic engineering threatens humanity with the specter of faux species, faux landscapes, and faux evolution. Already humanity is confronting new forms of discrimination based on using genetic databases to identify physical and mental limitations. In the long term, a people divide may occur between those who are genetically engineered and those who have not been.

11.1 Introduction

Designer eugenics is the next and perhaps the most challenging long-term problem facing humanity. It raises questions that were long the province of God. Humanity has the potential to reform the earth, the plants and animals that live upon it, and humanity itself. The big fear is "Can we trust ourselves to make the right decisions?" Can we depend on others to respect the sanctity of this planet and the planets we will colonize?

Humanity is frightened and allured by the powers of genetic engineering. Humanity already has the power to wipe out malaria by genetically modifying mosquitos, to raise gigantic genetically modified salmon, to grow genetically modified tomatoes that resist spoilage, and to alter genetically animal traits. Designer babies are on the horizon. What are the risks of genetic engineering?

V. Glass, *Humanizing the Digital Economy*, https://doi.org/10.1007/978-3-031-37507-1_11

Can they be measured? Can they be controlled? What are the chances that a lunatic uses genetic engineering to destroy us?

Humanity has a long record of reshaping the world and in doing so producing undesirable byproducts. The industrial revolution led to blacktopping the earth and pouring effluents into the sea and sky. These are difficult problems that humanity is still struggling to solve. Economists believe the answers lie in developing new types of property rights such as carbon taxes to control pollution.

Unintended consequences of human genetic engineering, in particular, are of a different order because American society treats human beings as sacred vessels – at least officially. It is difficult to see how a cocktail of legal changes in property rights, or limits on the profit motive, or government oversight will prevent human genetic experimentation that could have catastrophic consequences. People want to live forever and live healthy lives. Is this a realistic dream if humanity remains tied to the earth?

Even in the short term, progress in medical science is raising very difficult problems about the value of saving or extending human lives. A few decades ago, HIV was a death sentence; now it is a chronic disease, thanks to new drugs like AZT. People are living longer but end of life requires expensive healthcare. Expensive designer drugs are being developed to cure specific types of diseases. It is not surprising that healthcare costs are rising rapidly and cutting into budgets for other valuable services such as infrastructure and perhaps research to develop new approaches to reshaping the world.

11.2   A Brief History of Genetic Engineering

Before tackling the designer eugenics problem, let's look at evolution in a broad context to gain perspective about how much we should fear putting the power of God in the mind of man. For starters, genetic engineering stretches back at least as far as the birth of civilizations. According to Jared Diamond, for example, the great civilizations arose where wheat and rice grew naturally. People learned they were foodstuffs and began picking the stalks that were easiest to harvest for food. Without much forethought by humans, the plants yielding food began to expand their territory simply from the pattern of harvesting. Eventually, people started to cultivate these cereals without really understanding the genetics behind them.

In modern times, thanks to Gregor Mendel, plant breeders realized that a plant inherited dominant and recessive traits. From there, a systematic approach to cross-pollination led to new strains of all types of flowers. All you have to do is compare a wild rose to the hothouse variety to see enormous changes brought on by selective breeding. This type of scientific approach to plant breeding contributed greatly to the Green Revolution in the 1960s.

Selective breeding was also applied to cattle to enhance the stock in some defined way that paid off in the marketplace. Just compare longhorn livestock of the nineteenth century to today's massive, hornless cattle to see the dramatic increase in the beef yield produced by selective breeding.

When it came to human selective breeding, the ancient practices of hunter/gatherers and early farmers were not very different from the way they treated plants and livestock. Deformed babies were left to die after birth because they would prove a burden on the family and tribe. It was a common practice for a tribal chief to have many wives and many children as a means to enhance the stock of hunters and warriors. In civilized times, both practices became taboo, but they did not end until recent times. Midwives quietly snuffed out the lives of newborns born with obvious physical defects. Noblemen and later the rich had their mistresses.

This informal attitude toward genetics changed with the scientifically minded progressives of the nineteenth century and first four decades of the twentieth century. They tried to achieve twin goals: lessening suffering and enhancing the human stock by identifying people with genetic defects and those with superior genes. Educating the public was central to their strategy. People should know if they have inherited genetic defects and advise them not to have children. Public policies aimed at continence, contraception, and in special cases sterilization among high-risk groups would improve the human stock. Nazi nightmarish experiments on humans put an end to any thought of an American public policy that would use coercion to eliminate the unfit from society.

With the unique identification of chromosomes in the 1920s, a revolution in eugenics started to take off, slowly at first, but is gathering momentum and leading us to places humanity only dreamed off in science fiction and fantasy. It began with tests of fetuses in the womb for genetic defects. If the fetus had a defect, such as Down syndrome, a typical medical recommendation was a therapeutic abortion.

11.3 The Ethical Challenges of Genetic Engineering

Once genetics moved to the cellular level, a whole new landscape opened up to scientists. It wasn't filled with microscopic plants and animals. It was more like an industrial city. Cells were like factories that operate according to a DNA code – living software – that could be reprogrammed. The proteins built by this software became the hardware, the tools for building cells that produced output.

Imagine how exciting it is for a scientist to realize that humanity has the opportunity to reprogram these factories. They could manipulate diseased cells and build new ones that could bypass evolution's waste and delays in sorting out genetics that would make man into a superman. But genetic engineering could do so much more. No longer would it be necessary to raise and kill living creatures to produce food. The cellular factory could be redesigned to produce new materials, energy, and medicine and even become a data storage and processing unit far superior to inorganic ones. Innovators are working to mass produce designer DNA and stem cells. They are using cloud computing to store huge amounts of data that can be used to see how organs work in real time. New imaging processes will allow scientists to watch the brain reacting to different stimuli.[1]

Seeing life as an industrial belt led to experiments that would revolt even the most radical progressives. Scientists began combining human and animal cells in the hope of producing superior genetic combinations. Snipping genetic material from one place and pasting it elsewhere held the promise of turning genetically defective people into normal or even superior beings. This noble aim also opened the field to Frankenstein-like experiments.

The ethical challenges are often masked by scientific jargon. The identification of a human cell with a person is giving way to a systems approach in biology. Genes became stores of information that contained "assembly instructions and parts lists."[2] Life at the cellular level took on a "mechanical structure with what could be imagined as switches, dampers, and governors."[3]

Even with the shield of dehumanizing language and theories, scientists and policy makers are concerned about the possibility that life itself and certainly the preservation of humans as we know them is under threat. Scientists began reviewing the Nuremberg trials for guidance on the limits of acceptable genetic experiments. Universities developed guidelines and a review process for potentially dangerous experiments. The National Institute of Health issued regulations to prevent dangers to the public.

But how to enforce what could be almost unenforceable? Will any of these restrictions prevent dangerous experiments? The issues will look strangely similar to the other Black Swan examples. How effective can peer review be in limiting dangerous experiments? How capable are the government regulators when experiments operate at the leading edge of rapidly expanding science? A regulatory lag will always exist. Often, new rules are outdated before they even

---

[1] Indi Bio (2016, day 2), https://www.youtube.com/watch?v=WucEx8J_WM0. Accessed 1 May 2023.
[2] Comfort, N. (2012) The Science of Human Perfection: How Genes Became the Heart Of American Medicine Oxford University Press, London, p. 215
[3] Id., p. 215

become official. Cross-border control will be necessary but will likely also spawn genetic-engineering open zones.

Scientists want to push back frontiers. They want to develop new designer genes and systems within the body to go way beyond preventing genetic diseases, and the public wants them to push ahead.

The public senses the human fantasy of becoming gods can become a reality someday. They have already seen the first fruits of designer eugenics. Therapeutic abortions, in vitro fertilization, surrogate motherhood, and genetic screening have increased the odds of having healthy and perhaps superior babies.

The desire for control over fate is a very powerful inducement to move ahead with genetic engineering as rapidly as possible. Individuals themselves will pay a lot to keep looking young, feeling healthy, and knowing that genetic therapy of some sort could enhance them in novel ways. One can imagine lopsided wants as we've seen in China because of the one-baby rule. There, a preponderance of male children was born. Imagine if someone said, as Hermann Muller, the eugenicist once did, that if intelligence is good, more intelligence is better. We could see people with basketball heads being born outside the womb.

An unsettling byproduct may be an overemphasis on genetic engineering as the pathway to a good life. Upbringing, diversity, and the beauty of chance are likely to become too risky.[4] As a result, humanity begins to diverge in ways that we would agree could be nightmarish.

11.4 Government's Role

The role of government in a eugenics program may occur without needing a Hitler at the helm preaching racial purity. In a market-driven world, a way to escape personal responsibility for genetic decisions is to let the government take over. Ask yourself, why are there hospitals, orphanages, and insane asylums? Is it just because of economies of scale to best treat them under one roof, or is some other motivation the cause? Is it possible that people don't want seriously sick people around them, don't want to care for other people's children, and want protection from crazy people? Even religious institutions may not want the responsibility for supporting their own problem cases. They could become bankrupt.

---

[4] Id., p. 246

A government takeover may even have strong economic justifications. Health and well-being are already a market that is unlikely to operate efficiently. The market deals with human beings being treated as commodities. The people seeking insurance are likely to lie if they have an illness. Insurers don't want to ensure high-risk candidates, or the insurance premiums would not be affordable. People can plan but often believe they will live forever, and then an emergency occurs. People do not want catastrophic events to wipe anyone out because of the "There for the grace of God go I" empathetic reaction.

11.5 Genetic Engineering Is Re-engineering Core Values

One way or another, genetic engineering will attack America's core values, which depend on human nature as it existed before genetic engineering. In the last few centuries, "Man in the image of God" has been cut down by scientific discoveries. Many scientists agree with Darwin, as interpreted by Stephen J. Gould, that evolution shows no apparent design. Plants and animals adapt to their environment. The rise of complexity in human nature is mainly explained by a minimum barrier to life that requires certain basic materials and connections. The only way life can change, even if it changes randomly, is toward complexity. This is a passive form of evolution needing no overall design implanted in the first living entity.[5]

As Hayek pointed out, this is not true of culture. All three ideologies believe in purposeful cultural evolution, often with punctuated changes that overthrow a previous order. Knowledge and practices accumulate and are available to those who choose to tap them. Hayek, for example, said that business institutions are subject to a survival of the fittest battle in the marketplace. Nations can choose to adopt this wisdom and add to it or, as in the case of China and Japan centuries ago, turn their backs on the outside world. If Steven Pinker is correct, civilization has grown much more peaceful and prosperous with the takeoff in markets, in the rule of law and democracy, in knowledge of others gained from literacy, and in the conceptualizing of society and its populous that leads to fair treatment.

This separation between undirected natural evolution and directed cultural evolution is no longer plausible. We have the ability to alter both types of

---

[5] Gould, SJ. (1996) Full House: The Spread of Excellence from Plato To Darwin. Harmony Books, NY. p. 169

evolution at will. Designer eugenics will alter human nature and with it the core values that supported the best use of this nature. As with fire, gunpowder, and atomic power, we have no reason to presuppose that genetic engineering will be the end of us, but it will put humanity to the test, a test not readily answered by our three main ideologies. We will require new moral and religious insights to use this new power to enhance life.

Before getting carried away with man becoming a god, consider a squeamish example pointing in the opposite direction, of man becoming food. Scientists recently proclaimed they had made a cow burger from cow muscle grown in a laboratory. With great fanfare, someone fried the burger and offered it to three taste testers who ate it. They liked the texture, but the flavor was off, not enough fat. Not to worry, scientists will add fat cells to their cultured meat. This of course could be a great boon to humanity and to the millions of cattle killed each year. But let's consider an old Alfred Hitchcock episode, "The Specialty of the House." A person eats a meal at a private club and finds the food amazingly delicious. It turns out that the specialty of the house was human meat, and the invitee is served the following year as the main course. Suppose someone grows human muscle cells laced with fat and makes a special burger. Would society permit it? Could society prevent it? What will it do to humanity, to humanity's core values?

Volitional changes in human nature, whether the result of spontaneous marketplace demand or from government planning, are likely to disconnect us from future generations. The dark side of eugenics is obvious to a fan of science fiction. It can introduce in a new form the primitive urge to kill those with bad blood and nurture a new perfect man, perfect ethnic group, perfect society through genetic engineering.

Eugenics could ratchet up angst exponentially. People will expect their genes won't make the grade; they may not be able to articulate that failings and differences make life beautiful and interesting. Integrity could be lost in basic ways. A new form of prejudice could emerge. Non-altered and genetically modified humans may not want to have children with each other. Even more bizarre outcomes could occur. Richard Morgan, the science fiction author of *Altered Carbon*, predicted that men and women could exchange sexes or become unisex. When people can live forever, eternal physical torture done scientifically becomes a possibility. Genetic engineering could produce genetic haves and have nots, supermen, and primitive slaves.

Less dramatic, science may improve the predictability of human behavior and could lead to behavioral control by others, possibly government as in a Brave New World. This brings up a second path to designer eugenics, one that ties in with the other Black Swan examples. Manufactured implants have been used to save lives and lessen pain. Pacemakers, heart valves, and mechanical hearts are just a few examples. Those depending on electrical pulses are at risk of being jammed by outside sources such as cellphones. Smart implants expand the possibilities of tampering enormously. Already developed are computer chips that monitor well-being and alert rescue teams in cases where a patient is having a seizure. These devices give someone the ability to know the vital signs of the patient. By extension, any smart implant has the potential to allow some *Big Brother* to monitor and potentially control lives. Even more ominous are recent experiments with mice. Scientists are downloading instructions to create false memories in the brains of mice. Naturally, this technique could treat post-traumatic stress disorder, but it will also allow scientists to control the human mind, to make us in the image of someone else's creation. When memory is manipulated, what is the dividing line between reality and fantasy? Will we be able to download the memory of one person into another? Is that murder?

Besides direct gene manipulation, and manufactured implants, a third way approach to designer eugenics is through chemical alteration. Hunter-gatherer tribes sued mind-altering drugs such as peyote to unlock the spiritual world. Today, we have drugs to alter moods, to lessen pain, and to prevent disease. It is not unlikely that future drugs could even allow communal hallucinations or a person escaping to his own universe as Philip K. Dick suggested in *The Three Stigmata of Palmer Eldritch*.

The threats of genetic eugenics are real and hard to imagine with any degree of clarity. They are not issues that ideologues tackle in their historical story line. Would a strict libertarian simply say, "Let's set up gene markets"? They agree with outlawing slavery, so there are some limits in the marketplace. But what are they in this so-called market? It is not hard to imagine a dystopia where the profit motive leads to also sorts of hybrid life that would make us sick and fear for our future across future generations.

Would liberals want government to democratically control gene research and use so that all individuals benefit equally from genetic engineering? Who would decide on the genetic program? If we don't trust government with today's social and economic issues, would we trust government with our very being?

Would arch conservatives cut off genetic research that leads to lessening disease, infirmities, and enhancing life? Groping toward solutions when radical changes in humanity and life itself are in the offing may not be palatable even to the most inflexible conservative.

What would a nation do if keeping people alive indefinitely was both a reality and a tremendous burden on society and on future generations? Would a co-pay take care of the problem by allowing a person's life to end when his money is gone? Or should a team of government experts or theologians decide when a patient should accept a just and lasting peace?

And what about rogue states that are safe havens for mad scientists?

12

Unsettling Perspectives

Abstract This chapter reviews the unsettling effects of the coding revolution giving birth to digital networks, smart systems, big data, artificial intelligence, and genetic engineering. The message is that the coding revolution is altering life on many scales, from the cell to society to the earth's ecosystems and beyond. Humanity has reached the point of becoming a creator in the real world and a creator of virtual worlds. It is conquering inner space and outer space. As humanity travels to new realities of its own making, America's core values and story lines are undergoing stresses not easily understood but powerful, nonetheless.

I chose disruptive changes to society, each an unsettling example that traces effects of the coding revolution giving birth to digital bytes of data, digital networks, smart systems, big data, artificial intelligence, and genetic engineering. The message is that the coding revolution is altering life on many scales, from the cell to society to the earth's ecosystems and beyond. Humanity has reached the point of becoming a creator in the real world and a creator of virtual worlds. It is conquering inner space and outer space. As humanity travels to new realities of its own making, America's core values and story lines are undergoing stresses not easily understood but powerful, nonetheless.

Many of these issues are not new, and some authors have sounded the alarm already. Thomas Friedman articulated the "flat earth problem" that we have entered an era of low transportation and communication costs making it unlikely that one nation will dominate world affairs for long stretches of time. The flat earth problem also weakens the rule of law by allowing transactions to flow across borders with insufficient official oversight. Private property had become virtualized in cyberspace, allowing anyone with computer savvy to

V. Glass, *Humanizing the Digital Economy*, https://doi.org/10.1007/978-3-031-37507-1_12

steal, alter, and combine with other information, making it almost free to the taker. Terrorists whether they are the corporate variety or Jihadists, or rogue governments – and sometimes democratic governments – can spawn viruses and worms to attack and undermine competitors and enemies. In response, America has invested heavily in organizing counterterrorist palace guards, who, themselves, are threats to freedom and privacy themselves.

Paradoxically, scientists with noble intentions who are using genetic engineering techniques to solve problems plaguing humanity are also weakening America's core values. They are turning the human body into a specimen with the intent of transforming it into something invulnerable to disease or to aging and capable of being transformed into a super being. The surprise might be that humans merge, Borg-like, into a human-machine ecosystem.

Taken together, virtual reality allows people to escape into their own worlds, stealth security allows others to spy on the most private activities a person has, and genetic engineering threatens to transform human beings into something new.

A great transition is underway leading to unbalanced changes in society that is stressing American culture. The digital revolution, like earlier ones, is incomplete and evolving more rapidly in some dimensions than others. The most obvious and immediate disruptions are to market arrangements, both public and private. They have not caught up with the instantaneous, frictionless, global market that spawns new virtual products, including financial instruments that no one quite understands. Prices are inaccurate guides for the value of many products. Laws intended to protect the public from unfair practices such as bankruptcy laws can freeze markets. Human nature and social institutions have not caught up with stupendous changes created by the fast paced, open markets, often manipulated by anonymous characters that may be Americans or offshore speculators with their own agendas. Herding, out of fear or out of lust, used to be a localized phenomenon in the main. Now it is global. When the herd stampedes, there is nowhere to hide.

Private corporations are under pressure because internal safeguards are not up to the challenge of cyberspace competition. If AIG's top management can be believed, they did not know that their subsidiary was hemorrhaging billions of dollars on bad CDOs and CDSs, not to say the managers of AIG and other corporations sometimes have their own agendas at the expense of stockholders or even American interests. Eventually, losses pile up and a poorly managed company teeters on bankruptcy. Unfortunately, to attract global customers, companies have gotten so large and complex that allowing a poorly managed corporation to fail hurts the American economy. Is the pursuit of profits the path to corporate excellence? Joseph Stiglitz pointed out that America's best private corporations are its universities and the once insulated Bell Labs that only in name still exists. America has not really appreciated the irony of nonprofit organizations flourishing and profit-driven ones suffering from internal sickness.

From the public's perspective, bigness produces fear. Big government can control the lives of people within its jurisdiction. Big business can squeeze customers who need its services. Asymmetric power is at the heart of this fear: David and Goliath, but David has no sling. For some, the digital revolution is liberating, but for many others, this new technology disrupts their lives, turning known paths to fulfillment into dead ends.

The big online platforms have engendered fear because of their size. They are the focal point for the fears that the digital revolution has created. They have global reach and have created digital mosaics of billions of people. Their employees are anonymous, yet they can peer into the lives of anyone in their databases. Platforms have expanded the choices available to the public and reduced the search costs for the item desired. They even offer online assistants that will help make our choices. Is making decisions easier good for society in the long term? Should a social media platform filter online posts, or should the government do it, or should no one do it?

Once fear takes hold, it shows in the framing of issues. For instance, competition can easily be described as the desire to exploit people by extracting their payoffs from trades. Low prices are interpreted as predatory. High prices are monopolistic. Target pricing to cater to different market segments becomes price discrimination. Customizing products to cater to particular needs becomes behavioral manipulation. Private labels that supermarkets use suppress competition online. When a platform sets rules for trading on it, the rules become gateways that platforms close to keep competition out.

Those who study the emerging digital revolution are beginning to absorb its changes in how the economy operates. They are translating fears into concrete facts. Big business used to mean controlling a key product like steel or oil and the supply chains associated with these products. In the digital world, technology is the source of bigness and potential power. Big means controlling critical computer operating systems, browsers, server farms, virtual assistants, and online auctions. Measuring exploitation in this dynamic environment is difficult because platforms keep trying to capture new markets. In other words, market definitions, even software technology, keep morphing, sometimes in surprising ways.

In this type of environment, how does the government protect private property rights and competition? Personal data is floating through the Internet. Big platforms see it first, which gives them an advantage, but is it a permanent advantage when behavior and technology keep changing? Economists like to focus on consumer and producer surplus – gains from trade – as the benchmarks for seeing whether the public is being exploited. I suspect Daniel Bell, the sociologist, would cast a wider net. Like Lina Khan, he recognized that competition affects and is affected by government acts, by cultural norms, and by the rearrangement of competition caused by innovations. People sense when they are being exploited and want it stopped. The trouble is that the public is not monolithic.

Public policy like private decisions require tradeoffs. The public wants to even the power balance between themselves and big organizations. They want transparency. For instance, they want to know what a platform knows about them. They want to cut complexity or at least be insured against bad decisions because they do not understand the product they are buying. In a less chaotic world, food and drug labeling helped assure the public that what they ingested was nurturing, not poisonous.

Is government up to the challenge of somehow being a benign overseer of the online economy? Perhaps, perhaps not. It extends the government's power, but does it yield tangible benefits? So far, the jury is out. Government may not have the wherewithal to monitor and shape the online economy in ways that enrich society and spread the benefits.

One could reasonably argue that no amount of Jerry-rigging of government by adding congressional staff, or bureaucracies or subcontracting, will give governments the flexibility to establish order and fair rules and enforce fair play in cyber markets. Open borders, whether physical or virtual, limit social spending because welfare dollars could raise production costs and could hurt international competitiveness. Attempts to limit unequal distribution of wealth may lead to émigrés – both people and corporation – to new homes where tax laws are more favorable. This is not hard to imagine when transportation costs are low, communication is instant and global, and the psychic and material losses from a physical move are declining as world culture becomes integrated.

Despite the advent of big data and statistical techniques, anti-recessionary tools remain blunt. American policymakers still don't know with any precision the effects of deficit spending on the economy. Monetary expansion did not end the Great Recession as someone as Milton Friedman would have predicted. It is not clear if or to what extent American policy can lessen the damage caused by Black Swan events and policies that aim at ultimate security whether domestically or internationally often produce the opposite result, insecurity. America's desire to protect itself from communism and from oil delivery disruptions likely contributed to the international turmoil we see in the Middle East and elsewhere.

Government regulations are often out-of-date before they take effect in industries experiencing fast technological change. In many instances regulation did little to prevent corporate failures such as WorldCom and other communication giants, or Enron in the energy field, and many investment houses such as Merrill Lynch. Even worse, regulation gave the public a false sense of security that the government was protecting the public from shady dealings. It is not clear that government regulations of genetic engineering can be supple enough to prevent catastrophes and at the same time clear the way for important scientific research and genetically altered products and people.

Old definitions of sovereignty often seem outdated, if not downright wrong, when global coordination is necessary. Super national organizations are developing, but they lack enforcement power. America has walked away from many international rulings, from climate control to invading Iraq. Other nations such as Iran are doing what they feel is in their own interests and to hell with the rest of the world.

Myopic competition among states is undermining the rule of law. Nations with lax legal systems may in some cases attract shady but profitable businesses. Many markets have shifted to cyberspace. In a world with virtual borders, where a mouse click can shift billions of dollars or sensitive information, the rule of law becomes very hard to enforce. Failed states can harbor terrorist organizations such as Al-Qaeda. In the future, rogue states may become test beds for network viruses and homes for the type of genetic experiments described in melodramatic science fiction novels and movies.

Permanent war is feeding a covert sector of society that is drawing off resources and talent to combat terrorism. A dangerous tradeoff is underway between security and the rule of law, the basis of the freedoms we take for granted. Search and seizure in cyberspace are widespread with privacy as the victim. Laws limiting search should not cover up the fact that rules to uncover and prevent threats have been the legal tools used by kings and tyrants to suppress opposition.

With all these challenges, government gridlock may have occurred even without the ideology wars going on in America because it is not clear what policies are effective in this disruptive environment. As the scope of government ramped up, the expectations of the public ramped up. Failures and disappointments and cynicism are the products of setting unrealistic goals for policymakers. How do they protect property rights to adjusting them in an increasingly crowded civilization based on cyber technologies? How does government maintain a permanent war footing and keep Americans free from government intrusion?

The character of political marketing has taken a shameful turn, making a bad situation worse. Politicians have become the equivalent of brand names that are marketed to the public; they come with airbrushed pictorial histories and redacted resumes. After grueling primary contests, presidential candidates seem like a cross between prophet, superhero, and buffoon, sometimes with a touch of evil. Politic campaigns have become like a Hollywood blockbuster epic thriller, sometimes bordering on a film noire. Politicians position themselves as reformers who will cut out the rot and corruption in government instead of saying they will contribute to team building in government. To win, political candidates drum up expectations that are unattainable. Subject experts play supporting roles, often becoming key players. Lately, the scripts have become doctrinaire, out of touch with reality.

In the face of these potentially damaging trends, ideologues should feel uneasy. It is a bit too glib for libertarians to say as Joseph Stigler once said that private enterprise is a hardy weed and that left to its own, corporations will solve any problem, including the principal-agent problem because competition will force efficiency. It is also a bit glib to say that government sets up these problems with bailouts and supposed oversight that doesn't work gives investors a false sense of security. A more interesting line of thought is to pose questions to the faithful. How does cyberspace capitalism differ from traditional private enterprise? Are cyber networks more like public or private roads? How do you limit cyber invasion of private space when companies and governments can look at a person's communications? How does America's permanent war footing against terrorists affect the rule of law, privacy, and security? Who should define rules and enforce them for genetic research?

Conservatives think the problem is primarily ethical. They want to return to a time when professionalism was important, when buy, hold, and build trumped short-term greed, when patriotism and religion made people think in generations and about others instead of themselves. The issue is how this can be accomplished in an open, multicultural society where viewpoints differ on the meaning of community and patriotism. What will genetic research do to American culture, to religion, to the very meaning of self? What limits should America place on scientific research and who should set them?

Liberals want more government oversight to protect us from private enterprise gone amok; more government control to promote equal obligation such as universal medical care. Is this a realistic strategy? Does the government have the organizational capability to tackle problems in the cyber age? Does the government have the expertise to tackle complex, scientific problems? Can the American government continue to set policy on its own in the face of global markets and global national competitors that are shrinking America's power? Can the government really form communities? Which nations abroad have risen, the ones who received foreign aid and Peace Corps volunteers or the ones that struck out on their own? Can the government predict economic activity and manage the economy? Can the government act in loco parentis to many different ethnic groups?

All three ideologies have to find ways to uphold the integrity and sacredness of individuals, communities, and cultures in a future world where "boundaries are that of the imagination (Rod Serling)."

Part III

Reconciliation and Collaboration

Abstract I devote this final section to developing a narrative framework and analytic tools that allow ideologues to move out from where they are and explore new alternatives without having them shed their core beliefs. The centerpiece of the plan explained in Part III is this expansive American philosophy, which I call Religious Humanism. Next, I introduce new narrative and analytical tools and techniques drawn from Jewish mysticism, sociology, and systems theory to open new pathways for understanding societal and economic problems from a fresh perspective. In the process, Religious Humanism is then connected with the Coding Revolution. This marriage opens up new perspectives for solving current and impending social problems. This section ends with a series of proposed policy changes that could address particular privacy, security, and economic stability questions. The proposals are meant to be instructive sketches of how to use narrative tools developed in this section, not as final policy recommendations.

A political checklist often labels someone as a flaming liberal or red-necked conservative, or perhaps pale and wimpy if someone starts hedging. Sometimes a little more personal background helps refine the filter. A liberal Jew from New York conjures a whole set of images as does conservative republican from Idaho, or a member of the rainbow coalition hailing from San Francisco.

Getting by stereotypes is difficult. I chose ideological champions, cerebral ones, to show that America's ideologies have a lot to say about the workings of American politics and economics. They also have a lot in common when identifying flaws in society. On many issues, the champions I chose would probably agree with each other but operate differently. They would agree, for example, that a government guaranteed minimum standard of living is necessary to preserve human dignity and national stability.

Another less discussed strategy for working together is to identify a threat that requires common action. It seems much less palatable because the Fascists, Nazis, and communists used the specter of a foreign enemy to unite the people. Certainly the 9/11 attack united Americans against Jihadists, although the displays of patriotism quickly faded. Life went back to normal with people arguing over the same ideological battles. I chose a different approach: to identify a common threat to America's ideologies that is ongoing, that threatens the very core of their beliefs, which overturns or at least pushes around their ready answers to public policy. The threat I chose was the Coding Revolution, which puts into question the security of national borders, the rule of law, basic terms of human interaction, and even the genetic makeup of a human being. This is not to deny that humanity faces other threats. It is becoming clear the earth itself has limited carrying capacity and clashes of civilizations combined with weapons of mass destruction being stockpiled in states willing to use them could trigger wars that could kill millions in an instant.

I devote this final section to developing a narrative framework and analytic tools that allow ideologues to move out from where they are and explore new alternatives without having them shed their core beliefs. The starting point for reconciliation and collaboration is to realize that America's "isms" are like religions that split from a basic visionary insight. Capitalism, liberalism, socialism, and communism are secular religions based on the belief that the cause of crime and anti-social behavior is lack of resources. They predict that increases in per capita income will lead to a society that is trouble free – a heaven on earth of sorts. They simply differ on the level of central control and distribution of wealth.

Conservatives and environmentalists have a more traditional religious focus on overcoming humanity's sinful nature instead of on the lack of material goods as the source of human corruption. Conservatives believe that society should focus on abiding by God's wishes to usher in a Messianic Age. Environmentalists have their own religion based on humanity corrupting the environment. Worldly heaven will be restored if humanity restores nature to its pristine self. Arguably, libertarians and liberals would classify environmental damage results from not pricing pollutants correctly.

Each "ism's" view tries to develop myths and narratives that unify humanity toward a common purpose. Unimagined changes that shake the world require a new, usually, broader religious perspective. In Part I, I tried to make the case that conservatism, libertarianism, and liberalism formed to address societal crises. The idea already planted in Part II is that America is facing a new crisis caused by the Coding Revolution. In response, America needs a broader political philosophy and new narrative tools and techniques to recapture its sense of a unified mission.

A critical feature of America's "isms" is they are open to change and pluralistic. Liberals, libertarians, conservatives, environmentalists have different views of what their "ism" means and its methods. They absorb new ideas and develop new myths and visions. In a sense, they are part of a larger American philosophy that does not have a name. The centerpiece of the plan explained in Part III is this expansive American philosophy, which I call Religious Humanism. Like America's "isms" its basic elements are rationalism, pragmatism, romanticism, Deism, and mysticism. Like an alchemist, different proportions of these elements produce America's ideologies and many others, some as dark as Nazism. America's ideologies have picked different combinations and specific interpretations of the four elements to redeem, reform, and reinvent America. I will suggest ideologues can find new philosophical territory to explore and still keep their basic character. It is in these new spaces that collaboration is more likely.

Next, I introduce new narrative and analytical tools and techniques drawn from Jewish mysticism, sociology, and systems theory to open new pathways for understanding societal and economic problems from a fresh perspective. In the process, Religious Humanism is then connected with the Coding Revolution. This marriage opens up new perspectives for solving current and impending social problems. It also requires politicians, clerics, and philosophers to understand and adopt the language of the Coding Revolution. Suggested proposals for reform are described as examples of how new policy can be developed that offer enough bargaining space for political reconciliation and collaboration.

This section ends with a series of proposed policy changes that could address particular privacy, security, and economic stability questions. The proposals are meant to be instructive sketches of how to use narrative tools developed in the section, not as final policy recommendations.

Again, I do not expect this superstructure and set of narrative tools to create a new unity, only a new creativeness that could benefit everyone. Ideologies can develop very different views of the world but with enough overlap that they will have grounds to agree on shorter term policy.

Ideological reconciliation depends on realizing limitations in one's approach and looking for help from any source. My hope is that the culture-changers caused by the Coding Revolution that I have identified will allow ideologues to step back and realize what they don't know and challenge them to adjust their story lines to explain new realities. In the process, they may recognize that no science, no ideology, no culture, no religion has all the answers. From the basic assumptions of natural sciences to those of the social sciences, foolproof, objective knowledge of the workings of the universe are not there and become less certain as we move up the ladder of living creatures to the human level.

In America, common history tends to become fragmented, hyphenated, by an open society. Our saving grace is that we recognize eventually that a correction is necessary when the word doesn't match the deed. New frameworks, new paths, and new story lines are together the bridge to ideological conciliation. The challenge is to imagine the Coding Revolution as a new, higher stage of human existence with America as its guiding spirit. My aim in the next six chapters is to open new frontiers where America's ideologues can renew America's spirit by exploring new horizons.

13

Religious Humanism Defined

Abstract Religious humanism brings together major approaches to social problems that fall into the "religious" category: a collective focal point, a moral sense based on a covenant with ancestors, and an ongoing redemptive struggle with evil; "humanism" embodies the idea that humanity is the basic standard of value, enthroning the rational life; redemption depends on human effort alone. The key message is that religious humanism is a framework built from many strands of wisdom that can house many ideological and religious perspectives. Ultimately, religious humanism comes alive when these perspectives nurture each other. The question is how can this be accomplished?

American unity stems from a common religious spirit of tolerance that lets people live as they please so long as they do not hurt anyone. Different races, religions, and ethnic groups ennoble the human condition by showing we do not have to be alike to be part of a unified society. Respect for differences wears down barriers that isolate us and make us fearful of each other. America tries to make Jews, Christians, and Moslems ashamed to say that other religions are not as good as their own. It encourages families not to reject children who drift away from their heritage because other heritages also have their nobility. This is a grave threat to any fanatical religious group that knows its way is the only right way.

America's tolerance stems from a religious outlook on life that has its roots in the Enlightenment. It began as a rebellion against inherited wisdom, of believing that the Bible is the only fount of wisdom and that the right religion knew all the sacred truths. It led to a new religious view of the world that I define as "religious humanism." It is America's political religion – a religion without a formal name or formal services; it is a religion without rites of entry, but it exists and is incredibly vibrant.

The term "religious" embodies four ideas not easily contained in other terms: a collective focal point that binds and gives direction, a moral sense to help others in distress, a covenant with ancestors to keep their heritage alive, and an ongoing redemptive struggle with evil.

The first idea, the focal point, is a unifying purpose that symbolizes truths beyond rational thought built into our being that define the way we interact with the All and with each other. The human mind searches for ultimate causes to explain and cope with life. At the very limits of this search are ideals incarnated in a God-like spirit.

The importance of focal points lies in answering a simple question: How did we get here? What civilization did not have its gods. History suggests that humanity needs a spiritual focus that gives life meaning. This focus must invoke awe – at the very least for the existence of life on earth. It serves as a spiritual center that links the future with the past and, by doing so, gives a person's short, puny life a connection with eternity. This focal point is not necessarily fiction. Many people sense that beneath all the murkiness of existence, a path exists from those ruins of the past to a paradise they cannot even define. The universal process behind these visions deserves at least respect, perhaps even worship. And with it, life takes on a higher reality than day-to-day existence. Our lives gain meaning in a collective adventure in search of the Millennial Age.

The moral sense is also rooted in human nature and closely connected to the focal point. It presses a person to care for others without the hope of repayment. It prompts people to judge others and themselves by standards that have more to do with the salvation of humanity than with their contribution to gross domestic product. Moral duty explains the willingness of people to risk their own safety to prevent unfair dealing and bear the punishment for historical wrongs that they had no part in but benefit from. This moral sense, when properly directed toward treating every individual and every group with dignity, makes people want to make America a paradise.

From these inborn senses of reverence and obligation comes another idea the word religious captures: it is an abiding covenant with ancestors to keep their memories alive. More than in any other place, their spirits are palpable, still active, in ancient temples and graveyards. We act religiously when we pay homage to the greats of our people, when we support the institutions that keep our people together and try to honor the spoken and unspoken ways that our parents honored. All the symbols, ceremonies, and rituals that America has produced to honor its people are religious. Laying a wreath at the

Tomb of the Unknown Soldier is like an offering to God at a holy of holies. The inauguration of a president is like the selection of a pope, and Memorial Day is like a Passover Seder. Now we have a new holy site – Ground Zero.

The term religious also conjures the idea of redemption. In the Judeo-Christian tradition, humanity must struggle against evil, the corrupting force within the soul and nature itself that tries to destroy creation. Natural evils still kill innocent lives, destroy other worlds, and threaten the existence of the earth. Both nature and humanity, if you want to make the distinction, can use an overhaul. It is our religious duty to perfect the world by keeping evil in check and, where possible, transform evil into a productive power.

The humanistic label is much easier to defend because it does not depend on a supernatural being or force. Most Americans see humanity as the basic standard for measuring the value of existence. Beyond this, humanism stands for enthroning rational life. People believe that the human mind, no matter how puny, can solve the mysteries of the universe and use them to their benefit. They do not want to depend on a silent God for their redemption. They do not want to accept heritage as sacred. Any received wisdom must be assessed in each generation, and each generation should add its own wisdom to the human store.

Humanism suggests living with the tragedy of life. We will die, our heirlooms will turn to dust, future generations will not know us, our neighborhoods will disappear, and America's faces will look very different than they do today. The burden of life and memory turning to dust give our struggle to overcome death and the corruption of our works poignancy and urgency.

I do not want the humanistic label to sound too serious and dour. Humanism also represents the comical, sometimes absurd, side of human nature. Everything we do has a sense of unreality and phoniness about it. A business memo, the words of a politician, or a religious sermon do not ring completely true. Everyone is a player in some not always serious games. Man's ability to devise games sets him apart from the rest of the animal kingdom. In life's game, we play many roles. This fractured view of ourselves allows us to shift from one political position to another and accept many histories and meanings for a given situation. It depends on the role we decide to play.

Balance is crucial to understanding religious humanism. Visions of the sacred are often exclusionary and lead to witch hunts and death camps. Humanism has more subtle dangers. Overweening pride in American ingenuity led to the failures of key Great Society social and economic programs after World War II. Yet, the human standard, dedication to reason and truth, has led to fair laws, democratic government, and the large measure of personal freedom that Americans enjoy.

Its ecumenical spirit makes America's religion unique and compelling in this land of immigrants. Nowhere else has religious expression shed so many traditional trappings rooted in doctrine, race, or national origin. America tries to elevate newcomers by showing them that we all worship at the same altar. Whatever a person's religious beliefs or lack of them, the vast majority embrace the ideas that the Capitol building is America's temple; its two canonized Holy Scriptures are the Declaration and the Constitution, and America's days of remembrance and atonement are memorial and independence days. Lady Liberty embodies America's spirit of welcoming the oppressed and giving them hope that here, in the land of the free and the home of the brave, they can live their dreams if they have the will and energy to shape their futures.

America wants its newcomers to remember their pasts. Take Thanksgiving for example. It is a much more poignant holiday when a family sits down to a turkey dinner and reminisces about their uneducated ancestors who had little to eat and even less respect in the Old Country, who came here to start again, and who struggled and sacrificed so that their children would become American bigshots. Now the beneficiaries of that struggle sit at a sumptuous table and reflect that they are living an American dream.

America also wants newcomers to see that they are the lifeblood of its future. Colonization, westward expansion, slavery, mass immigration, America becoming a great power, and ethnic pride are America's Biblical stories. Like Abraham, Isaac, and Jacob, America's Founders committed shameful acts that would plague them and their progeny for many generations. Despite their shortcomings, we honor them because the founders wanted to build a righteous nation that honors freedom, equality, and the rule of law. Their descendants have tried to atone for their own and their ancestor's sins – sometimes reluctantly – by passing legislation outlawing discrimination. And because these old-American families have conceded power to newer groups peacefully and with a measure of grace, many Americans with little connection to the American Revolution see it as their struggle for freedom. So too we honor the other groups. Descendants of slaves championed civil rights following the noble example of Gandhi. Immigrants farmed the land, built the cities, and financed America's industry.

The weakest element of America's religion is its overly rational view of the world. Americans are experimental, skeptical of traditional solutions, skeptical of authorities that say, "This is the way we have always done it." But rationalism has the crucial weakness of treating people as indistinguishable. Everyone is free and equal – inherently the same. From a social perspective, treating people alike is critical to making a person comfortable so that he has a fair chance to succeed in life, but from a personal perspective, everyone wants to believe that he is special, that his life matters crucially in a larger context than his own little sphere.

A patriotic American must believe that in some small way his life is crucial to the creative unfolding of the American Dream and that his own sense of self would be incomplete without being an American. Loyalty requires faith in a golden vision of an America commonly held by all the distinct groups that live here. This vision need not be clearly defined, but its goal is to usher in a Messianic Age of peace, harmony, and virtue.

America should not underestimate how epics can unify a people. In Europe, many political movements drew wild support for their "Grand March" epics where a united people trooped toward a golden destiny. The communists offered a workers' paradise to those who followed them. The Nazis had their motley supporters whipped to a frenzy, with visions of a future filled with blond thoroughbreds. America has shied away from the epic because earlier ones – clearing the land and westward expansion – smack of white superiority. Instead, we rely on old saws about freedom and equality that seem as dry as an often-repeated wise saying to rally support for American causes.

This is unfortunate because America has a great storyline that should appeal to every person or group in danger. From a religious perspective, America's call to its people and to the world is for salvation. With an open heart, with the willingness to do what it takes, we can redeem the world and ourselves and usher in a Messianic Age if only we have the faith and fortitude to right the wrongs and heal the sufferings caused by man and nature. This nation is a living example of how the poor, the hungry, the illiterate, and the outcasts from many nations built the most powerful, richest, and arguably the most moral nation in human history. In the American epic, citizens don't march lockstep in formation, as an army of "right." It is more like a St. Patrick's Day Parade where people improvise and have a good time, but underneath it all, they have a serious purpose: to uphold traditions and declare that they remain strong even in this huge nation. Americans compete by building on their own strengths, not by tearing down the traditions of others.

Many seeming political oddities became clear when one sees America through a romantic lens where America's story becomes one's own. Why would John Doe – the invisible American – want to fight for his country? What does he get from his medieval loyalty? Only when one realizes that he stakes his salvation on the future of this country does his sacrifice make sense. No matter where his family came from, America is now part of his heritage and his homeland. Without America, he becomes a spiritual nonentity – an anonymous person living anywhere and nowhere.

Similarly, how do you explain Reagan calling Roosevelt his political father? I suppose you could say it was a cynical political move by Reagan to swing democratic voters to his side. I believe, however, that Reagan was sincere despite rejecting most of Roosevelt's political programs. Like Roosevelt, he was fighting to uplift the nation, but to Reagan, different times and conditions meant different policies. This religious perspective explains why many people besides Reagan shift from one political position to another without feeling that they are inconsistent or disloyal to their beliefs. They will support the plan they believe is most effective toward making America into the New Israel.

One of the greatest political oddities is that recent immigrants treat American history as their own. Why would they do that? It is because America honors these newcomers, gave them a chance to succeed, and honors them with a chapter in America's saga of salvation, which links them spiritually to the Founders of our nation.

Besides explaining patriotic fervor, America's salvation epic helps explain the nation's preoccupation with its never-ending struggle with evil – with helping the underdog beat the bully. In my case, I came to understand this side of the American epic from Jewish mystical sources – romantic interpretations of Biblical text that reveal mysteries of existence hidden in God's words – many of which I am sharing with you in this book. The chief text, the *Sefer Ha' Zohar* or *The Book of Splendor*, opened a new perspective on personal or national struggles closed to my rational mind.

From this book I learned that America's struggle with Ayatollah Khomeini's Iran was a soulful conflict at many levels. At the lowest, it was a struggle over who controls the world's oil or homeland security. At a higher level, it was a struggle between democracy and tyranny. At its highest level, it was a struggle between two cultures, Western and Middle Eastern, two approaches to salvation, Islamic fundamentalism and Western ecumenism.

Jewish mystics taught that evil has many levels and that the depths of evil are rooted in idolatry of self, of tribe, and oddly, of false "isms." How do you explain a Timothy McVeigh – or a Hitler? Should we write them off as psychotics or fringe people who turned their backs on Western culture? What about Osama Bin Laden, is he a religious fanatic or a holy man? The mystical approach would classify them as evil crusaders who wanted to tear down society and kill people to save a chosen few. They were evil because they violated the basic principle of religious mysticism: to preserve and enhance life whenever possible.

Tragically, evil often begins with a life story gone sour. In a fragile moment, the person seeks a sweeping and simple – an idolatrous – solution that will wipe away all his fears and shame. Their newfound faith assures them that their lives and those they kill are not as important as the Cause. The most passionate of them will blow themselves up to save society from the infidels.

Jewish mysticism teaches that you cannot disentangle good and evil. Traditionally, Americans have tended to divide the world into the good and bad guys, and whichever side they are on is, of course, the good side. Now we are not so sure. Jewish mysticism says that every act has a dark side to it, even an American one. You never know whether even your best motives or your most generous acts are truly sincere. This holds true in personal or political life. The best you can do is to understand dark urges and try to use them for productive ends. Ironically, Jewish mysticism warns not to try to wipe out evil. Those who try, like the Nazis, communists, and lately, radical Muslim groups, are fanatics who bring great destruction to the world.

Searching for the meaning of life revealed in sacred texts and images is an indispensable feature of any religion, including America's religion. Its motive force is the basis for composing epic stories and mythical images that define society's proper direction. No set of ethical rules or dogmatic principles will take the place of a story that explains a problem and offers a solution. In the religious humanistic mode, Americans use many models and standards of value to draw a broad outline of the world. Then they select useful kernels from this assortment of knowledge to fit a particular situation and build their storyline from there.

When I am developing my own grand policy statements, I act as if I were writing commentary on a Biblical story. I begin with standard political party commentaries. When I run into difficulties, I ask myself, what would Lady Liberty accept as just and merciful? Knowing that I am an amateur politico, I do not take my commentary too seriously unless the issue leads to war. If someone has an interesting suggestion, I am willing to rewrite my story line somewhat.

Sometimes I invoke Uncle Sam: He is a wheeler-dealer sharpie dressed in a huckster's top hat and tails. This "good ole" backslapper knows how to have a good time while making a few dollars. He is the perfect image for encapsulating pork barrel legislation that actually benefits the nation.

American policymakers and academics especially rely too much on theories and opinion polls to explain political behavior. They miss the importance of myths and sagas learned before going to school that shape a person's perspective on life. They do not examine methods of myth building and related mystical techniques that bind a person to a group and to a nation. Even a dry political theory such as libertarianism, which hammers away at social programs that take away personal choice, has a great story to tell of how it evolved, who were its champions, and why it is still such a vital political movement for making religious humanism come to life.

Most Americans subscribe to religious humanism implicitly; it is the spiritual core of our common culture; it is the basis for developing dual loyalty to America and to one's own particular background. It is the way to know yourself. Carlos Fuentes, the great Mexican author, said that individuality comes in contrast with others you know, your own society and culture. He called it self-definition rooted in heritage, or collective individuality. Whether you are a Jewish-American, Mexican American, or from another hyphenated group, you define yourself at least partly as an American because it is where you live.

Each of us has a hand in keeping and renewing religious humanism. When I tried to define my own life story, I noticed that I was borrowing themes from people I admired, many of whom are Jewish-Americans. Organically, I was becoming another character in the American tale. Sometimes, I believe I am adding to the American story. My reactions to September 11, like those of many others who saw the destruction of the Twin Towers, will eventually become part of American history.

Unifying America requires story building by American ethnic and racial groups who interpret events and the unfolding of American history differently. A catastrophic event like September 11 may have had a great effect on society. No person, no group, no generation has enough wisdom to draw out the moral lessons of such a cataclysmic event. The people who experienced it did not live long enough to feel its aftershocks. Those born afterward, who live in its wake, will not have experienced its terrors and exhilarations.

Each group in America may interpret differently the moral consequences of a historical event like September 11. The result will be a degree of inconsistency, but if these stories uphold religious humanism, the very inconsistencies will add depth to America's religious view of the world. The result will also be that each group feels that it was attacked, and it helped America overcome this tragedy.

America's main religious center is Ground Zero for the near future. Others exist where a great event, whether tragic or triumphant, has occurred. America's religious center was once on the Deck of the USS Arizona in Pearl Harbor, at Gettysburg, at Bunker Hill, and at Yorktown. It was in Utah when a golden spike completed America's intercontinental railroad and in Washington D.C. when the Lincoln Memorial was dedicated. It exists in a spirit that built the Golden Gate Bridge, in Silicon Valley, in the great American breadbasket, in Miami Beach, Coney Island, and Disneyworld. The land itself is a spiritual center. The Rockies, the Painted Desert, the lake districts of Minnesota and New York, and the coastlines are spiritual landscapes as diverse and grand as the people who live within their borders. America's religious center also lies in the places off the tourist maps, the places where people like me grew up, made their way – places called home. And it lies in a few pages of parchment – the Declaration and the Constitution.

14

Elements of Religious Humanism

Abstract Religious humanism is a broad creedal framework that comes to life when nourished by particular ideologies, religions, and cultural heritages. A critical challenge for religious humanism is to open new ideological pathways that stimulate experimentation. While ideologies have unique characteristics, religious humanism assumes they draw substance and spirit from four basic sources or perspectives: rational/pragmatic, romantic, deist, and mystical wisdom. The first two are in the humanist tradition and the second two are in the religious tradition. All four philosophical perspectives keep changing, especially at their outer edges, which suggests that America's ideologies are changing as well. But it is the mystical perspective that has the most potential for binding the wounds caused by social conflict if used in a nurturing way. The chapter ends with a model drawn from the mystical tradition that allows ideologs to see their beliefs in a new, more nuanced way. The model is then used to develop a mission statement for America and strategies for reexamining America's core values.

14.1 Introduction

The brief description of religious humanism leads naturally to ask a critical question: How can we use it to end the ideological wars at home and the cultural wars abroad?

The first step is to emphasize that religious humanism is a broad creedal framework that comes to life when nourished by particular ideologies, religions, and cultural heritages. They all have a place as long as they are inclusive of thoughts and imagery that honor the ultimate unity of all fields of learning and beliefs aimed at ennobling the highest aspirations of humanity. Religious humanism encourages the exploration of many paths leading to similar golden dreams. It exalts moral behavior built on experience and linked to religious traditions while encouraging voluntary trading of ideas and ways of living among peoples of all faiths and backgrounds. It seeks to unlock mysteries of the universe through study of sacred texts but sees scientific inquiry as a necessary part of man's purpose on earth. It champions harnessing evil inclinations toward productive use.

A critical challenge for religious humanism is to open new ideological pathways that stimulate experimentation. While ideological views have unique characteristics, religious humanism assumes they draw substance and spirit from four basic sources or perspectives: rational/pragmatic, romantic, deist, and mystical wisdom. The first two are in the humanist tradition and the second two are in the religious tradition.

All four philosophical perspectives keep changing, especially at their outer edges, which suggests that America's ideologies are changing as well. But as you will see, it is the mystical perspective that has the most potential for binding the wounds caused by social conflict if used in a nurturing way. At the end of the chapter, I offer a model drawn from the mystical tradition that allows ideologues to see their beliefs in a new, more nuanced way. I use this model to develop a mission statement for America and strategies for reexamining America's core values and educational program that can open fruitful discussions among even the most hardened ideologues.

14.2   Rational/Pragmatic: The Economic Man

The rational approach has English roots going back to the 1600s, beginning when Western philosophers tried to apply the scientific method to human problems. In all areas of social activity, rationalists were trying to look at problems objectively, classify them, examine data relevant to the problem, and come to some tentative conclusions.

Gradually, a mind shift occurred away from revealed wisdom written in holy books, away from tribal wisdom handed down from generation to generation, away from the wisdom of a ruling class, toward wisdom that honors the free-standing individual who defines his own life through force of will. He voluntarily competes and cooperates with others in a joint venture to enhance his and others lives.

As with any new trend, the shift to cultural individualism led to new theories of individuals in society. Instead of being a cell in the body of a nation, or a spirit trapped in a corrupt body, the individual became a part of a system with three types of decision-makers: the freely governed, the elected governors, and appointed judges. In England and America, the role of markets emerged as a wealth-bearing civilizing force. Buyers and sellers gained from trade; competition was peaceful and led to new ways to please customers. Equality, freedom, and fairness defined for individuals became primal values for developing legal and governmental policy. Rationalism was later extended to justify having government redistribute income from the rich to the poor and decentralizing power within society.

In Adam Smith's time, the rationalist was a trader who evaluated and priced his goods for sale. In the twentieth century, when corporations began to dominate the economy, the "man in the gray flannel suit" could serve as a model for the rational man. He was a member of a hierarchical team that examined customer needs methodically and then planned large-scale production of standardized products at low cost to meet these needs. Another model was a more heroic type, someone like John Galt in Ayn Rand's model, who created new products by using his mind.

In the late nineteenth century, pragmatists added a brake on extreme rationalism by recognizing that most of the time people don't have enough data to even classify a problem let alone define it. Faced with the need to do something, people fall back on rules of thumb that have worked in the past. If these rules don't work as expected, attempt to fix them in real time.

In the twentieth century, the rational approach began to crowd out pragmatism as a working model for public policy. Economists kept trying to imitate the harder sciences, and this is a basic flaw that still mars the profession. They built a model of human behavior built on strictly rational, egocentric principles of behavior. This "Economic Man" was characterized as a utility seeker who maximized personal benefits. As a private citizen, Economic Man picked an alternative that maximizes his satisfaction subject to the constraints facing him. In private life, the constraint is an annual or lifetime budget, but it could be other types such as the decisions of his family. Death, to him, is simply the end of his planning period, a number taken from an actuarial table.

His actual choices were the result of weighing the tradeoffs between alternative bundles of goods and services, including the combination of work and leisure he was willing to accept. The very act of deciding suggests losses from taking one bundle instead of another. He knew he could not have it all or try everything. His mode of operation was to act like a winning contestant on a game show who can pick package number 1, 2, or 3.

Economists did recognize a basic flaw in the Economic Man model: personal myopia, the inability to predict the future accurately. Keynesian economists gave as an example that each person's rational decision to save more for future spending could produce a recession if the reason for holding back demand was not communicated to businesspeople. Not to worry. From their perspective, government spending could offset private thriftiness. Economists, for a heady stretch in the 40-year period leading up to the Great Recession, believed in markets as the ultimate planning tool. They also believed they could keep the economy on a steady upward course by judicious use of monetary and fiscal policies.

According to the rationalist's view, politicians' behavior was also predictable. They will adopt policies that will win elections. They will support positions favored in opinion polls or pushed by large corporate contributors when their dollars will translate into votes. A way to overcome potential corruption was to put government policies on autopilot, using economic theories to develop these mechanisms such as triggered tax cuts during economic downturns.

The critical enablers of a good society, according to rationalists, are the rule of law, private property, competition, a sound financial system, a first-rate transportation system, and democracy. All of these features of government give an individual with drive the freedom to plan for success, however he defines it.

While the rational mind model has worked well, it is facing critical challenges that are undermining its power. Super-efficient networks on autopilot have created economic instability. Reactions to false news such as the assassination of President Obama sent stock prices into a tailspin because trading algorithms lined up in sell mode because they react in lockstep to certain triggers in the news and patterns in trading data. A herd mentality is at rational one level– to move with the herd instead of being trampled – but at another level, it drives assets prices to unsustainable levels, leading to market crashes. Through experimentation, behavioral economists keep uncovering human behavior patterns that explain herd mentality and other biases that suggest that markets can produce false signals that lead to inefficient behavior such as saving too little for retirement. The rise of online platforms is a new and potentially troubling reconfiguration of the marketplace. These platforms control so much information that they could potentially shape for their own gain buyer behavior, social behavior, and political behavior.

Cross-border trades and intrigues degrade the rule of law and the meaning of private property. It hardly recognizes that people and nations are driven by the need for power to control their environment and the demand for honor whether earned or not.

The redeeming feature of the rational approach is that its supporters know purely rational problem solving is not operational on its own. Rationalists recognize they don't have all the facts before and after a decision and have difficulty assessing the rightness of a decision even with the facts at hand. When automatic stabilizers fail, pragmatism kicks in. Pragmatic rationalists find ways to define workable policies that look familiar: ones that seemed to work in the past and have enough flexibility to offer a way out if they fail.

A rational pragmatist is likely to rely on policy experts to frame America's response to crises such as the financial meltdown in 2008 or the wars in the Middle East in high-blown cost-benefits terms such as acceptable losses, collateral damage, exit strategy, and long-term gains. This denatured approach to problem-solving has the advantage of leaning less on revenge as a justification for a strategy and more on long-term objective benefits. But it also gives enormous power to bureaucrats who are hidden from view and not punished for bad behavior and decisions.

14.3 Romantic: American Heroes

The romantic perspective is a product of the 1800s. It sprung up as a reaction against the scientific belief that human affairs could be boiled down to a series of formulas. A real person is vulnerable, fragile, lives a short life but has grand expectations, is prone to mistakes and regrets, and often angry at himself and others and tries to forget humiliations and slights as hard as that might be. Besides winning life's lotteries, he believes struggle and sacrifice are sources of self-satisfaction, especially when they left their mark on others who salute these noble gestures. A critical difference between the modern romantic in democratic lands and earlier incarnations is that the new romantic recognizes the humanity of others and tries to see life from the other's perspective. The "other" became an individual with rights, with similar needs for dignity and honor.

In comparison with the rationalist's triad of characters – the governed, the governors, and the judges – the romantic has his own triad of characters: the actor, the audience, and the role model. In England, the role model was the gentleman, the man of dignity and quiet strength who did the right thing, especially in stressful times.

A few versions of the English gentleman were carried over to America. The American cowboy is a popular one, a loner gentleman without pedigree.

Whether dressed in buckskins or a suit, he wanted to be left alone, but if he sees a wrong being committed, he, like John Wayne in his many Westerns or James Stewart in Mr. Smith Goes to Washington, would take on the bad guys, beat them up, and ride away into the sunset when the job was done.

Another version of the American ideal was popularized by Horatio Alger. His young adult stories showed that a poor boy from humble beginnings who goes to school, attends church, works hard, and cashes in on opportunities because he has prepared himself eventually rises to great heights in society. There are plenty of variations on this theme. The unconventional Thomas Edison or much later Steve Jobs dropped out of school but pursued a dream that brought them great fame.

American literature since World War II began to focus on a much less noble "me" type. Books such as *Revolutionary Road* gave us Franklin Wheeler, a man who thinks he is different from his conforming neighbors, who plans to quit his job and go to Paris but winds up staying the course, which leaves him with a dead wife and a hollow future. "Me against the Man" became a popular theme in the unsettled years of the 1960s and 1970s. The Hippie and love generation genres picked up on the anti-establishment American character.

Once the Vietnam War was over, a new, much more explicitly egocentric American romantic appeared. The new American character was not the starry-eyed dreamer who dies for love or country. His objective was far more self-serving. He was a self-actualizer who wanted to live a meaningful life but also wants comforts that money can buy. He wants to compose the best autobiography he can possibly write without feeling ridiculous. Education, readings, and the fine arts are not for economic payoffs; they are to raise the aesthetic level of his story – to make it more elegant. Unlike a rationalist who looks to the social sciences for answers, he turns to novels for his greatest insights into the human condition – preferably the deeply psychological ones drawn against a backdrop of a sweeping event like the Civil War, or the Great Depression, or the social revolutions that began in the 1960s and continues to this day.

This egocentric character has taken on many forms but often is portrayed adrift in a mass and alien society. One version is the psychologically tortured first- or second-generation ethnic American you find in a Philip Roth book or more recently in Jhumpa Lahiri's. Typically, the main character is keenly aware of his ethnic heritage, doesn't feel comfortable with the outsider habits of his parents' generation, longs to become a White Anglo-Saxon Protestant (WASP)-like American, knows he doesn't fit the role, and so feels estranged from everyone. Ironically, as John Updike chronicled so well, the WASP, at the same time, was having his own identity crisis. Small town WASPy life – sheltered, close-knit, claustrophobic, gossipy, often boring, with a few scandals thrown in for spice – was being invaded by outsiders who were turning downtown into a run-down battle zone, an edgy hostile landscape where anything goes if you have the guts. The only security from this alien threat was enough money to isolate yourself in a suburban community with a country club where wife swapping was a fun pastime.

The emerging American character was basically a fragile personality who pretended to be someone special. His supposed big ego is a ruse, a phony way of saying to others and himself that he was something other than what he really was – painfully ordinary. Nonetheless, he painted himself as vaguely heroic, a Master of the Universe that Tom Wolfe describes in *Bonfire of the Vanities*. In his own mind, family and friends, community and town, or neighborhood, people, profession, citizen, and so on – and not necessarily in that order – were supporting characters at best in the picture. Often, they were reminders of how trite his existence could be.

Tom Rachman summed up the absurdity of this emerging American character in his novel the *Imperfectionists* by announcing through one of his characters that ambition is the religion of Western Man. Everything we have touched or made has its roots in ambition: ambition to be heard, to be loved, to be better than others, to be immortal. Ambition produced cathedrals and sonnets, not love of God, not even love of life. If necessary, ambitious people will kill to succeed.

In his private life, this Master of the Universe's decisions focus less on bundles of goods and services and more on tradeoffs between personal dignity, social acceptance, and power. His choices are often a little whimsical and surprising. Unlike a rationalist who views work essentially as a necessary evil, work itself can be a liberating force, an outlet for self- development and sometimes a way for a person to step away from other problems.

In public life, an egocentric politician wants others to see him as a role model. He bestows benefits on his supporters and may even show generosity to win over his detractors. In the end, his dream is to secure his place in American history as someone who made a difference. This will require a tangible legacy, congressional bills with his name on them or footage of him leading the charge to fix a great American problem.

Whether a politician or private citizen, even an egocentric romantic's loyalty remains largely inherited. With only one life to live, and a short one at that, the new American romantic rushes to and clings to whatever makes him feel special. In his less grandiose mode, he becomes loyal to his own group because he grew up within it, and he can't repeat his youth. America is his home because he was born, or lived, or immigrated here; his friends are here and his other social connections.

Building social connections is important because they validate his personal story. He wants government and any organization he joins to make everyone feel like a valuable member. Common social values are important to him for setting yardsticks that measure personal success. To express them, he and his political representatives may use catch phrases for domestic policy such as "success without dominance," "allies in a common adventure," "common fears," "good leadership and role models," "see the other side," "show compassion," and "give them a break."

In the twenty-first century, America is moving away from the WASP ideal to a new form of tribalism – tribalism by choice. Perhaps because ethnic and racial mixing are increasing, loyalists to ethnic heritage and race are becoming more determined to validate their own fragile heritages. A positive outcome is a more in-depth understanding of the American experience as each group shows its contribution to American heritage. The fear is that it may lead to divisive views of American culture. The challenge is to overcome past injustices without forgetting that they occurred, to focus on the future instead of seeking revenge.

W. E. B. Du Bois, James Baldwin, Toni Morrison, Philip Roth, Thomas Sowell, and Cornel West offered a vision of this new American. Baldwin in *Notes of a Native Son* said that Americans are different than the people from their ancestral homeland. For instance, blacks in the United States are not Africans; they are Americans with African roots. They and other non-white minorities are beacons to the world. They can show that civilization is not synonymous with Europe. Yet, they have absorbed Western culture and made it part of their own. He and Cornel West[1] entreat American minorities to find a broader view of God's purpose on earth and to raise leaders with prophetic visions of inclusion. Americans in America were all once strangers in a strange land. Thomas Sowell said that ethnic groups should adopt the characteristics of groups that have succeeded despite being oppressed. He identified the middleman culture of the Chinese outside of China and the Jews.[2] Du Bois[3] asked the dominant whites to lend a hand and for freed slaves to learn western culture and skills to succeed in life, but not at the expense of bleaching their souls. The dilemma of wanting to honor the past and trying to pass for someone walking away from it is an uncomfortable theme in Morrison's *Tar Baby* and Roth's *The Human Stain*.

---

[1] West, C. (1991) Race Matters. Beacon Press, Boston.

[2] See, for example, Sowell, T. (1981) Markets and Minorities. Basic Books, NY.

[3] Du Bois, W. E. B. (1990) The Soul Of Black Folk *(1990* ed.) Vintage Press, NY.

One image of an American that continues to shine in the American consciousness is standing up for what is right even if no one comes to your aid. The classic figure of this persona is Gary Cooper in High Noon. Despite being a solid citizen and helping to make the town where he lived prosper, the townspeople made excuses for not helping him when criminals announced they were coming to town to settle an old score. Despite his fears, Cooper stayed, fought alone, and won.

This imagery sometimes carries over to public policy. Sometimes the results are tricky and dangerous. For instance, in the War on Terrorism, a romantic may talk of "a just war," "defending American honor," "punishing terrorists and liberating tortured people." For one type of romantic, losses of innocent American lives in combat trouble him greatly, but he still believes the American patriots who die for their country did so for the greater good of all freedom-loving people. America will honor them forever. This type of American romantic also tries sincerely to see the world through the other's eyes. If the other appears human and has a legitimate grievance, the American response becomes much more measured and humane. A second type of romantic is much more cynical. This is the show me type who doesn't want to be swept up in soaring rhetoric. He wants to know why he should fight a war against Jihadists. Like Dalton Trumbo's character in *Johnny Got His Gun*, he doesn't swallow that he should sacrifice his life for freedom, democracy, or national honor. For him, the fight in the Middle East is over a business deal gone wrong. Americans wanted access to cheap oil, and the Jihadists think they got a raw deal. If American politicians want to fight the Jihadists, let them pay people to protect our interests. Arguably, cynicism has become the common attitude of Americans, and this cynicism is self-fulfilling.

The digital revolution has incarnated a new Master of the Universe, the founders of the major online platforms: the notables include Bill Gates, Paul Allen, Jeff Bezos, Larry Page, Sergey Brin, Mark Zuckerberg, Steve Jobs, and Steve Wozniak. They helped found a new online world through the strengths of their imaginations. America is still trying to define their effect on the American psyche.

14.4 Deist: Grand Designers

Deism is another product of the Enlightenment with roots in England. It raises rationalism to a purposeful force that created and sustains the universe through an objective set of laws that makes all reality fit into a unity. These laws include both laws of nature and laws of society. If somehow we knew them all, humanity could usher in a Golden Age. Unfortunately, these laws are still far from known and may never be known, but a deist believes that all the wisdom uncovered so far points to a universe of conscious design with man as a special creation. On earth, and perhaps far beyond earth, man is the steward of creation. To abuse any part of this cosmic design is to desecrate the Light of Truth.

In essence, a deist tries to weave together a "theory of everything" with a conscious mind at its center. He is a doubter of older images of God though he believes in a creator who defined the laws that govern the universe. He is also a doubter of the afterlife but believes he is part of the cosmic design. He expects to live on spiritually and genetically after he dies.

American deism was popular among Founders, including Jefferson, Madison, Hamilton, and possibly Washington. As deists, they held people have natural rights, built into the fabric of existence, such as the right to life, liberty, and the pursuit of happiness. The belief in natural law influenced the Constitution and in particular the principles stated in the Bill of Rights. To the deist Founders, they are not simply hard-headed, instrumental values for a well-ordered society. Instead, they are rights that are in harmony with the laws governing the role of humanity in the creative process.

But are natural rights scientific? Weren't slaves considered a part of the natural order of society? People aren't born equal. Babies are born helpless.

Deist thinkers – some of whom are theists – tend to be enraptured by grand theories that explain the course of history. Adam Smith, a theist, gave us the Invisible Hand that guides self-centered individuals to satisfy society's needs and pushes society toward ever greater wealth and satisfaction. Marx and his disciples claimed they understood the true law of societies. They predicted that capitalism would destroy itself because of overproduction. Eventually, the proletariat would take over property and own it collectively. This classless society would give each according to his or her needs. Darwinist thinking led the Nazis to believe that by purifying the Aryan race through eugenics and mass extinctions of inferior races, they could speed the birth of the super-man race.

The irrationality of communism, Nazism, and religious fanatics makes it hard to believe in the likely evolution of well-ordered societies. The lust for power and national or religious purity trump economics as causes for war. Adam Smith's capitalism seems out of step with the rise of huge corporations with global reach.

Science didn't help the deist cause either. The rise of humans may have resulted from a meteor striking the earth 65 million years ago instead of a grand design built into the pattern of existence. Darwin and later Gould suggested that evolution is not progressive. It may seem as if evolution leads from simple life to complex, conscious life. But according to Gould, that progression is simply the only direction life could take. Life had a lower barrier on the forms it could take, but it had much more flexibility in becoming more complex. Wishful thinking on the part of humans may have equated survival of the fittest that is successful adaptation to the environment with a natural design leading to the human mind and beyond.

Few people call themselves deists today, but many Americans see the world as a deist would because they examine and test wisdom transmitted by scholars, religious leaders, and family members and try to mold them together assuming they all emanated from one unified set of natural laws. They will uphold moral and religious traditions and scientific practices that encapsulate the laws of Life and shed those that don't. Once uncovered, a deist believes he is saving the world from untold suffering by spreading universal truths to the unenlightened.

A deist has his own special tradeoffs in his quest to get beyond the facades, behind the masks, and above the petty details of everyday life and find the truth. He is more likely to act on a basic set of moral principles that have stood the test of time when expediency suggests being a bit more flexible in outlook. Unlike the rationalist who turns to experts and "how-to" manuals for advice or the romantic who turns to novels for insights, a deist looks to grand unified theories of society and nature as the basis for his actions.

In public life, a deist identifies with the statesman, a person who rises above petty prejudice to decide great issues fairly and compassionately. Like a model judge, he distances himself emotionally from a particular crisis, but his wise decisions set precedents for future generations. In his search for guidance, he uses the Constitution like a Bible. In there, he finds the inspiration to endow America with a better vision of itself.

The symbol of his approach to public policy is Lady Liberty. She represents a God of Light and Justice. She is a mythical figure with Judeo-Christian overtones. Loyalty to America depends on it being a righteous society that tries to redeem lost souls and care for those in distress. Its strength lies in appealing to the Judeo-Christian tradition for its outlook but with an emphasis on toleration for other religious ways.

The deist strongly believes that in the long term, the spread of freedom and democracy will overturn autocratic states. It is inevitable that truth will defeat ignorance. Even the existence of terror cells within the United States consisting of people who have lived among ordinary Americans and have seen American principles in action does not shake his confidence in the rightness and universality of his belief in the rightness of the rule of law, freedom, and democracy. America's challenge is to uphold its principles despite having an enemy within and without.

A more challenging conceptual issue facing deists is that if the laws and the universe fit neatly together, then does free will exist? A theory of everything, once discovered, would predict our every decision and our every action, but maybe not. Suppose the universal system is analogous to the Internet. A route from A to B can take many paths depending on the basic rules of the Internet and rules added on for particular reasons. It may seem as if the particular route chosen was the only route possible, but that would be wrong. Just as important nature may be subject to completely unpredictable Black Swan events that are the true drivers of the history of this planet. For humanity to ignore that chaotic swirls exist is to operate as if the universe is a gentle plain on which to travel. This happy fantasy could lead to humanity being sucked into a black hole.

14.5   Mystical: Soulful Covenants

The most unusual element of religious humanism is mysticism. It seems out of place as a tool for rational inquiry or even believable storytelling, but really isn't because mystical training sharpens the imagination to search for spiritual purpose in everyday existence. Even people who believe in strict rational thought have secret visions of becoming God-like.

Instead of describing the evolution of mysticism in America as a starting point for describing its features and flaws, I use Jewish mysticism as a starting point to show how this spiritual approach can reconnect a seemingly fragmented society and give it a source for creating new unifying visions. The basic model describes the soul as having three levels, which I will describe in more detail later in the section. For now, I will just list them and show how they apply to understanding the arts, economic and political dynamics, and religious practices. The three levels are (1) the vital force related to physical needs and sensory reactions, (2) the conscious force related to rational calculations and passions, and (3) the creative force of the mind that seeks inspiration and produces visions.

The following table summarizes how the spiritual levels can explain great works of art, loyalty to religions, private enterprise, and democracy.

	The arts			Religion	Private enterprise	Liberal democracy
	Music	Painting	Sculpture			
Creative	Evocative images, memories, feeling	Evocative images, memories, feeling	Evocative images, memories, feeling	Sacred, redemption	Invisible Hand	God or natural rights
Conscious	Harmonic chords	Mimesis using perspective	Mimesis, using perspective	Ethics, and practices	Markets	Representative government
Vital	Beat/rhythm	Colors	Texture	Ritual	Individual needs	Common psychic and physical essentials

For instance, a great work of art inspires a sense of wonder, shows that the artist has mastered the skills of an artist, and appeals viscerally to the viewer. In similar ways, great religions, private enterprise, and democracy produce inspired visions, lay out a path to a productive, meaningful life that satisfies basic needs.

When it comes to public policy, a mystic's challenge is to harmonize all three levels as societal conditions change. I am going to suggest that this model can help formulate domestic and foreign policy and act as a catalyst for generating new visions of America as a great society.

I will build up to this visionary dénouement in stages. First, I present a brief comparison between the rationalist and the mystic. Next, I describe the Jewish mystical model found in Kaballah. Afterward, a brief comparison of Jewish and Eastern mysticism is discussed. Next are discussions of the failings of mysticism to live up to its promises and offer a proposed update to the Jewish mystical model. My intent is to give it a more dynamic and modern look. Finally, I will apply my proposed changes to develop compelling American mission statements that could lead to national harmony and collaboration.

14.5.1 Rational and Mystical Perspectives Compared

As the historian Jacques Barzun said, an analytical mind has severe limitations. It seeks the essence, the bare outline of the real world, something like extracting circles, rectangles, and triangles from looking at a tree. These abstractions are devoid of qualities, leaving quantities and ideal shapes. The objective of scientific analysis is to master nature's laws. This inquiry is a special type of rationalism, a type that breaks down problems into manageable parts and attempts to solve them. As a result, according to Barzun, the scientific mind can never explain reality because scientific essences come from reality. Working up from essences to try to explain reality is doomed to failure. Imagine starting with circles, squares, and triangles and trying to reproduce reality. Imagine stitching together equations to reconstruct reality. It would look at best like a jigsaw puzzle.[4]

A theistic mystic, like a scientist, abstracts from life but life itself doesn't become an abstraction; life takes on an aura and a flow, a spiritual dimension lacking in the analytical mind. A traditional Judeo-Christian mystic looks beyond the everyday to uncover secret wisdom that can lead a searcher toward understanding the blueprint for creation: God's plan. The technique is not the scientific method; it is a well-honed sense of great imaginings that create myths and symbols that embody a culture, whether religious or secular.

Because their mystical practices attune the mind to think creatively, to look beyond the everyday and see the poetry underlying laws of nature and the workings of the human soul, mysticism and science can actually be partners in the creative process. Jewish mystics believed in mystical imagery that would be shocking to a regular attendee at religious services but would resonate with modern sensibilities.

14.5.2   Romantic and Mystical Perspectives Compared

American romantics like to tell stories of overcoming obstacles and realizing what matters in life. Sometimes they focus on relationships, sometimes on self-development, sometimes the stories are optimistic, sometimes tragic. The main theme is almost always self-centered. As you might expect, in the theistic mystical tradition, the romance is an encounter between man and God. I will describe this encounter in the Jewish Mystical Model section.[5] Here the key takeaway is that the romance is spiritual and eternal. It is a sacred covenant that crosses generations and focuses on redemption and renewal of humanity and all of God's creations. Each individual life is part of a sacred chain of life. To stare at oneself is to miss the beauty and pageantry of God's creations.

14.5.3   Jewish Mystical Model

As in many mystical traditions, the Force that created the universe had two inscrutable names, "No-Thing," and "Endless." This entity had no shape. But

---

[4] Barzun, J. (2000). From Dawn To Decadence: 500 Years Of Western Cultural Life. Harper Collins, NY. p. 167, for example.

[5] The main mystical text I use is the Zohar. There are many publications of it. See Daniel Matt's translation Pritzker Edition. Stanford University Press. or Sperling and Simon's translation (1984) Soncino Press, London.

from there, the mystical imagery takes on a Jewish character. This Force was inspired to create the physical universe because a universe of pure spirit is barren. The acts of creation allowed the Force to acquire a purposeful existence bound in the creative process. The crowning creation was man. Much like Adam, this Force wanted a counterpart, a "Thou." Man and God need each other to know themselves. The creation of man allowed the Force to take on new names familiar to the congregant such as Lord or Jehovah and others.

Another shocking idea was that this Force had created and destroyed previous universes, in effect saying that God's creations have flaws – that many creations are unstable because they lack balance of some kind, mainly a lack of balance in the universe between judgment and mercy.

A Jewish mystic believes that purposeful colored lights emanating from the Force contain the energy of creation, and the Hebrew letters embedded in that light are the genetic elements of the creative process. Proper letter combinations describe each unique facet of creation. By comparison, the coding revolution replaces bits or genetic lettering for the letters of the Hebrew alphabet – a major difference in inquiry but the same basic motivation that the universe has a genetic code, and the laser lights replace the lights of creation for producing virtual reality.

Treating Hebrew letters as a code does not fully capture the message Jewish mystics want to convey. To them, the letters are alive. They have spirit. Combinations produce the musical notes of creation. Sometimes they harmonize; sometimes they fight each other. Black letters separated by spaces in the bible are like fiery spirits. In a sense, they are like a spiritual binary code that can create universes, and if used improperly they corrupt and destroy creation. Humanity is in the process of actualizing a virtual dimension to life that Jewish mystics saw through a clouded window.

Similar to virtual reality, the Jewish mystic believes creations unfold in surprising ways. Unlike the deist who believes in a set of unchanging natural laws and a given purpose to existence, the Jewish mystic believes the purposeful dimension morphs because humanity has a role in shaping the universe. Done righteously, human actions will usher in a Messianic Age. Done with an evil intention or from ignorance, humanity's actions could potentially destroy God's creation.

The creative unfolding of the universe described by Jewish mystics is a surprisingly modern guide to the creative process. It begins with the will to create, stimulated by a lack of something. Then it awaits the inspiration that is necessary to find a solution to what is lacking. This inspiration is not like a data mining technique that looks for patterns in history. It is a faculty of the imagination. Once the inspiration has occurred, the next step is to understand it and develop a blueprint for action. The creator must then have the rigor to abide by the plan but the mercy to soften it if it creates hardships. While the creative process is underway, its unfolding beauty acts as a stimulant to carry on. The creative process requires endurance and the hope of victory. Once the new creation is fully formed, the birth of something precious comes into the world. As new desired needs surface, the process repeats itself.

This view is consistent with a secular description of humanity by Frank Knight, the University of Chicago economist, who preceded the "Chicago School" economists led by Milton Friedman. Knight believed that economics should recognize that people want to improve themselves by doing the right thing; only they do not know what they want, so choosing is an exploratory process. People learn about themselves by the actual choices they make. As they choose, goals once set in stone become pliable. They stretch and change, sometimes morph into new patterns. Values emerge that describe the choices made that measure one's accomplishments. The meaning of one's life changes as the debits and credits of past decisions fill the ledger of values and the options open for future change expand then narrow and then pass on to the next generation. This dynamic view of life and writ large for civilization is often surprising, sometimes playful, sometimes tragic, often frustrating, and repetitive. Yet the mixture of accomplishments, values, and purposes comprises the basic narrative elements of the Western epic story that keeps goading people to reach for new levels of mastery and personal humanity or suffer the consequences of stagnation.[6]

Returning to the Jewish mystical view, being God's partner bestows grandeur perhaps missing from Knight's description on what it means to be an American. Jewish mysticism elevates each person above self to seeing humanity as a whole in all its diversity having a critical role in redeeming the world, creating new worlds of the imagination, quickening dead worlds, and spreading conscious purpose through the cosmos.

A critical element in the creative process of the Jewish mystic is spiritual balance. According to Jewish mystics, evil is often the result of righteous anger taken to an extreme. The passion for rigor, for meting out judgment to people who corrupt the creative process leads to catastrophes. The most obvious application of the passion for vengeance is to the conflicts in the Middle East where Moslem, Christian, and Jew believe they have been wronged. It also has application in America, among ideologs, who often claim the other side is dragging America down a wrong path. A growing sense of victimhood and

---

[6] Frank H. Knight, FH. (1982) Freedom and Reform: Essays in Economics And Social Philosophy. Liberty Press, NY. pp. 279–290.

vengeance was apparent during the presidential campaign and after President Trump was elected. Extreme mercy is also destructive because it destroys the rules needed to maintain an ordered existence.

One of the most useful narrative tools drawn from Jewish mysticism is a layered perspective for visualizing problems common in other mystical traditions. This layering is associated with levels of the soul that I described briefly at the beginning of this section. It is a larger concept than the rational mind, closer to the animating and purposeful God's breath within the human body. Examination of the soul will pay off in many surprising ways. It will help show that an ideological viewpoint is really the product of different images of society, from everyday affairs to cosmic connections, which come together to produce an ideology. This soulful view will draw out even more clearly that America's three ideologies are special cases of religious humanism. Soulfulness will also point to the dynamics of creation needed to meet unexpected challenges and if done without proper spiritual balance can lead to destructive effects and great evil.

Here I describe the soulful levels in more detail to make them realistic tools for developing public policy. Jewish mystics believe the soul has three and sometimes five levels of consciousness. We will stick to three. The first and lowest level of the soul is its vital force. It is the animating force within the body including reflexes and other unconscious drives to survive. The vital force's prime directive is personal survival than survival of its species. At this level, land, kind, and "self" become blurred and sometimes form a physical unity needed for survival. Everyday habits and practices become tools for survival because the ones in use are likely to work. Time frames are measured in hours, days, weeks, perhaps a year – always closer to the immediate than to eons, and when time stretches it looks like eternal recurring cycles with no notion of meaningful change. Success is measured by physical survival and endurance to overcome obstacles.

The second level is the conscious force. It includes the faculties of logic and emotions directed toward deliberate goals. Its prime directive is to build a persona with the makings of a life plan aimed at building a consistent personal story line. The "rational" part of "rational passions" produces ideas such as the rule of law. The "passionate" part recognizes the impossibility of using rationality alone to make decisions. Without passion, it is impossible to weigh rational choices and come to a decision. It is even possible that rationality is a rationalization of emotional decisions.[7]

---

[7] See, for example, Jonathan Haidt, J. (2012) The Righteous Mind. Vintage Books, NY.

Judgment and mercy are two conscious force passions. When balanced they produce justice. When judgment becomes lustful, it leads to strict punishment that looks evil to a spectator. In this category is a type of vengeance I have called the Samson complex. It comes to life, when a hurt party who lacks power is willing to pull the house down, kill himself, just for the satisfaction of getting even with an enemy. Unchecked mercy is also dangerous because it doesn't recognize when crimes have occurred, and this produces even more evil because the merciful one becomes a dupe. This emotional imbalance has the label "irrational passions." They are the most dangerous corrupters of the conscious force.

Psychic time at this soulful level stretches beyond the limits needed by the vital force. It also becomes linear like a vector in the sense of purposely connecting the past to the future to achieve a goal. This goal may take years, even decades, depending on the required planning, organizing, and executing needed to complete the mission. Historical precedents become guides for future action because the past and future are part of the same process.

The third level is the creative force. A person learns about himself when he builds something new, becomes a parent, develops lasting relationships with others that crosses generations, or creates new worlds of imagination that all can share. The creative force begins with the will to change, to become better than before. Flashes of intuition beyond conscious control are the inspirational source for mythological imagery and creative themes found in epic stories. It hints at the existence of a blueprint for existence beyond the mind's capacity to grasp. Properly interpreted, these flashes produce discoveries, inventions, and insights into the human condition that permanently change the way humanity lives. America, the nation of nations, the city on the hill, the light unto the world, Lady Liberty, and Uncle Sam – mythical imagery – are the offspring of the Creative Force.

At its highest reaches, the creative force within the human soul begins to connect with the purposeful force that created, sustains, and changes the universe. It is a force within and yet apart from humanity. Its rules are the basis of humanity's spiritual intuitions. This force has a feeling of being impersonal and beyond time, yet so close as to be a personal God that cares deeply for every one of His creations. At this soulful level, time stretches to infinity; the human is not one; instead, he becomes part of something beyond number and grasp. At this level, all spiritual expressions from all religions and ideologies come together.

Each soulful layer has the equivalent of nodes that are its gateways. For instance, the creative force includes will, creative imagination, and understanding as its portals. The conscious force also has three nodes: judgment, mercy, and beauty. The vital force includes endurance, overcoming, fruitfulness, and the receptacle that holds and forms these spiritual impulses into real-world creations.

All three soulful levels are part of the same unity but generate different spiritual needs. Sometimes they clash, and other times they find grounds to cooperate. The conscious force itself, even when it seeks ways to organize life, can become contradictory and self-defeating. For instance, a person's rational impulse seeks to abstract from life ideas, natural laws, and overarching theories of everything. The emotional impulse, by contrast, seeks to define itself as a unique persona. Every decision and action chisel another defining line into the soul's image of its existential self. Less apparent but there as well are noble and dark motivations, called the side of light and the side of darkness that arguably operate at all three soulful levels. Many of these motivations like the willingness to die for a cause or kill without remorse are most easily classified as irrational because they defy logical explanations, but they are not. Even the darkest emotions are explainable as someone's excessive desire to justify the necessity and righteousness of getting even.

The righteous path often gets confused because of psychic timing contradictions. This is apparent in ideological discussions. Liberals, a la Keynes, say in the long run we are all dead, so let's develop policy for here and now. Conservatives believe every moment is the end of the long run, so we should think in generations to develop good policy. Libertarians believe in a timeless policy of aiming for a government that governs least.

In psychic-time, the soul can foreshorten real time so that ancestors separated by centuries become part of a nuclear family because they represent the unfolding character of a people. The Patriarchs of the Bible may be the product of this type of time compression as Thomas Mann the writer wrote in his Joseph saga. A catastrophe like September 11 can foreshorten time for those who experienced the attack. Planned futures fall away and only the present remains as they wonder what will happen next. At the same temporal time, people around the world are caught in different psychological time frames. Many continue to live life as before after the September 11 attack. But in psychic time, stupendous events like September 11 eventually affect the imagination of all peoples are part of the same sea of psychological time.

Psychic time lengthening is associated with spiritual maturity, and Jewish mystics identified longer horizons with the wise who have studied many years. Instead of following that path, one would suspect that older people, people who have lived and prospered in America, would favor a long view of redemption, so they would probably lean toward being conservative. Younger people, recent immigrants, may have a shorter time horizon and would, therefore, favor liberal policies.

Because the soul has such a complicated structure, someone who has studied Jewish mysticism would expect all but a few spiritual grandees to suffer from multiple visions of the proper course to take. I submit that most of America's ideologs have not achieved spiritual harmony, and if they recognized their shortcomings, they may become more flexible in outlook. They may even agree with the Jewish mystics that there are many righteous approaches to salvation.

The spiritual emanations of creation are not of light connected by pathways, and they are all connected with God's ultimate purposes for creation. In Jewish mysticism there are 32 righteous pathways. The number has mystical meaning because it is associated with the word "heart" in Hebrew. It means that with the right heart, there are many pathways to God. Applied to ideologies, it suggests that all of them are on the right path to renewing and enhancing America, but simply following a different set of policies. Properly executed, a libertarian, a conservative, or a liberal agenda could work to solve America's challenges. If this sounds far-fetched, consider they all share common values, even agree on basic shortcomings in society, and do recognize that a mix of private and public actions is necessary to solve America's problems.

A last humbling but important insight of the Jewish mystics is that humanity can never understand God's purposes for creating the universe, and likewise, a person will never understand his or her true purpose. The universe is a product of energy and matter, but the spiritual force that developed creation infuses them, but their origins will never be known.

The origin of Jewish mysticism is itself a mystery. It developed thousands of years ago, well before the first written documents, at a time when spirits dwelled in heaven and on earth. From this luxuriant spiritual world, a Being emerged among the Jews that personified them all and went even further. God exists but could not be named, He was becoming but to what no one knew. The Jewish God was personal yet remote and established the laws of nature by the Word and injected purpose into nature. Humanity, with all their defects, are His sacred offspring. The human persona bears features in common with those of God, and like God, some of their traits are within the realm of understanding. But the innermost or highest reaches of God as well as man are beyond human comprehension.

Jewish mystics believe humanity should imitate God. God is a lover of truth, but it is only one feature of His Being. He is also an emotional God, loving and compassionate to his creations, long-suffering because of their sins, and a fearful God who demands righteousness and is not above destroying His own creations if they reject Him.

A Jewish mystic's mindset differs from that of a deist's in two critical respects. First, a deist believes rational thought alone is the basis for human salvation. Without this divine faculty, human beings would be another animal species doomed by the cycles of nature to live and die and eventually become extinct. By contrast, a mystic is an existential believer. Behind everyday appearances lies a deeper spiritual reality. Every act and every phase of life shapes a person's soul and orients it toward good or evil. Even a seemingly insignificant good deed or sin can have cosmic consequences. Second, an even-minded deist tests his truths against facts, not limiting his inquiry to an ideology or fundamentalist view of religion. An open-minded mystic looks inward, into his soul, or into a divinely inspired book like the Bible to decipher God's plan for humanity. The search requires a higher level of awareness of reality that goes beyond everyday needs or rational thought to intuitions about the cosmic drama unfolding.

History is not just a series of events that may follow patterns to the mystic. Alongside secular history, a mystic plumbs sacred history for life's meaning. Sacred time has no beginning or end; it is alive; the days are alive and testify to our lives; and momentous events can still be relived. Myths populate sacred history. For the Jews, the Ten Commandments engraved on two tablets by the finger of God embodies the heart of Jewish religion.

14.5.4 Comparisons of Jewish and Eastern Mysticism

Though the goal of glimpsing ultimate reality is the same for mystics from different parts of the world, they differ in approach. Eastern mystics look inward to peel away layers of ignorance that cause suffering. When people try to hold onto possessions or fixed ideas in a changing world, they will suffer. Only by suppressing false constructs of the mind can a person experience that all creation is part is an organic whole. Then all the seeming conflicts in life fall away.

By contrast with Eastern mystics, Jewish and Christian mystics begin with a different premise about reality. Man is God's Thou. The world exists and humanity has corrupted it by sinning. Their objective is to redeem creation by restoring it to a purity that was lost early in the creative process, even before Adam's sin, and, by doing so, it burnishes God's image to its original splendor. They are like spiritual ecologists who want to harmonize their souls with the spirit of God. They seek to uncover the Wisdom that created natural laws, the Bible, and that resides in everyday affairs; and they want to stay away from impure spiritual and carnal influences or redeem their holy sparks and transform them from destructive fire to spiritual warmth.

Jewish and Christian mystics have a lively personal relationship with God. Man is a servant and potential partner in an "I and Thou" relationship with a loving but fearful God. The earthly world is a crude reflection of the heavenly one. A purposeful force emanating from God keeps the universe from becoming chaotic; the righteous acts of ordinary people strengthen this anti-entropic force. This God-emanating force infuses every real-world object and produces a spiritual aura. A house has the spiritual residue of those who lived there, and a man's life leaves a spiritual residue that floats across the generations. The everyday world is impermanent and coarse, but the spiritual world of "light" is permanent and pure. This spiritual light has much warmer, poetic, and artistic connotations than the deist's Light of Truth. It is a humane light that creates worlds and unites man to man and man to the cosmos. This mystical light emanates mythological images, consoling images, images that capture the essence of a people, their self-image and longings, images that no set of facts and figures, no objective history, and no philosophical utopia can capture.

14.5.5   The Need to Update Jewish Mysticism

Theistic mysticism lost much of its glamor since the Enlightenment. In a deep sense, it is because the mystics became encrusted in superstition. Originally, they were pathfinders who tried to see beyond the cycles of nature and looked for purpose in a threatening world. They searched for God, which led them to great insights into the human soul and into the creative process itself. Jewish mystics recognized that God did not create a perfect world. It was up to us to uncover God's natural laws and the meaning of God's religious laws that aimed at raising righteous people. They recognized the alphabet and numbers as seeds of creation and, when used properly, could identify patterns in creation; they even hinted that proper word orderings could alter the course of creation. Their insights produced reasonable theories of the universe's process of creative destruction and malevolent destruction. Jewish mystics also recognized in biblical passages that continuity built on a covenant with God and ancestors allowed wisdom to accumulate, and it was through wisdom built on righteous behavior that humanity would be redeemed, renewed, and ultimately uplifted. Their basic theme was making God smile and you and all who you touch will be blessed. Tragically, theistic mystics became reactionary over time. They didn't enlarge their field of inquiry to embrace new scientific discoveries. Instead, they fell back on preserving ancient teachings in secret cabals. Many mystics continued to believe magical incantations could tap into God's power and use it to heal humanity. If they could convince enough people to live righteously, the mystics believed it would usher in a Messianic Age. Then the righteous would be resurrected and the evil ones damned to oblivion. Their hunger for this new age led them to follow false Messiahs, yet they didn't lose faith in ultimate redemption. Their lust for righteousness turns many mystics into fanatics, even today. They are willing to die to honor God's will as they see it.

14.5.6 American Mysticism Is Alive But Needs Revitalization

Despite America's rejection theistic mystics, its spirit survives in muted tones. In private life, an American with a mystical bent sees tradeoffs between the obligations of everyday activities and time spent on spiritual search for God, and in the name of God he wants to redeem the world. He seeks to reconcile the almost irreconcilable: justice and mercy, leading and following, and giving and receiving. From esoteric and hidden texts, he learns that death is not a tragedy in the usual sense because his spirit returns to its Maker after death. Though he wouldn't miss a minute of living in this world, he somehow believes that the heavenly world is superior to the earthly one, justifying his life on earth as part of a divine plan that he must carry out. If he dies before fulfilling his obligations to the world, he may not enter Paradise in a timely fashion.

In public life, an American style "mystic" bears the added burden of leading people toward righteousness by example. His every thought and action aim at repairing society, renewing faith in a glorious vision of American society as a spiritual nation of nations. He is willing to become a political martyr to the cause if necessary. Polls will not sway him if the publics' demands go against his religious conscience.

The American mystical spirit reveals itself when someone gazes into the remote past and unforeseen future and conjures images of America as a Promised Land, a Light unto Nations, and a Land of Redemption and Fulfillment. Lady Liberty is the spirit of America. The war on terrorism is another manifestation of the struggle between good and evil that will be with us until the Millennium.

An American's mystical loyalty is tied up in spiritual visions of what this nation can become – a new Israel composed of the mixed multitude and separate tribes that are part of one nation, with each mixture and each group chosen and special. They are on a quest to show the world that holiness no longer means exclusion or one group better than another. By example, America will finally redeem the world by dignifying all. Linking personal imagination with national and cosmic visions is the strength of this perspective. His symbol is Jacob's ladder, a connection between heaven and earth for angels, spirits, and souls as they work to build this New World.

In the war on terrorism, an American mystic wants to restore Islam to a friendly sister religion of Judaism and Christianity. The struggle with the Jihadists is a struggle between good and evil with the outcome in doubt. The very existence of civilizations hangs in the balance, and it is up to America to lead the forces of light against the forces of darkness.

The great challenge of the American mystic is to embrace the idea that the most wondrous images of what America and humanity can become are the product of scientific advances. The coding revolution is pointing humanity toward becoming partners with God. What should humanity do now that it is beginning to reshape creation? Threats from designer genetics should not be a topic popularized solely by science fiction writers. A mystical saga should see the future unfolding with many surprises and challenges, and the pathway to God is endless. Soulful harmony should become a dynamic process instead of a static image of pure spiritual light, which God rebelled against.

Epic stories about cultural exchanges across borders are in short supply. The most prominent American writer of the epic genre, Cormac McCarthy, has updated the Sodom and Gomorrah stories, highlighting the threat from the alien culture that has sprung up along the border between Mexico and America. A more upbeat epic theme has remained unexplored. A new and troubling trend is to de-mythologize American heroes. While their flaws should be revealed, what they represented was not a glorification of a person. Instead, it was glorification of an ideal. Columbus may have been a cruel explorer, but mythical Columbus opened a new world to the oppressed of Europe.

The American mystical view needs to recognize as well that national cultural systems have extended across borders. For America to become a beacon of hope again, it must not simply become a platform for immigrants to re-launch their lives; it must also help other nations re-launch theirs.

Theistic mysticism isn't the only form of mysticism operating in America. Two important secular views of a hidden divine presence fall into the mystical category. Both have muted theistic overtones because many people no longer want their beliefs tied to God, the Creator. The one most discussed thus far in the book is the mysticism associated with Adam Smith's Invisible Hand that guides markets toward a better society. Market mysticism assumes that with clearly defined property rights and a pricing system that operates without government constraints, the market will solve virtually every social problem. In particular, it will eliminate the original sin that causes so much evil: poverty.

Market mystics believe profits charge creative inspiration. If fossil fuel reserves are diminishing, the profit motive will lead to alternative sources of fuel such as batteries. If pollution is becoming a concern, the cost of these negative externalities must be included in the property right. The added cost will limit pollution. Even saving species could have a price. Domesticated cattle are not at risk of extinction because they have market value. Rare species also have market value that if recognized would save them as well.

A wide range of objections to market mysticism has already been discussed. Ending poverty doesn't end conflicts. People and cultures struggle for power and honor. Sometimes the struggle ends in conflict. The market may not distribute income fairly. It may give firms undue market power for unacceptably long times.

One of the main pushbacks on market mysticism comes from environmental mystics. Not everything has a price. Nature has intrinsic value that environmentalists would consider sacred. Like Jewish mystics, the environmentalists have significant inconsistencies that should not weaken their basic message. They also have much in common. In Jewish mysticism, the earth is a spiritual being with a streak of evil to it because it wants to dominate the spiritual spheres. In modern environmentalism, Mother Earth has no such shortcomings.

The vision of the Garden of Eden to the staunchest environmentalists is of a pristine landscape populated with authentic species, protected from rapacious humans. The original sin for environmentalists is human agriculture. People began replacing natural ecosystems with farmland. The latest sin is the product of economic thinking. The earth became a supply house for mineral extraction, timber, and fuel. Dammed rivers destroyed wildlife. Antenna signals fill the air with invisible radio waves that may be endangering living creatures.

Environmentalists face a dilemma in connecting their imagery with scientific facts. Pristine nature doesn't exist. Humankind in the New and Old Worlds have altered the landscape. Images of the New World before the arrival of the Europeans as an untouched Eden are incorrect because Native Americans used controlled burns to maintain wildlife.

Darwinism suggests that survival of the fittest is the motive force among living creatures. They are all fighting tooth and claw. After perhaps millions of years, humans have won the struggle. They dominate the earth. Why is this bad?

Environmentalists once posited sustainable ecosystems as the reason for biodiversity. In its early formulations, ecosystems move toward more diversity, and when viewed from the heights, the seeming struggle is actual a grand harmony of life that tends toward a steady state. This sounds good, but the environment has never been in a steady state. Massive species extinctions have occurred several times in Earth's history. Now a mass extinction may be reversible. With genetic coding, humanity will soon have the ability to resurrect dead species such as the mammoths. Humanity is already creating mutations that improve harvest yields.

Another controversial issue is global warming. Is it okay if it is the product of a natural process? Is it okay if rising water levels and loss of ice sheets destroy life and coastal cities? Is it okay for humanity to counter this type of global warming?

The most persuasive case the environmentalists make is spiritual. Humanity are the stewards of the earth. It is not right for humanity to desecrate the land and destroy species. Human wealth is a source of sin because it makes people morally lax. Hubris sets in. The bible clearly states again and again, hubris leads to a fall, usually a major catastrophe – a flood, for example, that wipes out life. Setting aside zoos and parks and playing God with species will lead to a horrible fall.

14.5.7 Proposed Mystical Updates

A basic shortcoming of the Kabbalistic model is that its single dynamic is the proper use of God's ethical laws. Science has no play in this model as an independent constructive force. Individuality plays a secondary role to God's expectation of a person's role to play in the cosmic unfolding. Judgment and mercy play center stage in moral dramas. Much less emphasis is on the dialectic struggles between other complementary forces: power and obedience, control and trust, and honor and humility.

In the Western tradition, the will to power dominates human motivations. Warfare is no longer the desired method to dominate others, although the threat of warfare has its advantages. Market domination is another way to impose one's will on others by either paying them or embargoing them. The noncombative weapon in the digital world is information – surveillance in real time.

Using the three-level spiritual model as a base, one could imagine that the creative force now embodies human potencies that are growing in power. They can be used for both good and evil. These potencies allow people to imagine new purposes, new worlds of the imagination that are reifying, rolling horizons of the imagination of what humanity can become. Sparks of inspiration from the creative force ignite scientific breakthroughs, cultural revolutions, and radical social restructuring. Arguably, it is not channeled thinking of "new and improved" services or goods that are the source of great transformations of civilization. Rather, it is seizing the opportunities opened by the unexpected. The scientific world offers the easiest examples: that the world is spherical; that steam, gas, electricity, and atoms are controllable powers; that lasers can control beams of light; and that an Internet can open a virtual dimension to life.

At the conscious level, the working dynamics of blueprint and process turn some inspirations into practical uses. In science constant testing leads to discarding dead theories, pruning old ones, and planting new ones. The bank of knowledge keeps expanding. In the cultural realm of the arts, there is much less discarding because classics have their place among modern, and postmodern, bodies of work, and new artforms – cinema, digital art, and holograms – emerge. Social structures also change. The online economy will make the world's economies rethink the physical structure of cities, suburbs, and towns, the working rhythms of society, and the social relations of people who work for online platforms and those who use them.

At the vital force level, new aids, the product of science, could enhance human life. People will live longer; they will have mechanical and organic aids that will keep them active and healthy.

The spiritual energy from each level is bi-directional: moving up from the physical, moving down from the imagination. Physical needs spark the imagination. New inventions attend to physical needs. This spiritual dynamism lends itself easily to rejuvenating the image of "I and Thou." Humanity is a partner in creation with a universe that has rules. Humanity can uncover their purposes or give them purpose. After all, humanity is a product of the universe, and humanity seeks meaning to existence.

Another dimension of this model as I interpret tackles the issue of complexity. Life is complex, so pathways are difficult to define. This is true to some extent, but I believe overstated in crucial ways. I believe that at the creative level of the soul, all humanity has a common vision but imagined in different ways. This vision is to become a Thou to a cosmic purpose that seeks our support, whether this cosmic purpose is God or Brahman, or a force that cannot be defined yet regulates all things.

It is at the conscious level where complexity explodes. Each individual has his own view of life, and people come together to develop many pathways to becoming a Thou. Good and evil emerge as products of human decision-making. Evil is much more clearly defined because it results in physical or psychological harms that are damaging. Think of negative freedom as the product of rules to prevent damages. Good is much harder to define because it has many more possibilities for improving the lot of humanity. Think of positive freedom. It is much harder to define than negative freedom because it focuses on self-fulfillment. At the vital force level, complexity diminishes because all physical human bodies are roughly alike. Based on these assumptions, I offer my suggestions.

America's mission statement since its inception is in the Declaration of Independence: we hold these truths to be self-evident, that all men are created equal, that they are endowed by their Creator with certain unalienable rights, and that among these are life, liberty, and the pursuit of happiness. We can add a bold addition fit for future generations: to fertilize the universe, to bring purpose to it, to honor the dignity and preciousness of all life, to find ways to save the environment, and to and enhance our being at the same time. The search for higher levels of being is within the soul and the outer reaches of space. Surely, ideologs of all types can see the promise that a broad mystical outlook offers.

Next, consider America's core values – freedom, equality, private property, and security – from a mystical standpoint. This table has many flaws. My intension is simply to say that core values engage us at several soulful levels. To focus on the purely rational is to miss their breadth.

	Freedom	Equality	Property	Security
Creative	Power to imagine – broad connections to humanity – patriotism	Common destiny for humanity	The earth as an inheritance and bequest across generations	Protection from forces beyond personal control
Conscious	Power to choose – personal fulfillment	Fair treatment by others	Connection between work and ownership	Fair right to work rules
Vital	Power that enables – necessities	Necessities that assure basic human dignity	Physical possession of necessities	Legal protection from criminals

Another product of the mystical model is to realize that ideas like negative and positive freedom are not separate categories. It is better to see them as two poles that produce new definitions of core values. For instance, private and public properties are constantly morphing. Private property rights have become narrower in a society where people crowd together in cities as opposed to living in rural areas. They became narrower when people worked for huge corporations instead of being in business for themselves. They expanded with new products and services such as smartphones and property dimensions that will exist in virtual reality.

This soulful model has wide applicability that goes beyond America's mission and core values. I have already given practical applications of the three-level spiritual model at the start of the section. I showed that this new layered perspective can explain what constitutes art and how religion, private enterprise, and liberal democracy appeal to all levels of the soul.

Much of economic theory depends on two basic assumptions: consumers maximize personal utility and firms maximize profits. Higher levels of utility often translate into higher levels of consumption. This is not true from a soulful perspective. Finding your place in the God's creative process and doing your best to fulfill your obligation are the main goals in life. This search gives one's life meaning, and it is meaning much more than happiness that drives people to perfect themselves. Meaning, profit, and wealth (the accumulation of profits) have connections. Wealth provides security to pursue one's creative goals. Accumulating wealth opens possibilities for controlling one's life and raising one's status in society, both of which expand creative possibilities. Use of wealth allows a person to help thy neighbor or can be a vehicle for improving social conditions.

Increasingly, America's education is crowding out the arts in favor of analytics. Businesspeople and policymakers stress technical problem-solving, which they apply to supply chain disruptions or informational services. Intuition is considered either innate or learned on the job. The arts teach values. They train people to appreciate life at all the soulful levels. Arts and religion train students to open their minds to larger forces and by doing so learn how to discover new ideas. This type of training would complement people exploring virtual reality and genetic enhancements.

Another shortcoming of America's education system is a lack of exploration of corruption and evil. Examining the four philosophical approaches highlights the problem of an overly logical approach to evil. Rationalists assume that criminal behavior is a product of faulty societal incentives. If the payoff from stealing more than compensates for the cost of being caught and punished, the crime rate will rise. Romantics would attribute crime to a black heart produced by poor parenting and lack of social support. Deists would point to bad theories such as social Darwinism that suggest that survival of the fittest group is the right path to human development. Jewish mystics believe that evil is the product of excessive judgment against criminal acts that leads to vengeance or too little judgment against bad behavior that destroys the rules that shape society. The Jewish mystics did condemn corrupt sacred visions of God as profane. Yet none of them tackled the poisonous trickle up effect from the vital force (visceral) part of the soul that can infect conscious thought and prophetic visions. People or groups that feel threatened by real or fancied dangers become paranoic about strangers. This paranoia is most likely in a culture that is changing rapidly, when familiar landmarks and relationships become erased in a matter of years, when attacks against one group become sensationalized and isolated from other less visible everyday occurrences. America needs to grapple with this type of social poison because it separates people, turns society into a zero-sum game, and, even worse, motivates people to tear down society even it means being killed in the process. This is a recipe for American destruction.

15

Dynamic Integration of Ideological Perspectives

Abstract Four tasks remain to make the case that religious humanism can promote ideological collaboration. First is to identify elements of the four perspectives, namely, rational, romantic, deist, and mystical, that America's ideologies – libertarianism, conservatism, and liberalism – use and by implication do not use. Those missing spaces are areas for potential expansion of America's ideologies. Next, the objective is to show that ideologies have evolved to meet new changes and in some cases have drawn them together. Once done, the narrative turns to online platform dynamics discussed in earlier chapters to gain insights into the challenges ideologies face to remain major influences on public policy. Finally, the narrative shifts back to the mystical soulful ladder because the claim is that it is an important missing practice that can promote ideological collaboration.

15.1 Introduction

Four tasks remain to make the case that religious humanism can promote ideological collaboration. First is to identify elements of the four perspectives, namely, rational romantic, deist, and mystical, that America's ideologies – libertarianism, conservatism, and liberalism – use and by implication do not use. Those missing spaces are areas for potential expansion of America's ideologies. Next, is to show that ideologies have evolved to meet new changes and in some cases have drawn them together. Once done, the narrative turns to online platform dynamics discussed in earlier chapters to gain insights into the challenges ideologies face to remain major influences on public policy.

V. Glass, *Humanizing the Digital Economy*, https://doi.org/10.1007/978-3-031-37507-1_15

Finally, the narrative shifts back to the mystical soulful ladder because the claim is that it is an important missing method that can promote ideological collaboration.

15.2 Mapping America's Ideologies to Religious Humanism

The four perspectives – rational, romantic, deist, and mystical – are the constituent parts of Religious Humanism. Without too much effort, it is clear that America's three ideologies – libertarianism, liberalism, and conservatism – have adopted elements of these perspectives for their narratives. Libertarians are firmly in the rational camp and perhaps also in the deist with Man sometimes substituting for God as the apotheosis of creation, someone like the John Galt character in Ayn Rand's *Atlas Shrugged*, a superman who takes on the world and wins. Liberals are pragmatic and perhaps romantic in the sense of trying to help the helpless and nurturing the disadvantage to rise to "the gaze of nations" if they have the talent and will. Their deity is firmly in the deism category, a God of the Enlightenment with a touch of the mystical redeemer. Conservatives are more pragmatic than rational because they like to use rules of thumb for decision-making, often relying on best practices from the past. Horatio Alger is their romantic hero instead of a cowboy-like rescuer. Being religious in the traditional sense, they stress a covenant between an individual and his or her community and ancestors and God to be fruitful and faithful. Conservatives search mystically for a Promised Land where God, their savior, will reward the righteous and merciful. The libertarians would opt for market mysticism; the liberals for environmental mysticism; and the conservatives for redemption mysticism. Although you might not agree with these assignments in the particulars, I think most of you will agree that none of the ideologies covers the complete psychic terrain of religious humanism, meaning – and this is important – they all have room to expand their narratives in psychic space.

15.3 America's Ideologies Evolve

A reassuring tendency for ideological collaboration is to realize changes in descriptions of those three ideologies which have evolved to meet new challenges. Many libertarians believe in some government programs to help the helpless. Many conservatives are coming to accept gay marriage. Many liberals believe government spending can hurt the economy.

Ideologs also compromise. A good example is the Founders. They agreed on general principles of the nature of humanity largely taken from rational, deist, and religious sources and applied them to form the Constitution. Throwing in a bit of empirical data on man's sinful nature led to dispersing government power. Even so, the Founders disagreed on their particular visions of "These United States." Jefferson symbolized those who favored a loose federation of states populated by yeoman farmers. At the other end of the political spectrum was Hamilton who wanted a unified nation, strong central government, with a population engaged in commerce. Many of the Southern Founders also accepted the reality of slavery, while many Northerners believed it violated the Constitution and the biblical idea that all humanity descended from Adam and Eve.

Those particular visions are still recognizable in religious humanism but with a shift in perspective toward Hamilton's. The federal government's role of actively managing the economy arguably began with Teddy Roosevelt's trust-busting activities. Wilson put the economy on a war footing during World War I. The victory of Franklin Roosevelt over Herbert Hoover marked the beginning of a new creedal turn. America began to accept the federal government having an active role during peacetime planning and stabilizing the economy and in serving as a caregiver to its citizens. After World War II, the permanent war economy developed with a huge, specialized weapons industry emerging to produce weapons that could defeat communism. Libertarians like Milton Friedman accepted government's expansion as necessary to stabilize the economy and provide essential services, but he wanted to limit government discretion to pick and choose who received government benefits. Still, the libertarian vision of laissez-faire, of government leaving people to build their own lives, remains a check on government growth and so does the conservative vision of allowing communities to grow organically.

America's ideologies have morphed to accommodate the image of an American. After World War II, the image of the WASP as the essence of an American ideal began to wane. From then on, on a cultural level, America has been groping toward a creedal image that will justify a "diversity is beautiful" culture without erasing or effacing WASP culture. This new vision has not come into focus yet.

15.4   The Coding Revolution Challenges

In the past 150 years, technological change has altered the relationship of man and society. In the mid-1800s, Americans began moving from farm to city. By mid-1900s, the most educated men worked for big corporations. By the early 2000s, men and women were coding new products and services in Silicon Valley and other tech hotspots. Section 15.2 highlighted the ideological challenges of coding revolution: the fragility of economy because of the speed and complexity of the online economy; the increase in size and intrusiveness of online platforms; the biases of the media caused by fierce competition for viewers; the growth of spy agencies; and genetic engineering.

The financial system breakdown in 2008 and the ensuing panic began an extensive re-examination of private enterprise in cyber world. A few relatively anonymous players herded investors into a real estate frenzy financed by securities that were little understood. The sheer greed coupled with mass layoffs called into question America's materialistic culture. As the online economy developed into a virtual international system, the public has become concerned because basic values of freedom, equality, and opportunity are being threatened by fake or distorted news traveling at light speed in a virtual world without borders. The COVID-19 pandemic has changed attitudes toward work and family. People are less likely to commute to and from their workplace. Government, for the first time, shut down society to limit deaths. Countries closed their borders to protect themselves from infection.

Platforms like Amazon or Google are constantly under pressure to keep growing or die. Like older-generation huge corporations, they wield a great deal of power in the online economy, but they differ from them in a very important respect: the online platforms gather a great deal of personal information that allows them to know the intimate personal life of most Americans.

Digital exposure has occurred. People display themselves online. People give their opinions online. The vastness of communication volumes means that it is difficult for anyone or any group to stand out. This struggle to be noticed leads to exaggerated images of self and a constant stream of scandalous stories.

America's permanent war footing has boosted the size of America's spy agencies. They have become almost like a shadow government that monitors and sometimes controls private citizens and public officials. Security concerns led to limiting exports and imports of computer chips and smart communication and information devices.

The genetic engineering revolution threatens to alter life itself. How will altering our genes or putting implants into the body affect the image and integrity of a human life? "What do we want to be?" may no longer result from personal decisions on marriage, profession, and service. The new set of decisions will depend on the symbiosis of genes and technology that design the "self."

In this new environment, even die-hard libertarians are beginning to acknowledge that rational decision-making is often hard to prove because of so many unintended consequences that sometimes lead to financial panics and sharp economic downturns. Perhaps even the environmentalists have a point that a Black Swan event could threaten life on earth.

Future challenges are likely to be more spiritual than in recent decades. For instance, the ongoing war against Al-Qaeda and other Jihadists has accentuated the need to develop a new creedal synthesis that is more accepting of ethnic and religious diversity in the streets, in schools, in community life, and in world affairs. America cannot rely on ideological arguments backed by economic and military strength to bring peace to the world as it did during the twentieth century. America defeated Communism mainly because Western liberal democracy trumped Soviet-style regimes on any material yardstick from housing to warships. The war against fascism was also ideological with racial overtones tracing back to Social Darwinism of the nineteenth century. America won that war by enlisting people of all backgrounds in its fight.

Often, religions and ethnic groups gain strength from their seeming inferiority. For instance, Jihadists see themselves as the Islamic David against the American Goliath. They will not abide by a profane democratic ruling that violate the Laws of Allah like forcing women to uncover their heads.

15.5 The Value of the Soulful Ladder Technique for Promoting Ideological Reflection

So far, I have projected religious humanism as a cultural or philosophical superstructure that comes to life when filled with practical and spiritual wisdom aimed at improving public policy. Another way to look at it is to think of religious humanism as a specialized library of books, audios, and videos on public policy. Like the Dewey Decimal system, the library has a system for classifying material. One section is purely ideological; other sections are philosophical and religious. One section is political satire – a section with the likes of Will Rogers who tell us not to take ourselves too seriously because we all have shortcomings and blind spots. Another section contains different approaches to systems analysis with a growing list of references to digital systems. As with any library, the collection continues to grow, sometimes with new sections added.

My aim is to act like a librarian: to guide even the most rigid ideologues to material they might find interesting. And like a good librarian, I want ideologs to search among the growing list of sources without my help. Toward that end, I repurposed the soulful ladder from Jewish mysticism as a way for ideologs to expand their views without sacrificing their principles – and without someone telling them what the right way is. Soulful layering of a social problem opens new perspectives on public policy that any ideolog could accept and add to his or her interpretation of social issues. More than broadening one's outward perspective, I also hope the soulful ladder helps ideologs do a self-assessment of the strengths and limitations of their own beliefs.

A user of the soulful layering model should recognize that each ideology is part of a larger unity. They all have a place within the soulful model, but sometimes they are too confining as separate perspectives. Libertarians face the challenge of being accused that their ideology proposes that government run on autopilot. Everything will turn out well when private enterprise has free reign. Libertarianism defines the vital force in very egocentric terms. At this level, a person is like an animal, out to protect self by being dominant, having power over others and the natural world. The main weapon is the ability to think more clearly than others. Reason, forming concepts, and rational strategies stemming from the judgmental side of the conscious force enhance the likelihood of survival and separate humans from other animals, being the only species that can plan and remember. One tangible product of the conscious force is the rule of law that defines the terms of engagement among people. Moving up to the creative force level, libertarians focus on rational understanding and control of nature itself. Emerging from this search is a type of deism where each person or possibly as a voluntary collective humanity becomes God-like. Recognizing human vulnerability and a collective search for meaning may be fruitful areas for investigation. The soulful ladder offers defined pathways.

Conservatives focus on different areas of the soulful hierarchy. At the vital force level, again the main drive is for survival, but the strategy is to band together, to form a pack, to protect each other from danger. Communication, cooperation, and group sanctions like ostracism are their tools for keeping a little platoon together. At the conscious force level, they lean to the side of judgment, stressing obligations to self and society. Moral rules develop based on inherited wisdom such as the rule of law and living within one's means. Mercy does come into play but mainly for others they know. At the creative force level, they lean toward becoming chosen people to save humanity. Another, more ethereal longing is to achieve a type of marriage with God, or if the conservative happens to be a Hindu or Buddhist, to merge with God. Each person has a place in God's design to redeem the world. Critiques of conservatism point out that the market system and paternalistic government have stripped away the family and community as sources of security and self-development. A re-examination of the more rational side of the soulful ladder may help conservatives reinvigorate family and community in the Digital Age.

Liberals are somewhere in-between libertarians and conservatives. Their main focus is on the other, the poor and oppressed. At the vital force level, they focus on human weaknesses and prejudices, source of all types of prejudices and harmful acts. They too believe vital forces must be controlled at the conscious level with an approach distinctly "other oriented." They are judgmental to those on top and merciful for those at the bottom of society. They look to government, organized collective action, to accomplish their aims. At the creative force level, they focus much more on a blissful society where each receives according to need and all possess equal dignity, something like the communist dream without tyrannical rulers. Liberals lean toward deism at the creative force level but recognize that society becomes livable when it is merciful. An American liberal's most tangible image of what America can become is a nation of nations, at once a unity and a collection of distinctive cultures and races all adding their creative touches to the American dream. The imagery is compelling to many. Yet, it ignores the basic critique of liberalism as a justification for the inflated, inefficient public programs, and persistent deficit spending that have created divisive interest groups that fight for justice for their constituencies. Liberals could benefit from the searching the soulful ladder's judgment side for ways to ensure that government aims at national unity.

Ideologs implicitly weave together a particular set of motivations across all levels of the soul to produce a believable and satisfying solution to a problem. To produce a more expansive story, one that could lead to collaboration, ideologs have to realize the critical importance of not to letting one soulful perspective dominate. In the extreme, a narrow perspective often leads to close-mindedness and sometimes to fanaticism.

Notice, for religious humanism, the humanism part mainly resides in the logical side of the soul. It contains all the rational and pragmatic concepts for survival and mastery and aims toward man becoming God-like. The religious side of religious humanism resides on the emotional side of the soul. It is the very will to survive that is beyond reason, the passion to understand the world and to huddle together with the ultimate purpose of union with God or merging into God. Time is measured differently on both sides. On the logical side, time is in real terms, but as the horizon lengthens, it tends toward infinity, an undefined number without clear meaning in the logical sense. On the emotional side, time is much more psychic, sometimes bunching and stretching depending on the vividness of experiences and eventually meets at a paradoxical psychic dimension where no-time and eternity meet.

This added insight into religious humanism has important implications for policymakers in government and religious institutions. For both, it is clear that science, logic, emotions, and mystical longing are part of the same unity. They need each other. Without emotional longings, the will to create would not be a necessity. Rabbi Soloveitchik knew this implicitly when he explained God bestowed on humanity two creation stories: Adam One, the creator, and Adam Two, the lonely man of faith. They are complementary images of the human drive to become something better.[1]

Open-minded questioning and historical evidence are critical for developing a unified, emotionally uplifting, and realistic picture of an epic challenge to American culture. The Jewish mystical tradition offers a practical psychological technique for developing open-mindedness.

> A wise man knows for himself as much as is required, but a man of discernment apprehends the whole, knowing his own point of view and that of the other.[2]

An enduring story line must fit into the larger American saga. It must reaffirm long-held beliefs but also open new avenues of scientific, moral, and religious thought that justifies a new epic challenge's place in America's sacred history. The story line will also present an epic challenge as a series of related challenges covering multiple time horizons. The September 11 attack, for example, produced many challenges rippling out from Ground Zero: the cleanup, a fitting memorial, rebuilding, responding to the attack, an end game strategy, and absorbing the lessons from this cultural clash. The Coding Revolution ripples across reality and expands into virtual reality and is already changing how we live, how we connect with others, and how we see the future.

At no time will a viable story or group of viable stories remain fixed. Unfolding events and new insights valuable to the generation looking at them

---

[1] Rabbi Soloveitchik, JB. (1965) The Lonely Man of Faith (1965). OU Press, NY.
[2] THE ZOHAR, Translated by Sperling, H. and Simon, M. (1984) Volume 4. Soncino Press, London. Pp. 180–181.

assures the story will keep changing. But it will develop a basic outline and theme that takes on a permanent look.

Using this framework, America's twentieth-century epic challenges were primarily at the conscious force level – challenges to the way we organize, plan, and see ourselves from a largely rational perspective. It was private enterprise against command economies, and Everyman pitted against the Aryan. The Jihadist challenge is primarily a struggle between different perceptions of whether science or obedience to God as the creative force is the right pathway leading toward redemption. This struggle crosses all spiritual levels. It is also a struggle for oil (vital force) and a contest between theocracy, government under Sharia law, and democracy, under the rule of law (conscious).

America will reconcile with the Islamic world when it becomes clear that Allah would approve of our respect for all religions as He did. America must convince itself and the world that religious humanism points the way toward helping all America's religions and ethnic groups prosper and renew themselves instead of bartering their heritages for money and power. Perhaps it requires a new vision of God that will make even iconoclasts shed some of their petty, close-minded beliefs if they want to continue to have a following among their own congregants. It is a challenge as bold as the Israelites faced when they had to develop a cultural synthesis to explain their freedom and sustain them in their attempt to become a priestly nation. This time, America will have to show that it wants to become a priestly nation of nations, a friend and ally to all. The solution to the struggle with the Islamic world will also serve as a template for reconciliation and redemption among America's divided ethnic and racial groups. Religious humanism offers pathways for finding dignity in diversity.

The coding revolution is a twenty-first-century challenge. This challenge will test all levels of the soul. The main issue is whether cyber capitalism, stealth security, and eugenics will nurture the soul or corrupt it. In the mystical tradition, the prime question is whether our undertakings enhance God's creations or not. Power alone will not produce virtue and will not nourish creation unless conscience governs it. The pursuit of righteousness does not follow a clear roadmap. America's religions, philosophies, and ideologies are groping to find new visions, new policies, and new programs that harness the creative energies of the coding revolution. The soulful ladder is like a smart system: it widens the search in a systematically productive way.

16

Drilling for Oil in Alaska

Abstract Using drilling for oil in Alaska as a detailed case study, this chapter shows how religious humanism and associated mystical tools and techniques can improve the economic and environmental religious narratives for either drilling or not drilling for oil in Alaska. The narratives also uncover possible areas for collaboration.

16.1 Introduction

An example is perhaps the easiest way to see the four perspectives of religious humanism at work and the value of the mystical model for integrating them into understandable ideological story lines. Beyond that, the objective is to uncover areas for ideologues to collaborate and to suggest ways for them to work together to develop mutually satisfying policies.

Arguably, one of the more mundane policy debates that have little to do with the digital revolution occurred after the September 11 attack. It was whether to expand oil drilling in Alaska. The disagreements show clearly that many policy conflicts go well beyond the money trail. They have spiritual overtones that go even beyond seeing humanity as the measure of all things.

Many elements of the debate are familiar, but instead of laying them out in pro and con form and associating them with the Green Peace movement, oil interests, Republicans, Democrats, Alaskans, or other Americans, the debate here centers around each perspective of religious humanism. After describing the four perspectives in isolation, I then construct messages that would have worked at the 2012 party conventions using mystical narrative techniques. If

I'm successful, the narratives should cover all levels of the soul in a fair way that is very satisfying to ideologs.

One limitation of the example is that it applies to constructive conflicts only – people of good will try to solve a problem but offer contradictory advice. More challenging problems would attempt to convert destructive conflicts, where one side wants to defeat the other, into constructive ones.

16.2 Rationalist on Drilling: A Problem of Setting the Right Price

A rationalist treats oil drilling as a pure economic problem. His first decision is whether oil drilling in Alaska is a distinct problem or part of a larger one such as defining an American energy policy. In either case, he builds a mental income statement and picks the solution that produces the most profit. His greatest challenge is to quantify the costs and benefits that wind up on the income statement.

Taking a piecemeal approach first, he would say that on the plus side, drilling creates jobs, strengthens the economy, and lessens dependency on foreign oil. On the negative side, it slows the transition to other fuel sources and by doing so may make America even more dependent on foreign oil in the future or delay the transition to clean energy. Typically, drilling also causes oil spills and other environmental damages that someone will have to pay for.

The solution to the problem is simple in theory. It is to set the correct price for the oil drilling right. Assume that the government knows this price. If after all the calculations, the price is too high for the potential bidders, it signals the market that Alaskan oil is too expensive to bring to market. If the price is low enough to attract a bid, drilling will occur and the proceeds from the sale of this right will lead to the optimal rate of extraction and pay for cleaning up environmental damage.

The practical difficulty is not the decision to drill for oil but the price set for the right to drill. Because there are so many unknowns, like the expected cost of oil cleanups and the value of energy independence, so the debate goes on.

A broader view of the problem compounds the difficulties. If the decision to drill for oil in Alaska is part of America's energy strategy, it is just one of a host of options including raising the gasoline tax to reduce consumption and using the revenues to fund research into alternative fuels. The government could require auto manufacturers to build more fuel-efficient cars and pass along the expense to consumers. The government could also invest more in mass transit and raise tolls on roads. This brief list of possibilities shows that drilling for oil in Alaska is not a simple economic calculation with a straightforward solution. In this larger context, setting the price for oil drilling rights becomes a complex national input-output problem. A likely compromise is to define the problem pragmatically so that a decision is possible.

16.3 Romantic on Drilling: A Problem of Defining America's Message

Pragmatists argue over costs and benefits. Not so with romantics. They argue over story lines. Here are two conflicting themes or messages that an American romantic might choose. The first appeals to the American love affair with bigness and strength. A romantic of this type sees America as the brawny stacker of wheat, builder of cities. Drilling for oil in Alaska is a classic gigantic homegrown project that would showcase American technology – a pipeline thousands of miles long, drilling in permafrost, and once drilling is done, restoring Alaska to its original condition. The spot might even become a tourist attraction with pictures and videos making it clear that America's determined effort lessened America's dependence on foreign oil and was a fitting response to the 9/11 attack.

A different type of romantic would focus on America the Beautiful. Drilling will damage another American symbol: the Alaskan wilderness – big, pristine, and open, with no reminders of human exploitation. Rushing to drill for oil would send a message that the 9/11 attackers have pushed America to defile her northern wilderness. America should look elsewhere to cut its dependence on foreign oil.

16.4 Deist on Drilling: A Problem of Defining Man's Stewardship

A deist would try to look at the problem the way a rational God would. Humanity is the steward of life on earth but also part of its cycle of life. Any destruction of land or animals ultimately affects humanity. From a lofty view, a deist weighs the tradeoff between defiling the wilderness, endangering species like the Caribou, and the availability of cheap and reliable energy. Without oil, modern civilization cannot sustain itself. Drilling for oil in Alaska and conserving oil may be important stopgap measures, but it is not the solution to the world's problem. A deist would recommend a long-term coordinated plan to find new, sustainable, energy sources.

16.5 Mystic on Drilling: A Problem Harmonizing Human Needs with the Cosmic Plan

A mystic worships a God that grieves over the sins of humanity but, in His divine mercy, has built into creation the means for man to redeem himself. From this perspective, God hid oil deep in the frozen north for America's salvation and by extension to repair the world. But how should America use it and when to use it? Like the deist, the mystic tries to see beyond the near-term crisis to God's intentions, but he does not rely on scientific investigation. To find answers, he searches vertically along a spiritual dimension that is essentially a moral journey. At its highest reaches, the questions take on epic proportions. Should humanity abuse a pristine wilderness to protect itself from evil doers? Shall America allow nations that abuse their people and threaten Western civilization to profit by allowing them to monopolize the oil market? Perhaps a more positive view is in order. God wants humanity to see the use of oil as a steppingstone toward cleaner energy. Ultimately, humanity should develop clean, limitless energy.

16.6 Integrating the Four Perspectives Using the Soulful Hierarchy

The objective is to overlay the four perspectives onto the soulful model to develop unified messages that win the support of the American public.

Recall, in this mystical framework, the soul has five levels:

1. Vital force – reflexes and other unconscious drives to survive
2. Conscious force – logic and emotions directed toward deliberate goals; grand emotions and ideas, seat of storytelling, myth making, ideology, and fields of learning
3. Creative force – the force that created, sustains, and changes the universe, a force apart from humanity, yet it is also within life; produces flashes of intuition beyond conscious control hinting at a blueprint for existence beyond the mind's capacity to grasp

Consider two very stylized televised political messages for and against drilling for oil in Alaska as the products of this integration process. These dueling messages highlight political inconsistencies produced by a clash of story lines that conflict at every level of the soul.

The first message is pro-drilling. The segment opens with a line of frustrated car owners waiting their turns at the pumps to buy very high-priced gas. The narrator says, "America should not depend on foreign oil to keep our nation running." A sturdy pipeline then appears. It stands elevated above the frozen wilderness and disappears into the distant whiteness. A waving American flag superimposes over this serene display of American power. At the end of the message, the narrator says, "Keep America strong."

The second message is anti-drilling. This segment opens with a closeup of snow swept tundra; then the entire landscape comes into view. As it does, you see a wilderness gashed by oilrigs and pipelines. The narrator says, "America needs to stop gorging on fossil fuels; preserve the wilderness for your children and grandchildren." The message ends with a herd of Caribou standing near a pool of oil leeching into an icy stream.

Now, look at these messages. They appeal to all three levels of the soul yet use vastly different imageries to appeal to certain groups. The vital force is the most primitive part of the human soul; its first reflex is to survive. It wants to control any resource needed to keep the body healthy now because it measures time in minutes or days, not in generations. The pro-drilling message forces home the idea that without Alaskan oil people will not be able to heat their houses, or drive their cars – they will be stranded, isolated, and threatened with the loss of the basics of life. This message should appeal to Americans in the lower "48" states, but not to people who live near the drilling. Though some Alaskans may welcome the chance to earn more money from drilling, others may fear being poisoned by oil spilling onto coastal fishing beds or polluting land nearby.

At the conscious force level, the soul looks for consistent messages. It craves a set of neat rules to live by. Time begins to stretch out to a year or perhaps a generation. The pro-drilling side has packaged its case as an economic argument. Alaskan oil will lower gas prices and eliminate gas station lines. The conservationists have used an aesthetic argument. Oil drilling will despoil one of America's last nature preserves. Both sides use competing mythical images to win supporters, the American flag and a herd of Caribou. Both convey a holistic view of life that Americans cherish. The flag symbolizes power and independence; the Caribou symbolizes nature. Because both images are timeless, the argument has shifted subtly from real time to mythical time. It is a conflict between two eternal American symbols. A person senses he ought to pass along what he has inherited from nature like the Alaskan wilderness, but here too he wants to help those suffering because the price of oil is so high.

At the creative force level, the third and highest grade is where the focal point comes into play. Humanity's insignificance in the face of the overwhelming power of the cosmos checks him from wanting to exploit the planet for human purposes alone. Deciding to drill for oil in Alaska is not simply an economic decision, or even a political decision; it is a religious decision. Are we tampering with a cosmic plan? By drilling, we may be speeding up technological change needed to rescue the planet from eventual destruction, or we may be squandering resources that humanity will value far more at some future time.

The table below summarizes the viewpoints applied to the oil example.

The religious humanist's framework
Applied to drilling for oil in Alaska

Source	Perspective	Challenge
Humanist		
Rationalist	Economic problem	Set the correct price that reflects the social cost of extracting oil
Romantic	Storyline problem	Define America's message that Americans rally behind
Religious		
Deist	Objective cosmic truth problem	Tradeoff preserving the balance of nature, protecting Western culture, and assuring cheap energy to sustain modern civilization
Mystic	Subjective cosmic relationship problem	Use of oil as a steppingstone toward limitless clean energy

The table defines different perspectives often mixed together in political debates. Each one has its own inner tensions. Rationalists may disagree on the right price to set for a variety of reasons. They may disagree on the actual costs of drilling for oil. They may disagree on the scope of the project. Some may limit the analysis to the project itself. Others may look at it in a larger context. Those that take the broader approach may want to develop an energy policy that weighs the relative merits of other energy sources besides Alaskan oil. Romantics will disagree over the proper message America wants to project to the world. Deists may disagree on what truth is more appropriate to stress to evaluate oil drilling. Should it be preserving nature's balance, protecting Western cultural values, or assuring cheap energy to sustain American civilization? Mystics may differ on the moral implications of having such a valuable resource. Is this the right time to use it to redeem the world from fanatics?

Who will support one side or the other? Libertarians and conservatives would support drilling and the liberals would be against it. No surprise in these guesses. The bigger challenge is to sketch a narrative that would produce a satisfying political compromise. We can use the table as a starting point. If drilling is profitable, part of the profits should be banked to restore the environment to pristine condition and invested in alternative probably renewable energy sources, given as seed money through the National Science Foundation to researchers. The combined policy could show Uncle Sam building the pipeline carefully as a farmer who wants to preserve his land and eventually wanting to reclaim it. The meta-message would be that America is drilling reluctantly to keep the spiritual light on that lights the world.

17

Case Study: Sustainable Growth

Abstract America's three basic ideologies face the challenge of reframing their narratives and imagery to address Digital Revolution disruptions. In the previous chapter, I showed how using the perspectives associated with religious humanism can help construct policy narratives. In this chapter, I focus on policy strategies and actions. Using Bell's framework, any policy change affects techno-economic, cultural, and political arrangements. Here I combine Bell's framework with the "soulful model" to help frame the tradeoffs needed to implement a new policy. The case study I chose is a continuation of the debate on how to transition America from generating electricity using fossil fuels to clean renewables such as wind and solar. The first template is for domestic policy with the understanding that international spillovers occur. Later on in the chapter, I introduce a template that could apply to international relations with theocracies that control large oil reserves.

17.1 Introduction

America's three basic ideologies face the challenge of reframing their narratives and imagery to address Digital Revolution disruptions. In the previous chapter, I showed how using the perspectives associated with Religious Humanism can help construct policy narratives. In this chapter, I focus on policy strategies and actions. Using Bell's framework, any policy change affects techno-economic, cultural, and political arrangements. Here I combine Bell's framework with the "soulful model" to help frame the tradeoffs needed to implement a new policy. The case study I chose is a continuation of the debate on how to transition America from generating electricity using fossil fuels to clean renewables such as wind and solar. The first template is for domestic policy with the understanding that international spillovers occur. Later on in the chapter, I will introduce one that could apply to international relations with theocracies that control large oil reserves.

The table below uses the three soulful lenses to analyze the effects of a policy change on society from Bell's three perspectives: techno-economic, cultural, and polity. The best policies are in harmony with all three soulful levels and are consistent across Bell's three views of society. Not an easy task but one that gives ideologues many opportunities to place their imprint on government actions.

Domestic policy template			
	Techno-economic	Cultural	Polity
Creative force	Invention/innovation	Institutions reimagined	Oversight and support reimagined
Conscious force	Market changes and re-engineering of networks	Institutional changes required	Support and control policies
Vital force	Transactions updates	Behavioral updates	Compliance practices updates

Given this template, I could list hundreds of policy challenges facing America that this template could help solve. In many cases, a policymaker could face six policy goals:

1. Sustainable growth – stimulating innovation that is environmentally sensitive
2. Instability – lack of reliability and resilience once failure occurs
3. Distribution – transitioning Americans from one occupation to another
4. Privacy – protecting against digital overexposure
5. Security – the tradeoffs among import/export restrictions and military preparedness
6. Binding the nation – the challenges of diversity, immigration, and international relations

17.2 The Domestic Policy Case Study: Updating the National Power Grid

The current grid is composed of power generation, power transmission between generators and electric utilities, and power distribution from electric utilities to their customers. The grid is transitioning from power generation using fossil fuels and nuclear to renewables such as wind and solar. Wind and solar are less reliable than traditional fuel sources because wind is intermittent and the sun doesn't shine at night or shine through cloud coverings. As a result, the national grid must become smart to recognize supply instability and react to it quickly.

Demand patterns are also changing dramatically. Rooftop solar has become commonplace in many parts of the country. These customers may want to sell power back to the utility. Electric vehicles are becoming more popular. Owners charge them at home, typically at night. It has caused a blip in power consumption in evening hours. The grid will need to accommodate charging stations for these electric vehicles. Potentially, electric vehicles can supply power back to the grid, which means that the grid will tap into energy sources that are not in a fixed location.

Large companies and consortiums are developing their own microgrids, often as backup power for security purposes. These microgrids connect to the traditional power grid and use it either in emergencies or when the traditional grid is offering power at a lower cost. Any entity that both buys and sells power to the national grid is called prosumers. Once there is a two-way exchange of power, the national grid is vulnerable from hackers pretending to be customers.

The table below sketches these changes.

Sustainable growth objectives applied to the national grid			
	Techno-economic	Cultural	Polity
Creative force	Clean energy generation	Adoption of smart grid technology	Coordinated network policy updates
Conscious force	Macroeconomic effects	Energy industry transition – coal and gas market assets and labor reduced	Tax and subsidy policies. Equity and efficiency concerns. Oversight regulations. Privacy regulations associated with electric utilities and microgrids monitoring energy use. Security guidelines to limit malware
	Renewables with possible subsidies		
	Carbon "tax" market design	Changes in consumer product needs and use patterns	
	New market designs, for wholesale/retail energy, and network cost recovery. New market for charging/ recharging off premises	Effects on the distribution of income among grid users. Includes treatment of legacy motor vehicles	
	Network redesign		

(continued)

Sustainable growth objectives applied to the national grid			
	Techno-economic	Cultural	Polity
Vital force	Transaction updates: learning to operate in revised and new markets	Privacy and behavioral changes caused by switchover to smart electric examples: monitoring of appliances and recharging electric vehicles on the road	Compliance practices updates

17.2.1 Sustainable Growth

Innovations have spurred economic growth for the past 150 years. The list is large: autos, planes, appliances, computers, mobile devices, etc., fill in the rest. They have improved human well-being enormously in a wide range of dimensions from lengthening life spans to creature comforts. In recent decades, Americans have become increasingly concerned that humanity is treating the earth like a mine with unlimited resources. The thinking now is that abuse of the earth may threaten future generations. One response discussed here is to shift power generation from fossil fuels to wind and solar. This changeover will lower pollution and perhaps mitigate global warming.

Now to policy. I want to compare the economist's view of how to solve the problem to the expanded framework I articulated. An economist would treat pollution as an externality, whether it is greenhouse (GHG) gas emissions (carbon, dioxide, methane, and other gases such as sulfur hexafluoride) or particulates. An externality is a cost to society that is not captured by the market system. Air, for example, is a free good from a business' perspective but valuable from a social perspective. The economist's solution is to tax polluters.

A market-oriented economist, probably most comfortable in the libertarian camp, would recommend the government set up a carbon-trading market, where other greenhouse gases are turned into carbon equivalents. The government would set a target for carbon emissions and emission quotas or credits for particular industries. Then companies would trade credits. Polluters that produce valuable products can buy credits from low-value, low pollution enterprises. This allows the most efficient market outcome consistent with public policy.

A regulatory-oriented economist, probably most comfortable the liberal camp, might opt for controlling pollution at its source. Government could require factories to install pollution abatement devices. Conservatives might go along with this approach because a carbon tax translates into a factory dumping pollution on your front lawn for a fee.

The expanded framework has a much more expansive outlook that may help ideologues find common ground. Start with the creative force level. This is the least complicated level for developing policy. I believe all three ideologies are most likely to support a common vision of a future based on clean, renewable energy generation, a smart grid that can convert intermittent energy sources like wind and solar into reliable power sources and link the power grid with other essential grids – water and communication to name two. If you recall, the creative force has three connected soulful components: the will to change, the inspirational solution, and the basic blueprint for action. Begin with the will to change. It identifies something lacking in fulfilling the nation's mission, in this case, a grid that meets all six criteria. Each of America's ideologies would likely produce similar messaging. At the creative force level, the messaging will depend on the time horizon. The focus may be on wind and solar in the near-term transitioning in fusion power decades later. The point is that at this level, planning should be over many generations and consider many technologies and accommodate new power sources on the horizon. The planning blueprint should be flexible enough to adjust to unforeseen innovations.

Moving to the next soulful level – conscious force – complications begin to pile up. The liberals and libertarians will probably fight over a carbon tax or pollution regulation. All three ideologues would likely agree that the design and functioning of the grid would have to change. Wind and solar farms will be at different locations than coal generating plants, for example. Markets for new intermittent energy sources will require updates to power-generating markets because an unreliable unit of power should command a lower price than a reliable one.

At the vital force level, people who work in the industry will require new skills to assure that the grid operates reliably and is resilient to sudden unforeseen events that could cause blackouts. The message is that sustainable growth has costs, which I will continue to discuss when I take up the other policy challenges.

17.2.2 Instability

Renewable generation is intermittent as opposed to fossil fuel and nuclear generation, which are controllable during normal operations. Supply uncertainty presents a new challenge. So too does having solar energy produced by traditional customers of electric utilities. The expectation is that the grid will need to be reconfigured to accommodate thousands of small customer power sources. Instead of electric utilities supplying electricity to customers, customers may supply energy back to the grid and want to be paid from solar and electric vehicle discharges back to the grid. Unlike traditional power sources and power users, electric vehicles are not at a stationary location. Traditional customers are also working together so that they are a large enough entity to purchase and sell power in the wholesale market.

Engineers and economists have somewhat different approaches for assuring efficient, reliable, and resilient generation. The engineers want to redesign the networks to accommodate renewable generation. This will involve longer transmission lines between generation sources and electric utilities so that when solar is not available in one geographic area, it can be transmitted from another where the sun is shining. Same for wind. They want to install smart communications networks to ensure the grid is reliable and resilient. Based on their advice, electric utilities are installing smart meters at customer premises to measure electric usage and sensor devices in the grid to monitor performance and identify equipment and lines that are overheating or dysfunctional and alarms to signal that action is needed to prevent a brownout or blackout. This type of smart network can improve grid reliability, isolate, and restore power when lost, and lower the cost of providing electricity by time shifting demand when the system is under stress.

Economists have their own solutions to the problem of making the grid efficient, reliable, and resilient. They all center on efficient pricing through the introduction of market modifications. Today, there are wholesale markets for power generation run by independent system operators (ISOs) and regional transmission organizations (RTOs). Both types have a day-ahead market for committing generators for the next day and real-time markets that commit additional generators as needed. Prices are set based on the price offers by generator companies and demand for power from the electric utilities to serve their customers. The real-time market typically clears every 5 min. The delivered prices depend on transmission costs and congestion on particular transmission lines. With intermittent generation, the market mechanism will need to change to accommodate supply uncertainty. In effect, prices will rise to reflect extra power reserves needed as backup when particular wind and solar generators cannot deliver power. Economists are also developing plans to allow end users to aggregate their demand for energy and receive payment when the electric utility needs to cut demand.

In the distribution part of the network where customers will now buy and sell energy, economists want to introduce new localized trading markets and have customers pay for the option of using the electric utility's grid besides simply paying for power.

In comparison to the engineer's or economist's perspective, The Template I offer (first table) aims at more holistic solutions to overcome instability at a reasonable cost by looking across a broad swath of industries affected by a clean energy policy. For instance, policy solutions would include coordinated efforts to introduce new energy-efficient building materials and designs and retrofitting customer premises to improve energy efficiency.

Beyond that, the template's cultural and polity categories examine power and control transfers and their effects on social stability. For instance, electric utility companies would be losing power and control over networks. Fossil fuel and nuclear-generating companies would also lose power and control over their destinies. Policymakers need to develop incentives for electric utility, ISOs, and RTOs to accommodate market adjustments where they may lose profits, power, and control. Many of the adjustments within the electric utility companies will be cultural. It is difficult to transition from a monopoly mindset to a competitive one. This is an important issue that needs to be addressed.

17.2.3 Distribution

The coal industry is dying; gas companies are on notice that they are not part of America's plan for power generation; in the near term, nuclear will be in decline. Many people in these industries will lose their jobs. Whole regions of the country will suffer as a result of the transition from traditional fuel sources to renewables. Market economists would say that the strength of the market system is creative destruction. Firms and markets die, replaced by new ones that supersede them in some way. The American public was moving toward renewables even without government prodding. It would make economic sense to levy tariffs on imported goods from nations with lower pollution standards to offset their economic advantage in America's marketplace. Beyond that, unemployment insurance should help people transition between occupations. Another strategy for older workers is to retire or claim disability to receive government support.

At the conscious force level of the soulful model, empathetic and ethical considerations come into play. These include mercy and trust. When the government declares a profitable industry is no longer viable because of new-found rules on pollution, the government should compensate those hurt for their loss of income and for relocation and retraining costs. These types of costs should enter the calculus of shifting to renewables as a national goal.

When government subsidizes rooftop solar and electric vehicles, it benefits upper-income households because they have the funds to take advantage of these offers. Here again, for equity sake, for sake of preserving trust in government, poorer-income households should not subsidize the rich. A new tax of beneficiaries of subsidies is being considered in California. This is in line with the soulful approach.

17.2.4 Privacy

Privacy protection is a high-profile policy objective. Digital networks are a conduit for privacy invasions. Huge databases of personal information and the constant flow of data packets allow someone to capture your likeness and insert it into a digital hologram that is often distorted and almost devoid of the inner self. Anyone with a digital device has the capability of destroying a reputation, of making someone ashamed without really knowing if the image has any bearing on reality.

The electric utility companies will be collecting much more personalized data in the future. They are already installing smart meters on customer premises. These allow the electric utility to monitor usage in 15-min intervals. Simple statistical inferences will reveal when a customer is home or when the customer is using certain types of appliances. When smart appliances are connected to the grid, electric utilities will gather even more information. Future meters may directly identify appliance energy use.

The template suggests that the government needs to develop a strategy for protecting personal privacy that considers both economic and psychic costs. Economics would focus on the threat of identity theft or the increased likelihood of burglary. The template also identifies dangers to the sense of self when people are watching you.

The Daniel Bell approach comes into play. Privacy should be addressed from techno-economic, cultural, and political perspectives. Each one supplies different answers with different time frames. The economists and policymakers are following the techno-economic path to solve the problem. The cultural approach would consider a tradeoff between profits trust and honor. It may turn out that from a cultural perspective, profits may be sacrificed, or higher prices are necessary to assure privacy protection. Government rules will probably be necessary in this case.

17.2.5 Security

The move to open the grid to power injections by customers is a major security concern. Hackers can inject malware to compromise the network. Encryption typically protects private conversations. Here filters and firewall gateways will be necessary to protect customers from each other and the grid itself. As mentioned before, the government has banned Huawei communication equipment from being installed in America's communication networks.

The expanded framework again would arguably take a more holistic view of this strategy. The ban on equipment is a step in preventing an autocratic regime from spying on Americans. Perhaps the loss of the US market would weaken autocratic regimes like China financially and technologically. The larger framework would also raise the issue of the cost-effectiveness of import and export bans on goods from threatening nations versus strengthening the military. In both cases, there is a cost to private wealth production. The payoffs go beyond physical security. They extend to emotional security and spiritual protection against hostile forces.

17.3 Binding the Nation

Sustainable growth is a worthy new frontier in American policy. It has the potential to spark the nation's imagination with biblical imagery of restoring the environment and redeeming humanity's past sins of despoiling the gifts we inherited through no effort of our own. Political sincerity is an important consideration. Instead of saying sustainable growth is good for the economy or to protect the environment as if there are no sacrifices involved leads to cynicism. It sounds like a power grab wrapped in fine words. The truth is that sustainable growth will require sacrifices; there are uncertainties on the proper course of action; there will likely be mistakes. Policymakers must have a plan to handle the disruptions caused by this large change in government policy. The plan needs to be flexible so it can be adjusted. It should rely on private incentives instead of heavy-handed regulations. Since it is a government initiative, the government should pay for the transition – much like government shutting down the economy during the COVID-19 crisis. The cost should be transparent.

The great paradox of the creative process is that it is based on constructive conflicts among seemingly opposite forces that actually work together to form a unity. This imagery applies well to ideological struggles. "Freedom from" requires others not to interfere with what one is doing. This elbow room is most likely in a system that is creative, where people expect the future to be better than the past. In other words, people honor "freedom from" because of the hopes associated with "freedom to." Honoring traditions and having faith, two cornerstones of conservative ideology, are necessary for developing a creative environment. Material creations are reflections of spiritual imaginings, again a religious and secular connection. Growth is a means for realizing one's potential, and yet that potential requires the support of others. In a deep sense, proper support of others is the basis for creative growth.

Many paths lead to enlightenment. This hints at crucial idea: the necessity of faith in the future. Old, set orders are cast into disorder by technological change. In periods of disruption or stagnation, people have to stay the course, uphold basic American values, and believe in righteousness, in the creative spirit, because these are the ingredients of salvation.

Together, the economist's signals, the engineer's network designs, the computer scientists' algorithms, the psychologists' behavioral models, and the creative drives described by religious mystics open many new pathways for ideological collaboration on institutional reform. Economists urge policymakers to examine signals within and between organizations to see if they are working effectively. They also keep proposing new signals when old ones fail. Engineers urge policymakers to examine network designs to see if they have adequate capacity, good backup systems, and effective transmission paths. Computer scientists search for protocols and controllers to optimize the use of system information. Psychologists want modelers in all fields to use a more realistic model of decision-making. Mystics urge policymakers to encourage salvational longing. They, more than others perhaps, can imagine networks producing a new type of music.

George Gilder, an American economist, suggests America is truly a salvational society, shortchanged by an overly materialistic philosophy.[1] A touch of mysticism could raise the gaze of policymakers above what sometimes looks like modern economic graffiti. Analyzing financials is important, doing cost benefit analyses is important, accommodating vested interests is practical, but most importantly society needs to raise seekers of new lands and ideas, who build new industries, and invigorate humanity. These are soulful quests that require religious fervor.

---

[1] See, for example, George Gilder (1981). *Wealth and Poverty*. Basic Books.

17.4 International Relations with Theocracies that Control Large Oil Reserves

Here I develop a second template for examining international relations between the United States and a theocracy along the lines of Iran ruled by clerics.

International policy template – US and theocratic state			
	Techno-economic	Cultural	Polity
Creative force	US invention/innovation Aimed at standard of living Theocracy: just rewards from living righteously	US – secular focused, self-actualization Theocracy: religious focus; doing God's will	US – representative democracy Theocracy: rule by clerics
Conscious force	US markets, competition, competitive prices. Theocracy: just prices; just distribution of wealth	US core values focused on the individual Theocracy: core values based on religious aims of society	US free elections, rule of law Theocracy: restricted elections; God's law interpreted by clerics
Vital force	US primarily, each according to the value of product Theocracy: primarily, each according to his needs	US wealth is an indicator of success Theocracy: religious wisdom is an indicator of success	US compliance with secular laws Theocracy: compliance with religious law

This template shows immediately that the clash is not simply over control of oil; it is over a way of life and vision of the future. The United States' challenge is to find a common medium to exchange ideas that both sides can accept. This should be possible because Western culture and Islamic culture have a common vision: a longing for paradise. The challenge is not to demean the vision or pathway selected by a particular culture. Those visions are non-negotiable. Any outside group that threatens the vision becomes an enemy. In some cases, the weaker side will die for their faith and like Samsom be willing to bring down the others even if it means committing suicide.

18

A Macro-view Using Systems Analysis

Abstract In the last two chapters, I used the energy industry as a case study for using the templates I developed for creating narratives and analyzing a particular policy issue. In this chapter, I want to expand the scope to broad policy issues created by the digital revolution. Here I define "systems" as the mode of technology that underlies the economy. In almost Marxian fashion, I assume technology is the driving force changing economic, cultural, and political connections. The challenge is to identify the weak connections and barriers that make systems underperform. I offer policy recommendations based on using a systems approach to identify problems caused by the digital revolution and suggested solutions to these problems that ideologues can accept. I base some of the recommendations on examining the way platforms operate.

18.1 Introduction

In the last two chapters, I used the energy industry as a case study for using the templates I developed for creating narratives and analyzing a particular policy issue. In this chapter, I want to expand the scope to broad policy issues created by the digital revolution. Here I define "systems" as the mode of technology that underlies the economy. In almost Marxian fashion, I assume technology is the driving force changing economic, cultural, and political connections. The challenge is to identify the weak connections and barriers that make systems underperform. I offer policy recommendations based on using a systems approach to identify problems caused by the digital revolution and suggested solutions to these problems that ideologues can accept. I base some of the recommendations on examining the way platforms operate.

Although a system's approach is not new, systems in the digital revolution differ from previous ones by producing enormous amounts of data in real time that can assess the efficiency, reliability, and resilience of a system from moment to moment. In the Digital Age, networks are interconnecting and converging, making cross-system analyses possible. For instance, electricity networks and broadband networks now work together to identify and isolate breakdowns in the electricity grid.

The social disruption caused by the digital revolution is visceral to me. In the 1950s and 1960s, I had a small circle of friends and relatives and knew my father's business associates. When I bought something, I paid in cash. No one traced those dollars back to me. Now, I pay by credit card. I purchase products online. I suspect some online entity has produced a digital mosaic of me. My circle of acquaintances has expanded enormously online, but those contacts are often superficial. With so much data mining, I cannot trust online transactions. Government was also distant when I was young. For good or bad, now government has a say in almost everything I do. It monitors products for safety and offers a wide range of social services, from healthcare to job applications. The list is too long to enumerate.

To strengthen my case that the digital revolution has disrupted society, I take a more academic view. I offer a summary of three technical revolutions that have changed American society: pre-industrial, industrial, and digital. Of course, their dates and influences on society are subject to debate, but I think they convey the message that societal relations are very different than they were only a few decades ago. My other premise is that America's ideologies have not caught up with these disruptions. To make my case, I limit this section to the digital revolution because it is enough to highlight how the definitions of core American values need to change. The case would become even stronger if I had included the effects of genetic engineering.

System dynamics caused by techno-economic revolutions[a]

	Techno-economic	Cultural	Polity
Pre-industrial	Individual production. Physical products, customized services, local market. Time based on cycles of nature. Horsepower over dirt roads is the main transportation mode	Society: decentralized, largely rural. Ethnic clustering of groups from Western Europe. The "Protectant Ethic" is the norm for all groups. Work hard to succeed in this world and the world to come	Local
Industrial	Factory, physical products, regional/ national markets, ready to use uniform products. Time based on production process and shipment schedules Physical networks link markets – rail, roads, ships, and planes Communication – telegraph, then telephone	Business: organization – central/hierarchical control; separation of ownership and management Society: Move to urban areas Weakened community and religious loyalty Appliances such as the washing machine and indoor plumbing reduce drudgery and improve sanitation. Autos and telephones begin to overcome geographic limits Conspicuous consumption WASP Brahmin and country gentleman are standards of excellence	Federal control Industrial regulation and antitrust of particular industries Social services and social insurance Permanent large military using specialized weapons Government funds basic research. Produces Internet technology Federal prevention of crime and international spy services

(continued)

System dynamics caused by techno-economic revolutions[a]			
	Techno-economic	Cultural	Polity
Digital	Online platform, international markets, products software designed: virtual products, virtual reality, information. The Internet is the equivalent of the road network of the online economy Time periods in business in nanoseconds, in virtual reality, they are psychic	Business organization – centralized control; open use by application designers Society: breakdown of family Multicultural standard demanded Ideologies begin to displace traditional religions Return to home production via broadband connections that allow online work and videoconferencing Airbnb brings back borders for some Consumers become prosumers – receive and offer value online Photoshopped persona (digital mosaics) Virtually reality becomes the new dimension for creativity	Internationally dispersed control Regulation/ antitrust – broadband networks, core platform services, operating systems Supply chain becomes global Federal agencies aim to prevent crime and terrorism. Use spyware instead of field agents and weapons Video game-like weaponry

[a]This table is developed from several sources: (1) Thorstein Veblen (1904). *The Theory of Business Enterprise*. Charles Scribner and Sons. (2) Thorstein Veblen (1899). *The Theory of the Leisure Class: An Economic Study of the Evolution of Institutions*. Macmillan, and (3) Robert J. Gordon (2016). *The Rise and Fall of American Growth*. Princeton University Press

The pre-industrial stage was largely in effect when the United States formed into a nation. The image of a good society was decentralized. People produced and traded in local markets. Ethnic groups, mostly from Western Europe, clustered in specific areas. Religion was a powerful influence on behavior. People believed that working hard and being frugal were a proper way of life. The center of power was local government where people from the community decided on the types of public services they wanted. This was the template that formed the societal relations for Adam Smith in England and the Founding Fathers who backed Jefferson.

The next stage – the industrial revolution – led to the factory system and huge corporations. Property relations changed. People supposedly owned shares in a corporation but could not use corporate property for their own use. Managers, not owners, ran the corporations. Markets expanded; national transportation, electricity, and communications networks evolved. The telegraph, then the telephone, offered universal communication.

Society changed as people moved to cities to work in manufacturing. Ethnic mixing became more common. Communal connections weakened. Eventually personal income and wealth rose. Household appliances freed women from drudgery. Electricity and central heating reduced indoor pollution caused by fireplaces. Cars and telephones freed people from narrow geographical limits. Conspicuous consumption showed who was a success and who was not. The gold standard of success was the White Anglo-Saxon Protestant Brahmin of the likes of J. P. Morgan, Henry Ford, and John D. Rockefeller who ran mega-corporations.

Despite idolizing the wealthy protestant, the public began to fear big corporations and economic depressions. In response the federal government grew to meet national needs. The federal government attempted to harness big business by introducing industry regulation and antitrust. It began offering social insurance and services to protect the poor. It began shaping markets through taxation and subsidies.

Federal policing and military operations grew. Military equipment became specialized, leading to the fear of a military-industrial complex. In general, government operations and oversight became very complex because of coordination needs among federal, state, and local governments and special governmental agencies that may control local water systems.

The latest stage – the digital revolution – produced the online economy. Large platforms emerged that produced digital products and acted as brokers and dealers in physical goods. Software and information became competitive tools. Markets expanded internationally by using the broadband network to communicate and share information. Platforms operate almost like nation states. Their managers established their own government and rules for the platform. Unlike a typical government, a platform produces goods but also allows others to produce apps or trade on its platform.

America's culture was undergoing dramatic changes before the digital revolution took off. The social disruptions that began in the 1960s grew rapidly because of the massive increase in communication channels brought on by the digitalization of America's communications networks. Many groups developed their own channels to develop their own perspectives on American culture. Very quickly, multiculturalism began to replace the WASP cultural standard.

The development of online communities led to new voices in society. As a result, the definition of family and gender has undergone significant changes. Ideologies began to shape the major media outlets. They began to displace traditional religions as the source of cultural values. Interestingly, COVID-19 combined with the digital revolution marked the return to in-home work.

Instead of radiating success through conspicuous consumption of goods, people now Photoshop their persona to perfection. They are shifting from being consumers of goods and information to prosumers who sell online and share their beliefs. Their entertainment is increasingly online. Virtual reality is growing in importance. For many, online gaming has become an addiction.

Software continues to leverage human capabilities but sometimes lowers personal skills. For instance, Excel leverages math capability while eroding people's ability to count change. ChatGPT leverages writing and analytical capabilities while reducing the need to learn how to write or calculate. Note that many of these enhancements to a person's abilities to create virtual constructs do not appear in gross domestic product figures, which makes official statistics of well-being less reliable than before.

Networks are now at the center of the emerging information economy. Policymakers are attempting to master the basics of these new networks. Whether physical or biological, they have three common traits: (1) they have physical infrastructure for transmitting a product; (2) they have methods for encapsulating information that monitor a network's status; and (3) they have communication protocols to guide information through a network. All three traits are difficult to understand let alone control.

Using data mining and software algorithms, the government is attempting to find potential terrorists before they act. This has led to a marked increase in government surveillance of people within and outside the United States. Military equipment continues to become more like video-game equipment.

In the digital world, policymakers need to coordinate national policies with other nations because many digital markets, such as gaming and trading, are global. For instance, the European Union is defining rules to manage the activities of American platforms operating in Europe.[1] As I discuss public policy, it would be useful to refer to the following policy grid that encapsulates the challenges facing libertarians, conservatives, and liberals.

This table shows the basic approach of each major American ideology to analyzing public policy. My contention is that they are all valuable but too restrictive.

---

[1] See, for example, Friso Bostoen, *Understanding the Digital Markets Act*, Antitrust Bulletin, forthcoming June 2023.

Ideological policy perspective matrix			
Ideology	Techno-economic	Cultural	Polity
Libertarian: Transactional view			
Conservative:			
Communal view			
Liberal:			
Institutional view			

Recall that libertarians will look for private, transactional solutions to network issues. Conservatives may look to local control, where possible. Liberals will recommend changes in national policy. Each ideology should consider technology, economic arrangements, cultural values, and government institutional capabilities before offering a solution.

Many online challenges pose challenges that do not fit neatly into any policy strategy. For instance, the online economy has features of a public road network, which all three ideologies agree is in the public domain. But the big players in the online economy, the Internet service providers such as AT&T, and large platforms such as Google have characteristics of both public and private enterprises. They offer common transport and specialized services. They are planting intelligent devices in homes, businesses, and public places.

I have already suggested that religious humanism helps widen an ideologue's perspective. Here I want to use the characteristics of digital systems to justify widening ideological perspectives. As they widen, I expect that areas for ideological cooperation will increase.

I am going to explore, from a systems perspective, a few strategies for improving economic stability and societal trust. Arguably, the disaffection with American society has its roots in digital system failures. I reexam system breakdowns that contributed to financial panics, economic downturns, and lack of transparency about what big government and big enterprises are doing. My intention is also to spark the imagination of ideologues, to incent them to find answers wherever they can. This search could lead to ideological collaboration.

18.2 A Systems Approach to Public Policy

Economists evaluate a particular network's performance using four basic measures: efficiency, reliability, resilience, and innovation. A network is efficient if it produces output at least cost. Typically, efficient networks have backup capacity to assure that they can handle unexpected surges in demand. Sometimes a network crashes. When it does, a resilient network recovers quickly.

It is also useful to examine a particular network in its relationship with the rest of the economy. It is part of a system that produces a variety of products. Each entity in the system can affect the others. For instance, one way to reduce greenhouse gases is to use wind and solar for power generation. Another way is to better insulate buildings and use smart switches to turn on and off for water heaters and lighting. The new "smart" systems can talk to each other. Analysts can examine how the electric grid and building codes can work together effectively to reduce greenhouse gases.

"Smart" does not mean "stable." The distinguishing features of the new systems are speed and built-in intelligence. Sometimes, algorithms used by participants in the market are similar. This can lead to flocking or herding effects where everyone wants to act the same way, sometimes causing stampedes. Asymmetric intelligence can lead to anti-competitive behavior if one part of the network is large in relation to the others.

Another critical issue is to recognize that the systems in the Digital Age morph rapidly and the technical characteristics are complex. As a result, it is difficult to absorb the effect on the system of change in technology or behavior of a network or user of a network will have on the entire ecosystem.

18.2.1 Addressing Economic Instability

In the age of instant communication, we have seen that the financial industry is vulnerable to massive, almost instantaneous, withdrawals from financial institutions that can crash the financial system. The shift to wind and solar as the basic power sources for the national electric grid means that that grid is vulnerable to crashes if there is not enough sunlight or wind to power generators.

Research on online flocking patterns could be crucial for identifying and understanding causes of stampedes that could disrupt society. Many categories of models exist. Synchronization models explain flocking by showing how out of phase behavior can align after a particular event occurs. Information cascade models suggest that if enough people are behaving in a certain way, people follow their path even if privately they disagree with group behavior, until a break in the pattern occurs when an influential player departs from the flock, then others follow. There are many directions this research could take. Diffusion models explain adoption behavior as a combination of the intrinsic features of a product and adoption behavior of others. Tipping models predict that group behavior may turn if certain threshold conditions occur. Contagion models explain rapid shifts in behavior by examining local populations and how behavior flips in them and jumps to nearby groups. Infection models look to uncover susceptible types, infected types, and recovering types all in an effort to understand how one type of behavior can spread and then reverse itself.[2]

Any one of these model types could help identify potential financial panics and point the way toward preventing them. Unfortunately, not much is known about the psychology behind viral actions or about behavior during transitions, or chaotic periods. It is also difficult to gauge how international spillovers create panics. For instance, since bankruptcy laws freeze financial assets, investors want to get their assets out of threatened institutions immediately.

Another promising line of systems analysis is to recognize that uncertain outcomes are a fact of life and need to be addressed in system planning and operations. For instance, a solution to the uncertainty created by wind and solar power is to have an energy reserve strategy to assure reliable energy.

System incentive designs should be evaluated. For instance, the belief that options and insurance contracts can eliminate system-wide risk does not make sense. A system like the banking industry has an underlying variability that must be addressed. Simulation test beds can help analysts see what happens when different types of shocks affect the system. From there, policymakers can help define rules that make the system more resilient to unexpected shocks.

One likely outcome of a systems approach is that it will point toward standard network engineering strategies for producing a robust open network. Typically, engineers examine capacity needs to size a particular network; standard system-wide buffering techniques to limit bottlenecks; firewalls to protect users; pinging techniques, something like sonar, to identify system flaws; backup system to avoid failures; and disaster recovery techniques when systems do fail.

Buffering, in particular, is often used to prevent system failure caused by traffic contention for a limited transmission path – something like a traffic jam. Translated to financial industry language, for example, buffering could take the form of maintaining adequate reserves and placing limits on transactions that appear to indicate panic or other types of mania. Automatic controls are another technique to adjust the system when performance veers beyond a normal range, something like using a thermostat to keep home temperature within bounds.

---

[2] See, for example, Chiang, M. (2012) Networked Life: 20 Questions, *Chapter 8*, pp. 158–193. Cambridge University Press, NY.

Automatic intervention in fast-changing markets has the advantage of rapid response that sidesteps having to resort to lengthy political debate, something like unemployment insurance or tax reductions that automatically kick in when the economy dips toward recession.

Systems theory also stresses the importance of flexible but standardized rules of operations that must be consistent across geographic borders if a system is to operate efficiently and remain stable. Translated again to the financial system, systems theory would favor global organized coordinated regulations and procedures to improve the reliability of financial systems. None of the tools identified are really new to economic policy, but framing them in systems theory could change the perspective on economic policy.

From an economist's perspective, a systems approach will lead toward market designs that require truthful price/offers in markets. Good system market policies can moderate the likelihood of stampedes by placing limits on trading behavior. For instance, a market system that produces spot (immediate) prices, prices under long-term contracts, and market prices for future delivery at strike prices could reduce network costs and improve network reliability. In addition, all three types of pricing arrangements could secure enough energy capacity for the national grid to make it reliable. High spot, forward, and long-term contractual prices increase the profitability of investment in capacity. High reserve capacity is especially important when the national grid relies on wind and solar as the primary sources of energy.[3]

18.2.2 Addressing Anticompetitive Strategies

A systems approach geared to work in cyberspace could also help uncover hard to measure effects such as vested interests that block creativity and perhaps cause growing inequality of wealth in the United States. From a technical perspective, a large Internet service provider (ISPs) or online platform can use filters and gateways to hamstring competitors.

Niall Ferguson in *The Great Degeneration*[4] points to a matrix of culture of institutions that determine the effectiveness and fairness of a nation, again suggesting a systems approach would be useful to locate areas for reform in both the public and private sectors. The failure of the AT&T/Time Warner merger underscores the importance of cultural clashes in cyberspace. AT&T, a major Internet service provider, whose business was building networks,

---

[3] See, for example, Chao, H. and Wilson, R. Priority Service: Pricing, Investment, and Market Organization. American Economic Review (1987) 77: 899–916.

[4] Ferguson, N. (2013). *The Great Degeneration*. Allen Lane, UK.

bought Time Warner, a media giant. The merger created huge losses for AT&T and arguably lowered both companies' economic efficiency and innovativeness during this bad marriage.

One possibility for overseeing the online economy is to have an independent agency to gather information on political parties and interest group activities to identify undemocratic policies and procedures. On paper, this type of agency makes sense, but in practice it would face a host of challenges. Government salaries will not attract the type of expertise needed to monitor online activity. Subcontracting, instead, may lead to loss of government control. Of course, independence would be very difficult to achieve and maintain, and it would probably be blocked by vested interests. A new agency within government would threaten existing ones. For instance, the Federal Trade Commission and the Federal Communications Commission oversee parts of the operations of ISPs and platforms. Despite all these challenges, it may make the political process more transparent and democratic. But before voting yes for a new agency, analysts should do a systems assessment (including a cultural assessment) of how the agencies oversee the online economy individually and collectively.

This type of system analysis should consider a system's history whether it is in government or the private sector. Perceptions, expectations, and planning depend on historical patterns that have a degree of permanence to them. For instance, the telephone network was operated privately but was subject to regulation for many decades. As a result, many of its participants build their businesses assuming regulation would continue to exist. The breakup of the old Bell system in 1983 arguably benefitted society, but it had its costs. AT&T and other long-distance carriers failed. In 2015, the FCC chose to regulate the Internet – a decision reversed by President Trump's appointee, Ajit Pai. While the reversal resulted from a clash of ideologies, a basic challenge is to develop a strategy of transitions. It may be far less sexy as a goal but perhaps the most fertile source of collective innovation.

This new agency would also need a model of how the online economy is evolving as a benchmark for examining its failures. The most challenging online transitional situations are associated with the Internet which is morphing into a hybrid network of open and restricted communication channels and platforms expanding their reach into new markets. Some networks are leading the transition. Others will lag behind because of their investments in different vintages of technology with different capacity limits. Flash cut moves from one set of institutional arrangements to another set which are likely to disrupt markets and leave the public worse off unless the changeover date is well ahead, giving market participants plenty of time to plan for the changeover.

18.2.3 Policy Challenges

Before getting too ambitious about regulatory transitions, a bit of humbleness is in order. The description of the Internet suggests that experts have a precise model of how the new digital economy works. Not so. Even experts acknowledge that no one really knows how the Internet and related broadband networks will evolve. Often policymakers don't realize the tenuous connection between the actual operations of a system and its observed behavior. If someone had never learned the protocol layering of the Internet, imagine all the theories that could explain traffic patterns. The basic point is that a simple set of protocols can produce traffic pattern complexity. Unfortunately, with other, non-engineered systems, such as the ecosystem or even the political network, no such understanding of their workings exists, which can result in many theories that fit observed facts but not fit the underlying rules of behavior. Without leaping too far, this is a not so warning of putting too much weight on one or even several observations as proof that a specific event confirms a specific ideology. Events have their own idiosyncratic causes that are not easily tied to a simple causal model.

A good example of unpredictability caused by technological change is the Internet itself. Before it developed, a reasonable prediction of America's communication network would look like a bigger version of the old telephone network with bigger central switches and bigger pipes connecting them. Almost no one anticipated that a decentralized packet network would make this network obsolete in a few decades. Few would have anticipated the rapid development of fiber optics. Few would have thought that laying undersea cable would disrupt worldwide economic activities by allowing underdeveloped nations to compete with the United States for information processing supremacy. Hardly anyone believed that wireless technology would become a new medium for global communications.

Right now, a few scientists predict that quantum computing will replace digital computing. No one really knows where this new capability will lead, but at the very least, supposedly impenetrable encrypted information may be decrypted using quantum computing. Less dramatic is the push for software defined networks (SDNs) as a replacement for parts of the Internet. SDN's goal is to centralize network intelligence to improve network performance. This is at odds with the original intent of the Internet to decentralize network intelligence to make it flexible and scalable.

Nonetheless, political intervention is almost inevitable when the new technology is pervasive and disrupts traditional ways of operating. The Digital

Revolution fits this bill. While one can draw narrative tools from the operations of the internet and how it affects society, a more textured approach should merge it with traditional moral and spiritual prescriptions. Even in cyberspace, the values of propriety, prudence, benevolence, and trust are still critical, and so is a spiritual dimension that gives society a purpose.

In markets with clumps of market power, the question is whether the private sector can police itself. Will it develop best practice rules to avoid litigation? What are the impediments for private initiatives? Can the government prod private companies to develop industry standards of behavior? If so, the need for rigid regulations imposed by government is not necessary. An independent government agency could help identify best practices that could set future industry standards.

Findings may be paradoxical. Big companies are an easy target, but perhaps the main target of regulation should be small information providers because they may have a much shorter business time horizon than established platforms. Perhaps owners of operating systems have undue market power. But keep in mind that Microsoft no longer has the market dominance it once had.

18.3 Building Trust in a Networked Society

People are vulnerable to all sorts of inner doubts and outside pressures. From a public policy perspective, the issue is what types of vulnerability protection obligations should be assigned to the government. Here I limit the discussion to one key vulnerability caused by the digital revolution: 1984-style surveillance by private entities and the government itself. The challenge is to develop policies that the public believes in and supports. This requires a good deal of trust between institutions and the people.

No matter the state of technology, trust is the bedrock of a vibrant society. Without it, trade, whether in goods or ideas, begins to shrivel because of the fear of being exploited. Trust normally develops when outcomes from repeated transactions show that one can rely on the other to be honest without having to put a gun to his or her head. A society's institutions have an important role in building trust. People need to believe that both public and private institutions are stable and self-healing when problems arise.

Trustworthy institutions have a few common characteristics. America's Founders imagined that government is more trustworthy by separating it into branches so that one group in government did not manage commerce, the legal system, the police, and military. In general, government institutions tend to be trustworthy if they are open and inclusive. Pluralism tends to limit the power of any group to control the government. Democratic institutions fit this profile better than a dictatorial regime because a dictator, on a whim, can change government policy. As a result, private property becomes insecure and with it personal freedom. With the rise of giant corporations, the public feared they would dominate government by buying political influence. That fear led to trust busting and industry regulation. Now the public fears the power of large online platforms.

The rule of law – fair laws, fairly applied – is crucial for building trust in society. People need to know that lawbreakers will be punished whether they are huge corporations or government agencies. The law itself ought to evolve from a type of cultural unity in morals and behavior that lets people feel that others will treat them fairly. This is a challenge in a multicultural society where groups have different perspectives on upright behavior. This is not an insurmountable problem because the rule of law is constantly tested even within a homogenous society because jobs differ, incentives differ, wealth differs, community connections differ, and so on. The Digital Age presents new challenges because it is morphing rapidly, especially with the new breakthroughs in artificial intelligence. Yet, trust can evolve as long as people try to view conflicting claims through the eyes of an impartial judge. Not easy but doable.

18.3.1 Building Trust in the Private Sector

Many companies try to build reputations for honesty, even if the motivation is simply to boost profits. In some professions, the motivation to be trustworthy is an ethical obligation. A doctor has an obligation to patients that goes beyond offering services. Lawyers have codes of ethics. Business schools originally justified their existence by saying they would instill ethical behavior in their students. Business ethics focuses on a history of socially acceptable business practices.

The issue here is how to build trust in an online society where decision-makers are often anonymous, where they may be in another country, where they may be looking at your personal profile. One way is to avoid assuming others are trustworthy. Instead, build digital systems that are trustworthy. That is the basic rationale for blockchain technology. This technology time-stamps each trade irreversibly and has algorithms to validate a particular transaction. So far, it is used mainly for trading cryptocurrencies. In other words, this approach is not the answer.

Adding back the human touch, building trust in the online economy depends on the nature of the market. Internet service providers that own broadband networks are typically sophisticated buyers and sellers of network services. The number of providers is in the thousands. All that may be necessary for them to work together is the threat of government regulation. But when actors are more anonymous and number in the millions, building trust is much more difficult. Large platforms like Amazon devote resources to monitor platform transactions. When a platform identifies cheating, it typically punishes offenders by not allowing them to use their platforms. The immediate problem is that this type of personalized monitoring runs up against the right to privacy, which differs in the workplace and in the home.

Policymakers also need to identify market flaws that are long-lasting and costly to society that can be repaired at reasonable cost by government action, whether it is through a set of rules or tax incentives. A reasonable amount of transparency is necessary to judge behavior and performance. If prices, terms, and conditions of a contract are under nondisclosure, to what extent can this hurt the public? In the online economy, many network contracts are for bundles of services at multiple locations, often tailored to a customer's specific needs.

Related to transparency is developing proper signaling systems that convey meaningful information. Traditionally, price is the basic market signaling device about quality and cost. But prices for products and services carried on broadband pipes cannot easily be split out to particular services because network costs don't lend themselves to identifying costs associated with a specific service. After all, voice, data, and video are often transported over the same pipes, and they are not treated as services per se but as packet streams.

Wages are often a less effective market signal than the price of a product. A person's performance is hard to measure, especially in a team environment. Stock bonuses for top management may be even more problematic. Do stock bonuses improve corporate performance? The answer is by no means clear. With broadband networks, it is hard to allocate wage costs to specific services, again because the services themselves are treated as packets of information. Should more labor costs be allocated to video instead of voice simply because video requires more packets to produce an image?

Profits are not always a good signaling device. Often, the mission of an organization affects behavior and performance. For instance, imagine someone working for Sloan Kettering on a cure for cancer. Perhaps the person's motivation is nothing more than a selfish need to become famous. He probably also understands that if he finds a cure, many doctors and supporting staff won't have jobs anymore. Nonetheless, he strives and succeeds. Cancer ends. This same person could have had a much different motivation, maybe to work selflessly to end a horrible disease. In the end, his motivation didn't matter; it was results that counted; and those results depended on Sloan's mission to cure cancer.

Arguably some of our most treasured and successful institutions are ones not closely tied to performance measures based on profitability. Included in this category are America's major research universities and the hallowed Bell Labs that existed when AT&T was a monopoly. Recall that Bell Labs produced the transistor that started the electronics and digital revolutions and helped launch Japan as a major producer of radios and TVs. Cerf and Kahn, graduate students at UCLA, produced the transport protocols that enabled different types of equipment to work together. These protocols enabled the Internet.

Research companies have one basic idea in common: their employees want to create something new, something revolutionary, to uplift society. These examples are by no means an apology for research institutions because multinational corporations have also contributed to society greatly, but their employees operate under a much different objective – to build wealth and take a share of it.

18.3.2 Building Trust in the Government Sector

The problem of network transparency, the cornerstone of trust, carries over to the public sector. For instance, another popular source of institutional hand wringing was the cozy relationship between banks and government regulatory agencies before and arguably after the financial meltdown in 2008. To some extent, the relationship is far more than personal connections between key regulators and key financial executives. A cultural relationship had developed between the two types of organizations leading to certain types of expectations.

Using a wider systems lens, regulation has become more complex, with many government agencies overseeing the same institutions, none of which really has the expertise to regulate them effectively, especially as the market has become "virtual," crossing borders with the click of a mouse.

A particularly tough and dangerous problem is uncovering the web of relationships among America's secret services aimed at gathering intelligence and conducting covert operations because these institutions sometimes sidestep our legal system and routinely flout foreign laws. Even when secret services operate within the law, the laws that apply to them may permit snuffing out opponents instead of trying to settle disputes through negotiation.

Secret agents often work under the assumption that it is "us against them." Lurking among us are America's enemies. Most suggestions for building trust with secret service organizations are to set reasonable limits on their behavior by putting them under civilian control and subject to rigorous judicial review. A civilian agency could control secret databases, do the analysis for the security agencies, and leave it to such agencies as the CIA to investigate potentially dangerous trends. Nonetheless, the reach of America's secret services is expanding rapidly as more monitoring tools come online. No matter how many checks are in place, when government can develop a real-time video of a person's every move, privacy is lost. In many cases, judges defer to security agencies because they fear the consequences of a denial that leads to a terrorist attack.

Secrecy laws that cover sensitive research are also an issue. The government wants to protect the public from training and exporting terrorists in the United States. For instance, Congress passed the Public Health Security and Bioterrorism Preparedness and Response Act on June 12, 2002.[5] This law attempted to control biological products that can be used as weapons. Yet, arguably, the government itself may have collaborated with China on virus research that led to the COVID pandemic This and other acts such as the Patriot Act are making it difficult to form research teams with scholars from other nations and require great administrative costs associated with documenting research methods and results and can require that results cannot be published in scholarly journals. In other words, the need for secrecy to protect the public may undermine the very institutions that have produced the American economic miracle. No one really knows where the bounds need to be set on open collaboration.

18.4 Learning from the Platforms

Platforms have developed policies for assuring they remain popular with their users by building trust with their users. They are constantly experimenting with rules and design changes by altering its interfaces with some users while not changing them for others. The aim is to make users secure that the platform works to their benefit. Of course, any platform change will hurt some, which will lead to fairness complaints.

The fairness issue becomes especially important when a platform, like Amazon, for example, offers its own products while encouraging complementary and competing firms to trade on its platform. While the government continues to scrutinize Amazon's dealings, there are lessons to be learned from

---

[5] P.L. 107-88, H.R. 3448.

Amazon and other major platforms. In Amazon's case, despite private labeling Amazon's platform hosts more and more products and services.

Economists have focused on finding out when platforms exert undue market power to fend off competition. A natural outcome of competition is to protect one's turf and expand to new fields. Market rules can limit antisocial behavior that leads to markets that are less efficient and innovative. Allowing competition to thrive disperses economic power, which lessens the fear that a company may have too much political power.

I tried to highlight a less discussed analysis of platforms that is critical to ideological collaboration: the importance of corporate culture. These are my crucial takeaways:

- Platforms develop a corporate culture the evolves from its primary success in the marketplace.
- The core culture strengthens a platform's success for its core product offerings but limits flexibility in moving outside its cultural comfort zone. This is the equivalent of a cultural comparative advantage that leads to specialization.
- As opposed to previous big corporations, platform success depends crucially on converting dreams into products via virtual reality and artificial intelligence. This creative mindset is very similar to focusing on the creative level of the soulful mystical model, which I used to develop a mission statement for America.

By analogy, I believe that America's ethnic and racial groups have a core culture based on inherited traditions that give them a unique perspective on the human condition. Success in a multicultural society depends on recognizing, as the mystics did, that there are many pathways toward building an American dream. Each pathway is like a color that adds to the beauty and complexity of America's spiritual rainbow, or kaleidoscope if you prefer.

A limitation of representing a single cultural pathway in a multicultural society is that it makes each ethnic and racial group a bit myopic. Sometimes it can lead to culture wars. Many of the conflicts in America stem from focusing on the past or current position on the social ladder. These are important issues because any society has a collage of histories that make it special. Remembrance and respect are necessary conditions for harmony, but the crucial ingredient for unity is a meaningful mission that engages Americans from all backgrounds. Each group should strive to add its creative touch to what emerges; each can learn from the successes of and failures of others. Again, this vision is very similar to the message of religious humanism.

Besides learning from the platforms to regulate the online economy, government should also look inward to see how platform operations can improve their own offering to the public. To some extent, government policymakers could use the multiple levels of government to do systematic experiments about the services it offers.

The importance of culture is also important within government agencies. By necessity, government agencies require their people to follow rules set by legislation and interpretations of legislative intent. These rules limit personal discretion, which limits flexibility. As a result, it reduces an agency's ability to offer personalized services in comparison to the private sector.

Government agencies often have clashing cultures because they have different interests. Agencies compete for government dollars, which can cause turf wars. Security agencies that want to prevent terrorist attacks through covert surveillance and field operations have an antidemocratic streak. As government grows, politicians can use its resources to be reelected and enrich themselves. A new view of separations of powers needs development.

Government size also leads to two other challenges: complexity and partisanship. Any government act can alter the actions of parties that are seemingly remote from the action. For instance, giving the first people tax breaks who bought solar panels arguably raised electricity rates for poor people. Moreover, big projects draw many interested parties. In recent years, environmental and neighborhood concerns have made it difficult and costly to improve infrastructure because some group inevitable gets hurt.

Online exposure of a single outrage by a government agent can cause major social disruptions. For instance, no matter how many times conservative commentators like Larry Elder or Thomas Sowell point out that the police, in general, do not discriminate against African Americans, one video of a policeman beating or choking a black person will trump a thousand statistics. These images reinforce memories of the police brutalizing blacks. How to solve this problem besides bringing offending police to justice remains an open issue.

18.5 A Coordinated Multidisciplinary Approach to Policy Is Crucial

These examples suggest that no simple model along ideological lines describe optimal information transfer and institutional network arrangements for emerging broadband networks. Specific industries likely need their own special institutional relationships because of the types of products and services they offer. For instance, it does appear that so-called very efficient markets in which trades are made at very low costs sometimes become chaotic. Market stampedes happened as with the dot-com bubble and the housing bubble and financial panic that led to the Great Recession.

America's ideologies would do well to enlist a wide range of researchers and ethicists to help them adapt to a networked world. Economists have long examined physical flows among industries using input/output tables. They have also examined the effects of market power, mainly public utilities such as the local power company or Ma Bell.

Operations research specialists have focused on networks from a much more micro-perspective. They have developed techniques for minimizing transportation costs, balancing production lines, handling uncertainty within networks, and optimizing networks over time. As with economists, their focus is on physical inputs, connections, and outputs. In cyberspace, performance measures include dropped packets, delayed packets, jittery packets, serviced availability, and outages.

None of these models captures the physical network spillovers from one network to another in a way that would overcome decades of silo regulation of specific basic industries as if they were independent of each other. For instance, the power and broadband industries are largely regulated by separate regulatory agencies even though they are both competing to be the gateways into the "smart home" loaded with smart appliances that need to be controlled. The models certainly do not capture what one economist, Joseph Schumpeter, believed was the driving force in a market economy: creative destruction, the growth of new ideas and technologies that overthrow established firms and industries. They only superficially capture product and service flows between the public and private sectors. They do not show how public and private institutions adapt to the environment.

Data miners are examining the formation of social networks, which spring to life and have become massive almost overnight. The use of language processing and data mining could uncover corporate cultures deemed ethical and those that are not. This line of research could be expanded to evaluate the effectiveness of professional codes of ethics and see if they can be adapted to work effectively for other professional groups such as bioengineers. Big data tools could also help define character traits that produce cyberspace whistleblowers who risk their lives to uncover national scale wrongs and Wikipedia contributors who are willing to work together without pay to present facts to the public. Data mining can help distinguish those who look like they are trying to help but are actually hurting society. Its techniques can also help researchers evaluate effects on behavior of types of mission statements and internal policies across a wide range of industries and governmental agencies. Yet, these techniques should not be oversold. They depend on historical data to predict the future. One only has to look back a few decades and realize that historical data could not have predicted most changes in American society.

Economists and other social scientists and psychologists should focus on the importance of meaning in society and the marketplace. In the last decade, behavioral economics has become an important research field that tries to capture decision-making tendencies that are not fully consistent with rational choice. This new line of research has deepened economists' understanding of the causes of seemingly irrational behavior. Research on the meaning of life applied to personal and societal decisions is becoming crucial in the digital world because of so much economic and social turmoil. Applying "meaning" may go a long way toward understanding the breakdown of families, the loss of interest in hard work, the strife between ethnic and racial groups, and the loss of civic mindedness and patriotism.

Religious leaders also need to become more creative. The coding revolution is underway. Have religions absorbed the meaning of virtual reality and the possibility of man transcending himself? Have they understood the fears and hopes of humanity and translated them into new definitions of what is sacred and profane? The main visionaries are science fiction writers who attempt to imagine new worlds by mastering today's science, mathematics, political, economic, and social trends. Religious leaders need to offer their own visions that are compelling.

18.6 A Creative View of Public Policy

If America's ideologues could agree that the marketplace of Adam Smith's day or even of Franklin Roosevelt's day is not an adequate model, then there is room for accommodation. How does a nation operate when networks recognize no borders, where anyone can ship content around the world almost instantaneously at almost no cost, where a new application or a competitive move can disrupt the entire system, and where the usual is for cyberspace to morph in unexpected ways? Detailed regulation is often ineffective in fast-changing markets; international cooperation may not hold up when states are at odds with each other. A realistic evaluation of the government's capabilities and track record is necessary to avoid inflated policy pronouncement doomed to fail. Thinking of problems in network space, as connected systems, is a start to formulating new theories of marketplace and political behavior.

The real challenge is to overlay the systems approach on the template model where the rows are levels of the soul, namely, vital, conscious, and creative forces, and the columns are Bell's three perspectives on society – techno-economic, cultural, and polity. I kept Bell's columns in this chapter but left out the soulful lenses for simplicity. These lenses should not be ignored because they add depth to the analysis. Nor should the rational, romantic, deist, and mystical perspectives be shortchanged.

I used them to add a bold addition to America's mission statement fit for future generations: to fertilize the universe, to bring purpose to it, to honor the dignity and preciousness of all life, and to find ways to save the environment and enhance our being at the same time. The search for higher levels of being is within the soul and the outer reaches of space. Surely, ideologues of all types can see the promise that a broad mystical outlook offers.

All these perspectives and the mission statement I offered add a great deal of flexibility to any ideology, which gives any ideologue creative room because one should expect that ideologues will continue to apply their own perspectives to analyzing system problems, and that is a good approach because their basic perspectives are still valuable in a networked world. But the digital revolution and more so the coding revolution, with the challenge of genetic engineering included, require redesigning and reinterpreting ideological principles and core values and bringing them closer to religious aspirations for salvation and reconciliation in the digital world.

Starting with libertarians, I believe they would welcome any institutional innovations that could pass a market test. In their view institutions evolve according to a Darwinian process. New organizations producing better goods and services displace older ones. This creative destruction process produces an innovative society. From a libertarian's perspective, competitive networks morph in surprising ways because they adapt to solve new types of problems; operating in virtual reality is one of them. As a result of competitive pressure, institutions will latch onto trust-building practices and tools designed for a digital world. No matter the type of marketplace, libertarians believe institutions not based on the profit motive are flabby and, if they are government controlled, are generally poorly managed and potentially a political tool for coercing others. If the new tools point to less government, so much the better. The challenge for libertarians is to expand their approach as Milton Friedman did. He tried to transition public services back to the private sector. This happened with the Internet, which was originally a government-controlled network that was privatized. The experience can be applied to other public service sectors. A whole new dimension of the economy and society has emerged as a result of the digital revolution. How should property rights change? How should the meaning of negative freedom change? The old adage that your right to act ends at my nose does not apply easily to cyberspace.

Conservatives believe that a proper institution is peopled by stewards who carefully manage the assets given to them in trust. They would accept any tools that would place institutional networks on their target list to operate more ethically, and they have plenty on that list. Big financial institutions are suspect because employees often seem to look out for their own gains instead of working for stockholders and customers. Big platforms are too intrusive. Big government is suspect because employees are distant from local communities, and politicians seem to become rich in office or soon thereafter. I suspect conservatives would welcome new narrative tools that support communal behavior and personal decency fit for the Digital Age.

Liberals are open to using new tools for institutional reform because they are tinkerers with social systems. Like conservatives, they are also wary of profit-making institutions because they may exploit the poor or the disadvantaged. Unlike conservatives, they are wary of "old boy" networks that may lock outsiders out from opportunities. They don't shy away from big public institutions to solve national social problems. In their view, government institutions are sometimes inefficient, but they provide services that the private sector doesn't produce or produces too little. In specifics, liberals should accept any institutional arrangement in the real world or virtual reality that delivers needed services in an efficient and compassionate way. They will accept new network-based narratives that promote social justice and national security. Their challenge is to look inward at government operations and judge their performance fairly. Because they support government programs most, they should lead the way toward reform.

Perhaps the most unifying force that could bring ideologs to cooperate is America's determined will to create an inclusive society with a universal purpose. A certain type of person could be working in a patent office and yet be amazingly creative if his whole being is devoted to composing a living epic, or designing a temple, or giving birth to intellectual offspring, not so much for wealth, power, or fame but for the sake of being recognized by others as a partner, redeemer, or prophet who points the way to salvation. The will to create requires inspiration, something new in the world, something important that is missing, every spark of the creative imagination. America's ideologs may want to think beyond freedom and equality and focus on creativity and excellence. They both have strong ethical roots. Building a better society requires judging right from wrong, punishing lawlessness, but having mercy when mistakes happen. Endurance becomes a critical force. A creator needs the heft and strength to work long hours and the spiritual staying power to keep trying when paths lead nowhere. After much effort, victory, the "yes," occurs when finally, the prototype turns into a creation, which is then injected into the world, the fertile vessel of creation.

Bell Labs in its day, academic institutions, and when platforms like Microsoft or Google have opened, create new products and open new frontiers to the imagination. In particular, all of these institutions contributed to the digital revolution, a revolution that allows an ordinary person to tap into the world's knowledge, to build an online persona, explore the world from an armchair, and travel to imaginary worlds. The digital revolution with its algorithms and deep learning holds the promise to transform human activity into both eco- and human friendly. The digital revolution can become a worthy successor to the industrial revolution that built a comfortable, healthful America based on physical network expansions of water, gas, electricity, and telephone networks that were the hallmark of the twentieth century. A much less stellar product of the digital revolution is its effect on the financial industry that has devoted huge resources to developing financial instruments of limited value and for sucking many of the smartest minds into programmed trading.

The creative standard should be at the top of the policymaker's list of priorities, yet it is not the only social goal. One could argue that America's biggest problem now is the unfair distribution of wealth in the United States. The creativity/distribution debate raises many sets of questions. Are our national policies encouraging stable families, future directed behavior, and willingness to stay the course even if means sacrificing material benefits, or do our policies encourage a "me only" culture? Does the nation lack faith in its basic system when it adopts big social programs, or are national programs part of the creative process? Has America adopted an efficient approach to reform consistent with the creative development of institutions? Do the nation's tax policies encourage creative behavior or encourage creative uses of tax shelters? Do highly efficient markets break the connection between creativity and reward by bestowing riches on those first into the market, even by nanoseconds? Besides payoff to program traders, have electronic markets allowed producers of new products to reap huge rewards for simply beating competitors to the market in a tight race?

The distributional issue should modify the creative standard but not displace it. History suggests that battles over the distribution of wealth in society lead to economic stagnation and political instability. For instance, landed aristocrats in Europe tried to block merchants and industrialists from supplanting them. Acemoglu and Robinson have documented that nations fail when groups fight over who controls a nation's wealth instead of championing innovation.

It is a mistake to believe that a narrow set of rules will promote a virtuous creativity that ultimately benefits all groups in society. For instance, suppose the issue is lack of Internet privacy. If this problem persists, liberal economists will say it is a market failure requiring a new set of Internet rules or direct government intervention. Libertarian economists would counter that privacy will be accommodated when it pays off, and it will eventually. For instance, in a Wall Street Journal article, "Warning: government not always the solution". "No regulators were involved as WhatsApp used the open Internet to send secure messages."[6] This disrupted the costly traditional SMS text-messaging system used by telecom companies, which had been a $120 billion annual global business. WhatsApp already has more than 450 million users, almost half as many as Facebook. The Federal Trade Commission tried to protect privacy by forcing 20-year consent decrees on Facebook, Google, and Twitter that restrict their use of data they collect. This heavy-handed approach appears to be unnecessary, according to the authors. The real question is how long it will take. No easy answer is available because inventions and innovations are not the product of statistical analysis of the value of existing Internet characteristics. New products break the mold, are surprising, and only in retrospect seem inevitable. The great challenge for policymakers is to offer reasoned judgment, grounded in history, and act with the knowledge that any judgment is wrong and limiting of future actions, and any good decision is flexible enough to have within it the capability of being reversed.

Another mistake would be to assume American policy is applicable to all nations. Interconnected networks do not imply uniform global operations or risk. For instance, the dollar is the world's trading currency. Because America's debt is in dollars, not another currency, the government cannot formally default on its debt. Holders of dollars may lose if the dollar depreciates, but no country can tell America to pay up in a currency it doesn't have.

American policymakers must be aware of foreign policies. For instance, Neil Irwin, a New York Times writer, revealed the Fed had an open dollar facility with European banks and Korea right after Lehman collapsed to prevent an international collapse of the financial system. Global banks "did lots of business in dollars – buying up mortgage-backed securities, financing international trade between companies operating around the world." "But at that moment in 2008, private lending markets shut down." "Everybody was

---

[6] L. Gordon Crovitz (Feb. 23, 2014). "Crovitz: A WhatsApp Message for the Feds." WSJ Opinion. Available at https://www.wsj.com/articles/SB10001424052702304914204579397271366694950

hoarding dollars at once." The reason was that Lehman assets were frozen in Europe.

Consistent foreign policy that is fair and lawful are also musts. The Fed served as a lender of last resort to major banking centers even though it did not have the legal authority to do so. The Fed got around its legal constraints by swapping dollars for Euros for a fee. The Fed profited but what are the implications of bypassing Congress and developing its own international foreign policy?[7] The Fed chose not extend help to Indonesia, Turkey, and the Dominican Republic. They were not important to US economic interests. Were these inactions moral?

More importantly, other nations have very different histories than America. In many, colonial rule still burns into their psyche. Many post-colonial nations are really warring tribes kept together by generalissimos or religious autocrats. We've seen in Egypt and elsewhere, democratic rule fails when the spirit of compromise is absent. Russia has a history of autocratic rule and fears becoming vulnerable to Western power as former Soviet states such as the Ukraine align themselves with the West. It is unlikely that an American style democracy will take hold in Russia in the foreseeable future. Even the European Union, really a federation, is less stable than America. Europeans have a long history of national conflicts and territorial disputes. They will not easily give up national sovereignty. The obvious message is that the American model is not easily exported. Sometimes our success blinds us to alternatives that may not work here but would elsewhere. A network approach to foreign relations would help identify "transmission and application protocols" that could overcome seemingly insurmountable differences.

---

[7] Irwin, N. (2014). Fed's Aid in 2008 Crisis Stretched Worldwide. The New York Times. https://www.nytimes.com/2014/02/24/business/feds-aid-in-2008-crisis-stretched-worldwide.html. Accessed 1 May 2023.

19

Summary, Conclusions, and Outlook

Abstract The final chapter summarizes the entire presentation beginning with the basic problem of political gridlock, tracing its sources to ways for unblocking it. The theme in part emphasizes respect from better understanding of history and commonalities. Even so, all current ideologies face a credibility crisis caused by massive migrations and the coding revolution. Reconciliation and collaboration require finding new philosophical terrain that embraces a multi-vision view of the future that tolerates wide differences in imagery and image filtering. Religious humanism has this capability because it is a broad, flexible framework for American and world culture. Together with innovative analytical and narrative tools drawn from the coding revolution itself, religious humanism can reinvigorate America's core values and mythological images: Lady Liberty, Uncle Sam, Ground Zero, nation of nations, and city on the hill – all useful fictions can take on new tones and features. As Joseph Campbell said, unity is more likely when a nation has commonly accepted myths that embody a realistic and uplifting mission.

Imagine This Scene

A crowd of Americans is standing in front of the Statue of Liberty, eagerly awaiting its reopening ceremony. It is an imaginary August 2004, almost 3 years after the September 11, 2001, attack. The doors open, the crowd cheers, and then people begin to clap – the clapping becomes rhythmical. From an observation deck, reporters look down on all those ecstatic faces that could have come from a United Nations brochure.

"Americans Join Hands" is on the evening news – A gorgeous mosaic of America came to the Statue of Liberty today to reaffirm their faith in the American dream. "No terrorist group will make me afraid to come here. If we let them, they win," says Mr. Torres, a recent immigrant from the Caribbean.

"America has been good to me and my family," says Torres. "We came here with almost nothing and now we have a good life. Here my children go to school, and if they work hard, will live the American dream. I could have stayed home, but I could not."

"You know America is an amazing place. I read American history books and found that America is sorry for slavery and sorry for the way it treated my people. It makes me feel I am an American. When my family came to America, many helped us."

"I can't believe," Mr. Torres said, "that only a few months after the Twin Towers attack, no more rubble." "Downtown is clean." "You know, the new World Trade Center will be better than the old one, more beautiful and bigger." "I know it." "Where else would this happen?"

Though he may not say it, Mr. Torres understands that America's public policies have a spiritual dimension to them. The government doesn't run a deficit just to boost the economy; it does so to put people back to work for their own self-respect. This is word splitting, but nuances are important. The Statue's reopening ceremony is a statement to the world that America will overcome terrorism.

Mr. Torres has the makings of an American patriot. Any person who identifies his very being with America is such a person. A patriot cannot imagine living elsewhere. He will fight for America because America defines him. He is the incarnation of the New American. Not of European roots, he has taken on the American persona.

How does this happen? Knowing what causes this type of loyalty is a marketer's dream. Imagine someone saying I can't live without a particular car or designer shirt – hooked for life. Unrealistic as it sounds, this is what America still expects from its people. Immigrants or ethnics, no one is exempt. History shows that many newcomers are even more willing to sacrifice for America than homegrown Americans are.

Traditionally, people have given their lives for "Blood and Soil" or "God's true religion" to stimulate patriotic fervor. None of them applies to Mr. Torres. America is not his native land. Strictly speaking, it is not the native land of people with roots going back to the Mayflower. True, their history is now in America, but they recognize at some level that America is no group's land.

America has used a unique approach to patriotism. It spiritualizes the land. This is the new Israel. Instead of being a haven for an exclusive people to worship their God, it is a land of ingathering for all people to worship God as they please.

America shrinks from theories of land, folk, and God that explain why a person should die for his country. Instead, they want to live for this country, their own people, for their own self-development.

Americans must feel, in their bones, that this is a land worthy of sacrifice. If an ethnic-American group needs help, the rest of America's tribes and mixtures will treat it as family. They will fight to protect sons of liberty. When any American is captured or dies on the battlefield, a true patriot feels it as a loss of his own.

An American patriot spiritualizes his herding and territorial instincts and humanizes his visionary inspirations that suggest one right way to salvation. In a sense, he is a citizen of the world living in a land that upholds this vision.

And now imagine a similar scene but in the near future.

It is fourth of July; a crowd has gathered at Lady Liberty's base. The crowd is a bit thinner than in 2004 perhaps because the Twin Tower attack has receded into history, perhaps undocumented people decided to stay home. Overhead wiring looks like a necklace of cameras; police are everywhere; and undercover agents are dispersed among the crowd. Sharpshooters are crouched inside Lady Liberty. Police helicopters are overhead. Back at police command center, GPS and facial images are being fed into computers to identify suspected terrorists. People in the crowd are looking uneasily at anyone with backpacks or large objects. The big draw is not Lady Liberty, but a laser light show that will begin after dark. A rainbow of laser beams will shoot out of the torch. Lady Liberty herself will become a giant monument to virtual reality. Her features will change and so will her coloring. Something for everyone and yet something inauthentic – politically correct – an attempt to blot out Lady Liberty's white, European features.

An exaggerated scene perhaps but one that suggests America is losing its cultural center, losing its binding myths and metaphors, morphing into a society fearful of its future, a place where people cluster into defensive groups that are tired of talking and compromising. My intention in writing this book is to make America work again. I wanted to offer new pathways to overcome these fears, to help make America again the world's beacon for salvation.

I want Americans to conjure new imagery for Lady Liberty fit for the Digital Age. Archibald MacLeish sanctified the social security network set up during the Franklin Roosevelt administration by transforming Lady Liberty from a young woman who shines her light to guide the oppressed to American shores to a mother who nurtures her children. My non-poetic Lady Liberty lightshow is a prosaic attempt to picture a darkening American image of an inauthentic land addicted to special effects peopled by strangers no matter how close they are physically.

The digital revolution awaits a poet Laureate who can personify Lady Liberty in a new role that doesn't rely on changing Lady Liberty's features. Her torch could become a beacon of harmonious spiritual emanations guiding us toward a new and better society where we become partners of God in the best sense of ending the evils that afflict humanity, the evils that threaten life itself, the evils that are eating away at Earth's vitality, and the evils that freeze or burn countless lifeless heavenly bodies.

Are these images better suited for a science fiction story or a pulpit? Perhaps.

Instead of poetry, my advice for getting there reads a bit like a "how to" manual for self-improvement, not a biblical-style epic. Yet, my manual depends critically on understanding history. American ideologies were defined by overcoming catastrophes, by searching for meaning that rises above maximizing a faceless individual's utility.

My basic premise is that people will not change their basic life narrative by persuasion or factual evidence. People do change when their eyes open to a new set of challenges they can't explain or new possibilities they want to pursue. My objective is to offer new ways of seeing the world without threatening a person's core values. In this expanded field of vision lies the possibilities for ideologues to cooperate.

I offered a three-step method to restart a productive political dialogue in America. My first objective was to show that libertarians, conservatives, and liberals are insightful people worthy of respect for what they add to the political debate. To build the case, I showed they all support liberty, equality, the rule of law, and private property but interpret them differently, putting more stress on certain attributes. Libertarians and conservatives don't want government meddling in personal affairs. Liberals see government as a helpmate.

Emotional reactions to specific crises explain their ideological differences arguably much more so than vested interests or personal prejudices. From the eighteenth century onward, conservatives were repeatedly horrified by radicals who led mobs on a stampede to crush a paralyzed or corrupt ruling class then wound-up causing chaos, mass destruction, and murder of innocents and imposed a new and worse tyranny. As Burke might have warned, a mob leader is an abomination to civilization, a fanatic who would wipe away a noble heritage because of a wayward generation of legislators.

Libertarians reacted to the rise of tyrannies. From a more detached but still fearful perspective, they examined government failures that allowed a charismatic megalomaniac to topple an ineffective government and install his own gang at the top. The most glaring enabler was centralized control of society even when voted into being by a democratic process as was the case with the Weimar Republic. The great danger of centralized control is that it politicizes the economy. Disputing political factions cause political gridlock as they fight for their own pet projects and for control of society. Government management of large sectors of the economy leads to waste and corruption, so much so that the public yearns for a leader who will end the bickering and payoffs and make government work again.

Liberals increasingly felt guilty that as America rose to dominance from the late nineteenth century onward, local governments and private institutions were failing to care for the poor or protect its citizens from racism and prejudice or prevent speculative bubbles that led to periodic financial panics and economic depressions. They believed the federal government could and should act as the protector of society against the powerful rich and the powerful politicians who enforced Jim Crow in the South. The federal government could prevent catastrophic economic depressions as the world experienced during the 1930s.

Not surprisingly, these ideologies attracted people with different sentiments toward government and with their own political agendas. Conservatives and libertarians attracted supporters who wanted to limit government's reach by defining core American values such as liberty defined in the negative, "do not," while liberals put emphasis on opening opportunities, the "do" perspective on personal liberty.

I introduced champions to connect each ideology to a person so that they didn't sound like a set of principles devised by academics in their offices to explain society. These formulators lived through major crises, tried to make sense of them, tried to give us a way out, a solution. Burke lived through the French Revolution's murderous excesses. Hayek escaped to England as Nazism spread across Central Europe. Keynes keenly felt the Great Depression's economic devastation and potential threat to democracy.

Each one struggled to explain the crises. Their testaments have an honest and insightful feel of someone mingling objective and subjective observations and analyses to give us a truthful portrayal of society in trouble and ways to fix it. They were men of character, fair minded, who were looking out for us, the common citizen, and like prophets tried to warn us of impending disaster if we followed the wrong path: the road to serfdom for Hayek, the road to cultural dissolution for Burke, or the road to depression and riot for Keynes. These champions displayed the mastery of great novelists. They clearly understood the basic workings of society, followed certain principles either consciously or unconsciously, but knew the limitations of their beliefs as a guide to good policy. Hayek and Keynes were the best minds of the economics profession, admired private enterprise, but knew markets were not the solution to every problem. Sometimes markets don't form, or perform poorly, and sometimes people are not up to competing in the marketplace. I tried to build their case using their own words, often paraphrasing to pass along the tone of their observations and insights because they convey a crisis as they saw it. If I've succeeded in giving a good account of their ideas, supporters of a particular ideology should believe it more strongly and yet after reading the ideologies of the other champions have respect for them also as people of character, not a group of prejudiced people out for themselves.

I added other notables to show that each ideology has a living history filled with many distinguished characters that offered solutions to social problems in somewhat different ways. I introduced conservative thinkers who explained that local control, balanced budgets, and secure national borders are necessary to cultivate prudence, community, and national culture. I added libertarian scholars who applied economic theory to government operations and concluded that private groups, especially big businesses, will seek government benefits to boost their payoffs. From their perspective, government will tend to grow in ways distorted by political influence, and this must be stopped and rolled back. I picked liberal theorists who explored market failures in greater depth than Keynes and concluded they were the byproduct of persistent public myopia, prejudice, and skittishness, which a well-led government can overcome.

Each of America's ideologies gained devotees who were attracted to political leaders and thinkers that articulated their discontents. During the Great Depression, many African Americans switched from being Republicans to being liberal Democrats because Franklyn Roosevelt offered hope that the federal government would rescue them. Vietnam War demonstrations, street riots, and communes drove many Americans toward the security of conservative thought. Libertarianism gained strength with the failure of Great Society social programs to end poverty and racism. Triggering events often were the takeoff for an ideology's popularity, a labor riot, a bomb in a marketplace, a long bread line, or a march for freedom, and suddenly many accepted beliefs seemed wrong, and to accept society as it would make the aggrieved look like suckers if they didn't change political allegiances. Once they crossed to a new ideology, they couldn't turn back; they invested too much psychic energy to leave old beliefs behind and accept new ones. A feedback loop then developed from policy to opinions to ideology and back to policy. Supporters looked for evidence to support their positions and either ignored or reinterpreted evidence that weakened their political stands.

Followers of each American ideology pass along the wisdom of its champions knowingly or unknowingly. Reading aloud the Republican and Democratic platforms is like hearing yourself say something your parents would say. The statements and ideas in those documents sound surprisingly similar to those of the ideological champions I described, one of whom, Edmund Burke, lived more than 200 years ago. It's as if the writers paraphrased their ideas as I did but without attribution, changing somewhat dated yet amazingly vivid language fit for earlier generations into serviceably efficient modern plain speak.

Naturally, ideologs feel rejected and misunderstood when others don't see the obvious wisdom of their approach. An ideological no-man's land formed in early twenty-first-century America. Battle lines can't be breached by logical argument or case studies alone. In the real world, where controlled experiments are impossible on a large scale and the set of specific national issues keeps changing, none of these ideologies can be debunked. In the first section of the book, I suggested that each ideology may have an edge for solving specific types of problems, and they all add perspective to solving any problem.

I said sometimes that collaboration does occur using a novel policy twist. For instance, Milton Friedman was a master of taking social programs handed down from the New Deal and offering new approaches that built market incentives into them. He suggested school vouchers so that parents could pay for schools of their choice, and he suggested a negative income tax to give poor people the incentive to work.

All three ideologies recognize that institutions change to address unexpected changes in society. Innovative policy elasticizes general rules, making them flexible enough to be effective guides when unhappy surprises in society may require a government fix. As long as one side recognizes that the other side sees a policy issue from a different but legitimate perspective, constructive disagreements on implementation are possible. A record of minority opinions may actually serve as a catalogue of alternatives when a majority opinion fails, which will often happen.

Respecting the other side is one important approach for developing a collaborative spirit. Sometimes it works. Unfortunately, a compromising spirit seems lacking in America. William Gass said, "experience is broad and muddy ...it teaches mainly through pain, defeat, disappointment, loss."[1] From a skeptic's point of view, a "lofty hierarchy of explanations ... tables of statistics ...impose order on accident."[2]

---

[1] Gass, WH. (1995) The Tunnel. Dalkey Archive Press, IL. p. 20.
[2] Id., p. 31.

Recent history suggests that a string of losses or a sudden jolt from a common enemy is more likely to bring policymakers together as they try to present a united front to the American public and the enemy. As we saw after 9/11, a new crisis is an opportunity for creative cooperation. People from all political backgrounds recognize the need for new approaches, new techniques, and are willing to some extent to shed hide-bound stances.

My second objective was to suggest a crisis is developing that none of the ideologies addresses adequately. It is the coding revolution. This is not a sharply felt crisis like the 9/11 attack. If Burke were alive today, he would be amazed by all the new computer gadgetry but probably the car and jet would disorient him most because they allow a person to be transported physically to places where he only read about in novels during his day. Keynes and Hayek would be less shocked at the vast expansion of computing capacity but not overwhelmed. Nonetheless, they would wonder how the world was changing with 24-h communication becoming commonplace, with instant access to the world, with virtual reality, with lab techniques that are altering the very nature of life. Surely, this quiet revolution would make them unsure whether their core values such as the rule of law and the meaning of private property can be sustained in cyber world, a world that doesn't recognize national boundaries or enforce copyrights with much energy. Perhaps even more troubling to them would be genetic engineering because it is beginning to redesign human nature.

Using examples of the coding revolution – cyberspace capitalism, digital overexposure, stealth security, and designer eugenics – I attempted to fire a broadside against America's core values. In cyber worlds, a supposedly efficient market can become instantly chaotic by a hair trigger reaction to bad market news. In 2008, an economic storm rolled across the world in hours, giving policymakers little time to avoid financial collapse. Big platforms that want to meet and sometimes shape our needs in real time have gathered enormous digital dossiers on everyone that uses or may use their services. These digital profiles threaten to expose anyone to online bullying, opinion distortion, character assassination, identity theft, and potential legal liabilities. It just takes a few out-of-context quotes and Photoshopping to make anyone look like a criminal. Along those lines, I looked at the growing power of America's palace guard employed to protect us from terrorists that are becoming a potential menace to personal privacy. The very scale of its operations makes spying difficult to control because of the many ways to gather personal information. Anxious to avoid terrorist attacks, the public is reluctantly willing to let spy agencies operate sometimes beyond the limits of legality even if a small loss of life is at stake; honor demands we protect every citizen from harm. My last coding revolution example sounds much more like science fiction than reality – as of now. Artificial insemination, surrogate mothers, cloning, and genetically altered food, at first shocking or maybe unnerving, are becoming more acceptable, almost commonplace. Little by little, the sanctity and integrity of every living creation is being eroded, often with good intentions. A growing unease that someone will use genetic engineering in a monstrous way is a floating dread for many Americans. One genetic disaster or Frankenstein creation could cause a worldwide panic, worse than a major war.

My last objective was to offer a way out by expanding the range of each ideology by offering narrative tools and techniques and a broader framework that can help ideologs get beyond the ideological walls they've thrown up and find new collaborative solutions of the win-win sort, where everyone can point to some part of the plan and say it wouldn't work without a critical design feature or action plan.

The third section of the book introduced an expanded framework for developing and evaluating policy alternatives that would allow ideologs to collaborate without sacrificing their principles. I began by articulating an American political philosophy, which I defined as religious humanism. It is a composite of Enlightenment philosophy and traditional religious beliefs some only kept alive by a handful of religious scholars that encompasses America's ideologies as special cases. I defined the term "religious" to embody four ideas not easily contained in other terms: a collective focal point that binds and gives direction, a moral sense to help others in distress, a covenant with ancestors to keep their heritage alive, and an ongoing redemptive struggle with evil.

Ideologies have religious tinges to them. They impose meaning on life, offer core values to live by. They offer spiritual and scientific paths to overcome death and insecurity, and ways to enhance life, give it depth and relevance in a mass society. They strive for enlightenment, and the true champions are among the elect, chosen for immortality, like saints of old.

My belief is that America does not reject religious spirituality as superstition, or as a threat to reason and truth, or as a primary source of hate and vengeance, or as a guard against racial mixing and cultural pollution. In America it enhances a feeling of possibility, part of an imaginative spiritual voyage, part of a quest for redemption touching all parts of being, a poetic quest for a good and well-cultivated life.

Properly understood, American patriotism is an expression of religion at its best. It goes beyond tribe, beyond unreasoning calls to love it or leave it, to what religion calls for: redemption and renewal of humanity and all that humanity touches. American patriotism at its best aims at enlightening everyone, not by force but by seeing that our individual enlightenment depends crucially on enabling others to see a common golden path that humanity should journey toward.

I believe America has developed its own religion, religious humanism. It resembles a superstructure built from traditional religious thought but is ecumenical. It depends on traditional religions for its vitality. Paradoxically, America's religion can overcome divisiveness because it is steeped in the American culture of fairness. They will weigh whatever evidence is available and try to see events from all sides. Religious humanists respect religious differences and pray for guidance to a Deist God and their own traditional God. They are not sustainers of great religious movements, but they also don't cause great destruction so often associated with religious crusades based on unbridled passion.

America's ecumenical religion embraces science as a tool that needs to be directed toward ushering in a golden age. Scientific discoveries continue to uncover marvelous and threatening possibilities never even conceived by forebears. Science may cause great sorrow but on balance has been life supporting when directed by a belief that all life is sacred.

Plenty of religious stalwarts fill America's pews who are still at odds with science. This problem may have a solution in creative biblical commentary. For instance, which is more satisfying: a God that blows into dirt and produces a human, or blows into the dirt and creates a single cell that evolves into a human capable of self-reflection and understanding nature's laws? Perhaps the bible was less concerned with the transition than the end result. In ancient times, the world to come, the world of perfect ecstasy, was a place where the creator communed with the created in perfect harmony. Science offers a way for the human creator and his creation to merge as the composer merges with his music. Implicitly, I am saying America's religions must become more existential again, part of everyday life, and a practical influence on daily behavior if they want to remain vigorous in the Digital Age.

The humanistic label of religious humanism was much easier to defend because it doesn't depend on a supernatural being or force. Most Americans see humanity as the basic standard for measuring the value of existence. Beyond this, humanism stands for enthroning rational life. People believe that the human mind, no matter how puny, can solve the mysteries of the universe and use them to their benefit. They don't want to depend on a silent God for their redemption. They don't want to accept heritage as immutable. Any received wisdom must be assessed in each generation, and each generation should add its own wisdom to the human store.

My basic premise is that the humanistic spirit should not cut people off from their folkways. By discarding religion as superstition, or separating an individual's needs from his community, is like trying to describe a person from his shadow. The idea of God or whatever you want to call a divine purpose and judge is critical to America's culture.

Matthew Arnold once said that the Greeks developed the idea of consciousness and the Jews the idea of conscience.[3] Since World War II especially, after millions attended college and became rationalists, America has focused on consciousness. As a result, America has contributed little to the spiritual development of its people. In practice, by enticing the educated to follow their own dreams and build their own lives, America's post-war culture has weakened the religious and cultural superstructure that made America traditionally a place of salvation, of new beginnings and new opportunities to live a free and full life. One wonders whether America is raising egocentric materialists who walk away from heritage like throwing away an old piece of furniture. Are younger Americans becoming spiritually aimless, dissatisfied people with no greater cause than themselves? ##Do they see a society that worships youth and like children we are clamoring to be heard and be seen have little time to protect and comfort others?

Humanists need to see beyond the functional perspective – what works in the marketplace or in politics – to spiritual intangibles beyond self that give life coherence and purpose. Judaism, Christianity, and other religions are particular expressions of a more general answer to basic spiritual questions of who am I, why do I exist, do I have a purpose?

I identified four basic sources of wisdom that help define religious humanism and by extension, America's ideologies: logical/pragmatic, romantic, deist, and mystical. By extension, they are sources for ideological thought. Each of America's major ideologies draws on selections from these sources to develop its own logic and narrative. While selection is necessary to build a coherent ideology, it is also a limiting exercise if an ideology does not tap into these growing sources of wisdom.

Before exploring where an ideology could tap new fields of wisdom, I highlighted the selection process. I showed that libertarians stress logical decision-making with little tolerance for messy pragmatic compromises. They admire cowboy romanticism and a form of deism with man often substituting for a god as the creator. Liberals are both rational and pragmatic problem-solvers, romantic champions of the oppressed, and deist in their belief that natural laws exist to be controlled and used to enhance life. Conservatives are

---

[3] Arnold, M. Culture and Anarchy. Edited by Wilson, JD. Chapter 4, pp. 129–144, Hebraism and Hellenism. Cambridge University Press, London. https://en.wikisource.org/wiki/Culture_and_Anarchy/Chapter_4. Accessed 1 May 2023.

pragmatic, believers in Horatio Alger success stories, and mystical believers in a God who waits for us to uncover the mysteries of the universe and become God's creative partner. It should have been apparent that all three ideologies can expand into humanistic and religious frontiers to their advantage.

Then I tried to show that these sources of wisdom continue to grow. As they do, ideologs should absorb their new perspectives. One shortcoming with using the four characteristics of religious humanism to expand an ideolog's narrative range is that they seem like flattened philosophical terrain. It is as if one could step for logical/pragmatic to deism without any effort.

I needed a surprising new perspective that would allow ideologs to think along new dimensions, something like introducing someone to virtual reality before the Digital Age. That is where the mystical model came in. It is the fourth dimension to religious humanism. It is a dimension in psychic time that allows an ideologue to analyze economic, cultural, and political issues at three soulful levels that are like entangled purposeful force fields: the vital force, the conscious force, and the creative force. At each level time moves at different psychic speeds measured in hours at the vital force level, measured in planning horizons at the conscious level and not measurable, seemingly endless, at the creative level. Soulful levels have their positive and negative moral forces that need to balance to keep the soul from being distorted or destroyed, again something like positive and negative forces uncovered by physicists. The difference with physics is that the forces stay in balance through a constructive debate aimed at enhancing life. The debate is often between the supporters of judgment and the supporters of mercy.

I imagine the first reaction of a reader is that mystical narrative tools are gimmicks. But that is not true. I offered many practical uses of the mystical model. For instance, I suggested that the struggle between Islam and the West is at three spiritual levels: a struggle to control oil reserves, a struggle between democracy and theocracy, and a struggle between science and God as the path to redemption and renewal. I used an example of drilling for oil in Alaska to show that mystical narrative tools and techniques are useful for developing ideological narratives and finding ways for ideological collaboration. I also tried to show that America's ideologies have different spiritual outlooks and sense of psychic time. Liberals focus on group survival – the other, oppressed group; they tend to mercy instead of judgment and see redemption in tending nature's Garden, on preservation and fair distribution of its fruits. Conservatives also plan for group survival – their own first and move outward from there. They favor judgment and structure as more effective civilizing forces than mercy and flexibility. They, like liberals, want to preserve nature's gifts but not necessarily redistribute them as freely as liberals would. Libertarians are survivalists; "me" comes first. They favor good judgment and each according to his value in the marketplace over merciful handouts as the most humane path toward salvation of all, even the weak. They believe humanity's destiny is to control natural laws and use them to become creators, to bring life to the vast wastelands of the universe.

Even mystics need a practical template of how society works if they want to become effective policymakers. I introduced Bell's three societal perspectives as a complement that activates the soulful model. He examined society from three perspectives: techno-economic, cultural, and political. In his view a societal disruption affects all three categories in different ways and at different speeds. Technological change like the digital revolution rapidly supplants older equipment and buildings and, with a time lag, older ways of doing business. The effects of the digital revolution on culture has a different effect on history and the trajectory of society. Personal and group histories remain largely intact. Properly understood, the digital revolution can open new cultural possibilities. This takes time because even the effect of a computer took decades to affect people's lives. Political arrangements have also changed because of the large increase in the flow of information that can be processed in real time.

The Bell perspective helped me offer an operational template that policymakers of any ideological stripe could use for understanding physical and behavioral systems. Then I proposed to use a digital network perspective to help policymakers move away from the scientific practice of treating problems in isolation because this technique doesn't work well in an increasingly connected world.

My major focus was on avoiding Black Swan events and insulating society when they do occur. I artificially disassembled systems into physical and behavioral with the understanding that systems are designed by people for people – or their machines. Systems convey the idea of connectedness, and in the cyber age, most individuals are physically connected to networks and benefit or suffer from the actions of others. I artificially classified networks as hierarchical, with command and control given to top management, and horizontal connectivity like the Internet. I suggested that both vertical and horizontal systems have histories that one needs to understand before suggesting ways to improve them. Besides their history, many systems are changing rapidly as a result of the coding revolution.

Economists have examined management systems as if they were cat and mouse games with principals – top management or owners – as cats and managed employees as mice. While this model works to some extent, it doesn't capture the shifting coalitions of workers, entrepreneurs, and businesses worldwide that come together temporarily to build products, or the increasing connections among people with special skills who have more loyalty to their guild than to their employers, or the anonymous gambler who secretly trades or steals to make a fortune without having to physically batter someone.

Economists have understood the workings of the price mechanism for centuries as a primary tool for regulating behavior in the market – horizontal systems. They have only made small steps toward understanding the failures of prices in highly efficient cyber markets, or the use of prices as a complement to engineering practices aimed at stabilizing and improving the performance of physical networks such as the Internet. Real-time pricing and load shifting may now work because computers can monitor and process supply and demand patterns and shift loads when networks become congested. Many other issues such as pricing to interconnect networks and pricing of platforms that connect buyers and sellers are in their infancy.

Engineering design strategies can serve as powerful metaphors for determining public policy. The Internet is a classic example. It is a physical system built on simple protocols – rules for communication among machines and software – that has produced an enormously complex and flexible network. Built Lego-style, it has sharp edges and lacks a uniform, centralized design, but it works wonderfully because it can grow in unexpected directions as needs arise.

The systems approach leads to thinking of policy fixes like buffering in networks to prevent an overflow or system collapse. Pinging, high-frequency signaling, to test for network breaks suggests that tests of other systems like the effectiveness of monetary policy could be done with high-frequency changes in the stock of money. The translation of many products into bits of data may help policymakers move away from regulating specific products like plain old telephone service to regulating networks that provide communications. It may even turn out that rapid technological change should signal the end of regulation and perhaps usher in an age of granting funds and supplementing consumer income to provide universal telecommunications service. Policy discussions could include ideas such as self-healing networks, the percent downtime, the ability to deliver priority service, emergency service, the extent of a network's reach, and its capacity – many ideas rarely heard in general political discussions.

Engineers, economists, psychologists, and others are collecting enormous amounts of digital information about personal behavior. Like many others, I said data can help individually tailor goods and services for a perfect, personal fit. The data can also be used to spy on someone nonstop. One important idea, nothing new, that needs to be kept in mind: behavioral control will be countered. Data used to track cheaters may work for a while, but cheaters will learn. Machines may best other machines in high-frequency trading, but their edge has a short half-life. Countering will occur when the stakes are high for a particular transaction – a stock trade or a big theft of sensitive data.

Networks sprawl and getting used to this mindset will help policymakers think globally. Black Swans of many types can start with a virus or impulse that begins in a remote area or in the dark places of a huge metropolis. I offered examples to show that a systems approach can stimulate creative policymaking. I likened the loss of privacy in the Internet age to digital mosaic pollution, shards of personal information pieced together to produce faulty personal images. The pollution metaphor suggests that private and public actions can hold invasions of privacy within reasonable bounds. I used a systems approach to analyze the challenges of building a sustainable growth program.

Despite their complexity, systems have a basic blueprint. The Internet has an open systems interconnection model. Models have been developed for online platforms, called digital ecosystems. Models also characterize social systems. The operations of the major online platforms are an enormous trove of valuable insights into the future of the online economy. Platforms have learned how to encourage outsiders to use their platforms and enhance their offerings. They have learned how to monitor transactions to assure fair dealing by platform users. Their practices also illustrate the potential threats of allowing the platform overseers to set the rules for their platforms and being the enforcers of those rules.

All of the policy examples and thought experiments I've conducted hinge on a personal approach I've developed for using the narrative tools and techniques I've presented. I can summarize my narrative strategy as "soul, statutes, sales, and systems." I believe any creative policymaker must have the will to create and faith that inspiration will come (soul). Once the creative idea jells, it needs to be turned into a plan with a set of rules and procedures (statutes). The objective of a plan is a new set of goods or services that the public would welcome (sales). Finally, the product must fit into the web of products and services and enhance them (systems).

So much for basic strategy, the real challenge for creative collaboration is performing imaginative "what-ifs." I tried to imagine each American ideology as a system, as if I were in a control room and looking to put an ideological diagram on the main screen. The coding revolution was also my inspiration for renewing cultural and religious traditions by tapping into the vast resources uncovered by data mining and using them to understand the promises and dangers of policies aimed at making humanity a partner in creation that God would approve of. Ultimately, the measure of a policy's success is not its ideological purity or its innovations; the measure of its success is how much America has improved the quality of life and at what cost, and this bottom line may take decades to sort out.

I believe the spirit of creativity does not grow in a void or spontaneously. Morality matters; institutions matter; visions of the future matter. Digital systems open creative opportunities to civilize a new frontier. Raising creative adults relies heavily on moral training. This poem summarizes my moral ascent to humanity becoming partners in creation:

> In rearing lies ritual
> In ritual lies morality
> In morality lies the law
> In law lies judgment
> In judgment lies mercy
> In mercy lies reconciliation
> In reconciliation lies redemption
> In redemption lies renewal

A basic message is that the blueprint for ethical behavior is timeless. Underneath all the material trappings that seem to put distance between us and the ancient Israelites or Greeks is an unchanging soul with creative and purposeful aspirations A simple ethical test cuts through all the paraphernalia, blinking lights, equations, and simulations that camouflage modern man – it is the smile test. Would an ancient Israelite or Greek or any ancient nation smile at what we have done? They will frown if our souls have become unrecognizable.

I'll end with a warning and a wish. Firms die, markets die, political parties die, nations die, empires die – they all die when trust dies. What holds true for goods and service also holds true for the exchange of ideas. When people no longer believe an ideologue is willing to work with them, they reject the ideology. A person's ambition is often beyond happiness or financial security, or health; it is continuity of one's larger self; see it passed on to future generations (based on Staring at the Sun). A promising future depends on creative inspiration. This book's main goal was to help ideologs see a broader horizon than they had imagined and find new paths that look familiar and promising even as old ones recede in time. I hope I've succeeded.

Selected References

Akerlof GA, Shiller RJ (2009) Animal spirits. Princeton University Press, Princeton

Alinsky S (1971) Rules for radicals. Random House, New York

Arendt H (1976) The origins of totalitarianism. Harcourt Inc, New York

Armstrong K (2005) A short history of myth. Canongate Books, Edinburgh

Barnes J (1990) The history of the world in 101/2 chapters. Alfred A. Knopf, New York

Barnes J (1996) Cross channel. Random House, New York

Barrett W (1958) The irrational man. Doubleday, New York

Barzun J (2000) From dawn to decadence: 500 years of western cultural life. Harper Collins, New York

Bell D (1978) The cultural contradictions of capitalism. Basic Books, New York

Bell D (2000) The end of ideology: on the exhaustion of political ideas in the fifties. Harvard University Press, Cambridge

Berle A, Means G (2017) The modern corporation and private property. Routledge, New York

Berlin I (1997) The proper study of mankind. Farrar, Straus, and Giroux, New York

Bloom A (1987) The closing of the American mind. Simon and Schuster, New York

Bogel JC (2009) The battle for the soul of capitalism; enough: true measures of money, business, and life. Wiley, New York

Bogle JC (2011) Don't count on it. Wiley, New York

Bork R (2023) The antitrust paradox. Bork Publishing

Brooks D (2011) The social animal. Random House, New York

Burke E (1961) Reflections on the revolution in France and the rights of man by Thomas Paine. Doubleday and Co, Garden City

Burke E (1970) The Philosophy of Edmund Burke, Ann Arbor paperbacks. University of Michigan Press

Campbell J (1949) The hero with a thousand faces. Pantheon Books, New York

Carse J (1986) Finite and infinite games. The Free Press, New York

Cassier E (1968) Language and myth. Dover Publication, New York

Comfort N (2012) The science of human perfection. Yale University Press, New Haven

Crumpton H (2013) The art of intelligence: lessons from a life in the CIA's Clandestine Service. Penguin Books, New York

DeLong JB (2022) Slouching towards Utopia: an economic history of the twentieth century. Basic Books, New York

Dewey J (1927) The public and its problems. Swallow Press/Henry Holt and Co, Chicago

Dewey J (1963) Liberalism and social action. Capricorn Books/G. P. Putnam's Sons, New York

Diamond J (1997) Guns, germs, and steel. W.W. Norton, New York

Downs A (1957) An economic theory of democracy. Harper and Row, New York

Drucker P (1964) Concept of the corporation. Mentor Books, New York

Drucker PF (1969) The end of economic man. Harper Colophon Books, New York. Reprinted from 1939

Drucker P (1978) The age of discontinuity: guidelines to our changing society. Harper Colophone Books, New York

Eliade M (1957) The sacred and profane. Harcourt, Brace, and World, New York

Fairfield R (1966) The federalist papers. Anchor Books, New York

Ferguson N (2013) The great degeneration. Allen Lane, Bristol

Feuchtwanger L (1934) The Oppermanns. Carroll and Graf Press, New York

Fishman C (2006) The Wal-Mart effect: how the world's most powerful company really works – and how it's transforming the American economy. Penguin Press, New York

Freeman JB (2012) American empire: 1945–2000. Penguin Group, New York

Friedman M (1962) Capitalism and freedom. The University of Chicago Press, Chicago

Friedman M (1979) Free to choose. Harcourt Brace Jovanovich, New York

Friedman T (2002) The world is flat. Farrar, Straus, and Giroux, New York

Friedman M, Schwartz A (1963) A monetary history of the United States. Princeton University Press, Princeton

Gardner J (1983) The art of fiction. Vintage Books, New York

Gass WH (1995) The tunnel. Harper Collins, New York

Gilder G (1981) Wealth and poverty. Basic Books, New York

Gilder G (1992) Recapturing the spirit of enterprise, updated for the 1990s. ICS Press, San Francisco

Gilder G (2009) The Israel test. Richard Vigilante Books, Minneapolis

Glachen R (2008) Atmospheric conditions. Farrar, Strauss, and Giroux, New York

Goldberg R (2007) Liberal fascism. Doubleday, New York

Goodman A (1996) Katerskill falls and the family Markowitz. Washington Square Press, New York

Gordon RJ (2016) The rise and fall of American growth. Princeton University Press, New York

Gould SJ (1996) Full house. Harmony Books, New York

Green TH (1964) Political theory, John H. Rodman ed. Crofts Classics, New York

Ha-Am A (1962) Selected essays (trans: Simon L). Meridian Books and Jewish Publication Society of America, Philadelphia

Haidt J (2012) The righteous mind. Vintage Books, New York

Hartz L (1955) The liberal tradition in America. Harcourt Brace, New York

Hayek F (1944) The road to Serfdom. University of Chicago Press, Chicago

Hayek F (1960) The constitution of liberty. University of Chicago Press, Chicago

Hayek F (1979) Law, legislation, and liberty, vol 1, 1973; vol 2, 1976; vol 3. University of Chicago Press, Chicago

Hobhouse LT (1964) Liberalism. Oxford University Press, New York

Huber WD (2020) Corporate law and the theory of the firm. Routledge, New York

Ingersoll R (1944) Ingersoll's greatest lectures. Free Thought Press Association, New York

Johnson S, Kwak J (2011) 13 bankers: the wall street takeover and the next financial meltdown. Vintage Books, New York

Kahneman D (2011) Thinking fast and slow. Farrar, Straus, and Giroux, New York

Keynes JM (1965) General theory of employment, interest, and money. Harper Books, New York

Keynes JM (2004) The end of Laissez-Faire and the economic consequences of the peace. Prometheus Books, New York

Kindleberger CP, Aliber R (2005) Manias, panics, and crashes. Wiley International Classics, New York

Kirk R (1985) The conservative mind. Regnery Publishing, Washington, DC

Klein N (2007) The shock doctrine. Henry Holt and Co, New York

Knight F (1921) Risk, uncertainty, and profit. Pantianos Classics

Knight F (1947) Freedom and reform. Liberty Press, Indianapolis

Knight F (2014) The ethics of competition and other essays. Martino Publishing, Mansfield Centre

Knight F, Merriman T (2015) The economic order and religion. Martino Press

Krugman P (2013) End this depression now. W. W. Norton and Co, New York

Lakoff G (2006) Whose freedom? The battle over America's most important idea. Farrar, Straus, and Giroux, New York

Leuchtenburg WE (1963) Franklin D. Roosevelt and the new deal. Harper Torchbooks, New York

Levine R (2011) Free ride: how digital parasites are destroying culture, business, and how the culture business can fight back. Random House, New York

Lowi T (1969) The end of liberalism. W. W. Norton, New York

Macaulay T (1952) Prose and poetry, selected by G. M. Young, the Reynard Library. Harvard University Press, Cambridge

Manning DJ (1976) Liberalism St. Martins Press Inc, New York

Marshall A (2012) Principles of economics. Digireads.com Publishing

McGrath A (2004) The twilight of atheism. Doubleday

Mill JS (1956) On liberty. Bobbs-Merrill Co. Inc, New York

Niebuhr R (1932) Moral man and immoral society. Charles Scribner and Sons, New York

Niskanen W (1971) Bureaucracy and representative government. Aldine and Atherton/Wiley, New York

Nozick R (1974) Anarchy, state, and Utopia. Basic Books, New York

Pinker S (2002) The blank slate: the modern denial of human nature. Viking Press, New York

Pinker S (2007) The stuff of thought, language as a window into human nature. Viking Press, New York

Pinker S (2011) The better angels of our nature: why violence has declined. Viking Press, New York

Polanyi K (1944) The great transformation. Beacon Press, Boston

Posner R (1977) Economic analysis of law. Little Brown and Co, Boston

Posner R (1981) The economics of justice. Harvard University Press, Cambridge

Resnik DB (1998) The ethics of science. Routledge, London

Sandel MJ (1996) Democracy's discontent: America in search of a public philosophy. Belknap Press/Harvard University Press, Cambridge

Sandel MJ (1998) Liberalism and the limits of liberty, 2nd edn. Cambridge University Press, New York

Sandel MJ (2009) Justice: what's the right thing to do? Farrar, Straus, and Giroux, New York

Sandel MJ (2012) What money can't buy: the moral limits of markets. Farrar, Straus, and Giroux, New York

Schelling T (1978) Macromotives and microbehavior. W. W. Norton and Co, New York

Schumpeter J (1947) Capitalism, socialism, and democracy. Harper Torchbooks, New York

Shiller RJ (2005) Irrational exuberance, 2nd edn. Broadway Books, New York

Singer P (2011) The expanding circle, Revised edition 2011. Princeton University Press

Smith A (1952) An inquiry into the nature and causes of the wealth of nations. Encyclopedia Britannica Co, Chicago

Smith A (1976) The theory of moral sentiments. Liberty Classics, Indianapolis

Soloveitchik JB (2012) The lonely man of faith, Revised edition. OU Press, New York

Sorel G (1950) Reflections on violence (trans: TE Hulme, J. Roth). The Free Press, New York

Stephenson N (1999) Cryptonomicon. Avon, New York

Stiglitz JE (2010) Freefall. W. W, Norton and Company, New York

Taleb NN (2010) Black swans: the impact of the highly improbable, 2nd edn. Random House Trade Paperbacks, New York

Tate J, Knapp A (2019) Blockchain 2035: the digital DNA of internet 3.0. BlueShed LLC

Veblen T (1904) The theory of business enterprise. Charles Scribner and Sons, New York

Veblen T (2007) The theory of the leisure class. Oxford World Classics/Oxford University Press, New York

Weber M (1965) Politics as a vocation. Facet Books/Fortress Press

Wiener T (2007) Legacy of ashes (CIA). Doubleday, New York

Wills G (2010) Bomb power. Penguin, New York

Wilson EO (1998) Consilience: the unity of knowledge. Alfred A. Knopf, New York

Zelizer JE (2010) Arsenal of democracy. Basic Books, New York

Zinn H (1999) A people's history of the United States. Harper-Collins, New York

Zohar T (1984) Translated by Harry Sperling and Maurice Simon, 2nd edn. Soncino Press

Zohar T (2004) Translated by Daniel Matt, vol 1. Stanford University Press, Stanford

Index

Printed in the United States
by Baker & Taylor Publisher Services